NOT
QUITE
TWENTY

Stories, Poems, and a Play

NOT QUITE TWENTY

Stories, Poems, and a Play

RUTH F. EISENBERG
Pace College Westchester

Holt, Rinehart and Winston, Inc.
New York   Chicago   San Francisco   Atlanta   Dallas

Cover: Paper collage by Jerome Seckler

For Jay and Steve
and
Allen

Preface

The need to know, the desire to see for oneself, to experience life even if it entails meeting pain: these are characteristics that mark the adolescent. To take things for granted, to be a passive spectator, to lack curiosity: these are signs of old age, even in a ten year old child.

This is why "When I Awoke" is the opening work in this book. Actually, there is no way of knowing the age of either speaker. Yet, the female seems to speak for age: for prudence, caution, and safety in dealing with the reported disaster; the male for youth and involvement.

Not Quite Twenty—my son has questioned the title as patronizing, but I deny it vigorously—is a book about youth and dedicated to the spirit of youth. The ages of thirteen to nineteen served as boundary markers in choosing the material. Of nineteen prose pieces, eighteen are about people under twenty; fifty-seven poems reflect the same age group. Only for Conrad's "Youth" was this arbitrary limitation set aside. In it, Marlowe recalls his experiences when he was twenty, but his recollection seems to recreate and represent the spirit of all youth. Thus, for this book, the story serves as a kind of Epilogue.

Not Quite Twenty is, I believe, a unique book in its field. No other book known to me deals exclusively with fiction and poetry about teenagers—of our time and place and of distant times and places. No other text has brought together so many exceptional writers to comment on and disclose the problems and outlook of the adolescent.

There are four sections to the book: Initiation; Evaluation; Encounter; and Passage. Briefly, each deals with a different level of experience. *Initiation* is the introduction, usually painful and disillusioning, into the adult world. In *Evaluation*, youth appraises adult values like conformity and institutions like religion. *Encounter* contains stories about love and death. *Passage* carries the youth into the adult world for the taking on of adult responsibilities.

It is no secret that people like to read about themselves or those closest to them. It has seemed logical to me, therefore, to present to students a collection of readings of material that is both artistic and personally meaningful. The idea behind this book is essentially to encourage good reading and thoughtful evaluation; and, perhaps as a dividend, to inspire good writing.

For me, the book has been a labor of love: love for the material; love for my own sons, both in their teens when the project was begun; love for the hundreds of students I have taught, argued with, and learned from.

When I was nineteen, I made myself a pledge to try to keep alive the memory of the pleasures, passions, and pain of that year. *Not Quite Twenty* is an attempt to fulfill that pledge.

Ruth F. Eisenberg

White Plains, N. Y.
October 1970

Acknowledgments

From the beginning, when *Not Quite Twenty* was a shaky idea, I've had the constant encouragment and support of friends, relatives, and colleagues.

Almost from the first, ideas for inclusions were offered to me from colleagues, especially Alberta Avery, Mort Clark, and Robert Dell. Bob, my chairman, also made it possible for me to try out some of the stories in class.

MaryVye Cramblitt, Eva Reiman, and Rita Droesch of the Pace Library and Eileen Johnsmeyer were patient and friendly even when I kept books way overtime to have stories copied. And Paula Reich and June Richardson were prompt and efficient in getting the material out of the typewriters.

Also there were all the students who worked with me over the stories and poems. But a few I especially remember—the group who came to my home on post-class Friday nights to discuss some of the poems.

And, of course, there was the editorial help: from my sons, Jay and Steve; from the staff at Holt, Jane Ross, Dick Beal and my editor, Phil Leininger; from my good friends Allen Bachrach, Carol Swidorski, and Howard Livingston.

To all, enumerated or inadvertently overlooked, I am indebted and grateful, but especially to the three to whom this book is dedicated: it is as much theirs as it is mine.

CONTENTS

PART THREE   ENCOUNTER

NOT
QUITE
TWENTY

Stories, Poems, and a Play

Why Read?

The Function of Literature

The chief function of the arts is to reflect and to interpret life. With life as the subject matter, its treatment is a matter of media and capability. The variety of media extends from the solidity of the sculptor's stone and chisel to the abstraction of the composer's notes and rhythms. The writer's tool is also abstract; it is the words that he fashions into phrases, clauses, sentences, paragraphs or stanzas. Whether he writes prose or poetry, fiction or nonfiction, he will make decisions that will result in the creation of a form that will give expression to his thinking, his attitudes, and his emotions, so that others may share his experience—and evaluate it.

Although this book is concerned with fiction and poetry, let us first compare nonfiction and fiction prose. Nonfiction prose draws upon the observations, experiences, insights, researches, understanding, and logical capabilities of the writer for the purpose of explaining or describing a given situation, person, or problem. Further, the writer may analyze, comment on, or argue his thesis. Nonfiction prose is expressed in such forms as the article, essay, biography, history, and discourse. It is the basic writing technique of textbooks and the daily newspapers. Fiction, on the other hand, takes all of the above named factors—observation, experience, and so on—and adds to them the dimension of imagination. The fiction writer may deliberately distort or ignore some of these factors; he may, for instance, ignore logic to concentrate on the irrational; he may isolate a character within a fantasy world or situation. He uses imagination to make the real

1

seem more real as well as to create the utterly fanciful. It is the dimension of imagination, sparked by daydreams and wishes, or dredged out of nightmares and fears, that gives fiction its originality and its great appeal.

Nonetheless, we must hold firmly in mind the idea that literature reflects life. If the reflection is direct, honest, and undistorted, we call the literary result *realism*. If the reflection is real, but pessimistic, we call the literature *naturalistic*. If the reflection is reasonably accurate, but the glass is rose-tinted and we see everything a little better than it is, then we are dealing with a form of *romanticism*. But what if the glass is imperfect and the image is distorted? It is like a Coney Island funhouse mirror then; the image with its shrunken head, its bulbous belly and elongated legs is grotesque. It is like a *fantasy* or a *horror tale*, or even like a *satire* of the worst features of ourselves. Even if the image is distorted because the glass is curved or fragmented, the reflection is still that of the person standing before it. Even *science fiction* can be explained as a mirror reflection. But in this case the whole earth—man's civilization—is both the subject and the object. Worlds of the future or worlds yet unknown may be created, but they are conceived in terms of our known civilization.

What we may infer then is that no form of literature—or any other art for that matter—is so strange or so bizarre that it is actually divorced from life. Whether it is realism or surrealism, historical romance or the tale of terror, absurd farce or shattering tragedy, the writer and reader join in a collaborative effort to review and interpret life.

Pleasure Plus

One of the more infuriating experiences of life is to be thoroughly engrossed in a TV program, a book, or a magazine and have some one say, "What are you wasting your time on that junk for? Why don't you read something good for a change?" Up go the defenses and out goes judgment. Immediately, enjoyment is equated with value, as you respond, "I like it, and that's good enough for me." Or the tired business man cliché comes into play—"After a hard day at the office (school), I just want to relax. I don't want to think." The last sentence does unwittingly carry a built-in indictment; nevertheless, let us look at the statement positively. It is an admission that good literature gives us something to think about, and that, to a large extent, is what makes it good. "Why," you may ask, "isn't enjoyment enough?" Let us answer the question in a round-about way.

If one of the reasons that people read fiction is for enjoyment, another is for escape. The enjoyment may come in the form of laughter, tears, thrills, or admiration; whatever form it takes, the emotions are aroused. The escape comes when we enter into the world and the problems of the protagonist and thus temporarily forget our own. "I just couldn't put the book down, not even for a minute." Usually the more emotionally involved we become, the more likely we are to evaluate the experience as enjoyable. Many a red-eyed girl emerging from a Sandy Dennis movie has said, "It was just marvelous. I love a good cry," as she measures the value of the film in drenched hankies. But what made her cry did not move her escort to anything more than a yawn. She was enthralled; he was bored. Who is right? Neither or both?

Ultimately, enjoyment is a matter of taste and emotional satisfaction. While it can be developed or changed, taste cannot be legislated or ordered, and it is obvious that everyone has different emotional needs. Because we live in a high tension society, some people like their prose to keep pace—fast, punchy, and Hemingwayesque; others, resisting the pressure, want their literature leisurely, thoughtful, and heavily descriptive. Some bitter people enjoy only books that are critical, hostile, or that reveal and revel in the ugly and sordid in life. Some discouraged people want their fiction to free them from sordid reality and to show them a world of happy endings. Some people like being shocked; sex and dirty words—that's all they want, although they rarely admit it publicly.

A related problem is the fact that emotional needs and tastes change. Some books, like old clothes, we outgrow; some we grow into. *The Adventures of Huckleberry Finn*, read at fourteen, at nineteen, and at thirty will meet different needs. At fourteen, it's a funny adventure story; at nineteen, it's this plus a criticism of society; at thirty, it's both of these and a work of art. Maybe at fourteen, you didn't like it, didn't find it funny; you weren't ready for it. That doesn't mean that Huck Finn is lost forever. The book will stay the same; you will grow. Some books you will never like; this is not necessarily a negative comment on you or the book. As stated before, enjoyment is often a question of taste or need, and neither can be argued or ordained.

Obviously then, pleasure alone cannot be the criterion; it is too variable and unreliable. What else then, can determine whether a novel is good? Time, for one thing, insight for another.

The length of time a work has lasted is one valid way of measuring its worth. For two thousand years, Oedipus has stirred man as he relentlessly and tragically searches for his own identity. For over three hundred years, *Romeo and Juliet* has told of young love and of conflicts with parents. So do today's pop tunes. But the tunes, or most of them, disappear in a few months, while *Romeo and Juliet* continues to draw audiences, as it was originally written or as it was adapted in *West Side Story*. Holden Caulfield has been decrying phonies for more than twenty years, and he speaks to the idealism in all of us. Will he, however, appeal to your children and grandchildren?

When a work continues to speak to generation after generation all over the world, it is said to acquire timelessness, that is, it transcends its own time. Indeed it transcends space as well. It has reached the most basic human needs of men and women, needs that are intellectual, emotional, and/or spiritual.

The major determinant, however, in judging the value of a work is the insights it brings to the reader. Insight is more than just knowledge. *Literary insight* is an understanding of ourselves and of our world, gained as a result of evaluating our reading experience in relation to our life experience. It is the deepening of insight that humanizes us by making us both wiser and more compassionate. The work of fiction that gives us some insight is a good book; the work that gives us many insights is a great one. The insights we gain may be established on four levels that sometimes overlap—psychological, sociological, ethical, and metaphysical. Let us examine each.

A *psychological insight* enables us to answer, at least partially, the questions: Who am I? Why do I feel as I do? Why do I behave as I do? How typical are my feelings and actions? While most of us want to understand ourselves better, few of us want, need, or can afford psychiatric treatment. The gulf between the generations often makes it difficult for parents and teens to talk. Teenagers turning to friends find these friends are plagued by the same questions without answers. A book, however, can put a character through a similar experience and present a solution for consideration. The author may give no advice, but he has distance and objectivity toward the conflict. The reader "identifies"; he makes the necessary personal associations. Who has not dreamed of a weekend on the town with unlimited money and no responsibilities? We watch Holden Caulfield or Paul, in "Paul's Case" live it, and we see the pitfalls and problems that can occur when a daydream comes true. As a result, we feel very much more mature than either of these characters.

What young man has not wondered, like Henry Fleming in *The Red Badge of Courage*, if he would be a coward and run from battle? Crane reveals how men are not cowards or heroes, but creatures that react with their instincts like animals; the judgments on them are placed by others. We learn that fear is universal and nothing to be ashamed of.

Fiction, then, allows us to meet more people more intimately than we ever can in real life. In this way, we can measure them and ourselves.

A *sociological insight* opens the reader's eyes to the world he lives in—in both actual and historical time. Each of us occupies a tiny geographical space and an even smaller particle of time. Fiction allows us to travel as no jet airliner can.

There is no frigate like a book
To take us lands away.

was how homebound Emily Dickinson said it. *Julius Caesar* takes us to
the power struggle in ancient Rome where men conspired and intrigued
for leadership just as they do today. The politicking of ancient Rome is
not unlike modern Washington. The conspiracies at work in ancient
times can be found today in any country on the verge of revolt. On the
other hand, how many histories and sociological studies would we have
to read to get the picture of the migrants that *The Grapes of Wrath*
presents? The sociologist's picture, in black and white, lacks all the color
of Steinbeck's narrative.

Fortunately, we don't have to go to war to know its horror: read
The Naked and the Dead, Catch-22, or Steven Crane's poetry, *War is
Kind.* We can see the agonies of alcoholism or drug addiction, the miseries of prostitution or life in a slum, the terrors of sadistic brutality or
political suppression without having to experience them physically. Indeed, reading may protect us from the physical experience as we learn
vicariously about a world that is not immediate to our own backyard—
or about the world that is.

Of course, the travel can also be pleasant. We may enter villas and
drawing rooms with Henry James, go the length of the Mississippi on a
raft with Mark Twain, or embark for the South Sea Islands with a score
of writers from Melville to Maugham to Michener. We may travel endlessly in fiction and find that even where customs are exotic, people are
basically alike.

Ethical insights are much more difficult to deal with. Essentially,
our sense of right and wrong is established in our homes and via our religious beliefs. Whether or not one actually practices a faith, he is still
somewhat bound to its moral and ethical teachings. Even as we violate
the commandment, "Thou shalt not take the name of thy Lord in vain,"
we are aware that we are swearing.

But ethical decisions are not only the simple "thou shalts" and
"thou shalt nots" of the Bible. If we bend a rule, how much more will it
take to break it? While one cannot be a little bit pregnant, one can be
relatively honest. Or can one? Do special people merit special consid-
erations? Raskolnikov thought so before he murdered the old woman.
(His life, he decided, was of greater value and potential than hers.)
Crime and Punishment examines his decision and its results. Do special
situations demand a departure from age-old injunctions? This obviously
is a basic question of our time with the widespread civil dissent and the
so-called revolution in morality. In *Tea and Sympathy*, the professor's

wife decides that adultery is not immoral in face of the reassurance she can give the young man concerning his heterosexuality.

Then, too, we ask, aren't some sins worse than others? Hawthorne evidently thought so when he made Chillingworth the villain of *The Scarlet Letter* because he had violated the human heart. In effect, Hawthorne condoned the adultery of Hester Prynne and Arthur Dimmesdale as he allowed them to work out their own salvations.

It must be made very clear, however, that except for a very small body of didactic tales, like Aesop's or Fontaine's *Fables*, or stories with a moral from the Bible or Sunday School texts, most literature does not clearly tell us what to do, what decision to make, or what turn to take. Most stories merely present the situation and show the possible ramifications. The protagonist's decision and subsequent responses will indirectly reveal the writer's views.

Lastly, we come to the most important question of all. When we speak of *metaphysical insights*, we are really addressing ourselves to the simplest, yet most complex questions. What is man's relation to God? What purpose is there in the universe? What meaning does life hold— especially if one doubts that there is life after death? Since no writer is God, no writer has the answer to these questions, and literature is not bound to supply pat answers. Replying to a criticism of Archibald MacLeish's play, *J.B.*, a critic once wrote that it is not necessary that a writer supply the answers; it is sufficient that he asks good questions.

How much can man dare to know—so little that he was forever damned after eating the apple in the Garden of Eden?—so little that Prometheus was chained to a rock by Zeus as a punishment for bringing knowledge to men? So challenging is the question that Ahab fought the very forces of nature itself in the enormous white whale Moby Dick, "thrusting through the wall . . .," and risked his own destruction and that of his crew.

Even a discussion of metaphysics resolves itself into questions. Can man ever see the face of God?—ever know His will? What paths are there for modern man who denies the existence of God or who believes that God is unconcerned with man? Explore the mysteries of T. S. Eliot's *The Wasteland*; puzzle over Huck's moral decision to go to hell; wonder with Hamlet if man has the right to send himself to "The undiscovered country from whose bourn /No traveler returns—" and assume for himself God's control over man's life and destiny.

The greatest works are those that address themselves to all these questions. Oedipus, in seeking to know himself as a man, is also aware of his responsibilities as a king. He is tormented by the fact that the man he killed by the roadside was a king. Worse, the man, it turns out, was his own father. Oedipus is guilty of having challenged the gods by trying to change his preordained fate. For his sins, he blinds himself in punishment. Modern man forgives Oedipus as Oedipus could not forgive himself. Hamlet's anguish is for his inability to act: his inability to decide whether it is right or wrong to avenge the death of his father; his inability to resolve his conflict between being a loyal son to his mother or his father, a loyal subject to the living king or the dead one; his inability to give full love to Ophelia; his inability to live his life or end it. Sophocles and Shakespeare each wrote plays to attract and engage the audience, but at the same time each addressed himself to the human dilemma.

Perhaps the reader has already noted that the many illustrations given to clarify insight have all come from full-length works. This is partly because more people are familiar with the chosen works. It is also because the writer often needs the length and scope of a novel or a full-length play to develop his ideas fully. The compression of the short forms is both a delimitation and a discipline. One does not expect as much from a short work; when one receives several insights then, indeed, it is a great story or poem to give so much in so little.

While short fiction can rarely achieve the depth of full-length works, it does deal essentially with the same material. The stories, the play, and the poems in this collection were not originally written for a classroom audience, but for the general reading public. Some undoubtedly will give you pleasure. Some of the protagonists have conflicts that will be familiar to you and, perhaps, with which you may identify. With reflection after reading and perhaps some classroom discussion, you may gain some insights. Then, too, hopefully you will learn how the craft of the writer enabled you to share in his experience, for content cannot be separated from form. But this is the subject of the next section.

The Craft of
Fiction

Virginia Woolf once wrote, "Perhaps the quickest way to understand the elements of what a novelist is doing is not to read but to write; to make your own experiments with the dangers and difficulties of words."[1] The dangers and the difficulties of words and their structured organization represent the basic challenges to the writer, whether he is an essayist, a novelist, a dramatist, or a poet. The experiments that Miss Woolf speaks of are the writer's conscious use and deliberate manipulation of words, even such minutia as the choosing of prepositions and conjunctions. His experimentation with words, the choosing and arranging of them, and his final selections and decisions are what give variety, individuality, and distinction to his work. Altogether they represent what is called the writer's style.

But no writer evolves a style overnight. The distinctiveness of a style is determined by several factors: the writer's own personality, the type of verbal fluency he utilizes, and his knowledge and practice of the craft of his chosen form. Knowledge of his craft is basic, for even if a man attempts to revolutionize a form, he still has to know what he is breaking away from.

The average reader of fiction doesn't think about all of this. He is content to read for the story alone, what it is and how it will come out. The intellectually alert reader, however, once his curiosity and emotional needs have been satisfied, will begin to consider *how* the story satisfied, *how* the words manipulated his response—in other words, *how* the story

[1] Virginia Woolf, "How Should One Read a Book," *The Second Common Reader*, (Harcourt, Brace and World, 1932), p. 283.

worked. It is at this point that analysis begins. When one reads good writing, recognition of the writer's craft augments the reader's appreciation. He is satisfied in two ways—emotionally and intellectually, with one experience enriching the other.

However, before going any further into analysis, let us stop and apply Miss Woolf's advice.

> *Assignment*: Write a short story, any length.
> *General authorial advice:* Deal with material you know.
>
> Where do you begin? Usually with a character, perhaps yourself, in a situation that you participated in or one you know of. The problem is to dramatize or make meaningful what otherwise might just be an anecdote. Is there a point to the whole thing? Is there a recognizable meaning to the experience that the reader can share?
>
> For the sake of an arbitrary beginning here, the protagonist will be a teenage girl. But some questions arise—specifically, how old? in high school? or college? or working? Does she live at home or away from home? Where is home? Where is away? Is the character satisfied or dissatisfied or indifferent to be where she is? Why? Is there possibility of change?
>
> If you examine what is happening so far, you'll see that questions about characterization and setting have begun to intrude and to force answers or possibilities.
>
> Now to intensify the possibilities. What, for instance, if the girl is a stranger? What if she is black? What if she is crippled? What if she is ignorant or countryfied? What if she is brilliant and restless? Conflicts are now beginning to arise.
>
> And so it goes. . . . Conflicts will give rise to intensification and, hopefully, to a meaningful resolution.
>
> At this juncture, no words have been set down because, until your own feeling about the girl and her problem is established, you can't write. You must decide whether you sympathize with her or not, and whether she is somehow funny, pathetic, or even tragic. Does her situation make you angry? Resentful? Or is she just another "pawn in the game of life?" The writer's attitude must be fixed, for it will determine the actual verbal choices for the narrative and the dialogue.
>
> When you clearly know your protagonist and her conflict, and how you feel about the total situation, it is time to begin to write. There is probably still more to work out, but a first draft or a preliminary character sketch can be started.

If the reader analyzes what has just been done, he should understand some of the experimentation and manipulation that go into the creation of a well-structured short story. By examining a few of the endless possibilities of manipulation, the writer comes to recognize the imperatives of control.

This, all in all, is the joint concern of theme and form. *Theme* is the reason or idea behind the manipulative process. *Form* is the process itself. Behind the fictive form are six components: Characterization, Plot, Theme, Setting, Tone, and Language.

Characterization

Every story must have a *protagonist*—a central character around whom the main action revolves. In standard potboiler fiction, the protagonist is usually a hero type—square of jaw, shoulder, and head. In good fiction, the protagonist may be a hero or a coward, a cranky old man, or a confused little girl. He, or she, may be anyone, even someone unreal. He may be a symbolic figure designed to represent others like him in class, station in life, or national type. More often, though, he will be an individual, recognizable and distinct, a person with whom the reader may have some sense of identification.

In order to reveal the personality of the protagonist—and the other characters as well—the writer has several techniques he may use. Most simply, he may *tell* about the man: his name, occupation, appearance—the kind of information one might get when meeting a stranger. In addition, the author may tell of the character's thoughts and feelings, —"She thought wistfully of home," or, "He sensed something awful was going to happen." The reader does not have to work material out for himself; the writer places it clearly before him.

The more subtle means of revealing character are those that the writer employs to *show* his protagonist's personality, such as through dialogue or action. *Dialogue* is the most obvious way of showing character; what the character says, as well as his diction and grammar, reveals his education, his background, and his temperament. In "The Three Day Blow," Hemingway reveals, in their conversation, the boys' interest in baseball, reading, and hunting, and gives information about the family of each. He implies the age of the boys and their schooling. The characters' *actions* also supply a key, and are often revealed in verbs. A man who stomps across a room is very different from one who steals across it, or minces. Immediately, three different images come to mind.

Still other ways of revealing character are through the uses of *setting* and *symbol*. In "Paul's Case," Paul's red carnation, with all its bravado and its short life, stands for Paul himself. The symbol reinforces an understanding of the personality. Johnny's sign, "Debbie Go Home," speaks for his attitude toward whites and their policies, but the setting of the story, in a working-class colored home in South Africa, also tells us something of the family and its problems. Setting can also be relevant to the character's conflict, and may thus reveal his personality and attitudes. In "The Rendezvous" it is the setting that makes it possible for the narrator to observe secretly the young couple who meet in the woods.

The writer can also show the *reactions of other characters* to the protagonist, through their attitudes, actions, and/or dialogue. The teachers feel threatened by Paul's nonconformity in "Paul's Case"—but why? What is it about Paul that makes those who have power over him so vindictive and mean?

An examination of the opening paragraph of "The Man Jones" will reveal how much information a reader can be given when a writer ably blends many techniques. For instance, we are told Jim's full and rather unusual name and his various nicknames—the one he prefers, and the one some friends call him. We see his action with the jonquils and realize his self-consciousness because of his "furtive" look and his loud-sounding footsteps. We learn that he is a college student, between classes, who isn't quite sure he should be in the building he is entering. Pieces of information, revelations of personality, and even an intimation of his conflict are all deftly worked in.

Related to the use of other characters and their attitudes toward the protagonist is the use of the *foil* character, one whose behavior or personality in some way complements another character in order to emphasize significant information or traits. Barbara, with her postcard "Safe," is the foil for Jim in "The Man Jones." The bloke, with his "blank" mood, is the foil for the father with his "black" moods in "On Saturday Afternoon"; it is in contrasting the two characters that the narrator understands them and himself.

Mention might also be made of the stream of consciousness technique, which takes the reader directly into the mind of the character so that the thinking-dreaming process itself is revealed in all its complexities, tangents, and fragments. This technique is not illustrated in this collection though there are intimations of it in Shaw's "Gunner's Passage."

There is one more thing to be said about the protagonist that makes him come alive and draws our interest. Usually it is the problem he faces, either within or outside himself, and how he goes about handling it. The force, person, or people against which the protagonist is struggling is known as the *antagonist*. The nature of the conflict determines the plot of the story, the second main element in the construction of fiction.

Plot

There are two ways of defining plot. One is to say that it is the vehicle or device that carries the theme of the story. The other is to say that it is the presentation of a conflict that the protagonist will attempt to resolve. Either way, the plot is the story line, and its success, for most readers, lies in its ability to hold one's interest.

However, plot, as a technical device, consists of two parts—exposition and action. *Exposition* is the revealing, actually, the exposing, of all the relevant background material, such as setting, action antecedent to the story, and what the characters know and feel about one another and themselves. *Action* is the development of the conflict; once the conflict is set, its intensification begins. In a short story this must come quickly; a novelist can be more leisurely. Poetry, too, even non-narrative poetry, employs conflict to set up a tension between opposing forces.

The conflicting forces that determine the action of a story may generally be described in, or reduced to, four categories:

> Man against himself
> Man against man or men
> Man against the elements or the forces of nature
> Man against God.

The first of these, *Man against himself*, is concerned with the protagonist's inner emotional struggle and is implicit in the psychological story. The protagonist's main problem is himself. The story may also have a second or external conflict, but the real battle is within. The resolution of the conflict is the solution of his problem, a solution that may be final, as in "Paul's Case" or temporary, as in "Almos' a Man."

Man against man is the basic plot device of both action tales and sociological stories. It is the main ingredient of all westerns, private eye and war stories, and most love stories. It also represents man against a whole segment of society. In the love story it is seen in the popular, "boy meets girl, boy loses girl, boy gets girl" idiom. It is the good guys against the bad; the white hats versus the black hats. But it is also the politician against the crowd, or the virtuous reformer against the corrupt bosses. Generally speaking, the action relies on confrontation and showdown.

In stories in which man against man is not the dominant plot device, it is often employed in a secondary capacity.

Man against the elements is the plot device that pits the protagonist against those natural forces that he cannot control—volcanic eruptions from which he must flee, an empty desert onto which he has crashed, a disease or wound that he cannot survive. The biological self, as well as the individual's powers of endurance, is in conflict with hostile powers of overwhelming strength that are utterly indifferent to man's fate—any man's fate. Tales of heroism, physical and/or moral, rise from such conflicts.

Man against God is a form of inner conflict, but it is one particularly concerned with the meaning of life and death. It is the basic conflict of the philosophical story. In it, the protagonist examines the meaningfulness or meaninglessness of his sense of being or non-being.

He may openly defy God or negate God or come to reaffirm his belief in God. More than an emotional conflict, it is a spiritual and ethical conflict that examines the very core of the protagonist's existence. It is more than confrontation with life; it is confrontation with life's force in the abstract.

The reader has probably already recognized that it is possible for a story, and more especially for a long story or a novel, to develop more than one conflict and more than one kind of conflict. It is, however, the reader's job to determine which one is dominant. It is in isolating the main conflict and examining its climax that the reader finds the story's theme, but this point will be developed more fully later.

The conflict or conflicts, once established, are, as already indicated, then intensified to move the action of the story forward. The moment of *climax*, the so-called turning point, occurs when the protagonist acts on or resolves his conflict. This may be a very dramatic or exciting moment—as when the cavalry arrives in the nick of time—or it may be a very quiet one, as in "Sophistication" when two young people, not even speaking to one another, come to the joint realization that their youth is ending.

What follows the climax is called the *dénouement* or *resolution*. Dénouement comes from the French word meaning unknotting or unraveling, and it is the aftermath, the working out, the life-continuing phase that closes the story. Not all stories have a dénouement because, in some stories, like Poe's horror tales, the climax comes in the last paragraph, sometimes in the last sentence. The climax, however, may appear anywhere after the two-thirds to three-quarter mark of the story. The climax never occurs in the first half; the story builds to and ends with the climax and the dénouement.

A few stories have no climax. In a sense, perhaps, they have no plot. Instead, they have a series of intensified moments that never resolve the conflict. These are subtle tales and they reveal to us that some of life's problems are never resolved.

To sum up: the plot is the chief literary vehicle that carries the theme; it is the action of the story; it is built on conflict; in traditional form, it works its way through to climax and resolution.

Theme

The *theme*, briefly, is the idea behind the story, its point, purpose, and intention; it is the meaning that underlies the action. It is usually a generalization built from the nature of the protagonist, his conflict, and its resolution. If the plot is the vehicle, the theme is the cargo carried.

In didactic tales, like Aesop's or La Fontaine's *Fables*, the lesson is explicitly stated at the end. In tales of popular morality, good conquers evil, the poor get their reward, and father knows best. In serious literature, the theme is not often so easy to find or generalize, but it is inevitably some kind of comment on life and its values. The narrator of "On Saturday Afternoon" learns that black rage against life is healthier than blank despair.

If the theme is difficult to find or articulate, the reader should first examine the protagonist's main conflict and then the climax. Is the working out affirmative or negative? Is the turning point a victory or a loss or an inevitability? Does the protagonist end the story in a stronger or a weaker position than where he began? From these speculations, a generalization may be drawn; that generalization is the theme.

Setting

Setting is essentially a matter of time and place. If a story is abstract and the setting is "nowhere" then "nowhere" becomes a place, as "tomorrow" becomes now. The two divisions of setting each have separate parts that function in two ways.

The place of a story is both its generalized geographical area and the specific location (the room or rooms or outdoor locale) in which the action is unfolded. The need to know the entire location of a story varies. For instance, it is important to ascribe the nationality of the narrator of "On Saturday Afternoon" (he can only be English), but "The Rendezvous" could happen in almost any country. Nevertheless, in "The Rendezvous" the woods are important because they conceal the narrator from the young couple in the clearing. The detailed descriptions Willa Cather gives for Cordelia Street and the New York hotel are important if the reader is to understand what Paul is running from and what he is running to. Yet while the flavor of "Paul's Case" is American, the story could occur to a boy in Germany or England or almost any country where standardization and materialism are culturally dominant.

It was indicated earlier that setting can also aid in characterization. Since setting also includes weather conditions, it also adds to the mood or the atmosphere of the story.

The time factor operates in a somewhat similar double way. First there is the *place in time*—when the story occurs: sometime in the past, or what Thornton Wilder called the "perpetual present," or, as in science fiction, the future. In some stories the author is specific enough to name the year, the season, even the day of the week or the hour of the day. Often the season or time of day contributes to the symbolic meaning of the work; this is particularly true in poetry. Spring is the season of youth, as is the morning or early afternoon representative of youth's place in time. Many of the stories and poems in this collection, such as "The Saint" and "The Picnic," take place in the spring.

The other factor of time is *duration*—or the time needed in order to enact the plot. Generally speaking, short stories cover a much shorter time span than novels, but there are many exceptions that can be found and much variation within each form. The duration of "Agostino" lies within a few crucial weeks of the summer. "The Three Day Blow," however, covers only the few hours of an afternoon in which two boys get drunk and sober up again.

Sometimes an author extends duration by use of *flashback*. Thus, in "Gunner's Passage" although Stais waits just a few hours before emplaning to return home, we are projected back several weeks through his memory to the crash that wounded him.

Tone

One of the governing factors of all writing, not just fiction, is tone. *Tone*, quite simply, is the expressed attitude of the author toward his material. It is how he feels about his subject matter and/or his characters. It is what lies behind the writer's decision about whether his material should be treated for laughs, suspense, or tears. If he is angry, for example, the question of how that anger should be handled would come up; should it be controlled and understated, blatant and forceful, or satiric?

Tone is closely tied to the meaning of the story, but it reveals the author's emotional, rather than his intellectual, viewpoint. When we read "The Blue and the Green," we sense a feeling of painful, tender reminiscence, as though the author himself, not just the narrator, has never been able to reconcile himself to the heartbreak of the end of his first love affair. On the other hand, Updike's notion of the absurdity of the situation in "A & P" adds to the humor of the narrator's act of "chivalry."

The impact of tone on the material can best be measured by asking, "what if the author had felt differently?" We are sympathetic to Paul partly because Willa Cather is. Suppose, however, she had treated him with contempt, that her attitude was like that of Paul's teachers or the kids in his class. Might he not then be only a fresh misfit, an odd ball—even some kind of phony queer with his red carnation and his wild stories, who deserved what he got? If Moravia had thought "Agostino" was funny—a young boy like that visiting a brothel—the story would lack much of its sympathy and perhaps all of its pain.

What then, it may be asked, is the difference between mood and tone? One explanation is that if *tone* is the author's attitude, *mood* is the way he makes the reader feel. Tone is the conveyor; mood is what is conveyed. Tone, therefore, governs mood.

Language

There is no irony in the fact that language comes so late in this discussion. Although readers think of stories as primarily consisting of words, writers realize that the particular choosing of, or final "experimentation with," words comes only after all the other conscious decisions about the story have been made. It should be understood that some decisions are not conscious ones.

Essentially, the writer has three basic language choices to consider; he must decide if the story is to be narrated in formal English, through the stream of consciousness technique, or in the vernacular.[2] The writer will reach his decision about the language of his narration after he has determined the point of view (to be discussed next) from which he will tell the story.

Formal English as a narrative device needs little explanation. The story is related in standard English, and only in the dialogue does the writer violate the commonly accepted rules.

In using formal English, the good writer is not only concerned with the grammatical construction of his sentences; he is also cognizant of poetic devices, such as metaphor and imagery, that enrich and sparkle his prose. Two masters of poetic prose are Joseph Conrad and F. Scott Fitzgerald. A reading of two entirely different stories—"Youth," representing nineteenth century England and "The Ice Palace," representing twentieth century America—can amply illustrate the versatility of formal English.

It was in the revolutionary words of Mark Twain's Huck Finn, "You don't know about me, without you have read a book by the name of 'The Adventures of Tom Sawyer,' but that ain't no matter," that the *vernacular*, the ordinary idiomatic speech of people, was introduced as the narrator's language. It had long been used in dialogue, but not consistently. (Often one of the reasons old novels appear stilted is that the dialogue is not in the vernacular, but is as formal as the language of the narrative itself.) When the vernacular is used in the narrative, the author pretends to direct his outlook through the perceptions and the mouth of the narrator. Vernacular narration lends itself particularly well to humor, as in "A & P" or "On Saturday Afternoon" or in the more famous full-length novel, *The Catcher in the Rye*.

There now remains one last device to discuss concerning fiction before turning to the stories themselves, and that is Point of View.

Point of View

If theme and tone express the author's *meaning* and *attitude*, *point of view* expresses the author's perspective on his material. Nevertheless, it seems to be one of the most misleading and confusing terms in writing. It is commonly understood to mean the author's attitude of mind

---

[2] The stream of consciousness technique, which tries to reproduce the thinking-dreaming process, using disjointed, fragmented language to do so, will not be discussed further here as there are no stories in this book that utilize it.

or opinion (his viewpoint), but this would mean that point of view and theme are the same thing, which is not true. Point of view is actually the position he takes to look at his story; it is his *point of perspective* or, geographically, his *point of stance*.

Perhaps an illustration will help clarify the differences. Let us assume a front page story—a campus riot with students beaten up, several arrests, and the academic community in an uproar. Questions come up: What happened? How did it start? Why did it start? How long previously had there been unrest? Attitudes are expressed, some conflicting with others: compassion for the victims; outrage at brutality or at the affront to the university itself; anger at loss of property or the stoppage of classes; perplexity at why these things continue to reoccur from campus to campus; disgust against either agitating students or stand-pat administrators. Any of these feelings or a combination of several of them express an attitude and will create the tone behind the reportage of the story.

But the problem is deciding from what angle the event will be reported so that it will be faithful to the truth and the emotional response. It is not unlike working with a camera. Should one write a series of closeups or interviews with selected individuals? Or show a panoramic view of the broad story and its even broader implications? Should one find an eyewitness to present his own account? Or make an intensive study of one "typical" situation that might somehow represent the totality? Should one get most of the material from the administration, the faculty, or the student body? Or should one write a report based on a policeman's testimony? One can surely see how many different versions of "the truth" there are likely to be.

The selection of the "angle" is essentially the problem and decision connected with perspective or point of view. And while this illustration pretended to handle a nonfiction reporting situation, the exact application can be made to fiction with one significant difference. The writer of fiction can go into a character, can know him from the inside out, in a way the nonfiction writer cannot. The fiction writer may pretend to assume an identity and enter the story as narrator. He may view it from the outside, as a newspaper reporter might, and only tell what can be seen, heard, and sensed. He may play God and remove himself to a distance from the material, but he still knows what goes on within the characters' minds and bodies. His decision will shape his story, and he will have chosen his point of view.

The three possibilities just established actually describe the three basic points of view, from which the writer opts to use one. (A novelist may shift point of view in different sections of his book; a short story usually remains unified.) These three points of view are called the personal or first person, the objective, and the omniscient.

The *personal* or *first person* point of view is readily distinguished because the story is told by "I," an "I" who, to the reader's annoyance, is sometimes nameless. A chief reason for the author to choose to tell his story from the first person is that it lends to it a sense of truth, of actuality and immediacy—that is, I was there; I saw it; I ought to know. The common error of the reader is to consider the narrator the disguised spokesman for the author himself. This is generally not so; the narrator is an invented character like all the others.

The sense of believability usually works to the author's advantage, but not always, because of the tendency to confuse the author with his narrator. Many people mistakenly believe Edgar Allen Poe was out of his mind because most of his short stories were written in the first person, and several of his narrators were deranged. For Poe, the mastery of his technique turned against him; his personal reputation has always suffered because people have assumed him as mad as the men in his horror tales.

There are, however, other disadvantages; for instance, the narrator can only be in one place at a time, so he has to use ruses to discover what is happening elsewhere—such as finding a diary or receiving a letter or accidentally overhearing a conversation. Also, he can only *know* what goes on in his own head; he must guess at what other characters think or feel unless they tell him, in dialogue or a letter. The personal point of view, therefore, is limited to the perspective of the narrator.

The narrator's function in the story, however, can vary. He may be cast only as a spectator, not a participant, in the action he describes; this is largely the way Turgenev uses him in "The Rendezvous." On the other hand, he may be a spectator-participant as in "A & P." T. S. Pritchett, in "The Saint," gives us still a further refinement; he has his narrator view his own action of several years earlier to indicate how he, the narrator, has reevaluated the experience.

The *objective* point of view is the one, as already indicated, taken by a good journalist in reporting a personally observed story. Only the external details are given by an anonymous third person viewer who does not enter the narrative. The account is written in such a way that the writer's own personality does not intrude on the facts, and the reader will feel that he himself was an active observer.

The objective point of view calls for the self-discipline of the writer; he must not tempt himself with the internal workings of the characters' minds and bodies. It also calls for creative reading, as the reader must supply what the story does not state—characters' attitudes, states of mind, or emotional responses. Objective material often necessitates a quick reading followed by long thinking.

Few writers use this technique, but two Americans, both journalists by training, have used it well, Stephen Crane and Ernest Hemingway. In "The Three Day Blow," Hemingway shows the degrees by which the boys are getting drunk and then drunker by reporting their conversation and the care with which Nick walks.

As will be seen in the next section, drama relies chiefly on objective point of view presentation.

The *omniscient* point of view is more simply known as the God's eye view. The writer plays God, and can see a muscle spasm, a throat tighten, or feet grow cold. He can feel a girl's pleasure begin before her cheek blushes or can think through a boy's decision. He can reveal silent prayer. The writer can do this with as many characters as he chooses.

He may want to observe intensely only one character, and, by writing the story in the *third* person, he may develop this one person's character above all others. Joyce does this in "Eveline." Shaw, in "Gunner's Passage," explores Stais' thoughts while all the other characters reveal themselves through dialogue. In these stories, the reader is allowed to enter the mind of just one character.

On the other hand, the writer may play God with all his characters, with his whole invented world. In "Susanna at the Beach," Gold supplies the reader with a wealth of closely observed external detail; he interprets this material as a good newspaper editor might, but, more than that, he slips in and out of the characters' minds: "He wanted to float up an inner tube and go out someplace to think about it," or of Susanna, ". . . if she thought of her body at all, thought only of her skill . . ." or ". . . the old Polish woman shivered at her own memories of paleness, of resiliency, of pink colors."

The range available to the writer who uses the omniscient point of view is enormous. He can look at his material closely or from a distance, objectively or subjectively, individually or collectively. Unlike the God of Genesis, who labored six days on the world and said, "This is good," and rested on the seventh, the omniscient writer may labor longer and rest less; he may also say, "This is good," but in his "genesis" he can also say, "This is bad." His best characters may never know what it is to suffer death as they live eternally in his story. Eternally they pass from one generation of readers to the next.

This is the great reward that the craft of fiction offers its masters.

Reading Drama
and Poetry

Speed reading ads would have everyone believe that speed is the cardinal virtue in reading achievement. Students caught in the overwhelming whirl of course requirements are likely to agree. But a moment's reflection quickly reveals a fallacy. Some material demands slow reading, and, in addition, repeated reading. This is the kind of reading all fine literature should receive, especially drama and poetry.

A slow reading of drama and poetry is essential because of the need to read in. The demands of form made on the writer make it imperative for him to use implication, ambiguity, or, sometimes, deliberate omission. This means that what the writer implies, the reader must infer; what the writer leaves out, the reader must supply. Speed reading does not help accomplish this kind of reading skill.

This section will not attempt to accomplish a thorough introduction to drama and poetry as art forms. All that will be presented here are some of the distinguishing features of each form and some time-tested suggestions for better comprehension in the reading and analysis of each.

Drama

With the exception of some poetry, drama is the most visual of the verbal arts. A play is written primarily to be seen. All the great ancients whose work we still read, such as Sophocles, Euripedes, Aeschylus, Aristophanes, wrote for the spring festival of Dionysus or the lesser known Lenaea. At these festivals new plays were presented before huge audiences, and a panel of judges selected the best of the festival. William Shakespeare wrote his plays primarily for Richard Burbage to enact before the large clamoring crowds that came to the Globe Theater whenever the flag was flown. Shakespeare hoped for immortality through his poetry, his sonnets, not through his drama. Even George Bernard Shaw wrote for a mass audience, though the printed editions of his plays often come equipped with prologue and epilogue that could only have been written for a reader, not a theatergoer.

It is drama's visual quality that the reader must always bear in mind when slumped in a chair with the play in his hand in the privacy of his room. If a play is not being played, it is up to the reader to "play it," to stretch his imagination to see characters cross the stage or to hear the lines delivered. The playgoer has the double advantage—or disadvantage—of having two people who make interpretations of the lines for him. First, the director, with or without consultation with the writer, brings his interpretation to the lines; then the actor does the same. Thus the playgoer is two times removed from the original. This is why there can be so many interpretations of a role. The reader, on the other hand, must deal with the unspoken words before his eye and must try to spring them into action and intonation. This is a difficult job and calls for a different kind of reading skill from that given to the short story or the novel.

In the last chapter, it was indicated that the dramatist works essentially from the objective point of view in presenting his material. He "removes" the "fourth wall" from his setting and allows the audience to view the action on stage with him. Even material presented in arena theaters or theaters-in-the-round generally maintains the objective view while exploring subjective expression. The problem for the dramatist is how to have his characters reveal their thoughts directly to the audience.

In Shakespeare's time this was done in essentially two ways—the aside and the soliloquy. In both, the actors directly address the audience. The assumption is that when they speak in this manner they always speak the truth. Iago, that consummate liar and flatterer, always tells the truth of his motives and aims in his asides and soliloquies. The essential difference between the two is their length. The soliloquy is much longer.

Another device that has been used for centuries is the use of a narrator, like the famous stage manager in *Our Town* or Tom in *The Glass Menagerie*. The narrator is allowed to reveal his own thoughts as he presents the rest of the play to the audience.

Eugene O'Neill experimented with different devices in order to try to establish omniscience on stage. He met with varying degrees of success. In *The Great God Brown* he revived the Greek mask; when the character spoke his thoughts, he lifted the mask; when he spoke his dialogue, he removed the mask. In *Strange Interlude*, O'Neill revived the aside and used it quite extensively. This way the audience could compare the characters' true feelings and ideas with what they actually said to one another.

An unusual device was employed by Samuel Beckett in his short play *Krapp's Last Tape*; he used a tape recorder playing back memories of an old man, Krapp, to the same old man.

Probably the most frequently used device today is the "dream sequence" and its several variations. In a sense, the audience is presented with a play within a play, or a scene within a scene. Probably, the most brilliant use of the technique occurs in Shaw's *Man and Superman*. In a special dream act, he presents his characters, slightly disguised, in Hell; this is the famous *Don Juan in Hell*, which can be played with or without the rest of *Man and Superman*, just as *Man and Superman* can be played without the dream sequence.

A more fluid use of the dream sequence is one that makes the action of the dream run concurrent with the action of the main plot. In *Death of a Salesman*, Willy Loman periodically transcends time and space as he reenacts his memories within the frame of the outer action, which shows his life just before his suicide.

Other devices include the use of mixed media—slides projected on a screen, off-stage voices, or movies flashed briefly. The contemporary Theater of the Absurd and the Theater of Cruelty have used the world of the insane, in which characters speak whatever seems to occur to them; the audience is assumed to be part of the madhouse.

In these ways, the writer tries to go beyond the third dimension, beyond the limitations of the conventions of the stage. But in the last analysis, these are just devices, for the main tool of the dramatist is *dialogue*. The words his characters speak carry most of the burden of characterization, action, theme, and tone. The words the characters address to one another or about one another are, therefore, doubly loaded with significance because they convey the unspoken as well as the spoken. They give impetus to the action, not only by carrying forward the story line, but by implying gesture, nuance, and volume.

Dialogue, under any circumstances, but most particularly in a play where so much depends on it, is most difficult to write. To be good, dialogue must sound natural, like real speech. But most real speech, especially idle conversation, is banal and without significant direction. To reproduce it accurately would bore an audience to death. Therefore, the writer, in general conformance with his knowledge that the theater is essentially an imitation of life and an artificial device, uses dialogue in a way that can only be called "really fake." It pretends to be real, but it is not. It can only be fake because real conversation does not serve dramatic purpose. The principle problem of dialogue, therefore, is to make really fake talk sound genuine.

The playwright, knowing the limitations as well as the possibilities of dramatic convention, can utilize his dialogue to reveal character. As in real life, two people gossip about a third, but in the theater they only drop relevant clues to the absent one's personality and indicate their attitudes toward him or her. In this way, background and other expository material are supplied.

After completing a play, the reader would find it helpful to go back and reread the dialogue of the opening scene to search out the expository material and to see how, and if, the play has been integrated. The writer, especially the modern writer, supplies additional clues if the reader is wise enough to use them. These clues are revealed by some of the other devices legitimately allowed the playwright, chiefly setting and character description.

It has already been pointed out in the previous section that setting is an aid to characterization. One can take the old cliché about clothes being the man and extend it to show that a man's home reveals his personality. Even if the setting is away from home, as it is in *A Memory of Two Mondays*, it is carefully described so we can see it as a backdrop against which the different and differing lives of the various characters are played out.

Settings also function symbolically, even realistic ones. It is significant that Chekhov's *The Cherry Orchard* opens and ends in a nursery. When the author indicates a nonrealistic or semirealistic setting, the reader can be additionally certain that symbolic interpretations are in order.

A part of the script that many readers unfortunately skip over is the description given to a character upon his or her entrance into the action. Ancient dramatists did not give us the advantage of full descriptions like the ones that modern playwrights supply. We cannot precisely fix Hamlet's age, know the color of his hair, or know whether he was generally more studious than athletic or vice versa. Thus, actors can play him as being anywhere from eighteen to twenty-five, blond or brunet, and so on. On the other hand, Arthur Miller deftly sketches pictures of his people in *A Memory of Two Mondays*. On Bert's first entrance into the shipping room of the auto parts warehouse, he is described as coming in with three things—his lunch, a thick book, and the *New York Times*. The last two mark him immediately as being different from the kind of person one thinks of as working in such a setting. His first action is to clear a table so that he can read the newspaper.

The reader should not skip over these clues, but use them to create his own picture of the persons described, both as individuals and as representative of particular types.

Thornton Wilder once described a play as being an act of collaboration in which the writer's chief function is that of an originator. The playwright establishes the details for action, set, costumes, and lighting, but only so that other experts—the director, set and costume designers, lighting experts, and so on—can then join in and develop the writer's ideas. This is what the reader must also do; he must visualize the set, place the imaginary furniture, and turn on the lamps or the sun. The more actively he participates, the more he will get from the play itself.

Poetry

No attempt will be made here to define poetry, for if there is general agreement about anything in literature, it is that an attempt at a definition of poetry is hopeless. Words like "verse" and "rhyme" and "rhythm" and "metaphor" fly about. Young practitioners talk earnestly about "expressing emotions" or ideas—to no avail. Poetry involves all of these and, sometimes, only one or two of these. Principally poetry is made of words, or, as Hollis Sommers once said, "A poem is not in other words; it's in these words."

We will therefore look at poetry here as the verbal art form most particularly concerned with words, or more specifically with the single, individualized, separate word. Poetry is also involved with lines, sentences, and stanzas, but the word is first and foremost—what it means, how it sounds, how it beats or syllabifies and whether it conveys a picture or an action.

In speaking of the word and what it means, we refer to both its denotation and its connotation. Poetry, by its very nature, relies on compression—of words, that is, not of meaning. Poetry, on the one hand, paradoxically must be absolutely precise in its word use while, on the other hand, it must allow for metaphoric extension and make use of ambiguity. This means that the dictionary is the most valuable tool in a poet's library as he must know or check meanings, as well as derivations and shades of meaning. The careful reader of poetry should show a similar reliance on his dictionary.

The *denotation* of words is to be found in standard reference works, chiefly the dictionary. A word's meaning or its multiple meanings, as well as other information such as its syllabification, pronunciation, and derivation, are given. It is because words have a definable denotative meaning that men can communicate. It is because so many words have several meanings that the writer, particularly the poet, is able to play with ambiguities and multiple possibilities to make his poem a richer experience. The last two lines of the first poem in this book, "When I Awoke" by Raymond Paterson, read:

I have to see
He said.

This is grammar school simple. But as one responds to the word "see," meaning "to use one's eyes," simultaneously other meanings are being recorded—"to learn, to inspect, or to look over, to know." All of these function for a combined impact. Looking up the verb "have" reveals meanings concerning possession—"to possess, to be possessed," —but "have" also means to perform; its synonyms are "hold, possess, and own." In spite of this, the reader probably supplied the definition "must," or even the less grammatical "got to" when he read, "I have to see" because there is so much urgency in the line, an urgency that has been developed by the earlier statements of the poem.

If every poem were read this carefully with so much attention to detail, it is conceivable that much less poetry would be read in this world. It is also understandable that, for a large number of people, to read poetry this way would destroy its esthetic experience. The illustration, however, is given chiefly to illustrate the point made about denotation: words that have several meanings are used as such knowingly by the poet to intensify impact. If the reader does not feel the necessity of checking familiar words, nevertheless, he must check out the unfamiliar—new words, mythological references, and so on. To take short cuts is to cut off a full comprehension of what a poem says.

But poems are not only intellectual experiences. It is unfortunate if the only question asked of a poem is, "what does it mean?" Readers who ask only this forget or ignore the fact that poetry draws on a vast reservoir of human feeling.

To ignore the emotional impact of poetry in a busy search for *meaning* will cause the reader to lose much of poetry's beauty; it will also shortchange the reader as a human being. As poetry appeals to the intellect, it also appeals to the five senses and to human emotions.

Therefore, two other legitimate questions to ask of poetry are "what does it make me feel?" and "what has the poet done to draw this reaction from me?" The second question can be answered by referring to the poet's use of several techniques, chiefly imagery, metaphor, and word connotation. We will consider this last one next.

If denotation is the explicit definition of words, *connotation* is the implicit response or responses that we associate with a word with which we enlarge the definition. It calls forth emotional responses based on experience, reactions that are largely unconscious. "Mother," for instance, may be "the female parent of a plant or animal" in Webster's *New World Dictionary*, but mother is also part of the fabled trio, mother, God, and country; she is the mom of apple pie fame and conversely "Mommy" of Albee's *The American Dream*; she is the candy, hearts and flowers of official and unofficial mother's day, and the nag who is always after you to pick up your socks and brush your teeth. Mother is, in short, a complex of symbolic and emotional responses, not all of which are conscious, responses that go way beyond the denotation of the word.

The poet exercises a conscious choice of words to elicit both these conscious and unconscious responses from the reader. This is only one reason why every poem is owed more than one reading. The minimum number of times a poem should be read is three, and one of these should be out loud. Often the ear catches what the eye could not grasp.

Consideration of the sound of poetry introduces the categories of rhythm and rhyme. To consider *rhythm* first, it is still helpful to consider the word rather than the line. A word consists of one or more syllables. At least one of these syllables is stressed; the others are unstressed. Fooling with sounds creates these varieties of the word "syllable":— *sil*/a/bl; si/*lah*/bl; sil/a/*bull* (the italicized portion receives the stress). Obviously only one, the first, is correct. The easiest way to recognize where a stress or accent belongs is to shift the emphasis and try to say the word wrong. The importance of stress shifts can be demonstrated in another way. Some words radically change their meaning by shifting the accent. Try saying subject, content, or present changing the stress. Not only do the meanings change, but so do the parts of speech, that is, nouns become verbs, adjectives become nouns, and so on.

As each word has a stress or unstress or a number of such combinations, each word, therefore, has a built-in beat or rhythm. Stringing words together on a line may or may not produce a regular rhythm, but the poet will be conscious of their beat—even in free verse—and may choose his words for rhythm to reinforce meaning. The lines, I "have to see/He said," are in the basic iambic rhythm, even though this poem is written in free verse. Iambic, the most frequently used rhythm in English and American poetry, is the basic beat of the English language; it is also the heart beat, pulse beat, or life beat.

When rhythm gets so pronounced that the reader is in danger of getting lost in it, the rhythm is called singsong. But a strong rhythm, from the hands of a skilled poet, will have subtle breaks, as Edward Arlington Robinson's "John Gorham" or e.e. cumming's "a pretty a day" does. Complete regularity is not necessarily desirable.

Another way that rhythm is expressed, a way that perhaps many students do not think about, is in stanza patterns—either internal or the more familiar external patterns. In Archibald MacLeish's poem, "Not Marble nor the Gilded Monuments," each stanza of four lines has three long lines and one short one, that is, each except the fifth and sixth stanzas which consist of five lines and then three lines but nevertheless maintain the three long, one short pattern. One might speculate on why MacLeish introduced the variation.

Formal external stanza patterns are in such combinations as the quatrain, which has four lines; the sestet or sextet, which has six lines; the octet, of eight lines; or alternating combinations. "Boy with His Hair Cut Short" by Muriel Rukeyser has an unusual five line stanza. In free verse there are any number of variations and there may be no immediately discernible pattern, but sometimes there is one that the more careful reader will spot.

Rhyme, or as it is sometimes spelled, rime, is concerned with sound that all words, and even nonwords like nonsense syllables, are made of. Rhyme is actually concerned with "sound alikes." It is not, however, only a matter of the end words of a line sounding alike—sound, bound, found; it has more diversity. When the last words on a line sound alike, it is called *end rhyme*, a sensible title for it tells what it does.

There is, in addition to sound-alike rhyme, a kind of rhyme based on words looking alike—sound, bound, wound; is that last one the past tense of wind, or is it the word meaning injury? If it is the latter, it is an illustration of *eye rhyme* or *approximate rhyme*. English is a much poorer end-rhyming language than French or Spanish, for instance, and therefore the poet will sometimes rely on approximate or slant rhyme. Emily Dickinson made much use of approximate rhyme, and her earlier and more pedestrian editors used to revise her poems to "clean up" her rhymes and make them more regular!

Rhyme, however, is not exclusively concerned with the end of the line. It also includes such within-the-line devices as alliteration, assonance, and *consonance*, the last of which is often used in approximate rhyme because the rhyming is in the final consonants only. *Assonance* is the repetition of vowel sounds. In X. J. Kennedy's "First Confession," the opening line almost stutters its fright because of the repeated "uh" sound: "Blood thudded in my ears, I scuffed." Miller Williams combines assonance with *alliteration*, the repetition of the first consonant sound, in a series of words in the line "Poor dreamer of dust and dungeon." In free verse, the poet may use end rhyme here and there; more often he doesn't use it at all, but he always uses the other rhyming devices. Rhyme is only one of the many characteristics that distinguish free verse from prose.

All in all, it can be said that the several devices of rhyme give the melody to poetry, and supply the poet with the techniques with which he tries to lift the word to music.

The art of the poet must appear at times to be particularly frustrating: He must try to make music without notes or any instrument but the human speaking voice, and he must try to make pictures without brush, paint, or canvas. But words do have a picture-making potential because they stimulate the imagination to see—and hear, touch and smell—what is not actually a literal object. Their picture-making potential functions in two ways. The first is simply the arrangement on the page; this is particularly true of free verse with its more open forms. The second is the choice of words to stir the reader to "see" a picture in his mind; this is called *imagery*. Hollis Summer's line, "The traffic light blushes its carnal hope," animates a red light in a way no engineer ever dreamed possible. Archibald MacLeish, speaking of "The Young Dead Soldiers," says, "They have a silence that speaks for them at night and when the clock counts." The line is full of paradox and pictures—a speaking silence and counting clock (representing yet another device called personification).

MacLeish's line also uses the poetic device known as *metaphor*. While there are many forms of metaphor, and experts specialize the term into divisions like simile, metonomy, and synecdoche, it is only important to remember that all metaphors are implied comparisons. The silence of death is like the silence of a quiet night when even a clock can be heard ticking. In e.e. cummings' poem, "a pretty a day," the lines read "(but born are maids/to flower an hour/in all, all)." Obviously maids don't flower by showing petals that sooner or later fade and fall off. Almost instantly the reader converts the literal expression into the figurative one—a girl's prettiness and its short life is like a flower's prettiness and its short life.

Some metaphors have almost been standardized into a routine predictability. Those are the ones concerned with the ages of man. Man's life is so often compared to the time of the day or the season of the year that a chart can be drawn to show the equivalents with the attendant emotions usually ascribed to each period:

BIRTH, INFANCY AND CHILDHOOD	YOUTH ADULTHOOD	MIDDLE AGE	OLD AGE, DEATH
Morning, dawn	Noon, after-noon	Sunset, evening	Night
Spring	Summer	Autumn, fall	Winter
Hope, innocence, joy, anticipation	Fulfillment, early maturity	Ripeness, some anxiety, full maturity, reflection	Fear, termination, anxiety, regret, coldness

Understanding this metaphor system can help clear up many a puzzling line; understanding can also lead to an extension of the symbolic meaning.

Metaphors appear within a line, but they have another broader use. Sometimes a whole poem is a metaphor; the situation described is really like something else, something more abstract, something that speaks to man's more generalized condition. It is the joint use of metaphor (this is *like* that) and symbol (this means that) that leads to the explorations of concealed meanings. Together they lead in turn to both the puzzlement and the excitement of reading and discussing poetry.

The poet, therefore, gives us a lot in a little. Since poetry is the most compressed of the verbal arts, every single word and phrase must carry its own weight. Nothing can be superfluous. Poetry is concerned with concentration and intensity; the writer selects and narrows his focus, while the reader fixes his attention, expands the poem, and enlarges it. John Ciardi once said, "A good poem doesn't say something; it leaves something." A good poem becomes *more* than the sum of all its parts.

The reader of poetry must then read attentively. And he should read aloud. If he has trouble finding the meaning of the whole poem even after he has identified the individual words, he should try to read the poem for sentences, as he would read prose. Ezra Pound, in an essay on poetry, wrote, "Poetry ought to be at least as well written as prose." The reader should feel free to ignore temporarily the line breaks; he should hunt up the subject and the verb if they are far separated, and rephrase the sentence for himself. When the meaning of the sentence becomes clear, the reader can wonder why the poet divided the lines as he did. In describing his craft, Robert Frost is supposed to have said, "To write poetry is to go a-sentencing," and he was a man who scorned free verse. Thus in all verse forms, the reader too should go a-sentencing.

To facilitate understanding, the reader should also try to identify the speaker of the poem and to whom the poem is addressed. Perhaps the poet is speaking in his own voice directly to the reader, but perhaps not. The poet may assume a *persona*, a kind of mask; the reader should then try to characterize the speaker: age, sex, position in life, and so on. Then the question should be answered, to whom is the poem addressed? Is the speaker talking to himself, to another person, to God, or to the reader? These are the main possibilities.

Since a poem, according to Hollis Summers "doesn't start with a form, but with a statement," the reader should try to put the statement into his own words. With many poems it is helpful to read the first and last stanzas again (sometimes in reverse order) to try to isolate the problem or conflict and its solution or resolution. Once one sees where a poem wants to go and where it arrives, he can reexamine how it got there.

Despite all this talk about the meaning of poetry, it is a mistake to think of poetry as having *only* meaning. It also has sense and feeling and sound and image. Poetry may be hard to define, but it does not need to be justified. It brings pleasure; it expresses the inexpressible, and it deepens understanding. A poem can, of itself, be a happening. Archibald MacLeish almost says it all in his great closing line of "Ars Poetica,"

> A poem should not mean
> But be.

Part One

INITIATION

When I Awoke

Raymond Patterson

>When I awoke, she said:
>Lie still, do not move.
>They are all dead,
>She said.
>
>Who?
>I said.
>
>The world,
>She said.
>
>I had better go,
>I said.
>
>Why?
>She said,
>What good
>Will it do?
>
>I have to see,
>I said.

*Stories of initiation are concerned with an individual's encounter
with the realities of life. Such stories tell of a loss of innocence, a fall
from grace, a smashing of illusion, an awakening from dreams. Life is
presented as being full of ambiguities, as puzzling, and sometimes
brutal or cruel. Seeing the world as unsafe, the individual becomes
aware of the precariousness of his own position.*

*In a sense all stories about teenagers are initiation stories; each
reveals an encounter with some aspect of life previously unnoticed or
irrelevant to the child's world. Some stories, however, make this
awakening the central concern; such a one is "Agostino."*

*"Agostino" is not really a short story; it is far too long. It falls more
into the category of the novella—longer than a short story and shorter
than a novel. As a story of initiation, it relates the crucial summer in
Agostino's life when he starts his "rite of passage" from the world
of childhood and innocence into the world of the adult.*

Agostino

Alberto Moravia

During those days of early summer Agostino and his mother used
to go out every morning on a bathing raft. The first few times his mother
had taken a boatman, but Agostino so plainly showed his annoyance at
the man's presence that from then on the oars were entrusted to him.
It gave him intense pleasure to row on that calm, transparent, early
morning sea; and his mother sat facing him, as gay and serene as the
sea and sky, and talked to him in a soft voice, just as if he had been a man
instead of a thirteen-year-old boy. Agostino's mother was a tall, beautiful woman, still in her prime, and Agostino felt a sense of pride each
time he set out with her on one of those morning expeditions. It seemed
to him that all the bathers on the beach were watching them, admiring
his mother and envying him. In the conviction that all eyes were upon
them his voice sounded to him stronger than usual, and he felt as if all
his movements had something symbolic about them, as if they were part
of a play; as if he and his mother, instead of being on the beach, were
on a stage, under the eager eyes of hundreds of spectators. Sometimes
his mother would appear in a new dress, and he could not resist remark-
ing on it aloud, in the secret hope that others would hear. Now and again

she would send him to fetch something or other from the beach cabin, while she stood waiting for him by the boat. He would obey with a secret joy, happy if he could prolong their departure even by a few minutes. At last they would get on the raft, and Agostino would take the oars and row out to sea. But for quite a long time he would remain under the disturbing influence of his filial vanity. When they were some way from the shore his mother would tell him to stop rowing, put on her rubber bathing cap, take off her sandals and slip into the water. Agostino would follow her. They swam round and round the empty raft with its floating oars, talking gaily together, their voices ringing clear in the silence of the calm, sunlit sea. Sometimes his mother would point to a piece of cork bobbing up and down a short distance from them, and challenge him to race her to it. She gave him a few yards start, and they would swim as hard as they could toward the cork. Or they would have diving competitions from the platform of the raft, splashing up the pale, smooth water as they plunged in. Agostino would watch his mother's body sink down deeper and deeper through a froth of green bubbles; then suddenly he would dive in after her, eager to follow wherever she might go, even to the bottom of the sea. As he flung himself into the furrow his mother had made it seemed to him that even that cold, dense water must keep some trace of the passage of her beloved body. When their swim was over they would climb back onto the raft, and gazing all round her on the calm, luminous sea his mother would say: "How beautiful it is, isn't it?" Agostino made no reply, because he felt that his own enjoyment of the beauty of sea and sky was really due above all to his deep sense of union with his mother. Were it not for this intimacy, it sometimes entered his head to wonder what would remain of all that beauty. They would stay out a long time, drying themselves in the sun, which toward midday got hotter and hotter; then his mother, stretched out at full length on the platform between the two floats, with her long hair trailing in the water and her eyes closed, would fall into a doze, while Agostino would keep watch from his seat on the bench, his eyes fixed on his mother, and hardly breathing for fear of disturbing her slumber. Suddenly she would open her eyes and say what a delightful novelty it was to lie on one's back with one's eyes shut and to feel the water rocking underneath; or she would ask Agostino to pass her her cigarette case or, better still, to light one for her himself and give it to her. All of which he would do with fervent and tremulous care. While his mother smoked, Agostino would lean forward with his back to her, but with his head on one side so that he could watch the clouds of blue smoke which indicated the spot where his mother's head was resting, with her hair spread out round her on the water. Then, as she never could have enough of the sun, she would ask Agostino to row on and not turn round, while she would take off her brassière and let down her bathing suit so as

to expose her whole body to the sunlight. Agostino would go on rowing, proud of her injunction not to look as if he were being allowed to
take part in a ritual. And not only did he never dream of looking
around, but he felt that her body, lying so close behind him, naked in the
sun, was surrounded by a halo of mystery to which he owed the greatest
reverence.

One morning his mother was sitting as usual under the great beach
umbrella, with Agostino beside her on the sand, waiting for the moment
of their daily row. Suddenly a tall shadow fell between him and the
sun. He looked up and saw a dark, sunburnt young man shaking hands
with his mother. He did not pay much attention to him, thinking it was
one of his mother's casual acquaintances; he only drew back a little,
waiting for the conversation to be over. But the young man did not
accept the invitation to sit down; pointing to the white raft in which he
had come, he invited the mother to go for a row. Agostino was sure his
mother would refuse this invitation as she had many previous ones; so
that his surprise was great when he saw her accept at once, and immediately begin to put her things together—her sandals, bathing cap and
purse, and then get up from her chair. His mother had accepted the
young man's invitation with exactly the same spontaneity and simple
friendliness which she would have shown toward her son; and with a
like simplicity she now turned to Agostino, who sat waiting with his head
down, letting the sand trickle through his fingers, and told him to have
a sun bath, for she was going out for a short turn in the boat and would
be back soon. The young man, meanwhile, as if quite sure of himself,
had gone off in the direction of the raft, while the woman walked sub-
missively behind him with her usual calm, majestic gait. Her son, watching them, could not help saying to himself that the young man must
now be feeling the same pride and vanity and excitement which he himself always felt when he set out in a boat with his mother. He watched
her get onto the float: the young man leaned backward and pushed with
his feet against the sandy bottom; then, with a few vigorous strokes,
lifted the raft out of the shallow water near the shore. The young man
was rowing now, and his mother sat facing him, holding onto the seat
with both hands and apparently chatting with him. Gradually the raft
grew smaller and smaller, till it entered the region of dazzling light which
the sun shed on the surface of the water, and slowly became absorbed
into it.

Left alone, Agostino stretched himself out in his mother's deck
chair and with one arm behind his head lay gazing up at the sky,
seemingly lost in reflection and indifferent to his surroundings. He felt
that all the people on the beach must have noticed him going off every
day with his mother, and therefore it could not have escaped them that
today his mother had left him behind and gone off with the young man

of the bathing raft. So he was determined to give no sign at all of the disappointment and disillusion which filled him with such bitterness. But however much he tried to adopt an air of calm composure, he felt at the same time that everyone must be noticing how forced and artificial his attitude was. What hurt him still more was not so much that his mother had preferred the young man's company to his as the alacrity with which she had accepted the invitation—almost as if she had anticipated it. It was as if she had decided beforehand not to lose any opportunity, and when one offered itself to accept it without hesitation. Apparently she had been bored all those times she had been alone with him on the raft, and had only gone with him for lack of something better to do. A memory came back to his mind that increased his discomfiture. It had happened at a dance to which he had been taken by his mother. A girl cousin was with them who, in despair at not being asked by anyone else, had consented to dance once or twice with him, though he was only a boy in short trousers. She had danced reluctantly and looked very cross and out of temper, and Agostino, though preoccupied with his own steps, was aware of her contemptuous and unflattering sentiments toward himself. He had, however, asked her for a third dance, and had been quite surprised to see her suddenly smile and leap from her chair, shaking out the folds of her dress with both hands. But instead of rushing into his arms she had turned her back on him and joined a young man who had motioned to her over Agostino's shoulder. The whole scene lasted only five seconds, and no one noticed anything except Agostino himself. But he felt utterly humiliated and was sure everyone had seen how he had been snubbed.

And now, after his mother had gone off with the young man, he compared the two happenings and found them identical. Like his cousin, his mother had only waited for an opportunity to abandon him. Like his cousin, and with the same exaggerated readiness, she had accepted the first offer that presented itself. And in each case it had been his fate to come tumbling down from an illusory height and to lie bruised and wounded at the bottom.

That day his mother stayed out for about two hours. From under his big umbrella he saw her step on to the shore, shake hands with the young man and move slowly off toward the beach cabin, stooping a little under the heat of the midday sun. The beach was deserted by now, and this was a relief to Agostino, who was always convinced that all eyes were fixed on them. "What have you been doing?" his mother asked casually. "I have had great fun," began Agostino, and he made up a story of how *he* had been bathing too with the boys from the next beach cabin. But his mother was not listening; she had hurried off to dress. Agostino decided that as soon as he saw the raft appear the next day he would make some excuse to leave so as not to suffer the indignity of being left behind again. But when the next day came he had just started away when he heard his mother calling him back. "Come along," she said, as she got up and collected her belongings, "we're going out to swim." Agostino followed her, thinking that she meant to dismiss the young man and go out alone with him. The young man was standing on the raft waiting for her. She greeted him and said simply: "I'm bringing my son, too." So Agostino, much as he disliked it, found himself sitting beside his mother facing the young man, who was rowing.

Agostino had always seen his mother in a certain light—calm, dignified and reserved. During this outing he was shocked to see the change which had taken place, not only in her manner of talking but, as it seemed, even in herself. One could scarcely believe she was the same person. They had hardly put out to sea before she made some stinging personal remark, quite lost on Agostino, which started a curious, private conversation. As far as he could make out it concerned a lady friend of the young man who had rejected his advances in favor of a rival. But this only led up to the real matter of their conversation, which seemed to be alternately insinuating, exacting, contemptuous and teasing. His mother appeared to be the more aggressive and the more susceptible of the two, for the young man contented himself with replying in a calm, ironical tone, as if he were quite sure of himself. At times his mother seemed displeased, even positively angry with the young man, and then Agostino was glad. But immediately after she would disappoint him by some flattering phrase which destroyed the illusion. Or in an offended voice she would address to the young man a string of mysterious reproaches. But instead of being offended, Agostino would see his face light up with an expression of fatuous vanity, and concluded that those reproaches were only a cover for some affectionate meaning which he was unable to fathom. As for himself, both his mother and the young man seemed to be unaware of his existence; he might as well not have been there, and his mother carried this obliviousness so far as to remind the young man that if she had gone out alone with him the day before, this was a mistake on her part which she did not intend to repeat. In the future she would bring her son with her. Agostino felt this to be decidedly insulting, as if he was something with no will of its own, merely an object to be disposed of as her caprice or convenience might see fit.

Only once did his mother seem aware of his presence, and that was when the young man, letting go the oars for a moment, leaned forward with an intensely malicious expression on his face and murmured something in an undertone which Agostino could not understand. His mother started, pretending to be terribly shocked, and cried out, pointing to

Agostino sitting by her, "Let us at least spare this innocent!" Agostino trembled with rage at hearing himself called innocent, as if a dirty rag had been thrown at him which he could not avoid.

When they were some way out from shore, the young man suggested a swim to his companion. Agostino, who had often admired the ease and simplicity with which his mother slipped into the water, was painfully struck by all the unfamiliar movements she now put into that familiar action. The young man had time to dive in and come up again to the surface, while she still stood hesitating and dipping one toe after another into the water, apparently pretending to be timid or shy. She made a great fuss about going in, laughing and protesting and holding on to the seat with both hands, till at last she dropped in an almost indecent attitude over the side and let herself fall clumsily into the arms of her companion. They dived together and came up together to the surface. Agostino, huddled on the seat, saw his mother's smiling face quite close to the young man's grave, brown one, and it seemed to him that their cheeks touched. He could see their two bodies disporting themselves in the limpid water, their hips and legs touching, and looking as if they longed to interlace with each other. Agostino looked first at them and then at the distant shore, with a shameful sense of being in the way. Catching sight of his frowning face, his mother, who was having her second dip, called up to him: "Why are you so serious? Don't you see how lovely it is in here? Goodness! what a serious son I've got"; a remark which filled Agostino with a sense of shame and humiliation. He made no reply, and contented himself with looking elsewhere. The swim was a long one. His mother and her companion disported themselves in the water like two dolphins, and seemed to have forgotten him entirely. At last they got back onto the raft. The young man sprang on at one bound, and then leaned over the edge to assist his companion, who was calling him to help her get out of the water. Agostino saw how in raising her the young man gripped her brown flesh with his fingers, just where the arm is softest and biggest, between the shoulder and the armpit. Then she sat down beside Agostino, panting and laughing, and with her pointed nails held her wet suit away from her, so that it should not cling to her breasts. Agostino remembered that when they were alone his mother was strong enough to climb into the boat without anyone's aid, and attributed her appeal for help and her bodily postures, which seemed to draw attention to her feminine disabilities, to the new spirit which had already produced such unpleasant changes in her. Indeed, he could not help thinking that his mother, who was naturally a tall, dignified woman, resented her size as a positive drawback from which she would have liked to rid herself; and her dignity as a tiresome habit which she was trying to replace by a sort of tomboy gaucherie.

When they were both back on the raft, the return journey began.

This time the oars were entrusted to Agostino, while the other two sat down on the platform which joined the two floats. He rowed gently in the burning sun, wondering constantly about the meaning of the sounds and laughter and movements of which he was conscious behind his back. From time to time his mother, as if suddenly aware of his presence, would reach up with one arm and try to stroke the back of his neck, or she would tickle him under the arm and ask if he were tired. "No, I am not tired," he replied. He heard the young man say laughingly: "Rowing's good for him," which made him plunge in the oar savagely. His mother was sitting with her head resting against his seat and her long legs stretched out; that he knew, but it seemed to him that she did not stay in that position; once, for instance, a short skirmish seemed to be going on; his mother made a stifled sound as if she were being suffocated and the raft lurched to one side. For a moment Agostino's cheek came into contact with his mother's body, which seemed vast to him—like the sky—and pulsing with a life over which she had no control. She stood with her legs apart, holding on to her son's shoulders, and said: "I will only sit down again if you promise to be good." "I promise," rejoined the young man with mock solemnity. She let herself down again awkwardly on to the platform, and it was then her body brushed her son's cheek. The moisture of her body confined in its wet bathing suit remained on his skin, but its heat seemed to overpower its dampness and though he felt a tormenting sense of uneasiness, even of repugnance, he persisted in not drying away the traces.

As they approached the shore the young man sprang lightly to the rower's seat and seized the oars, pushing Agostino away and forcing him to take the place left empty beside his mother. She put her arm round his waist and asked how he felt, and if he was happy. She herself seemed in the highest spirits, and began singing, another most unusual thing with her. She had a sweet voice, and put in some pathetic trills which made Agostino shiver. While she sang she continued to hold him close to her, wetting him with the water from her damp bathing suit, which seemed to exude a violent animal heat. And so they came in to the shore, the young man rowing, the woman singing and caressing her son, who submitted with a feeling of utter boredom; making up a picture which Agostino felt to be false, and contrived for appearance' sake.

Next day the young man appeared again. Agostino's mother insisted on her son coming and the scenes of the day before repeated themselves. Then after a few days' interval they went out again. And at last, with their apparently growing intimacy, he came to fetch her daily, and each time Agostino was obliged to go too, to listen to their conversation and to watch them bathing. He hated these expeditions, and invented a thousand reasons for not going. He would disappear and not show himself till his mother, having called him repeatedly and hunted for him everywhere, succeeded at last in unearthing him; but then he came less in response to her appeals than because her disappointment and vexation aroused his pity. He kept completely silent on the float, hoping they would understand and leave him alone, but in the end he proved weaker and more susceptible to pity than his mother or the young man. It was enough for them just to have him there; as for his feelings, he came to see that they counted for less than nothing. So, in spite of all his attempts to escape, the expeditions continued.

One day Agostino was sitting on the sand behind his mother's deck chair, waiting for the white raft to appear on the sea and for his mother to wave her hand in greeting and call to the young man by name. But the usual hour for his appearance passed, and his mother's disappointed and cross expression clearly showed that she had given up all hope of his coming. Agostino had often wondered what he should feel in such a case, and had supposed that his joy would have been at least as great as his mother's disappointment. But he was surprised to feel instead a vague disappointment, and he realized that the humiliations and resentments of those daily outings had become almost a necessity of life to him. Therefore, with a confused and unconscious desire to inflict pain on his mother, he asked her more than once if they were not going out for their usual row. She replied each time that she didn't know, but that probably they wouldn't be going today. She lay in the deck chair with a book open in her lap, but she wasn't reading and her eyes continually wandered out to sea, as if seeking some particular object among the many boats and bathers with which the water was already swarming. After sitting a long time behind his mother's chair, drawing patterns in the sand, Agostino came round to her and said in a tone of voice which he felt to be teasing and even mocking: "Mamma, do you mean to say that we're not going out on the raft today?" His mother may have felt the mockery in his voice and the desire to make her suffer, or his few rash words may have sufficed to release her long pent-up irritation. She raised her hand with an involuntary gesture and gave him a sharp slap on the cheek, which did not really hurt, probably because she regretted it almost before the blow fell. Agostino said nothing, but leaping up off the sand in one bound, he went away with his head hanging down, in the direction of the beach cabin. "Agostino! . . . Agostino! . . ." he heard his name called several times. Then the calling stopped, and looking back he fancied he saw among the throng of boats the young man's white raft. But he no longer worried about that, he was like someone who has found a treasure and hastens to hide it away so that he may examine it alone. For it was with just such a sense of discovery that he ran away to nurse his injury; something so novel to him as to seem almost incredible.

His cheek burned, his eyes were full of tears which he could not keep back; and fearing lest his sobs should break out before he got into shelter, he ran doubled up. The accumulated bitterness of all those days when he had been compelled to accompany the young man and his mother came surging back on him, and he felt that if only he could have a good cry it would release something in him and help him to understand the meaning of all these strange happenings. The simplest thing seemed to be to shut himself up in the beach cabin. His mother was probably already out in the boat and no one would disturb him. Agostino climbed the steps hurriedly, opened the door and, leaving it ajar, sat down on a stool in the corner.

He huddled up with his knees tucked into his chest and his head against the wall, and holding his face between his hands, started weeping conscientiously. The slap he had received kept rising up before him, and he wondered why, when it seemed so hard, his mother's hand had been so soft and irresolute. With the bitter sense of humiliation aroused in him by the blow were mixed a thousand other sensations, even more disagreeable, which had woundered his feelings during these last days. There was one above all which kept returning to his mind: the image of his mother's body in its damp tricot pressed against his cheek, quivering with a sort of imperious vitality. And just as great clouds of dust fly out from old clothes when they are beaten, so, as the result of that blow to his suffering and bewildered consciousness, there arose in him again the sensation of his mother's body pressed against his cheek. Indeed, that sensation seemed at times to take the place of the slap; at others, the two became so mixed that he felt both the throbbing of her body and the burning blow. But while it seemed to him natural that the slap on his cheek should keep flaring up like a fire which is gradually going out, he could not understand why the earlier sensation so persistently recurred. Why, among so many others, was it just that one which haunted him? He could not have explained it, but he thought that as long as he lived he would only have to carry his memory back to that moment in his life in order to have fresh against his cheek the pulse of her body and the rough texture of the damp tricot.

He went on crying softly to himself so as not to interrupt the painful workings of his memory, at the same time rubbing away from his wet skin with the tips of his fingers the tears which continued to fall slowly but uninterruptedly from his eyes. It was dark and stuffy in the cabin. Suddenly he had a feeling of someone opening the door, and he almost hoped that his mother, repenting of what she had done, would lay her hand affectionately on his shoulder and turn his face toward her. And his lips had already begun to shape the word "Mamma" when he heard a step in the cabin and the door pulled to, without any hand touching his shoulder or stroking his head.

He raised his head and looked up. Close to the half-open door he
saw a boy of about his own age standing in an attitude of someone on
the lookout. He had on a pair of short trousers rolled up at the bottom,
and an open sailor blouse with a great hole in the back. A thin ray of
sunshine falling through a gap in the roof of the cabin lit up the thick
growth of auburn curls round his neck. His feet were bare; holding the
door ajar with his hands, he was gazing intently at something on the
beach and did not seem to be aware of Agostino's presence. Agostino
dried his eyes with the back of his hand and said: "Hello, what do you
want?" The boy turned around, making a sign not to speak. He had an
ugly, freckled face, the most remarkable feature of which was the rapid
movement of his hard blue eyes. Agostino thought he recognized him.
Probably he was the son of a fisherman or beach attendant, and he had
doubtless seen him pushing out the boats or doing something about the
beach.

"We're playing cops and robbers," said the boy, after a moment,
turning to Agostino. "They mustn't see me."

"Which are you?" asked Agostino, hastily drying his eyes.

"A robber, of course," replied the other without looking around.

Agostino went on watching the boy. He couldn't make up his mind
whether he liked him, but his voice had a rough touch of dialect which
piqued him and aroused his curiosity. Besides, he felt instinctively that
this boy's hiding in the cabin just at that moment was an opportunity—
he could not have explained of what sort—but certainly an opportunity he must no miss.

"Will you let me play too?" he asked. The boy turned round and
stared at him rudely. "How do you get into it?" he said quickly. "We're
all pals playing together."

"Well," said Agostino, with shameless persistence, "let me play too."

The boy shrugged his shoulders. "It's too late now. We've almost
finished the game."

"Well, in the next game."

"There won't be any more," said the boy, looking him over doubtfully, but as if struck by his persistence. "Afterwards we're going to the
pine woods."

"I'll go with you, if you'll let me."

The boy seemed amused and began to laugh rather contemptuously.
"You're a fine one, you are. But we don't want you."

Agostino had never been in such a position before. But the same
instinct which prompted him to ask the boy if he might join their game
suggested to him now a means by which he might make himself accept-
able.

"Look here," he said hesitatingly, "if you . . . if you'll let me join
your gang, I . . . I'll give you something."

The other turned round at once with greedy eyes.

"What'll you give me?"

"Whatever you like."

Agostino pointed to a big model of a sailboat, with all its sails attached, which was lying on the floor of the cabin among a lot of other toys.

"I'll give you that."

"What use is that to me?" replied the boy, shrugging his shoulders.

"You could sell it," Agostino suggested.

"They'd never take it," said the boy, with the air of one who knows. "They'd say it was stolen goods."

Agostino looked all round him despairingly. His mother's clothes were hanging on pegs, her shoes were on the floor, on the table was a handkerchief and a scarf or two. There was absolutely nothing in the cabin which seemed a suitable offering.

"Say," said the boy, seeing his bewilderment, "got any cigarettes?"

Agostino remembered that that very morning his mother had put two boxes of a very good brand in the big bag which was hanging from a peg; and he hastened to reply, triumphantly, "Yes, I have. Would you like some?"

"I *don't* think!" said the other, with scornful irony. "Are you stupid! Give them here, quick."

Agostino took down the bag, felt about in it and pulled out the two boxes. He held them out to the boy, as if he were not quite sure how many he wanted.

"I'll take both," he said lightly, seizing the boxes. He looked at the label and clicked his tongue approvingly and said: "You must be rich, eh?"

Agostino didn't know what to answer. The boy went on: "I'm Berto. What's your name?"

Agostino told him. But the other had ceased to pay any attention. His impatient fingers had already torn open one of the boxes, breaking the seals on its paper wrapping. He took out a cigarette and put it between his lips. Then he took a match from his pocket and struck it against the wall of the cabin; and after inhaling a mouthful of smoke and puffing it out through his nose, he resumed his watching position at the crack of the door.

"Come on, let's go," he said, after a moment, making Agostino a sign to follow him. They left the cabin one behind the other. When they got to the beach Berto made straight for the road behind the row of beach cabins.

As they walked along the burning sand between the low bushes of broom and thistles, he said: "Now we're going to the Cave . . . they've gone on past . . . they're looking for me lower down."

"Where is the Cave?" asked Agostino.

"At the Vespucci Baths," replied the boy. He held his cigarette ostentatiously between two fingers, as if to display it, and voluptuously inhaled great mouthfuls of smoke. "Don't you smoke?" he said.

"I don't care about it," said Agostino, ashamed to confess that he had never even dreamed of smoking. But Berto laughed. "Why don't you say straight out that your mother won't let you? Speak the truth." His way of saying this was contemptuous rather than friendly. He offered Agostino a cigarette, saying: "Go ahead, you smoke too."

They had reached the sea-front and were walking barefoot on the sharp flints between dried-up flower beds. Agostino put the cigarette to his lips and took a few puffs, inhaling a little smoke which he at once let out again instead of swallowing it.

Berto laughed derisively.

"You call that smoking!" he exclaimed. "That's not the way to do it. Look." He took the cigarette and inhaled deeply, rolling his sulky eyes all the while; then he opened his mouth wide and put it quite close to Agostino's eyes. There was nothing to be seen in his mouth, except his tongue curled up at the back.

"Now watch," said Berto, shutting his mouth again. And he puffed a cloud of smoke straight into Agostino's face. Agostino coughed and laughed nervously at the same time. "It's your turn now," said Berto.

A trolley passed them, whistling, its window curtains flapping in the breeze. Agostino inhaled a fresh mouthful and with a great effort swallowed the smoke. But it went the wrong way and he had a dreadful fit of coughing. Berto took the cigarette and gave him a great slap on the back, saying: "Bravo! There's no doubt about your being a smoker."

After this experiment they walked on in silence past a whole series of bath establishments, with their rows of cabins painted in bright colors, great striped umbrellas slanting in all directions, and absurd triumphal arches. The beach between the cabins was packed with noisy holiday-makers and the sparkling sea swarmed with bathers.

"Where is Vespucci?" asked Agostino, who had to walk very fast to keep up with his new friend.

"It's the last one of all."

Agostino began to wonder whether he ought not to turn back. If his mother hadn't gone out on the raft after all, she would certainly be looking for him. But the memory of that slap put his scruples to rest. In going with Berto he almost felt as if he were pursuing a mysterious and justified vendetta.

Suddenly Berto stopped and said: "How about letting the smoke out through your nose? Can you do that?" Agostino shook his head, and his companion, holding the stump of his cigarette between his lips, inhaled the smoke and expelled it through his nostrils. "Now," he went on, "I'm going to let it out through my eyes. But you must put your hand on my chest and look me straight in the face." Agostino went up to him quite innocently and put his hand on Berto's chest and fixed his eyes on Berto's, expecting to see smoke come out of them.

But Berto treacherously pressed the lighted cigarette down hard on the back of his hand and threw the butt away, jumping for joy and shouting: "Oh! you silly idiot! You just don't know anything." Agostino was almost blind with pain, and his first impulse was to fling himself on Berto and strike him. But Berto, as if he saw what was coming, stood still and clenched his fists, and with two sharp blows in the stomach almost knocked the breath out of Agostino's body.

"I'm not one for words," he said savagely. "If you ask for it you'll get it." Agostino, infuriated, rushed at him again, but he felt terribly weak and certain of being defeated. This time Berto seized him by the head, and taking it under his arm almost strangled him. Agostino did not even attempt to resist, but in a stifled voice implored him to let go. Berto released him and sprang back, planting his feet firmly on the ground in a fighting stance. But Agostino had heard the vertebrae of his neck crack, and was stupefied by the boy's extraordinary brutality. It seemed incredible that he, Agostino, who had always been kind to everyone, should suddenly be treated with such savage and deliberate cruelty. His chief feeling was one of amazement at such barbarousness. It overwhelmed him, but at the same time fascinated him because of its very novelty and because it was so monstrous.

"I haven't done you any harm," he panted, "I gave you those cigarettes . . . and you . . ." He couldn't finish. His eyes filled with tears.

"Uh, you crybaby," retorted Berto. "Want your cigarettes back? I don't want them. Take them back to Mamma."

"It doesn't matter," said Agostino, shaking his head disconsolately. "I only just said it for something to say. Please keep them."

"Well, let's get on," said Berto. "We're almost there."

The burn on Agostino's hand was hurting him badly. Raising it to his lips he looked about him. On that part of the beach there were very few cabins, five or six in all, scattered about at some distance from each other. They were miserable huts of rough wood. The sand between them was deserted and the sea was equally empty. There were a few women in the shade of a boat pulled up out of reach of the tide, some standing, some lying stretched out on the sand, all dressed in antiquated bathing suits, with long drawers edged with white braid, all busy drying themselves and exposing their white limbs to the sun. A signboard painted blue bore the inscription: "Amerigo Vespucci Baths." A low green shack half-buried in the sand evidently belonged to the bath man. Beyond this the shore stretched away as far as the eye could see, without either cabins or houses, a solitude of windswept sand between the sparkling blue sea and the dusty green of the pine trees.

One entire side of the man's hut was hidden from the road by sand dunes, which were higher at this point. Then, when you had climbed to the top of the dunes, you saw a patched, faded awning of rusty red, which seemed to have been cut out of an old sail. This awning was attached at one end to two poles driven into the sand, and at the other to the hut.

"That's our cave," said Berto.

Under the awning a man seated at a rickety table was in the act of lighting a cigarette. Two or three boys were stretched on the sand around him. Berto took a flying leap and landed at the man's feet, crying: "Cave!" Agostino approached rather timidly. "This is Pisa," said Berto, pointing to him. He was surprised to hear himself called by this nickname so soon. It was only five minutes ago that he had told Berto he was born at Pisa. Agostino lay down on the ground beside the others. The sand was not so clean as it was on the beach; bits of coconut shell and wooden splinters, fragments of earthenware and all sorts of rubbish were mixed up in it. Here and there it was caked and hard from the pails of dirty water which had been thrown out of the hut. Agostino noticed that the boys, four in all, were poorly dressed. Like Berto they were evidently the sons of sailors or bath men. "He was at the Speranza," burst out Berto, without drawing breath. "He says he wants to play at cops and robbers too, but the game's over, isn't it? I told you the game would be over."

At that moment there was a cry of "It's not fair! It's not fair!" Agostino, looking up, saw another gang of boys running from the direction of the sea, probably the cops. First came a thickset, stumpy youth of about seventeen in a bathing costume; next, to his great surprise, a Negro; the third was fair, and by his carriage and physical beauty struck Agostino as being better bred than the others. But as he got nearer, his ragged bathing suit, full of holes, and a certain coarseness in his handsome face with beautiful blue eyes, showed that he too belonged to the people. After these three boys came four more, all about the same age, between thirteen and fourteen. The big, thickset boy was so much older than the others that at first it seemed odd that he should mix with such children. But his pasty face, the color of half-baked bread; the thick, expressionless features, and an almost brutish stupidity were sufficient explanation of the company he kept. He had hardly any neck, and his smooth, hairless torso was as wide at the waist and hips as at the shoulders. "You hid in a cabin," he shouted at Berto. "I dare you to deny it. Cabins are out of bounds by the rules of the game."

"It's a lie!" retorted Berto, with equal violence. "Isn't it, Pisa?" he added, suddenly turning to Agostino. "I didn't hide in a cabin, did I? We were both standing by the hut of the Speranza, and we saw you go by, didn't we, Pisa?"

"You did hide in my cabin, you know," said Agostino, who was incapable of telling a lie. "There, you see!" shouted the other, brandishing his fist under Berto's nose. "I'll bash your head in, you liar!"

"Spy!" yelled Berto in Agostino's face. "I told you to stay where you were. Go back to Mamma, that's the place for you." He was filled with uncontrollable rage, a bestial fury which amazed and mystified Agostino. But in springing to punish him one of the cigarette boxes tumbled out of his pocket. He stooped to pick it up, but the big boy was quicker still, and darting down he pounced on the box and waved it in the air, crying triumphantly: "Cigarettes! Cigarettes!"

"Give them back," shouted Berto, hurling himself upon the big boy. "They're mine. Pisa gave them to *me*. You just give them back."

The other took a step back and waited till Berto was within range. Then he held the box of cigarettes in his mouth and began to pummel Berto's stomach methodically with his two fists. Finally he kicked Berto's feet from under and brought him down with a crash. "Give me them back!" Berto went on shouting, while he rolled in the sand. But the big boy, with a stupid laugh, called out: "He's got some more . . . at him, boys." And with a unanimity which surprised Agostino all the boys flung themselves upon Berto. For a moment there was nothing to be seen but a writhing mass of bodies tangled together in a cloud of sand at the feet of the man, who went on smoking calmly at the table. At last, the fair boy, who seemed to be the most agile, disentangled himself from the heap and got up, triumphantly waving the second box of cigarettes. Then the others got up, one by one; and last of all Berto. His ugly, freckled little face was convulsed with fury. "Swine! Thieves!" he bellowed, shaking his fist and sobbing.

It was a strange and novel impression for Agostino to see his tormentor tormented in his turn, and treated as pitilessly as he himself had just been. "Swine! Swine!" Berto screamed again. The big boy went up to him and gave him a resounding box on the ear, which made his companions dance for joy. "Do you want any more?" Berto rushed like a mad one to the corner of the hut and, bending down, grabbed hold of a large rock with both hands and flung it at his enemy, who with a derisive whistle sprang aside to avoid it. "You swine!" yelled Berto again, still sobbing with rage, but withdrawing himself prudently behind a corner of the hut. His sobs were loud and furious, as if giving vent to some frightful bitterness, but his companions had ceased to take my interest in him. They were all stretched out again on the sand. The big boy opened one box of cigarettes, and the fair boy another. Suddenly the man, who had remained seated at the little table without moving during the fight, said: "Hand over those cigarettes."

Agostino looked at him. He was a tall, fat man of about fifty. He had a cold and deceptively good-natured face. He was bald, with a curious saddle-shaped forehead and twinkling eyes; a red, aquiline nose with wide nostrils full of little scarlet veins horrible to look at. He had a drooping mustache, which hid a rather crooked mouth, and a cigar between his lips. He was wearing a faded shirt and a pair of blue cotton trousers with one leg down to his ankle and the other rolled up below his knee. A black sash was wound round his stomach. One detail in particular added to Agostino's first feeling of revulsion, the fact that Saro—for this was his name—had six fingers instead of five on both hands. This made them look enormous, and his fingers like abbreviated tentacles. Agostino could not take his eyes off those hands; he could not make up his mind whether Saro had two first or two middle or two third fingers. They all seemed of equal length, except the little finger, which stuck out from his hand like a small branch at the base of a knotty tree trunk. Saro took the cigar out of his mouth and repeated simply: "What about those cigarettes?"

The fair boy got up and put his box on the table. "Good for you, Sandro," said Saro.

"And supposing I won't give you them?" shouted the elder boy defiantly.

"Give them up, Tortima; you'd better," called out several voices at once. Tortima looked all round and then at Saro, who with the six fingers of his right hand on the box of cigarettes, kept his half-closed little eyes fixed on him. Then, with the remark: "All right, but it isn't fair," he came over and put his box down on the table too.

"And now I'll divide them," said Saro, in a soft, affable voice. Without removing his cigar, he screwed up his eyes, opened one of the boxes, took out a cigarette with his stumpy, multiple fingers, which looked incapable of gripping it, and threw it to the Negro, with a "Catch, Homs!" Then he took another and threw it to one of the others; a third he threw into the joined palms of Sandro; a fourth straight at Tortima's stolid face—and so with all the rest. "Do you want one?" he asked Berto, who, swallowing back his sobs, had come silently back to join the others. He nodded sulkily, and was thrown one. When each of the boys had received his cigarette, Saro was about to shut the box, which was still half-full, when he stopped and said to Agostino: "What about you Pisa?" Agostino would have liked to refuse, but Berto gave him a dig in the ribs and whispered: "Ask for one, idiot, we'll smoke it together afterward." So Agostino said he would like one, and he too had his cigarette. Then Saro shut the box.

"What about the rest? What about the rest?" shouted all the boys at once.

"You shall have the rest another day," replied Saro calmly. "Pisa, take these cigarettes and go and put them in the hut." There was complete silence. Agostino nervously took both boxes and, stepping over the boys' prostrate bodies, crossed to the shed. It appeared to consist of one room only, and he liked its smallness, which made it seem like a house in a fairy tale. It had a low ceiling with whitewashed beams, and the walls were of unplaned planks. Two tiny windows, complete with window sill, little square panes of glass, latches, curtains, even a vase or two of flowers, diffused a mild light. One corner was occupied by the bed, neatly made up, with a clean pillowcase and red counterpane; in another stood a round table and three stools. On the marble top of a big chest stood two of those bottles which have sailboats or steamships imprisoned inside them. Sails were hung on hooks all around the walls, and there were pairs of oars and other sea tackle. Agostino thought how he should love to own a cottage as cosy and convenient as this. He went up to the table, on which lay a big, cracked china bowl full of half-smoked cigarettes, put down his two boxes and went out again into the sunlight.

All the boys were lying face downward on the sand around Saro, smoking with great demonstrations of enjoyment. And meanwhile they were discussing something about which they did not seem to agree. Sandro was just saying: "I tell you it *is* him."

"His mother's a real beauty," said an admiring voice. "She's the best looker on the beach. Homs and me got under the cabin one day to see her undress, but her chemise fell just above the crack we were looking through and we couldn't see anything at all. Her legs, gee, and her breasts. . . ."

"You never see the husband anywhere about," said a third voice.

"You needn't worry, she satisfies herself. . . . D'you know who with? That young guy from Villa Sorriso . . . the dark one. He takes her out every day on his raft."

"He's not the only one either. She'd take anyone on," said someone maliciously.

"But I know it's not him," insisted another.

"Say Pisa," said Sandro suddenly. "Isn't that your mother, that lady at the Speranza? She's tall and dark, with long legs, and wears a striped two-piece bathing suit . . . and she's got a mole on the left side of her mouth."

"Yes, why?" asked Agostino, nervously.

"It *is* her, it *is* her," cried Berto triumphantly. And then, in a burst of jealous spite: "You're just their blind, aren't you? You all go out together, her and you, and her gigolo. You're their blind, aren't you?" At these words everyone roared with laughter. Even Saro smiled under his mustache. "I don't know what you mean," said Agostino, blushing and only half-understanding. He wanted to protest, but their coarse jokes aroused in him a curious and unexpected sense of sadistic satisfaction. As if by their words the boys had, all unawares, avenged the humiliations which his mother had inflicted on him all these days past. At the same time he was struck dumb with horror at their knowing so much about his private affairs.

"Innocent little lamb," said the same malicious voice. "I'd like to know what they're up to; they always go a long way out," said Tortima with mock gravity. "Come on, tell us what they do. He kisses her, eh?" He put the back of his hand to his lips and gave it a smacking kiss.

"It's quite true," said Agostino, flushing with shame; "we do go a long way out to swim."

"Oh yes, to swim!" came sarcastically from several voices at once.

"My mother does swim, and so does Renzo."

"Ah, yes, Renzo, that's his name," affirmed the boy, as if recovering a lost thread in his memory. "Renzo, that tall dark fellow."

"And what do Renzo and Mamma do together?" suddenly asked Berto, quite restored. "Is it this they do?" and he made an expressive gesture with his hand, "And you just look on, eh?"

"I?" questioned Agostino, turning around with a look of terror.

They all burst out laughing and smothered their merriment in the sand. But Saro continued to observe him attentively, without moving. Agostino looked around despairingly, as if to implore aid.

Saro seemed to be struck by his look. He took his cigar out his mouth, and said: "Can't you see he knows absolutely nothing?"

The din was immediately silenced. "How do you mean, he doesn't know?" asked Tortima, who hadn't understood.

"He just doesn't know," repeated Saro, simply. And turning to Agostino, he said in a softer voice: "Speak up, Pisa. A man and a woman, what is it they do together? Don't you know?"

They all listened breathlessly. Agostino stared at Saro, who continued to smoke and watch him through half-closed eyelids. He looked round at the boys, who were evidently bursting with stifled laughter, and repeated mechanically, through the cloud which seemed to cover his sight: "A man and a woman?"

"Yes, your mother and Renzo," explained Berto brutally.

Agostino wanted to say "Don't talk about my mother," but the question awoke in him a whole swarm of sensations and memories, and he was too upset to say anything at all. "He doesn't know," said Saro abruptly, shifting his cigar from one corner of his mouth to the other. "Which of you boys is going to tell him?" Agostino looked around bewildered. It was like being at school, but what a strange schoolmaster! What odd schoolfellows! "Me, me, me! . . ." all the boys shouted at once. Saro's glance rested dubiously on all those faces burning with eagerness to be the first to speak. Then he said: "You don't really know either, any of you. You've only got it from hearsay. . . . Let someone tell him who really knows." Agostino saw them all eyeing each other in silence. Then someone said: "Tortima." An expression of vanity lit up the youth's face.

He was just going to get up when Berto said, with hatred in his voice: "He made it all up, himself. . . . It's a pack of lies. . . ."

"What d'you mean, a pack of lies?" shouted Tortima, flinging himself upon Berto. "It's you who tells lies, you bastard!" But this time Berto was too quick for him, and from behind the corner of the hut he began making faces and putting out his tongue at Tortima, his red, freckled face distorted by hatred. Tortima contented himself with threatening him with his fist and shouting: "You dare come back!" But somehow Berto's intervention had wrecked his chances, and the boys with one accord voted for Sandro. His arms crossed over his broad brown chest on which shone a few golden hairs. Sandro, handsome and elegant, advanced into the circle of boys stretched out on the sand. Agostino noticed that his strong, bronzed legs looked as if they were dusted over with gold. A few fair hairs also showed through the gaps in his bathing trunks. "It's quite simple," he said in a strong, clear voice. And speaking slowly with the aid of gestures which were significant without being coarse, he explained to Agostino what he now felt he had always known but had somehow forgotten, as in a deep sleep. Sandro's explanation was followed by other less sober ones. Some of the boys made vulgar gestures with their hands, others dinned into Agostino's ears coarse words which he had never heard before; two of them said: "We'll show him what they do," and gave a demonstration on the hot sand, jerking and writhing in each other's arms. Sandro, satisfied with his success, went off alone to finish his cigar. "Do you understand now?" asked Saro, as soon as the din had died down. Agostino nodded. In reality he hadn't so much understood as absorbed the notion, rather as one absorbs a medicine or poison, the effect of which is not immediately felt but will be sure to manifest itself later on. The idea was not in his empty, bewildered and anguished mind, but in some other part of his being; in his embittered heart, or deep in his breast, which received it with amazement. It was like some bright, dazzling object, which one cannot look at for the radiance it emits, so that one can only guess its real shape. He felt it was something he had always possessed but only now experienced in his blood.

"Renzo and Pisa's mother," he heard someone say close beside him. "I'll be Renzo and you be Pisa's mother. Let's try." He turned suddenly and saw Berto, who with an awkward, ceremonious gesture was making a bow to another boy. "Madam, may I have the honor of your company on my raft? I'm going for a swim. Pisa will accompany us." Then suddenly blind rage took possession of him and flinging himself upon Berto he yelled: "I forbid you to talk about my mother." But before he knew what had happened he was lying on his back on the sand, with Berto's knee holding him down and Berto's fists raining blows on his face. He wanted to cry, but realizing that his tears would only be an opening for more jeers, he controlled them with great effort. Then, cov-

ering his face with his arm, he lay as still as death. Berto left him
alone after a bit, and feeling very ill-treated he went and sat down at
Saro's feet. The boys were already busy talking about something else.
One of them suddenly asked Agostino: "Are you rich, you people?"

Agostino was so intimidated that he hardly knew what to say. But
he replied: "I think so."

"How much? . . . A million? Two millions? . . . Three millions?"

"I don't know," said Agostino, feeling bothered.

"Got a big house?"

"Yes," said Agostino; and somewhat reassured by the more courteous turn of the conversation, pride of possession prompted him to
add: "We have twenty rooms."

"Bum . . ." came incredulously from someone.

"We've got two reception rooms and then there's my father's
study . . ."

"Aha!" said a scornful voice.

"Or it *used* to be my father's," Agostino hastened to add, half-hoping
that this detail might make them feel a little more sympathetic towards
him. "My father is dead."

There was a moment's silence. "So your mother's a widow?" said
Tortima.

"Well, of course," came from several mocking voices. "That's not
saying anything," protested Tortima. "She might have married again."

"No, she hasn't married again," said Agostino.

"And have you got a car?"

"Yes."

"And a chauffeur?"

"Yes."

"Tell your mother I'm ready to be her chauffeur," shouted someone.

"And what do you do in those reception rooms?" asked Tortima,
on whom Agostino's account seemed to make more impression than on
anyone else. "Do you give dances?"

"Yes, my mother has receptions," replied Agostino.

"Lots of pretty women, you bet," said Tortima, as if speaking to
himself. "How many people come?"

"I don't really know."

"How many?"

"Twenty or thirty," said Agostino, who by now felt quite at his
ease and was rather gratified by his success.

"Twenty or thirty . . . What do they do?"

"What do you expect them to do?" asked Berto ironically. "I suppose they dance and amuse themselves. They're rich . . . not like us. They
make love, I suppose."

"No, they don't make love," said Agostino conscientiously, for the sake of showing that he knew perfectly well what they meant.

Tortima seemed to be struggling with an idea which he was unable to formulate. At last he said: "But supposing I was to appear at one of those receptions, and say: 'I've come too.' What would you do?" As he spoke he got up and marched forward impudently, with his hands on his hips and his chest stuck out. The boys burst out laughing. "I should ask you to go away," said Agostino simply, emboldened by the laughter of the boys.

"And supposing I refused to go away?"

"I should make our men turn you out."

"Have you got menservants?"

"No, but my mother hires waiters when she has a reception."

"Bah, just like your father." One of the boys was evidently the son of a waiter.

"And supposing I resisted, and broke that waiter's nose for him, and then marched into the middle of the room and shouted, 'You're a lot of rogues and bitches, the whole lot of you.' What would you say?" insisted Tortima, advancing threateningly upon Agostino, and turning his fist round and round, as if to let him smell it. But this time they all turned against Tortima, not so much from a wish to protect Agostino as from the desire to hear more details of his fabulous wealth.

"Leave him alone . . . they'd kick you out, and a good thing too," was heard on all sides. Berto said sneeringly: "What have you got to do with it? Your father's a boatman and you'll be a boatman too; and if you did turn up at Pisa's house you certainly wouldn't shout anything. I can see you," he added, getting up and mimicking Tortima's supposed humility in Agostino's house . . . " 'Excuse me, is Mr. Pisa at home? Excuse me . . . I just came . . . Oh, he can't? . . . Never mind, please excuse me . . . I'm so sorry . . . I'll come another time.' Oh, I can see you. Why, you'd bow down to the ground."

All the boys burst out laughing. Tortima, who was as stupid as he was brutal, didn't dare stand up to their taunts. But in order to get even he said to Agostino: "Can you make an iron arm?"

"An iron arm?" repeated Agostino.

"He don't know what an iron arm is," said several voices, derisively. Sandro came over and took hold of Agostino's arm and doubled it up, and told him to stay with his hand in the air and his elbow in the sand. Meanwhile Tortima lay face downward on the sand and placed his arm in a similar position. "You push from one side," said Sandro, "and Tortima will push from the other."

Agostino took Tortima's hand. The latter at one stroke brought down his arm and got up triumphantly.

"Let me try," said Berto. He brought down Agostino's arm just as easily and got up in his turn. "Me too, me too!" cried all the others. One after another they all beat Agostino. At last it was the Negro's turn, and someone said: "If you let Homs beat you, well, your arm must be made of putty." Agostino made up his mind not to let the Negro beat him.

The Negro's arms were thin, the color of roasted coffee. He thought his own looked stronger. "Come on, Pisa," said Homs, with sham bravado, as he lay down facing him. He had a weak voice, like a woman's, and when he brought his face to within an inch of Agostino's, he saw that his nose, instead of being flat, as you might have expected, was almost aquiline, and curved in on itself like a black, shiny curl of flesh, with a pale, almost yellow mole above one nostril. Nor were his lips broad and thick like a Negro's, but thin and violet-colored. He had round eyes with large whites, on which his protuberant forehead and its great mop of sooty wool seemed to press. "Come on, Pisa, I won't hurt you," he said, putting his delicate hand with its thin, rose-nailed fingers in Agostino's. Agostino saw that by raising himself slightly on his shoulder he could easily have brought his whole weight to bear on his hand, and this simple fact allowed him at first to keep Homs under his control. For quite a while they competed without either of them getting the upper hand, surrounded by a circle of admiring boys. Agostino's face wore a look of great concentration; he was putting his whole strength into the effort; whereas the Negro made fearful grimaces, grinding his white teeth and screwing up his eyes. Suddenly a surprised voice proclaimed: "Pisa's winning!" But at that very moment Agostino felt an excruciating pain running from his shoulder right down his arm; he could bear no more, and gave in, saying: "No, he's stronger than me." "You'll beat me next time," said the Negro in an unpleasantly honeyed voice, as he rose from the ground. "Fancy Homs beating you too, you're good for nothing," sneered Tortima. But the other boys seemed tired of ragging Agostino. "How about a swim?" asid someone. "Yes, yes, a swim!" they all cried, and they set off by leaps and bounds over the hot sand to the sea. Agostino, trailing behind, saw them turning somersaults like fish into the shallow water, with shouts and screams of joy. As he reached the water's edge Tortima emerged, bottom first, like a huge sea-animal, and called out: "Dive in, Pisa. What are you doing?"

"But I'm dressed," said Agostino.

"Get undressed then," returned Tortima crossly. Agostino tried to escape, but it was too late. Tortima caught hold of him and dragged him along, struggling and pulling his tormentor over with him. He only let him go when he had almost suffocated him by holding his head under water. Then with a "Good-bye, Pisa," he swam off. Some way out Agostino could see Sandro standing in an elegant posture on a raft, in the middle of a swarm of boys, all trying to climb on to the floats. Wet and panting he returned to the beach and stood a few moments watching the raft going further and further out to sea, all alone under the blinding sunshine. Then hurrying along the burnished sand at the water's edge, he made his way back to the Speranza.

It was not so late as he feared. When he reached the bathing place he found that his mother had not yet returned. The beach was emptying; only a few isolated bathers still loitered in the dazzling water. The majority were trailing languidly off in single file under the midday sun up the tiled path which led from the beach. Agostino sat down under the big umbrella and waited. He thought his mother was staying out an unusually long time. He forgot that the young man had arrived much later than usual with his raft and that it was not his mother who had wanted to go out alone, but he who had disappeared; and said to himself that those two had certainly profited by his absence to do what Saro and the boys had suggested. He no longer felt any jealousy about this, but experienced a new and strange quiver of curiosity and secret approval, as if he were himself an accomplice. It was quite natural for his mother to behave like that with the young man, to go out with him every day on the float, and at a safe distance from prying eyes to fling herself into his arms. It was natural, and he was now perfectly well able to accept the fact. These thoughts passed through his mind as he sat scanning the sea for the return of the lovers. At length the raft appeared, a bright speck on the sea, and as it drew rapidly nearer he could see his mother sitting on the bench and the young man rowing. Every stroke of the oars as they rose and fell left a glittering track in the water. He got up and went down to the water's edge. He wanted to see his mother land, and to discover some traces of the intimacy at which he had assisted so long without understanding, and which, in the light of the revelations that Saro and the boys had made, must surely be brazenly advertised in their behavior. As the raft came near the shore his mother waved to him, then sprang gaily into the water and was soon at his side. "Are you hungry? We'll go and have something to eat at once. . . . Good-bye, good-bye till tomorrow. . . ." she added in a caressing voice, turning to wave to the young man. Agostino thought she seemed happier than usual, and as he followed her across the beach he could not help thinking there had been a note of joyous intoxication in her farewell to the young man; as if what her son's presence had hitherto prevented had actually taken place that day. But his observations and suspicions went no further than this; for apart from her naïve joy, which was something quite different from her customary dignity, he could not really picture what might have happened while they were out together, nor imagine what their relations actually were. Though he scrutinized her face, her neck, her hands, her body with a new and cruel awareness, they did not seem to bear any trace of the kisses and caresses they had received. The more Agostino watched his mother the more dissatisfied he felt. "You were alone today . . . without me . . ." he began, as they approached the cabin; almost hoping she would say: "Yes, and at last we were able to make love." But his mother only seemed to treat this remark as an allusion to the slap she had given him, and to his running away. "Don't let's say any more about that," she said, stopping and putting her arm around his shoulders, and looking at him with her laughing, excited eyes. "I know you love me; give me a kiss and we won't say any more about it, eh?" Agostino suddenly felt his lips against her neck—that neck whose chaste perfume and warmth had been so sweet to him. But now he fancied he felt beneath his lips, however faintly, a stirring of something new, as it were a sharp quiver of reaction to the young man's kisses. Then she ran up the steps to the cabin, and he lay down on the sand, his face burning with a shame he could not comprehend.

Later, as they were walking back together, he stirred up these new mysterious feelings in his troubled mind. Before, when he had been ignorant of good and evil, his mother's relations with the young man had seemed to him mysteriously tinged with guilt, but now that Saro and his disciples had opened his eyes, he was, strange to say, full of doubt and unsatisfied curiosity. It was indeed the frank jealousy of his childish love for his mother which had first aroused his sensibilities; whereas now, in the clear, cruel light of day, this love, though as great as ever, was replaced by a bitter, disillusioned curiosity compared with which those early, faint evidences seemed insipid and insufficient. Formerly, every word and gesture which he felt unbecoming had offended without enlightening him, and he wished he had not seen them. Now that he came to look back, those small, tasteless gestures which used to scandalize him seemed mere trifles, and he almost wished he could surprise his mother in some of the shameless attitudes into which Saro and the boys had so recently initiated him.

He would never have hit so soon on the idea of spying on his mother with the direct intention of destroying the halo of dignity and respect which had hitherto enveloped her, had he not that very day been driven by chance to take a step in that direction. When they reached home mother and son ate their luncheon in silence. His mother seemed distrait, and Agostino, full of new and, to him, incredible thoughts, was unusually silent. But after lunch he suddenly felt an irresistible desire to go out and join the gang of boys again. They had told him they met at the Vespucci bathing place early in the afternoon, to plan the day's adventures, and when he had got over his first fear and repugnance the company of those young hooligans began to exercise a mysterious attraction over him. He was lying on his bed with the shutters closed; it was warm and dark. He was playing as usual with the wooden switch of the electric light. Few sounds came on him from outside; the wheels of a solitary carriage, the clatter of plates and glasses through the open windows of the *pension* opposite. In contrast with the silence of the summer afternoon the sounds inside the house seemed to stand out more clearly, as if cut off from the rest. He heard his mother go into the next room and her heels tapping on the tiled floor. She went to and fro, opening and shutting drawers, moving chairs about, touching this and that. "She's gone to lie down," he thought suddenly, shaking off the torpor which was gradually invading his senses; "and then I shan't be able to tell her I want to go on the beach." He sprang up in alarm at the thought, and went out on the landing. His room looked over the balcony facing the stairs, and his mother's room was next to his. He went to her door, but finding it ajar, instead of knocking as he generally did, he gently pushed the door half open, moved perhaps by an unconscious desire to spy upon his mother's intimacy. His mother's room was much bigger than his, and the bed was by the door; directly facing the door was a chest of drawers, with a large mirror above it. The first thing he saw was his mother standing in front of the chest of drawers. She was not naked, as he had pictured and almost hoped when he went in so quietly; but she was partly undressed and was just taking off her necklace and earrings in front of the glass. She had on a flimsy chiffon chemise which only came half-way down her loins. As she stood leaning languidly to one side, one hip was higher and more prominent than the other, and below her solid but graceful thighs her slender, well-shaped legs tapered to delicate ankles. Her arms were raised to unfasten the clasp of her necklace and, through the transparent chiffon, this movement was perceptible all down her back, curiously modifying the contours of her body. With her hands raised thus, her armpits looked like the jaws of two snakes and the long, soft hair darted out of them like thin black tongues, as if glad to escape from the pressure of her heavy limbs. All her splendid, massive body seemed to Agostino's fascinated eyes to lose its solidity and sway and palpitate in the twilight of the room, as if nudity acted on it as a leaven and endowed it with a strange faculty of expansion; so that at one moment it seemed to billow outwards in innumerable curves, at another to taper upwards to a giant height, and to fill the space between floor and ceiling.

Agostino's first impulse was to hurry away again, but suddenly that new thought, "It is a woman," rooted him to the spot, with wide-open eyes, holding fast to the door handle. He felt his filial soul rebel at this immobility and try to drag him back; but the new mind which was already strong in him, though still a little timid, forced his reluctant eyes to stare pitilessly at what yesterday he would not have dared to look upon. And during this conflict between repulsion and attraction, surprise and pleasure, all the details of the picture he was contemplating stood out more distinctly and forcibly: the movements of her legs, the indolent curve of her back, the profile of her armpits. And they seemed to correspond exactly to his new conception, which was awaiting these confirmations in order to take complete sway over his imagination. Precipitated in one moment from respect and reverence to their exact opposite, he would almost have liked to see the improprieties of her unconscious nudity develop before his eyes into conscious wantonness. The astonishment in his eyes changed to curiosity, the attention which riveted them and which he fancied to be scientific in reality owed its false objectivity to the cruelty of the sentiment controlling him. And while his blood surged up to his brain he kept saying to himself: "She is a woman, nothing but a woman," and he somehow felt these words to be lashes of insult and contempt on her back and legs.

When his mother had taken off her necklace and put it down on the marble top of the chest of drawers, she began with a graceful movement of both hands to remove her earrings. In order to do so she held her head slightly to one side, turning a little away from the glass. Agostino was afraid she might catch sight of him in the big standing mirror which was nearby in the bay window; for he could see himself in it, standing furtively there, just inside the folding door. He raised his hand with an effort, knocked at the doorpost and said: "May I come in?"

"One moment, darling," said his mother calmly. Agostino saw her disappear from sight and, after rummaging about for a while, reappear in a long blue silk dressing gown.

"Mamma," said Agostino, without lifting his eyes from the ground, "I am going down to the beach."

"Now?" said his mother, abstractedly. "But it's so hot. Hadn't you better sleep a little first?" She put out one hand and stroked his cheek, while with the other she rearranged a stray lock of her smooth black hair.

Agostino suddenly become a child again, said nothing but remained standing, as he always did when any request of his had been refused, obstinately dumb, and looking down, his chin glued to his chest. His mother knew that gesture so well that she interpreted it in the usual way. "Well, if you really want to very much," she said, "go to the kitchen first and get them to give you something to take with you. But don't eat it now . . . put it in the cabin . . . and mind you don't bathe before five o'clock. Besides, I shall be out by then and we'll swim together." They were the same instructions she always gave him.

Agostino made no reply, and ran barefooted down the stone stairs. He heard his mother's door close gently behind him. He put on his sandals in the hall and went out on to the road. The white blaze of the midday sun enveloped him in its silent furnace. At the end of the road the motionless sea sparkled in the remote, quivering atmosphere. In the opposite direction the red trunks of the pine trees bent under the weight of their heavy green cones.

He debated with himself whether to go to the Vespucci Baths by the beach or by the forest; but chose the former, for though he would be much more exposed to the sun he would be in no danger of passing the baths without seeing them. He followed the road as long as it ran by the sea, then hurried along as fast as he could, keeping close to the walls. Without his realizing it, what attracted him to the Vespucci, apart from the novel companionship of the boys, were their coarse comments on his mother and her supposed amours. He was conscious that his former disposition was changing into quite a different feeling, crueller and more objective, and he thought that their clumsy ironies, by the very fact that they hastened this change, ought to be sought out and cultivated. Why he so much wanted to stop loving his mother, why he even hated himself for loving her, he would have been unable to say. Perhaps because he felt he had been deceived and had thought her to be different from what she really was, or perhaps because, not being able to go on loving her simply and innocently as he had done before, he preferred to stop loving her altogether and to look on her merely as an ordinary woman. He was instinctively trying to free himself once for all from the encumbrance of his old, innocent love which he felt to have been shamefully betrayed; for now it seemed to him mere foolishness and ignorance. And so the same cruel attraction which a few minutes ago had kept his eyes fixed on his mother's back now drove him to seek out the humiliating and coarse companionship of those boys. Might not their scoffing remarks, like her half-revealed nakedness, help to destroy the old filial relationship which was now so hateful to him? When he came within sight of the baths he slowed down, and though his heart was beating violently so that he could hardly breathe, he assumed an air of indifference.

Saro was sitting as before at his rickety table, on which were a half-empty bottle of wine, a glass, and a bowl containing the remains of fish soup. But there seemed to be no one else about, though as he got nearer the curtain opened and he saw the black body of the Negro boy Homs lying on the white sand.

Saro took no notice at all of the Negro, but went on smoking meditatively, a dilapidated old straw hat rammed down over one eye. "Aren't they here?" asked Agostino in a tone of disappointment. Saro looked up and observed him for a moment, then said: "They're gone to Rio." Rio was a deserted part of the shore, a few kilometers further on, where a stream ran into the sea between sandbanks and reeds.

"Oh dear," said Agostino regretfully, "they've gone to Rio . . . what for?"

It was the Negro who replied. "They've gone to have a picnic there," and he put his hand to his mouth with an expressive gesture. But Saro shook his head and said: "You boys won't be happy till someone's put a bullet through you." It was clear that their picnic was only a pretext for stealing fruit in the orchards; at least, so it seemed to Agostino.

"I didn't go with them," put in the Negro obsequiously, as if to ingratiate himself with Saro.

"You didn't go because you didn't want to," said Saro calmly.

The Negro rolled in the sand, protesting: "I didn't go because I wanted to stay with you."

He spoke in a honeyed, singsong voice. Saro said contemptuously: "Who gave you permission to be so familiar, you little nigger? We're not brothers as far as I know."

"No, we're not brothers," said the other in an unruffled, even triumphant tone, as if the observation gave him profound satisfaction.

"You keep your place then," said Saro. Then, turning to Agostino: "They've gone to steal some corn. That's what their picnic'll be."

"Are they coming back?" asked Agostino anxiously. Saro said nothing but kept looking at Agostino and seemed to be turning something over in his mind. "They won't be back very soon," he replied slowly; "not till late. But if you like we'll go after them."

"But how?"

"In the boat," said Saro.

"Oh yes, let's go in the boat," said the Negro. He sprang up, all eagerness, and approached Saro, but the latter did not give him a glance. "I have a sailboat . . . in about half an hour we shall be at Rio, if the wind's favorable."

"Yes, let's go," said Agostino happily. "But if they're in the fields how shall we find them?"

"Never you fear," said Saro, getting up and giving a twist to the black sash round his stomach. "We shall find them all right." Then he turned to the Negro, who was watching him anxiously, and added: "Come on, nigger, help me carry down the sail and mast."

"I'm coming, Saro, I'm coming," reiterated the jubilant Negro, and he followed Saro down to the boat.

Left by himself Agostino stood up and looked round him. A light wind had sprung up from the northwest, and the sea, covered now with tiny wavelets, had changed to an almost violet blue. The shore was enveloped in a haze of sun and sand, as far as the eye could see. Agostino, who did not know where Rio was, followed with a nostalgic eye the capricious indentations of the lonely coast line. Where was Rio? Somewhere out there, he supposed, where earth, sky and sea were mingled in one confused blackness under the pitiless sun. He looked forward intensely to the expedition, and would not have missed it for worlds.

He was startled from these reflections by the voices of the two coming out of the hut. Saro was carrying on one arm a pile of ropes and sails, while in the other he hugged a bottle. Behind him walked the Negro, brandishing like a spear a tall mast partly painted green. "Well, let's be off," said Saro, starting down the beach without glancing at Agostino. His manner seemed to Agostino curiously hurried, quite different from his usual one. He also noticed that those repulsive red nostrils looked redder and more inflamed than usual, as if all their network of little branching veins had suddenly become swollen with an inrush of blood. "*Si va . . . si va . . .*" intoned the Negro behind Saro, improvising a sort of dance on the sand, with the mast under his arm. But Saro had nearly reached the huts and the Negro slackened his pace to wait for Agostino. When he was near, the Negro signaled him to stop. Agostino did so.

"Listen," said the Negro, with an air of familiarity. "I've got to talk something over with Saro . . . please oblige . . . please . . . by not coming. Go away, please!"

"Why?" asked Agostino, much surprised.

"I told you I've got to talk something over with him . . . just the two of us," said the other impatiently, stamping his foot on the ground.

"I *must* go to Rio," replied Agostino.

"You can go another time."

"No—I can't."

The Negro looked at him, and his eyes and trembling nostrils betrayed a passionate eagerness which revolted Agostino. "Listen, Pisa," he said, "if you'll stay behind I'll give you something you've never seen before." He dropped the mast and felt in his pocket and brought out a slingshot made of a fork of pinewood and two elastics bound together. "It's lovely, isn't it," and the Negro held it up.

But Agostino wanted to go to Rio. Besides, the Negro's insistence aroused his suspicions. "No, I can't," he said.

"Take it," the other said again, feeling for Agostino's hand and trying to force the slingshot into his palm. "Take it and go away."

"No," repeated Agostino, "I can't."

"I'll give you the slingshot and these cards, too," said the Negro, feeling his pocket again; and he drew out a small pack of cards with pink backs and gilt edges. "Take them all and go away. You can kill birds with the slingshot . . . the cards are quite new."

"I told you I won't," said Agostino.

The Negro turned on him an eye of passionate entreaty. Great drops of sweat shone on his forehead, his whole face was contorted in an expression of utter misery. "But why won't you?" he whined.

"I don't want to," said Agostino, and he suddenly ran towards the bath man, who was now standing by the boat. As he reached Saro he heard the Negro call after him: "You'll be sorry for this." The boat was resting on two rollers of unplaned fir a short way up the beach. Saro had thrown the sails into the boat and seemed to be waiting impatiently. "What's he up to?" he asked Agostino, pointing to the Negro.

"He's just coming," said Agostino.

And in fact the Negro came running over the sand with great leaps, holding the mast under his arm. Saro took hold of the mast with the six fingers of his right hand, and with the six fingers of his left reared it up and planted it in a hole in the middle seat. Then he got into the boat, fastened the sail and loosened the sheet. Saro turned to the Negro and said: "Now let's shove off from underneath."

Saro stood beside the boat, grasping the edges of the prow, while the Negro made ready to push from behind. Agostino, not knowing what to do, looked on. The boat was of medium size, part white and part green. On the prow, in black lettering, was written *Amelia*. "*Ah . . . issa,*" commanded Saro. The boat slid forward on its rollers over the sand. As soon as the keel passed over the hindmost roller the Negro bent down and took it in his arms, pressing it to his breast like a baby; then leaping over the sand as in a novel kind of ballet, he ran and placed it under the prow. "*Ah . . . issa,*" repeated Saro.

The boat slid forward again quite a distance, and again the Negro gamboled and caracoled from stern to prow, with the roller in his arms; one last shove, and the prow of the boat dipped into the water and it was afloat. Saro got in and placed the oars in the rowlocks; then, grasping one in each hand, he motioned to Agostino to jump in, excluding the Negro as if by prearrangement. Agostino entered the water up to his knees and tried to climb in. He would never have succeeded had not the six fingers of Saro's right hand seized him firmly by one arm and pulled him up like a cat. He looked up. Saro was lifting him with one arm, without looking in his direction, for he was busy adjusting the left-hand oar. Agostino, in disgust at being grasped by those fingers, went off and sat in the stern. "Good," said Saro, "you stay there; now we are going to take her out."

"Wait for me, I'm coming too!" shouted the Negro from the shore. Exhausted by his efforts he sprang into the water and seized the edge of the boat. But Saro said: "No, you're not coming."

"What am I to do?" cried the boy, in an agony of disappointment. "What am I to do?"

"You can take the trolley," answered Saro, standing up in the boat and pulling hard. "You'll get there before us, see if you don't."

"But why, Saro?" wailed the Negro, thrashing along in the water beside the boat. "Why, Saro? I want to go too."

Without a word Saro dropped his oars, bent over and covered the Negro's face with his enormous hand. "I've told you you're not coming," he said quietly, and with one push sent the Negro over backward in the water. "Why, Saro?" he went on wailing. "Why, Saro?" and his melancholy voice, mingled with the splashing of the oars, made an unpleasant impression on Agostino and aroused in him an uneasy sense of pity. He looked at Saro, who smiled and said: "He's such a nuisance. What do we want with him?"

The boat was already some way from the shore. Agostino looked round and saw the Negro get out of the water and, as he thought, shake his fist threateningly at him.

Saro silently took out the oars and laid them down in the bottom of the boat. Then he went to the prow, undid the sail and fastened it to the mast. The sail fluttered uncertainly for a moment, as if the wind were blowing on both sides of it at once; then suddenly, with a violent shock swelled in the wind and leaned over to the left. The boat obediently settled down on its left side too, and began to skim over the waves, driven by the light breeze. "Good," said Saro, "now we can lie down and rest a bit." He settled down in the bottom of the boat and invited Agostino to lie beside him. "If we sit in the bottom," he explained, "the boat goes faster." Agostino obeyed, and lay down beside Saro.

The boat made swift progress in spite of its heavy build, rising and falling with the little waves and occasionally rearing up like a foal which feels the bit for the first time. Saro lay with his head resting against the seat, and one arm behind Agostino's neck, controlling the rudder. For a while he said nothing; then: "Do you go to school?" he asked at last.

Agostino looked up. Saro was half-lying and seemed to be exposing his wide, inflamed nostrils to the sea air, as if to refresh them. His mouth was open under his mustache, his eyes half-shut. His unbuttoned shirt revealed the dirty, grey, ruffled hair on his chest. "Yes," said Agostino, suddenly trembling with fear.

"What class are you in?"

"The third."

"Give me your hand," said Saro; and before Agostino could refuse he seized hold of it. To Agostino his grasp felt like a vice. The six short, stumpy fingers encircled his whole hand and met below it. "What do they teach you?" Saro went on, stretching himself out more comfortably and sinking into a kind of ecstasy.

"Latin . . . Italian . . . geography . . . history . . ." stammered Agostino.

"Do they teach you poetry . . . lovely poetry?" asked Saro, in a low voice.

"Yes," said Agostino, "poetry as well."

"Recite some to me."

The boat plunged, and Saro shifted the rudder without changing his beatific attitude. "I don't know what . . ." began Agostino, feeling more and more embarrassed and frightened. "I learn a lot of poetry . . . Carducci . . ."

"Ah yes, Carducci," repeated Saro mechanically. "Say a poem by Carducci."

"*Le fonti del Clitunno*," suggested Agostino, terrified by that hand which would not let him go, and trying little by little to escape from it.

"Yes, *Le fonti del Clitunno*," said Saro in a dreamy voice.

> *Ancor dal monte che di foschi ondeggia*
> *frassini al vento mormoranti e lunge*

began Agostino in a shaky voice.

The boat sped on, and Saro, still stretched at full length with closed eyes and his nose to the wind, began to move his head up and down as if scanning the lines. Agostino clung to poetry as the only means of escape from a conversation which he intuitively felt to be dangerous and compromising, and went on reciting slowly and clearly. Meanwhile, he kept trying to release his hand from those six imprisoning fingers; but they held him more tightly than ever. With terror he saw the end of the poem drawing near, and not knowing what to do he joined the first line of *Davanti a San Guido* on to the last line of *Fonti del Clitunno*. Here would be proof, if any were needed, that Saro didn't care a bit about the poetry but had something quite different in view; *what*, Agostino could not understand. The experiment succeeded. *"I cipressi che a Bolgheri alti e schietti"* suddenly began without Saro giving the faintest sign of noticing the change. Then Agostino broke off and said in an exasperated voice: "Let go, please," and tried at the same time to pull his hand quite away.

Saro started, and without letting go of him, opened his eyes and turned to look at him. He must have read such violent antipathy and such obvious terror on Agostino's face that he suddenly realized that his plan, for he certainly had a plan, was a complete failure. He slowly withdrew one finger after another from Agostino's aching hand and said in a low voice, as if speaking to himself: "What are you afraid of? We're going ashore now."

He dragged himself to his feet and pulled round the rudder. The boat turned its prow towards the shore.

Still rubbing his cramped fingers, Agostino got up from the bottom of the boat without a word and went to sit in the prow. By now the boat was not far from the shore. He could see the whole beach, the white stretch of sun-bleached sand which at that point was very wide, and beyond the beach the dense, brooding green of the pines. Rio was at a gap cut out in the high dunes, overhung by a greenish-blue mass of reeds. But before they got to Rio, Agostino saw a group of people on the beach, and from the center of this group there rose a long thread of black smoke. He turned to Saro, who was sitting in the stern controlling the rudder with one hand. "Is this where we get out?"

"Yes, this is Rio," replied Saro indifferently.

As the boat drew nearer and nearer to the shore Agostino saw the group gathered round the fire suddenly break up and start running down to the water's edge, and he at once saw that it was the boys. He could see them waving and probably calling out, but the wind carried their voices away. "Is it them?" he asked nervously.

"Yes, it's them," said Saro.

The boat drew nearer still and Agostino could clearly distinguish the boys. They were all there: Tortima, Berto, Sandro, and the others. And there was the Negro Homs, leaping along the shore and shouting with the others, a discovery which for some reason gave him a very uncomfortable feeling.

The boat made straight for the shore where with a rapid turn of the rudder, Saro brought it in crosswise, and throwing himself upon the sail clasped it in both arms and lowered it to the deck. The boat swung motionless in the shallow water. Saro took a small anchor from the bottom and threw it into the water. "Let's go ashore," he said. He climbed over the edge of the boat and waded through the water to meet the boys who were waiting on the beach.

Agostino saw the boys crowding around him and apparently offering him congratulations, which Saro received with a shake of his head. Still louder applause greeted his own arrival, and for a moment he was deceived into thinking they were welcoming him cordially. But he soon realized he was mistaken. Their laughter was mocking and sarcastic. Berto called out: "Good old Pisa, he enjoys going out for a sail," while Tortima, putting his fingers into his mouth, gave a rude whistle. The others imitated him. Even Sandro, usually so reserved, looked at him with contempt. As for the Negro, he did nothing but jump about around Saro, who went on ahead towards the fire the boys had lit on the beach. Surprised and vaguely alarmed, Agostino went and sat down among the others around the fire.

The boys had made a sort of rough oven out of damp compressed sand. Inside was a fire of dried pine cones, pine needles and twigs. Heaped up in the mouth of the oven were about a dozen ears of corn, slowly roasting. Spread out on a newspaper near the fire were masses of fruit and a watermelon. "He's a fine one, is our Pisa," said Berto, when they had sat down. "You and Homs are buddies now, you ought to be sitting together . . . you're brothers, you two; he's black, you're white . . . that's all there is to it . . . and you both like going for a sail."

The Negro chuckled appreciatively. Saro was bending down to give the corncobs another turn in front of the fire. The others laughed derisively. Berto went so far as to give Agostino a push which sent him against Homs, so that for a moment their backs were touching; one chuckling with depraved self-satisfaction, the other bewildered and disgusted. "But I don't know what you mean," said Agostino suddenly. "I went out in the boat; what harm is there in that?"

"Aha, what harm is there in that? He went out in the boat. What harm is there in that?" repeated many scoffing voices. Some were holding their sides with laughter.

"Yes, indeed, what harm?" repeated Berto, turning to him again. "No harm at all! Why, Homs thinks it's grand, don't you Homs?"

The Negro assented ecstatically. And now the truth began dimly to dawn on Agostino, for he couldn't help seeing some connection between their taunts and Saro's odd behavior in the boat. "I don't know what you mean," he declared. "I didn't do anything wrong in that boat. Saro made me recite some poems, that's all."

"Ah, ah, those poems," was heard on all sides.

"Isn't it true what I say, Saro?" cried Agostino, red in the face.

Saro didn't say yes or no; he contented himself with smiling, watching him all the while with a certain curiosity. The boys interpreted his air of pretended indifference, which was really a cloak for his treachery and vanity, as giving the lie to Agostino. "Oh, of course," they all struck up together: "He asks the host if the wine is good, eh, Saro? That's a good one! Oh, Pisa, Pisa!" The Negro was having his revenge, and enjoying himself particularly. Agostino suddenly turned on him, trembling with rage, and said: "What is there to laugh at?"

"I'm not laughing," he replied, edging away.

"Now, don't you two quarrel," said Berto. "Saro will have to see about making you friends again." But the boys lost all interest when the issue seemed to be settling itself peacefully, and were already talking of other things. They were telling how they had crept into a field and stolen corn and fruit; how they had seen the enraged farmer coming towards them with a gun; how they had run away, and the farmer had fired salt at them without hitting anyone. Meanwhile, the ears were ready, beautifully toasted on the embers. Saro took them out of the oven and with his usual fatherly air parceled out one to each. Agostino took advantage of a moment when they were busy eating, and sprang across to Sandro, who was sitting a little apart, eating his corn grain by grain.

"I don't understand," he began. The other gave him a knowing look and Agostino felt he need say no more. "The Moor came by trolley," said Sandro slowly, "and he said you and Saro had gone sailing."

"But what harm is there in that?"

"It's no business of mine," replied Sandro, casting down his eyes. "It's up to you . . . you and the Moor. But as for Saro," he stopped and looked at Agostino.

"Well?"

"Well, I wouldn't have gone out alone with Saro."

"But why?"

Sandro looked carefully round him, then in a low voice gave the explanation which Agostino somehow expected, without being able to say why. "Ah," he said . . . but he could say no more and went back to the others. Squatting in the middle of the boys, with his imperturbable, good-natured head on one side, Saro had the air of a kind paterfamilias surrounded by his sons. But Agostino felt a deep loathing when he looked at him, greater in fact than he felt for the Negro. What made Agostino hate him more was his silence when appealed to, as if he wanted the boys to believe that what they had accused him of had really taken place. Besides, he could not help noticing that their scorn and derision had set a wide gulf between him and his companions—the same gulf which he now realized separated them from the Negro; only the Negro, instead of being humiliated and offended, as he himself was, seemed somehow to relish it. He tried more than once to turn the conversation on to the subject which so tormented him, but was met with laughter and an insulting indifference. Moreover, in spite of Sandro's only too clear explanation, he still could not quite grasp what had really happened. Everything seemed dark around him and within him, as if instead of beach, sea and sky, there were only shadows and vague, menacing forms.

Meanwhile, the boys had finished eating their roasted corn and tossed the bare cobs away in the sand. "Let's go swim at Rio," suggested someone, and the proposal was immediately accepted. Saro went with them, for it was agreed that he should take them all back to Vespucci in the boat.

As they walked along the sand Sandro left the others and came over to Agostino. "If you're offended with the Moor," he said, "why don't you put the fear of God into him?"

"How?" asked Agostino, in a discouraged tone.

"Give him a good hiding."

"But he's stronger than me," said Agostino, remembering the duel of the iron arm. "Unless you will help me."

"Why should I help you? It's your concern . . . yours and his." Sandro pronounced these words in such a way as to make it quite clear that he took the same view as the others as to the reason for Agostino's hatred of the Negro. A sense of terrible bitterness pierced Agostino to the heart. So Sandro, the only one who had shown him any kindness, believed that calumny too. After giving him this advice Sandro went off to rejoin the others, as if he were afraid of being seen with Agostino. From the beach they had passed through a forest of young pines; then they crossed a sandy path and entered the reed beds. The reeds grew thick and tall, and many had a white, plumy crest; the boys appeared and disappeared between their long green spears, slipping about on the damp earth and pushing the stiff, fibrous leaves aside with a dry, rustling sound. At last they came to a place where the reed bed widened around a low, muddy bank; at sight of them big frogs leaped from all sides into the opaque, glassy water; and here they began to undress, all together, under the eyes of Saro, who sat fully clothed on a rock overlooking the reeds, and appeared to be absorbed in his cigar, but was really watching them all the time through his half-closed eyelids. Agostino was ashamed to join them, but he was so afraid of being laughed at that he too began to unbutton his trousers, taking as long as he could about it and keeping an eye on the others. The rest seemed to be over-joyed at getting rid of their clothes, and bumped into each other shout-ing with glee. They looked very white against the background of green reeds, with an unpleasant, squalid whiteness from groin to belly, and this pallor only emphasized a sort of graceless and excessive muscu-larity which is especially to be found in manual workers. The graceful, well-proportioned Sandro, whose pubic hair was as fair as that of his head, was the only one who hardly seemed to be naked, perhaps because his skin was equally bronzed over his whole body; in any case his naked-ness was quite different from that repulsive nakedness displayed in the public baths.

Before diving in the boys played all sorts of obscene pranks; open-ing their legs wide, poking and touching each other with a loose prom-iscuity which astounded Agostino, to whom this sort of thing was quite new. He was naked too, and his feet were black from the cold, filthy mud, but he would have liked to have hidden himself in the reeds, if only to escape the looks which Saro, who sat hunched up motionless like one of those huge frogs native to the reed bed, darted at him through half-closed eyes. But as usual his repugnance was less strong than the mysterious attraction which bound him to the gang; the two were so in-dissolubly mixed up together that it was impossible for him to distin-guish between his horror and the pleasure which underlay it. The boys displayed themselves each in turn, boasting of their virility and bodily prowess. Tortima, the vainest of all, and in spite of his disproportionate strength the most squalid and plebeian looking, was so elated as to call out to Agostino: "Suppose I was to appear before your mother, one fine morning, naked like this, what would she say? Would she go along with me?"

"No," said Agostino.

"And I tell you that she'd come along at once," said Tortima. "She'd just give me one good look over, to see what I was good for, and then she'd say: 'Come along, Tortima, let's be off!'" The gross ab-surdity of his suggestion made them all laugh, and at his cry: 'Come, Tortima, let's be off!' they flung themselves one after another into the water, diving in head over heels, just like the frogs whom their coming had disturbed.

The shore was so entirely surrounded by reeds that only a short stretch of the river was visible. But when they got into the middle of the stream they could see the whole river which, with an imperceptible mo-tion of its dark, dense waters, flowed toward the mouth further down among the sandbanks. Up-stream the river continued between two lines of large silvery bushes which cast delightful reflections in the water; till one came to a little iron bridge, beyond which the reeds, pines and poplars were so dense as to prevent further passage. A red house, half-hidden among the trees, seemed to keep guard over this bridge.

For a moment Agostino felt happy, as he swam in that cold, powerful water which seemed to be trying to bear his legs away with it; he forgot for a moment all his wrongs and crosses. The boys swam about in all directions, their heads and arms emerging from the smooth green surface. Their voices resounded in the limpid, windless air; seen through the transparency of the water their bodies might have been the white shoots of plants blossoming out of the depths and moving hither and yon as the current drew them. Agostino swam up to Berto, who was not far off, and asked: "Are there many fish in this river?"

Berto looked at him and said: "What are you doing here? Why don't you keep Saro company?"

"I like swimming," replied Agostino, feeling miserable again; and he turned and swam away.

But he was not so strong or experienced a swimmer as the others; he soon got tired, and let the current carry him towards the mouth of the river. He had soon left the boys and their clamor behind him; the reeds grew thinner; through the clear, colorless water he could see the sandy bottom over which grey eddies flowed continually. At last he came to a deeper green pool, the stream's transparent eye as it were; and when he had passed this his feet touched the sand, and after struggling a moment against the force of the water he climbed out on to the bank. Where the stream flowed into the sea it curled round itself and formed a knot of water. The stream then lost its compactness and spread out fanwise, growing thinner and thinner till it was no more than a liquid veil thrown over the smooth sands. The tide flowed up into the river with tiny foam-flecked wavelets. Here and there in the watery sand, pools forgotten by the stream reflected the bright sky. Agostino walked about for a little, naked on the soft, mirroring sand, and enjoyed stamping on it with his feet and seeing the water suddenly rise to the surface and flood his footprints. There arose in him a vague and desperate desire to ford the river and walk on and on down the coast, leaving far behind him the boys, Saro, his mother and all the old life. Who knows whether, if he were to go straight ahead and never turn back, walking, walking on that soft white sand, he might not at last come to a country where none of these horrible things existed; a country where he would be welcomed as he longed to be, and where it would be possible for him to forget all he had learned and then learn it again without all that shame and horror, gently and naturally as he dimly felt that it might be possible. He gazed at the dark, remote horizon which enclosed the utmost boundaries of sea and shore and forest and felt drawn to that immensity as to something which might set him free from his bondage. The shouts of the boys racing across the shore to the boat roused him from his melancholy imaginings. One of them was waving his clothes in the air, and Berto was calling: "Pisa, we're off!" He shook himself and walked along at the edge of the sea to join the gang.

The boys were thronging together in the shallow water. Saro was warning them in fatherly tones that the boat was too small to hold them all, but he was clearly only teasing them. Screaming, the boys flung themselves like mad upon the boat; twenty hands at once clutched the sides, and in a twinkling the boat was filled with their gesticulating bodies. Some lay down on the bottom, others sat in a heap in the stern around the rudder, some in the prow, others on the seats; others again sat on the edge and let their feet dangle in the water. The boat really was too small for so many, and the water came almost to the top.

"We're all here then, are we?" said Saro in great good humor. He stood up, let out the sail, and the boat sped out to sea. The boys cheered its departure loudly.

But Agostino did not share their happy mood. He was looking out for a favorable opportunity to prove his innocence and remove the unjust stigma which oppressed him. He took advantage of a moment when the other boys were deep in some discussion, to scramble up to the Negro who was sitting alone in the bow and resembled in his blackness a new kind of figurehead. Squeezing one arm hard, Agostino demanded: "What did you go and say about me just now?"

It was a bad moment to choose, but it was Agostino's first opportunity of getting near the Negro who had taken good care to keep at a distance while they were on shore. "I spoke the truth," said Homs, without looking at him.

"What is the truth?"

The Negro's reply terrified Agostino. "It's no good your squeezing my arm like that. I only spoke the truth. But if you go on setting Saro against me I shall tell your mother everything. So look out, Pisa."

"What!" cried Agostino, seeing an abyss open beneath his feet. "What do you mean? Are you crazy? I . . . I . . ." He stammered, unable to follow up in words the frightful vision his imagination suddenly summoned up. But he had no time to continue. Shouts of derision broke out all over the boat.

"Look at them both side by side," laughed Berto. "Look at them! What a shame we haven't got a camera to take them both together." Agostino turned round, his face burning, and saw them all laughing. Even Saro was smiling under his mustache, as with half-closed eyes he puffed at his cigar. Agostino drew back from the Negro, as from the touch of a reptile, and with his arms around his knees sat watching the sea, his eyes full of tears.

On the horizon the sun was setting in clouds of fire above a violet sea, shot with pointed, glassy rays. The wind had risen and the boat made slow progress, listing heavily to one side under its load of boys. The prow of the boat was turned out to sea and seemed to be directed towards the dark profiles of far-off islands which rose among the red smoke of sunset like mountains at the end of a distant plateau. Saro, holding firmly between his knees the boys' stolen watermelon, split it open with his seaman's knife and cut off large slices which he distributed to them paternally. They passed the slices and bit into them greedily, spitting out the seeds and tearing off pieces of the flesh. Then one after another the sections of red, close-gnawed rind flew overboard into the sea. After the melon it was the turn of the wine flask, which Saro solemnly produced from under the stern. The bottle made the round of the boat, and even Agostino was obliged to swallow a mouthful. It was warm and strong and at once went to his head. When the empty bottle had returned to its place Tortima sang an indecent song, and they all joined in the refrain. Between verses they pressed Agostino to sing too, for they had noticed his black mood; but no one spoke to him except to tease him and incite him to sing. Agostino felt within him a heavy weight of pent-up grief which the windy sea and magnificent fires of sunset on the violet waters only made more bitter and unbearable. It seemed to him horribly unjust that it was on such a sea and under such a sky that a boat like theirs should be sailing, so crowded with malice, cruelty, falsehood and corruption. That boat, overflowing with boys gesticulating like obscene monkeys, with the fat and blissful Saro at the helm, was to him an incredible and melancholy sight in the midst of all that beauty. At moments he wished it would sink; he would have liked to die himself, he thought, and no longer be infected and stained by all that impurity. How far away seemed the morning when he had for the first time looked upon the red awning of the Vespucci Baths; far away and belonging to an age already dead. Each time the boat rose on an unusually high wave they gave a yell which made him shudder; each time the Negro addressed him with his revolting and hypocritically slavish humility, he tried not to listen and drew back still further into the prow. He was dimly conscious of having on that fatal day entered upon an age of difficulties and miseries from which he could see no way of escape. The boat made a long trip, going as far as the port and then turning back again. When they at last touched land Agostino ran off without saying good-bye to anyone. But he had not gone far before he slackened his pace and looking back saw the boys helping Saro to pull the boat up on the beach. It was already getting dark.

That day was the beginning of a dark and troubled time for Agostino. On that day his eyes had been opened for him by force, but what he had learned was too much for him, a burden greater than he could bear. It was not so much their novelty as the quality of the things he had learned which oppressed and poisoned him; they were too appalling and too portentous for him to assimilate. He thought, for example, that after that day's disclosures about his mother his relations with her would have become clarified; that the uneasiness, distaste and even disgust which, after Saro's revelations, her caresses awoke in him would somehow, as if by enchantment, be resolved and reconciled in a new and serene consciousness. But it was not so; the uneasiness, distaste and disgust remained, rising in the first instance from the shock and bewilderment to his filial love occasioned by his obscure realization of his mother's femininity, and after that morning in Saro's tent rising from a bitter sense of guilty curiosity which his traditional and abiding respect for his mother rendered intolerable to him. At first he had unconsciously tried to break loose from that affection by an unjustified dislike, but now it seemed to him a duty to separate his newly won reasoned knowledge from his sense of blood relationship with someone whom he wanted to consider only as a woman. He felt that if only he could see in his mother what Saro and the boys did—just a beautiful woman—then all his unhappiness would disappear; and he tried with all his might to seek out occasions which would confirm him in this belief. But the only result was that his former reverence and affection gave place to cruelty and sensuality.

At home his mother did not hide herself from him any more than she had before, and was unaware of any change in his attitude towards her. As his mother, she had no sense of shame; but to Agostino it seemed that she was wantonly provocative. He would hear her calling him, and would go to her room to find her at her toilet, in negligee and with her breasts half-uncovered. Or he would wake to find her bending over him to give him his morning kiss, with her dressing gown open so that he could clearly see the shape of her body through her fragile, crumpled nightgown. She would go to and fro in front of him as if he were not there; putting on or taking off her stockings, putting on her clothes, applying perfume or make-up; and all those acts which Agostino had once thought so natural now seemed to him the outward and visible signs of a much more embracing and more dangerous reality, so that his mind was torn between curiosity and pain. He kept saying to himself: "She's only a woman," with the objective indifference of a connoisseur. But a moment later, unable to endure either her maternal unselfconsciousness or his own watchfulness, he would have liked to shout: "Cover yourself up, go away, don't let me see you any more, I'm not the same as I used to be." But his hope of judging his mother as a woman and nothing more almost immediately suffered shipwreck. He soon saw that even if she had become a woman she remained in his eyes all the more his mother; and he realized that the cruel sense of shame which he had at first attributed to the novelty of his feelings would now never leave him. He saw in a flash that she would always remain for him the person he had loved with such a free and pure love; she would always mix with her most feminine gestures those purely affectionate ones which for so long had been the only ones he knew; never would he be able to separate his new conception of her from his now wounded memory of her former dignity. He did not for a moment doubt that the facts of her relationship with the young man really were as reported by the boys in Saro's tent. And he wondered secretly at the change which had taken place in him. At first he had only felt jealousy of his mother and antipathy towards the young man; both feelings being rather veiled and indefinite. But now, in his effort to remain objective and calm, he would have wished to feel sympathy for the young man and indifference towards his mother. But this sympathy seemed somehow to make him an accomplice, and his indifference to make him indiscreet. He very seldom went out with them now on the raft, for he generally contrived to avoid being invited. But whenever he went he was conscious of studying the young man's gestures and words almost as if he wanted him to overstep the limits of permitted social gallantry, and of studying his mother almost in the hope of having his suspicions confirmed. At the same time these sentiments were intolerable to him because they were the exact opposite of what he wanted to feel, and he would almost have liked to feel again the pity which his mother's foolish behavior had once aroused in him; it was more human and affectionate than his present merciless dissection.

Those days of inner conflict left him with a confused sense of impurity. He felt that he had exchanged his former state of innocence, not for the manly calm he had hoped for, but a dark, indeterminate state in which he found no compensating advantages, but only fresh perplexities in addition to the old. What was the good of seeing clearly, if this clarity only brought with it deeper shades of darkness? Sometimes he wondered how older boys than himself managed to go on loving their mother when they knew what he knew; and he concluded that such knowledge must at once destroy their filial affection, whereas in his own case the one did not banish the other, but they existed side by side in a dreary tangle.

As sometimes happens, the place which was the scene of these discoveries and conflicts—his home—became almost intolerable to him. The sea, the sun, the crowd of bathers, the presence of many other women at least distracted him and deadened his sensibilities. But here, between the four walls of his home, alone with his mother, he felt exposed to every kind of temptation, beset by every kind of contradiction. On the beach his mother was one among many other sun bathers; here she seemed overpowering and unique. Just as on a small stage the actors seem larger than life, so here every gesture and word of hers stood out with extraordinary definition. Agostino had a very lively and adventurous sensibility in regard to the familiar things of his home. When he was a child every passage, every nook and corner, every room had had for him a mysterious and incalculable character; they were places in which you might make the strangest discoveries and live through the most fantastic adventures. But now, after his meeting with those boys in the red tent, these adventures and discoveries were of a quite different kind, so that he did not know whether to be more attracted or frightened by them. Formerly he used to imagine ambushes, shadows, spirits, voices in the furniture and in the walls; but now his fancy, even more actively than in his exuberant childhood, attached itself to the new realities with which the walls, the furniture, the very air of the house seemed to him to be impregnated. And in place of his old innocent excitement which his mother's good-night kiss and dreamless sleep could always calm, he was tormented by a burning and shameful curiosity which at night grew to giant proportions and seemed to find in darkness more food for its impure fire.

Everywhere in the house he seemed to spy out traces of a woman's presence, the only woman whom he had ever known intimately; and that woman was his mother. When he was with her he felt as if he were somehow mounting guard over her; when he approached her door he felt he was spying on her; if he touched her clothes he felt as if it was herself he was touching, for she had worn these clothes, they had held her body. At night he dreamed with his eyes open, and had agonizing nightmares. He would sometimes imagine himself to be a child again. afraid of every sound, of every shadow, and would spring up to run and take refuge in his mother's bed; but as soon as his feet touched the ground he realized, sleepy and bewildered though he was, that his fear was only a cunning mask for curiosity and that directly he was in his mother's arms his nocturnal vision would reveal its true purpose. Or he would wake suddenly and wonder whether by chance the young man of the raft were there at that very moment in his mother's room on the other side of the wall. Certain sounds seemed to confirm this suspicion, others to contradict it; he would toss restlessly in bed for a while, and at last, without the smallest idea how he had got there, would find himself in the passage in his nightshirt, listening and spying outside his mother's room. Once he could not resist the temptation of going in without knocking, and he stood motionless in the middle of the room in the diffused moonlight which entered through the open window, his eyes fixed on the bed where he could distinguish his mother's black hair spread out over the pillow and her long, softly rounded limbs. "Is that you, Agostino?" she asked, waking up. Without saying a word he turned and hurried back to his room.

His reluctance to remain alone with his mother drove him more and more to Vespucci. But here other torments awaited him, and made the place as odious to him as his home. The boys' attitude towards him after he had been out alone in the boat with Saro had not changed at all; it had in fact assumed a definite and final form, as if founded on an unshakable conviction. For he was the one who had accepted that signal and sinister favor from Saro; it was impossible to get that idea out of their mind. So that, in addition to the jealousy and contempt they had felt for him from the first on account of his being rich, was now added another source of contempt . . . his supposed depravity. And in the minds of those young savages the one seemed to justify the other, the one to grow out of the other. They seemed by their humiliating and cruel treatment of him to imply that he was rich and therefore naturally depraved. Agostino was quick to perceive the subtle relation between these two charges, and he dimly felt that they were making him pay for being different from them and superior to them. His social difference and superiority were expressed in his clothes and his talk about the luxury of his home, in his tastes and manner of speech; his moral difference and superiority impelled him to refute the charge of having had any such relations with Saro, and kept showing itself in open disgust at the boys' manners and habits. So at last, prompted by the humiliating position in which he found himself rather than exercising any definite choice of his own, he decided to be what they seemed to want him to be . . . that is, just like themselves. He began wearing his oldest and dirtiest clothes, to the great surprise of his mother, who noticed that he no longer took any pride in his appearance; he made a point of never mentioning his luxurious home, and he took an ostentatious pleasure in ways and habits which up to that time had disgusted him. But worst of all, and it needed a great effort to nerve himself to it, one day when they were making their usual jokes about his going out alone with Saro, he said that he was tired of denying it, and that what they accused him of had really happened, and that he didn't care whether they knew it or not. Saro was startled by these assertions, but perhaps from fear of exposing himself did not deny them. The boys were also very much surprised to hear him admitting the truth of gossip which had seemed to torment him so much before. He was so timid and shy that they would never have given him credit for so much courage, but they very soon began raining down questions on him as to what had really happened; and then he lost heart, got red in the face and refused to say another word. Naturally the boys interpreted his silence in their own way, as being due to shame and not, as it really was, to his ignorance and incapacity to invent. And the usual load of taunts and low jokes became heavier than ever.

But in spite of this breakdown he really had changed. Without being conscious of it himself, without really trying to, he had, by dint of spending so much time with the boys every day, ended by becoming very like them, and had lost his old tastes without really acquiring any new ones. More than once, in a mood of revolt against Vespucci, he had joined in the more innocent games at Speranza, seeking out his playmates of earlier in the summer. But how colorless and dull those nicely brought-up boys now seemed to him, how boring their regulation walks under the eye of parents or tutors, how insipid their school gossip, their stamp collections, books of adventure and such-like. The fact is that the company of the gang, their talk about women, their thieving expeditions in the orchards, even the acts of oppression and violence of which he had himself been a victim, had transformed him and made him intolerant of his former friendships. It was during this time that something happened which brought this home to him more strongly. One morning when he arrived late at Vespucci he found no one there. Saro was off on some business of his own, and there were no boys to be seen. He wandered gloomily to the water's edge and seated himself on a float. Suddenly, as he was watching the beach in the hope of seeing at least Saro come in sight, a man and a boy about two years younger than himself appeared. He was a small man, with short, fat legs under a protruding stomach, a round face and pointed nose confined by pince-nez. He looked like a civil servant or professor. The boy was thin and pale, in a suit too big for him, and was hugging a large and evidently new leather ball to his chest. Holding his son by the hand, the man came up to Agostino and looked at him doubtfully for some time. At last he asked if it was possible to go for a row.

"Of course," replied Agostino, without hesitation.

The man considered him rather suspiciously over the top of his glasses, then asked how much it would cost to go out for an hour on a bathing raft. Agostino knew the prices and told him. Then he realized that the man had mistaken him for the bath man's son or for one of his boys, and that somehow flattered him. "Very well," said the man, "we will go."

Agostino didn't need telling twice. He at once took the rough pine log which served as roller, and placed it under the prow of the boat. Then, grasping the ends of the two floats in both hands, his strength redoubled by this singular spur to his pride, he pushed the raft into the water. He helped the boy and his father to get on, sprang after them and seized the oars.

For a while Agostino rowed without speaking. At that early hour the sea was quite empty. The boy hugged his ball to his chest and kept his pale eyes fixed on Agostino. The man sat awkwardly, with knees apart to make room for his pauch. He kept turning his fat neck to look about him, and seemed to be enjoying the outing. At last he asked Agostino who he was, the bath man's son, or employed by him. Agostino replied that he was employed by him. "And how old are you?" asked the man.

"Thirteen," replied Agostino.

"There," said the man, turning to his son, "this boy is almost the same age as you, and he's already at work." Then to Agostino: "And do you go to school?"

"I should like to, but how can I, sir?" he answered, assuming the hypocritical tone which he had heard the boys put on when asked a question like that. "We've got to live, sir."

"There, you see," said the father to his son. "This boy can't go to school because he has to work, and you have the face to make a fuss about your lessons."

"There's a lot of us in the family," said Agostino, rowing vigorously, "and we all work."

"And how much can you earn a day?" asked the man.

"It depends," replied Agostino. "If many people come, about twenty or thirty lire."

"Which of course you give to your father," interposed the man.

"Of course," replied Agostino, without a moment's hesitation, "except what I make in tips."

This time the man didn't think it necessary to point him out as an example to his son, but he nodded his head approvingly. His son said nothing, but hugged his ball still closer and kept his pale, watery eyes fixed on Agostino. "Would you like to have a leather ball like that, boy?" the man suddenly asked Agostino. Now Agostino had two identical balls, which had been lying about for a long time in his room and his other toys. But he said: "Of course I should, but how am I to get one? We have to buy necessities first." The man turned to his son and said to him, probably half in fun: "There now, Peter, give your ball to this boy who hasn't got one." The boy looked first at his father and then at Agostino, and greedily hugged his ball tighter; but still he didn't say a word. "Don't you want to?" asked his father gently. "Don't you want to?"

"It's my ball," said the boy.

"Yes, it's yours, but if you like you may give it away," persisted the father. "This poor boy has never had one in all his life; now, don't you want to give it up to him?"

"No," said his son emphatically.

"Never mind," interposed Agostino at this point, with a sanctimonious smile, "I don't really want it. I shouldn't have time to play with it . . . it's different for him."

The father smiled at these words, pleased at having found such a useful object lesson for his son. "He's a better boy than you," he went on, stroking his son's head. "He's poor, but he doesn't want to take away your ball, he leaves it to you; but whenever you want to grumble and make a fuss, I hope you'll remember that there are lots of boys like this in the world, who have to work, and who have never had balls or any toys of their own."

"It's my ball," repeated the boy obstinately.

"Yes, it's yours," sighed his father, absent-mindedly. He looked at his watch and said in a tone of command: "It's time we went back; take us in, boy." Without a word Agostino turned the prow towards the beach.

As they approached the shore he saw Saro standing in the water watching his maneuvers attentively, and he was afraid the bath man would give him away. But Saro didn't say a word; perhaps he understood, perhaps he didn't care; he gravely helped Agostino pull the boat up the beach. "This is for you," said the man, giving Agostino the sum agreed on and something over. Agostino took the money and gave it to Saro. "But I'm going to keep the tip," he added, with an air of self-satisfied bravado. Saro said nothing; scarcely even smiling, he put the money inside the sash bound around his stomach and walked off slowly across the beach to his hut.

This little incident gave Agostino a definite feeling of not belonging any more to the world in which boys of that sort existed, and by now he had got so used to living with the poor that the hypocrisy of any other kind of life bored him. At the same time he felt regretfully that he wasn't really like the boys of the gang. He was still much too sensitive. If he had really been one of them, he thought sometimes, he would not have suffered so much from their coarse and clumsy jokes. So it seemed that he had lost his first estate without having succeeded in winning another.

One day, towards the end of the summer, Agostino went with the boys to the pine woods to chase birds and look for mushrooms. This was what he enjoyed most of all their exploits. They entered the forest and walked for miles upon its soft soil along natural aisles, between the red pillars of the tree trunks, looking up in the sky to see if somewhere between those tall trunks there was anything moving among the pine needles. Then Berto or Tortima or Sandro, who was the most skillful of all, would stretch the elastic of his slingshot and aim a sharp stone in the direction they thought they had seen a movement. Sometimes a sparrow with a broken wing would come hurtling down, and go fluttering lamely along with pitiful little chirps till one of the boys seized it and twisted its neck between his fingers. But more often the chase was fruitless, and the boys would go wandering on deeper and deeper into the forest, their heads thrown back and their eyes fixed on some point far above them; going even farther and farther till at last the undergrowth began and a tangle of thorny bushes took the place of bare, soft soil covered with dry husks. And with the undergrowth began their hunt for fungi. It had been raining for a day or two and the leaves of the undergrowth were still glistening with wet, and the ground was damp and covered with fresh green shoots. In the thick of the bushes . . . there were the yellow fungi, glittering with moisture; sometimes magnificent single ones, sometimes families of little ones. The boys put their fingers through the brambles and picked them delicately, holding the head between two fingers and taking care to bring the stalk away too, with earth and moss still clinging to it. Then they threaded them on long, pointed sprigs of broom. Wandering thus from patch to patch of undergrowth, they would collect several kilos for Tortima's dinner, for he, being the strongest, confiscated their finds. That day their harvest had been a rich one, for after wandering about a good deal they had found some virgin undergrowth where the fungi were growing closely packed together in their bed of moss. It was getting late before they had even half-explored this undergrowth; so they began to tramp slowly homeward, with several long spits laden with fungi and two or three birds.

They generally followed a path which led straight down to the shore; but this evening they were led farther and father in pursuit of a teasing sparrow which kept fluttering along among the low boughs and continually gave the illusion of being just within reach, so that they ended by walking the whole length of the forest, which to the east came to an end just behind the town. It was dusk as they emerged from the last pine trees on to the piazza of a remote suburb, with rubbish heaps and thistles and broom scattered about and a few ill-defined paths winding over it. Stunted oleanders grew at intervals around the edge; there were no pavements, and the dusty gardens of the few little villas which bordered it alternated with waste ground enclosed by bits of fencing. These little villas were placed at intervals all round the piazza and the wide expanse of sky over the great square added to the impression of loneliness and squalor.

The boys cut diagonally across the piazza, walking two and two like a religious order. At the end of the procession came Tortima and Agostino. Agostino was carrying two long spits of fungi and Tortima held a couple of sparrows in his great hands, their bloody heads dangling.

When they had reached the far end of the piazza Tortima nudged Agostino with his elbow and, pointing to one of the little villas, said cheerfully: "Do you see that? Do you know what that is?"

Agostino looked. The villa was very like all the others; a little bigger perhaps, with three stories and a sloping slate roof. Its façade was gloomy and smoke-grimed, with white shutters tightly closed; while the dense trees in the garden almost hid it from view. The garden did not look very big; the wall around it was covered with ivy, and through the gate one could see a short path with bushes on either side, and a double-paneled door under an old-fashioned porch. "There's no one there," said Agostino, stopping.

"No one, eh?" laughed the other; and he explained to Agostino in a few words who it was lived there. Agostino had several times heard the boys talking about houses where women lived alone, and how they shut themselves in all day, and at night were ready to welcome anyone who came, in return for money; but he had never seen one of these houses before. Tortima's words roused in him to the full the sense of strangeness and bewilderment which he had felt when first he heard them discussing it. And now as then he could hardly believe that there really existed a community so singular in its generosity as to dispense impartially to all that love which seemed to him so far away and so hard to come by; so he now looked with incredulous eyes on the little villa, as if he hoped to read on its walls some trace of the incredible life that went on inside it.

Compared with his imaginary picture of rooms on each of which a naked woman shed her radiance, the house looked singularly old and grimy. "Oh yes," he said, with pretended indifference, but his heart had already begun to beat faster.

"Yes," said Tortima, "it's the most expensive in the town." And he added a number of details about the place and the number of women, the people who went there and the time you were allowed to stay. This information was almost displeasing to Agostino, substituting as it did sordid details for the confused, barbaric image he had formed when he first heard tell of these forbidden places. But assuming a tone of idle curiosity he put a great many questions to his companion. For, after the first moment of surprise and disappointment, an idea had suddenly sprung up in his mind and soon laid fast hold of him. Tortima, who seemed to be well informed, gave him all the information he needed. Deep in conversation they crossed the piazza and joined the others on the esplanade. It was now almost dark and the party broke up. Agostino gave his fungi to Tortima and started home.

The idea which had come to him was clear and simple enough, however complicated and obscure its origin. He had made up his mind to go to that villa this very night and sleep with one of the women. This was not just a vague desire, it was an absolutely firm, almost desperate resolution. He felt that this was the only way he could escape from the obsession that had caused him such intense suffering all that summer. If he could only possess one of those women, he said to himself, it would forever prove the boys' calumny to have been ridiculous, and at the same time sever the thin thread of perverted and troubled sensuality which still bound him to his mother. Though he did not confess it to himself, his most urgent aim was to feel himself forever independent of his mother's love. A simple but significant fact had convinced him of this necessity, only that very day.

Up to now he and his mother had slept in separate rooms; but that night a friend of his mother's was arriving to spend a week with them. As the house was small it had been arranged that their guest should have Agostino's room, while a cot was to be made up for him in his mother's room. That very morning he had been disgusted to see the cot set up beside his mother's, which was still unmade and covered with bedclothes. His clothing and books and washing things had been carried in with the cot.

The fact of sleeping together only made Agostino hate still more that promiscuity with his mother which was already so hateful to him. He thought this new and still closer intimacy must suddenly reveal to him, without hope of escape, all that up to now he had only dimly suspected. Quickly, quickly he must find an antidote, and set up between his mother and himself the image of another woman to whom he could turn his thoughts if not his eyes. And the image which was to screen him from his mother's nakedness, and which would restore her dignity by removing her femininity . . . one of those women in the villa on the piazza was to supply that image.

How he was to get himself received in that house and how he would choose the woman and go off with her were matters to which Agostino did not give a thought—indeed, even if he had wanted to, he would never have been able to picture it. In spite of Tortima's information, the house and its inmates and everything belonging to it were surrounded by a dense atmosphere of improbability, as if one were not dealing with reality but with the most daring hypothesis which might at the last moment prove fallacious. The success of his undertaking depended on a logical calculation; if there was a house, then there were women too, and if there were women there was the possibility of meeting one of them. But it was not quite clear to him that the house and the women really were there; and this was not so much because he doubted Tortima's word as because he was totally lacking in terms of comparison. Nothing he had ever done or seen bore the faintest resemblance to what he was about to undertake. Like a poor savage who has heard about the palaces of Europe, and can only picture them as a slightly larger version of his own thatched hut, so he, in trying to picture those women and their caresses, could only think, with slight variations, of his mother; the love making could only be conjecture and vague desire.

But, as so often happens, his very inexperience led him to busy himself with practical aspects of the question, as if once these were settled he could also solve its complex unreality. He was particularly worried by the question of money. Tortima had explained to him in great detail exactly how much he would have to pay and to whom; and yet he could not quite grasp it. What was the relation between money, which is generally used for acquiring quite definite objects with recognizable qualities, and a woman's caresses, a woman's naked flesh? Was there really a price, and was that price really fixed, and not different in each particular case? The idea of giving money in exchange for that shameful and forbidden pleasure seemed to him cruel and strange, an insult which the giver might find pleasant but which must be painful for the one who received it. Was it really true that he would have to pay the money directly to the woman, and in her very presence? He somehow felt he ought to hide it and leave her with the illusion of a disinterested relationship. And then, wasn't the sum Tortima had mentioned too small? No money would be enough, he thought, to pay for such an experience . . . the end of one period of his life and the beginning of another.

Faced with these doubts he decided to keep strictly to what Tortima had told him, even if it turned out to be false, for he had nothing else on which to base his plan of action. He had found out from his friend how much it cost to visit the villa, and the figure did not seem higher than the amount he had been saving for a long time in his terra-cotta money box. With the small coins and paper money it contained he must surely be able to get the amount together, and it might even prove to be more. His plan was to take the money out of the money box, then wait till his mother had gone to the station to meet her friend, when he would go out in his turn, fetch Tortima and set off with him to the villa. He must have enough money for Tortima too, for he knew him to be poor and certainly not in the least disposed to do him a favor unless he was going to get something out of it himself.

This was his plan, and though it still seemed to him desperately remote and improbable he resolved to prepare for it with the same care and certainty as if it had only been an outing in a boat or some expedition into the pine woods.

Eager and excited, freed for the first time from the poison of remorse and impotence, he almost ran all the way home from the distant piazza. The front door was locked, but the french windows of the drawing room stood open, and through them came the sound of music. His mother was at the piano. He went in; the two subdued lights over the piano lit up her face while the rest of the room was in darkness. His mother was sitting on the piano stool, and beside her, on another, sat the young man of the raft. It was the first time that Agostino had seen him in their house, and a sudden presentiment took his breath away. His mother seemed to divine his presence, for she turned her head with a calm gesture of unconscious coquetry, a coquetry of which Agostino felt the young man to be the object rather than himself. She at once stopped playing when she saw him, and called him to her. "Agostino, what do you mean by coming in at this hour? Come here."

He went slowly up to the piano, full of revolt and embarrassment. His mother drew him to her and put her arm around him. He noticed that his mother's eyes were extraordinarily bright and young and sparkling. Laughter seemed to be on the brink of bubbling up through her

lips, making her teeth glitter. She quite frightened him by the impetuos-
ity, almost violence, with which she drew him to her, as if she were trembling with joy. He was sure that these manifestations had nothing to do
with him personally. And they reminded him strangely of his own excitement of a few minutes before, as he ran through the streets in his eagerness to fetch his savings and go with Tortima to the villa and possess a
woman.

"Where have you been?" his mother went on, in a voice which
was at once tender, cruel and gay. "Where have you been all this time,
you naughty boy?" Agostino made no reply; he did not feel his mother
really expected one. That was just how she sometimes spoke to the cat.
The young man was leaning forward, clasping his knees with both hands,
his cigarette between two fingers, and gazing at his mother with eyes as
sparkling and smiling as her own. "Where have you been?" repeated
his mother. "How naughty of you to play truant like that." She rumpled
up his hair on his forehead and then smoothed it again with her warm,
slender hand, with a tender but irresistible violent caress. "Isn't he a
handsome boy?" she said proudly, turning to the young man.

"As handsome as his mother," the young man replied. She smiled
pathetically at this simple compliment. Full of shame and irritation,
Agostino made an effort to free himself from her embrace. "Go and
wash yourself," said his mother, "and make haste, because we are soon
going in to supper." Agostino bowed slightly to the young man and left
the room. Behind him, he immediately heard the music taken up again
at the very point where he had interrupted it.

But once in the passage he stood still and listened to the sounds his
mother's fingers were drawing from the keys. The passage was dark, and
at the end of it he could see through the open door into the brightly lit
kitchen, where the cook, dressed in white, was bustling about between
the table and the kitchen range. His mother went on playing, and the
music sounded to Agostino gay, tumultuous, sparkling, exactly like the
expression in her eyes while she held him to her side. Perhaps that really
was the character of the music, or perhaps his mother read into it some
of her own fire and sparkle and vivacity. The whole house resounded
to the music, and Agostino found himself thinking that out in the road
lots of people must be stopping to listen, wondering at the scandalous
wantonness which seemed to pour from every note.

Then, all at once, in the middle of a chord, the sounds stopped,
and Agostino was convinced—he could not have told how—that the passion which had found expression in the music had suddenly found another
outlet. He took two steps forward, and stood still on the threshold of the
drawing room. What he saw did not much surprise him. The young man
was standing up, and kissing his mother on the lips. She was bending
backward over the low stool, which was too small to hold her body;

one hand was still on the keyboard and the other was round the young man's neck. Even in the dim light he could see how her body was arched as it fell backward, with her chest thrust forward, one leg folded behind her, and the other stretched out toward the pedal. In contrast to her attitude of passionate surrender, the young man preserved his usual easy and graceful carriage. As he stood, he held one arm round the woman's neck, but apparently more from fear lest she might fall over than from any deep emotion. His other arm hung at his side and he still had a cigarette between his fingers. His white-trousered legs, planted far apart, expressed deliberation and complete mastery of the situation.

The kiss lasted a long time and it seemed to Agostino that whenever the young man wanted to interrupt it his mother clung to his lips more insatiably than ever. He really could not help feeling that she was hungry . . . famished for that kiss, like someone who has been starved too long. Then, at a casual movement of her hand two or three solemn, sweet notes sounded in the room. Suddenly they sprang apart. Agostino took a step forward and said: "Mamma." The young man wheeled about, and standing with his legs apart and his hands in his pockets, pretended to look out the window.

"Agostino!" said his mother.

Agostino went to her. She was breathing so violently that he could distinctly see her breasts rising and falling through her silk dress. Her eyes were brighter than ever, her mouth was half-open, her hair in disorder; and one soft, pointed lock, like a live snake, hung against her cheek.

"What is it, Agostino?" she repeated, in a low, broken voice, doing her best to arrange her hair. Agostino felt a sudden oppression of pity mingled with distaste. He would have liked to cry out to her: "Calm yourself, don't pant like that . . . don't speak to me in that voice." But instead, he put on a childish voice and said, with exaggerated eagerness: "Mamma, can I break open my money box? I want to buy a book."

"Yes, dear," she answered, putting out a hand to stroke his brow. At the touch of her hand Agostino could not help starting back. His movement was so slight as to be almost imperceptible, but to him it seemed so violent that he felt every one must notice it. "Very well then, I'll break it," he said. And he left the room quickly, without waiting for a reply. The sand on the stairs made a gritty sound as he ran up to his room. The idea of the money box had really only been a pretext; the fact was he didn't know what to say when he saw his mother looking like that. It was dark in his room; the money box was on a table at the far end. Through the open window a street lamp lit up its pink belly and great black smiling mouth. He turned on the light, picked up the money box and flung it on the ground with an almost hysterical violence. It broke at once and from the wide opening poured a quantity of money of every description. There were several notes mixed with the coins. He went down on hands and knees and frantically counted the money. His fingers were trembling and, while he counted, the image of those two down in the drawing room kept getting mixed up with the money that was lying scattered over the floor—his mother, hanging backwards over the piano stool, and the young man bending over her. But when he had finished counting he discovered that the money did not amount to the sum he needed.

What was he to do? It flashed through his mind that he might take it from his mother, for he knew where she kept it, and nothing would have been easier; but this idea revolted him and he decided simply to ask her for it. But what excuse could he make? He suddenly thought of one, but at that moment he heard the gong sounding for supper. He hastily hid his treasure in a drawer and went downstairs.

His mother was already at table. The window was wide open and great velvety moths flew in from the courtyard and beat their wings against the white lampshade. The young man had gone and his mother had again assumed her usual dignified serenity. Agostino, as he looked at her, wondered why her mouth bore no trace of the kisses which had been pressed on it a few minutes before, just as he had wondered that first time, when she went out on the raft with the young man. He could not have defined what feelings this thought awoke in him. A sense of pity for his mother, to whom that kiss seemed to be so disturbing and so precious; and at the same time a strong feeling of repulsion, not so much for what he had seen as for the memory which remained with him. He would have liked to expel that memory, to forget it altogether. How was it possible that such troublous and changing impressions could enter through one's eyes? He foresaw that the sight would be forever stamped on his memory.

When they had finished, his mother rose from the table and went upstairs. Agostino thought he would never find such an opportune moment to ask for the money. He followed her up and went into her room with her. His mother sat down at the dressing-table and silently studied her face in the glass.

"Mamma," said Agostino.

"What is it?" she asked absentmindedly.

"I want twenty lire."

"What for?"

"To buy a book."

"But didn't you say you were going to break open your money box?" asked his mother, gently passing the powder puff over her face.

Agostino purposely made a childish excuse.

"Yes, but if I break it I shan't have any money left. I want to buy a book without opening my money box."

His mother laughed fondly. "What a baby you are." She studied herself a moment more in the glass, then she said: "You'll find my purse in the bag on my bed. Take out twenty lire, and put the purse back again." Agostino went to the bed, opened the bag, took out the purse and took twenty lire from it. Then clutching the two notes in his hand he flung himself on the cot beside his mother's. She had finished her make-up and came over to him. "What are you going to do now?" "I'm going to read this book," he said, taking a book of adventures at ransom from the bed table, and opening it at an illustration.

"Very well, but remember before you go to sleep to put out the light." His mother was still moving about the room, doing one thing and another. Agostino lay watching her, with his head pillowed on his arm. He obscurely felt that she had never been so beautiful as on that evening. Her dress of glossy white silk showed off brilliantly her brown coloring and the rich rose of her complexion. By an unconscious reflowering of her former character she seemed to have recovered all the sweet, majestic serenity of bearing she used to have; but with an indefinable breath of happiness. She was tall, but Agostino had never seen her look so imposing before. Her presence seemed to fill the room. White in the shadow of the room, she moved majestically about, with head erect on her beautiful neck, her black eyes calm and concentrated under her smooth brow. Then she put out all the lights except above the bed table, and bent down to kiss her son. Agostino drank in again the perfume he knew so well, and as he touched her neck with his lips he could not help wondering if those women . . . out there in the villa . . . would be as beautiful and smell as sweet.

Left alone, Agostino waited about ten minutes to give his mother time to have gone. Then he got up from the cot, put out the light, and tiptoed into the next room. He felt about in the dark for the table by the window, opened the drawer and filled his pockets with coins and notes. He felt with his hand in every corner of the drawer to see if it was really empty, and left the room.

When he was on the road he began to run. Tortima lived at the other end of the town, in the caulkers' and sailors' quarter, and though the town was small he had a long way to go. He chose the dark alleys bordering on the pine woods, and walking fast and occasionally running, he went straight ahead until he saw, appearing between the houses, the masts of the sailboats in the dry dock. Tortima's house was just above the dock, beyond the movable iron bridge which spanned the canal leading to the harbor. By day this was a forgotten, dilapidated spot with tumble-down warehouses and shops bordering its wide, deserted, sun-baked quays, pervaded by the smell of fish and tar, with green, oily water, motionless cranes and barges laden with shingle. But now the night made it like every other part of the town, and only a ship whose bulging sides and masts overhung the footpath, revealed the presence of the harbor water lying deep in between the houses. Agostino crossed the bridge and headed toward a row of houses on the opposite side of the canal. Here and there a street lamp irregularly lit the walls of these little houses. Agostino stopped in front of an open lighted window, from which came the sounds of voices and clatter of plates, as if they were having a meal. Putting his fingers to his mouth he gave one loud and two soft whistles, which was the signal agreed upon between the boys of the gang. Almost at once someone appeared at the window. "It's me, it's Pisa," said Agostino, in a low, timid voice. "I'm coming," answered Tortima. He came down, still eating his last mouthful, red in the face from the wine he had been drinking. "I've come to go to that villa," said Agostino. "I've got the money here . . . enough for both of us." Tortima swallowed hard and looked at him. "That villa the other side of the piazza," Agostino repeated. "Where the women are."

"Ah," said Tortima, understanding at last. "You've been thinking it over. Bravo, Pisa. I'll be with you in a moment." He ran off and Agostino walked up and down, waiting for him, his eyes fixed on Tortima's window. He was kept waiting a long time, but at last Tortima reappeared. Agostino scarcely recognized him. He had always seen him as a big boy with trousers tucked up, or half-naked on the beach and in the sea. Now he saw before him a young working man in dark holiday clothes: long trousers, waistcoat, collar and tie. He looked older too, because of the brilliantine with which he had plastered down his usually unruly hair; and his spruce, ordinary clothes brought out for the first time something ridiculous and vulgar in his appearance.

"Shall we go now?" said Tortima as he joined him.

"But is it time yet?" asked Agostino, hurrying along beside him as they crossed the bridge.

"It's always time there," said Tortima with a laugh.

They took a different road than the one Agostino had come by. The piazza was not far away, only about two turnings further on. "But have you been there before?" asked Agostino again.

"Not to that one."

Tortima did not seem to be in any hurry and kept his usual pace. "They'll hardly have finished supper and there'll be no one there," he explained. "It's a good moment."

"Why?" asked Agostino.

"Why, don't you see, we can choose the one we like best."

"But how many are there?"

"Oh, about four or five."

Agostino longed to ask if they were pretty, but refrained. "What do we have to do?" he asked. Tortima had already told him, but the sense of unreality was so strong in him that he felt the need of hearing it reaffirmed.

"What does one do?" said Tortima. "Nothing simpler. You go in . . . they come and show themselves . . . you say: 'Good evening, ladies,' you pretend to talk for a bit, so as to give yourself the time to look them well over . . . then you choose one. It's your first time, eh?"

"Well," began Agostino rather shamefacedly. "Go along!" said Tortima brutally. "You're not going to tell me it isn't the first time. Tell that to the others, if you like, but not to me. But don't be afraid. She does it all for you. Leave it to her."

Agostino said nothing. The image evoked by Tortima of the woman initiating him into love pleased him . . . it had something maternal about it. But in spite of these facts he still remained incredulous. "But—but do you think they'll want *me*?" he asked, standing still suddenly and looking down at his bare legs.

The question seemed to embarrass Tortima for a moment. "Let's go on," he said, with feigned self-assurance. "Once there, we'll manage to get you in."

They came through a narrow lane to the piazza. The whole of it was in darkness, except for one corner where a street lamp shone peacefully down on a stretch of uneven sandy earth. In the sky above the piazza the crescent moon hung red and smoky, cut in two by a thin filament of mist. Where the darkness was thickest Agostino recognized the villa by its white shutters. They were closed, and no ray of light showed through them. Tortima, without hesitation, crossed over to the villa. But in the middle of the piazza, under the crescent moon, he said to Agostino: "Give me the money, I'd better keep it."

"But I . . ." began Agostino, who did not quite trust Tortima. "Are you going to give it me or not?" persisted Tortima harshly. Agostino was ashamed of all that small change, but he obeyed and emptied his pockets into Tortima's hands. "Now keep your mouth shut, and come along with me," said his companion.

As they came near to the villa, the darkness grew less dense, and they could see the two gateposts, the garden path and the front door under the porch. The gate was not locked, and Tortima pushed it open and entered the garden. The front door was ajar. Tortima climbed the steps and went in, motioning to Agostino not to make a sound. Agostino, looking curiously about him, saw a quite empty hall, at the end of which was a double door, with brightly lit panes of red and blue glass. Their entrance was the signal for a ringing of bells and almost immediately the massive shadow of someone seated behind the glass door rose against the glass, and a woman appeared in the doorway. She was a kind of servant, middle-aged and very stout, with a capacious bosom, dressed in black with a white apron tied round her waist. She came forward, sticking out her stomach, and with her arms hanging down. She had a swollen face and sulky eyes which looked out suspiciously from under a mass of hair.

"Here we are," said Tortima. Agostino saw from his voice and manner that even he, who was usually so bold, felt intimidated.

The woman scrutinized them hostilely for a moment; then she made a sign, as if inviting Tortima to pass inside. Tortima smiled with renewed assurance, and hastened toward the glass door. Agostino made as if to follow him. "Not you," said the woman, putting her hand on his shoulder.

"What!" cried Agostino, at once losing all his fear. "Why him and not me?"

"You've really neither of you any business to be here," said the woman firmly; "but he will just pass, you won't."

"You're too little, Pisa," said Tortima mockingly. And he pushed the door open and disappeared. His stunted shadow stood out for a moment against the panes of glass; then it vanished in the brilliant light.

"But what about me?" insisted Agostino, exasperated by Tortima's treachery.

"You get off, boy, go away home," said the woman. She went to the front door, opened it wide, and found herself face to face with two men who were just coming in. "Good evening . . . good evening," said the first, who had a red, jolly face. "We're agreed, eh?" he added, turning to his companion, a pale, thin young man. "If Pina's free, I'm to have her . . . and no nonsense about it."

"Agreed," said the other.

"What's this little fellow doing here?" the jovial man asked the woman, pointing to Agostino.

"He wanted to come in," said the woman. A flattering smile framed itself on her lips.

"So you wanted to go in, did you?" cried the man, turning to Agostino. "At your age, home's the place at this hour. Home with you," he cried again, waving his arms.

"That's what I told him," the woman said.

"Suppose we let him come in?" remarked the young man. "At his age I was making love to the maid."

"Well, I'm blest! Get away home . . . home . . . *home*," shouted the other, scandalized. Followed by the fair man he entered the folding door, which banged-to behind them. Agostino, hardly knowing how he got there, found himself outside in the garden.

How badly it had all turned out; he had been betrayed by Tortima, who had taken his money, and he himself had been thrown out. Not knowing what to do, he went up the garden path, looking back all the time at the half-open door, the porch, the façade with its white shutters closed. He felt a burning sense of disappointment, especially on account of those two men who had treated him like a child. The laughter of the jovial man, the cold, experimental benevolence of his companion, seemed to him no less humiliating than the dull hostility of the woman. Still walking backward, and looking round at the trees and shrubs in the garden, he made his way to the gate. Then he noticed that the left side of the villa was illuminated by a strong light coming from an open window on the ground floor. It occurred to him that he might at least have a glimpse of the inside of the villa through that window; and making as little noise as possible he went towards the light.

It was a window open wide on the ground floor. The windowsill was not high; very quietly, and keeping to the corner where there was less chance of his being seen, he went up to the window and looked in.

The room was small and brilliantly lighted. The walls were papered with a handsome design of large green and black flowers. Facing the window a red curtain, hanging on wooden rings from a brass rod, seemed to conceal a door. There was no furniture visible, but someone was sitting in a corner by the window for he could see crossed legs with yellow shoes stretched out into the room. Agostino thought they must belong to someone lying in an armchair. Disappointed at not seeing more, he was going to leave his post when the curtain was raised and a woman appeared.

She had on a full gown of pale blue chiffon which reminded Agostino of his mother's nightgown. It was transparent and reached to her feet; looking at her long, pale limbs through that veil was almost like seeing them float indolently in clear sea water. By a vagary of design the neck of her gown was cut in an oval reaching almost to her waist; and from it her firm, full breasts seemed to be struggling to escape, so closely were they pressed together by the dress, which was gathered round them into the neck with many fine pleats. Her wavy brown hair hung loosely on her shoulders; she had a large flat, pale face, at once childish and vicious, and there was a whimsical expression in her tired eyes and mouth, with its full, painted lips. She came through the curtain with her hands behind her back and her bosom thrust forward, saying nothing and standing quietly, in an expectant attitude. She looked at the corner where the man with the crossed legs was lounging; then, silently as she had come, she turned and disappeared, leaving the curtain wide open. At the same time the man's legs vanished from the sight of Agostino. He heard someone get up and withdrew from the window in alarm.

He returned to the path, pushed the garden gate open, and came out on the piazza. He felt a keen sense of disappointment at the failure of his attempt, and at the same time a feeling almost of terror at what awaited him in days to come. Nothing had happened, he had not possessed any woman, Tortima had gone off with all his money, and tomorrow the same old jokes would begin again and the torment of his relations with his mother. Years and years of emptiness and frustration lay between him and that act of liberation. Meanwhile he had to go on living just as before, and his whole soul rebelled at the bitter thought that what he had hoped for had become a definite impossibility. When he got home, he went in without making any noise; he saw the visitor's luggage in the hall and heard voices in the sitting room. He went upstairs and flung himself on the cot in his mother's room. He tore off his clothes in the dark, and throwing them on the floor got into bed naked between the sheets. . . .

After a little he became drowsy and at last fell asleep. Suddenly he woke with a start. The lamp was lit and shone on his mother's back. She was in her nightgown and with one knee on the bed was just going to get in. "Mama," he said suddenly, in a loud, almost violent voice.

His mother came over to him. "What is it?" she asked. "What is it, darling?" Her nightgown was transparent, like the woman's at the villa; the lines and vague shadows of her body were visible, like those of that other body. "I want to go away tomorrow," said Agostino, in the same loud, exasperated voice, trying to look not at his mother's body but at her face.

His mother sat down on the bed and looked at him in surprise. "But why? . . . What is the matter? Aren't you happy here?"

"I want to go away tomorrow," he repeated.

"Let us see," said his mother, passing her hand gently over his forehead, as if she were afraid he was feverish. "What is it? Aren't you well? Why do you want to go away?"

His mother's nightgown reminded him so much of the dress of that woman at the villa: the same transparency, the same pale, indolent, acquiescent flesh; only the nightgown was creased, which made this picture even more intimate and secret. And so, thought Agostino, not only did the image of that woman not interpose itself as a screen between him and his mother, as he had hoped, but it actually seemed to confirm the latter's femininity. "Why do you want to go away?" she asked again. "Don't you like being with me?"

"You always treat me like a child," said Agostino abruptly, without knowing why.

His mother laughed and stroked his cheek. "Very well, from now on I'll treat you like a man. . . . Will that be all right? But you must go to sleep now, it's very late." She stooped and kissed him. Then she put out the light and Agostino heard her get into bed.

"Like a man," he couldn't help thinking before he fell asleep. But he wasn't a man. What a long, unhappy time would have to pass before he could become one.

Theme Questions

1. The opening paragraph of the story is unusually long. Study it in detail in relation to: characterization, indications of conflict and indications of plot development (foreshadowing), setting, symbols, and tone. Show specifically how the paragraph prepares the reader for the story that develops.

2. "... it had been his fate to come tumbling down from an illusory height and to lie bruised and wounded at the bottom." Expand on this as a thematic sentence for an examination of Agostino's initiation, and indicate his illusion, the sense of its height, his fall, and the nature of his wound.

3. The story has six sections. Analyze each in terms of the plot structure and development, the changes in Agostino; note when the climax occurs, and the nature of the dénouement.

4. Two important symbols in the story are water and the forest. Find and analyze the many meanings of water. At what point do the two symbols come together? How do you interpret this?

5. Psychologically, theologically and structurally, Agostino is a study in good and evil, sin or the fall from grace, guilt and anxiety or alienation. Analyze the story for these contrasts and other dualities and/or ambiguities.

. . . **also by Albert Moravia**   *Two Adolescents*
The Woman of Rome
More Roman Tales
The Lie

Preoccupation with sex and its incessant physical and psychological demands engages more hours than either teenagers or adults are likely to admit. Speculation, curiosity, fear, and experimentation are all part of the sexual initiation, as shown in Nemerov's "Young Woman," Shapiro's "The First Time," and, in a less direct way, Jerome's "Deer Hunt."

Young Woman

Howard Nemerov

Naked before the glass she said,
"I see my body as no man has,
Nor any shall unless I wed
And naked in a stranger's house
Stand timid beside his bed.
There is no pity in the flesh."

"Or else I shall grow old," she said,
"Alone, and change my likeliness
For a vile, slack shape, a head
Shriveled with thinking wickedness
Against the day I must be dead
And eaten by my crabbed wish."

"One or the other way," she said,
"How shall I know the difference,
When wrinkles come, to spinster or bride?
Whether to marry or burn is bless-
ed best, O stranger to my bed,
There is no pity in the flesh."

The First Time

Karl Shapiro

Behind shut doors, in shadowy quarantine,
There shines the lamp of iodine and rose
That stains all love with its medicinal bloom.
This boy, who is no more than seventeen,
Not knowing what to do, takes off his clothes
As one might in a doctor's anteroom.

Then in a cross-draft of fear and shame
Feels love hysterically burn away,
A candle swimming down to nothingness
Put out by its own wetted gusts of flame,
And he stands smooth as uncarved ivory
Heavily curved for some expert caress.

And finally sees the always open door
That is invisible till the time has come,
And half falls through as through a rotten wall
To where chairs twist with dragons from the floor
And the great bed drugged with its own perfume
Spreads its carnivorous flower-mouth for all.

The girl is sitting with her back to him;
She wears a black thing and she rakes her hair,
Hauling her round face upward like moonrise;
She is younger than he, her angled arms are slim
And like a country girl her feet are bare.
She watches him behind her with old eyes,

Transfixing him in space like some grotesque,
Far, far from her where he is still alone
And being here is more and more untrue.
Then she turns round, as one turns at a desk,
And looks at him, too naked and too soon,
And almost gently asks: *Are you a Jew?*

Deer Hunt

Judson Jerome

Because the warden is a cousin, my
mountain friends hunt in summer when the deer
cherish each rattler-ridden spring, and I
have waited hours by a pool in fear
that manhood would require I shoot or that
the steady drip of the hill would dull my ear
to a snake whispering near the log I sat
upon, and listened to the yelping cheer
of dogs and men resounding ridge to ridge.
I flinched at every lonely rifle crack,
my knuckles whitening where I gripped the edge
of age and clung, like retching, sinking back,
then gripping once again the monstrous gun—
since I, to be a man, had taken one.

Theme Questions

1. A common denominator of "Young Woman," "The First Time,"
and "Deer Hunt" is fear. How is it demonstrated in each poem?
What other emotions are revealed?

2. Clarify the problem of each protagonist. What kind of answers
do the poems supply to the problems?

From *Light in the West*. Published by The Golden Quill Press. Reprinted by permission of Ann Elmo Agency, Inc., 52 Vanderbilt Ave., New York, N.Y. 10017.
Copyright © 1962.

Prehistory shows man as a hunter, and killing his first quarry made a boy into a man in the eyes of the tribe. Anthropologists reveal that the initiation to the hunt is a secret rite among many primitive people, as it is also the initiation to manhood. William Faulkner in The Bear *gives us a literary transcription of such rites.*

The weapon of the hunter, in modern times the gun, has also taken on, for some, this ritualistic aspect. The gun, usually a symbol of destruction and death, paradoxically also becomes a symbol of sex as well as manhood. This was just seen in "Deer Hunt"; it is also implicit to Richard Wright's "Almos' a Man."

Almos' a Man

Richard Wright

Dave struck out across the fields, looking homeward through paling light. Whut's the usa talkin wid em niggers in the field? Anyhow, his mother was putting supper on the table. Them niggers can't understan nothing. One of these days he was going to get a gun and practice shooting, then they can't talk to him as though he were a little boy. He slowed, looking at the ground. Shucks, Ah ain scareda them even ef they are biggern me! Aw, Ah know whut Ahma do. . . . Ahm going by ol Joe's sto n git that Sears Roebuck catlog n look at them guns. Mabbe Ma will lemme buy one when she gits mah pay from ol man Hawkins. Ahma beg her t gimme some money. Ahm ol ernough to hava gun. Ahm seventeen. Almos a man. He strode, feeling his long, loose-jointed limbs. Shucks, a man oughta hava little gun aftah he done worked hard all day. . . .

He came in sight of Joe's store. A yellow lantern glowed on the front porch. He mounted steps and went through the screen door, hearing it bang behind him. There was a strong smell of coal oil and mackerel fish. He felt very confident until he saw fat Joe walk in through the rear door, then his courage began to ooze.

"Howdy, Dave! Whutcha want?"

"How yuh, Mistah Joe? Aw, Ah don wanna buy nothing. Ah just wanted t see ef yuhd lemme look at tha ol catlog erwhile."

"Sure! You wanna see it here?"

"Nawsuh. Ah wans t take it home wid me. Ahll bring it back to-morrow when Ah come in from the fiels."

"You plannin on buyin something?"

"Yessuh."

"Your ma letting you have your own money now?"

"Shucks. Mistah Joe, Ahm gittin t be a man like anybody else!"

Joe laughed and wiped his greasy white face with a red bandanna.

"Whut you plannin on buyin?"

Dave looked at the floor, scratched his head, scratched his thigh, and smiled. Then he looked up shyly.

"Ahll tell yuh, Mistah Joe, ef yuh promise yuh won't tell."

"I promise."

"Waal, Ahma buy a gun."

"A gun? Whut you want with a gun?"

"Ah wanna keep it."

"You ain't nothing but a boy. You don't need a gun."

"Aw, lemme have the catlog, Mistah Joe. Ahll bring it back."

Joe walked through the rear door. Dave was elated. He looked around at barrels of sugar and flour. He heard Joe coming back. He craned his neck to see if he were bringing the book. Yeah, he's got it! Gawddog, he's got it!

"Here, but be sure you bring it back. It's the only one I got."

"Sho, Mistah Joe."

"Say, if you wanna buy a gun, why don't you buy one from me? I gotta gun to sell."

"Will it shoot?"

"Sure it'll shoot."

"Whut kind is it?"

"Oh, it's kinda old. . . . A lefthand Wheeler. A pistol. A big one."

"Is it got bullets in it?"

"It's loaded."

"Kin Ah see it?"

"Where's your money?"

"Whut yuh wan fer it?"

"I'll let you have it for two dollars."

"Just two dollahs? Shucks, Ah could buy tha when Ah git mah pay."

"I'll have it here when you want it."

"Awright, suh. Ah be in fer it."

He went through the door, hearing it slam again behind him. Ahma git some money from Ma n buy me a gun! Only two dollahs! He tucked the thick catalogue under his arm and hurried.

"Where yuh been, boy?" His mother held a steaming dish of black-eyed peas.

"Aw, Ma, Ah jus stopped down the road t talk wid th boys."

"Yuh know bettah than t keep suppah waitin."

He sat down, resting the catalogue on the edge of the table.

"Yuh git up from there and git to the well n wash yosef! Ah ain feedin no hogs in mah house!"

She grabbed his shoulder and pushed him. He stumbled out of the room, then came back to get the catalogue.

"Whut this?"

"Aw, Ma, it's jusa catlog."

"Who yuh git it from?"

"From Joe, down at the sto."

"Waal, thas good. We kin use it around the house."

"Naw, Ma." He grabbed for it. "Gimme mah catlog, Ma."

She held onto it and glared at him.

"Quit hollerin at me! Whut's wrong wid yuh? Yuh crazy?"

"But Ma, please. It ain mine! It's Joe's! He tol me t bring it back t im termorrow."

She gave up the book. He stumbled down the back steps, hugging the thick book under his arm. When he had splashed water on his face and hands, he groped back to the kitchen and fumbled in a corner for the towel. He bumped into a chair; it clattered to the floor. The catalogue sprawled at his feet. When he had dried his eyes, he snatched up the book and held it again under his arm. His mother stood watching him.

"Now, ef yuh gonna acka fool over that ol book, Ahll take it n burn it up."

"Naw, Ma, please."

"Waal, set down n be still!"

He sat down and drew the oil lamp close. He thumbed page after page, unaware of the food his mother set on the table. His father came in. Then his small brother.

"Whutcha got there, Dave?" his father asked.

"Jusa catlog," he answered, not looking up.

"Yawh, here they is!" His eyes glowed at blue and black revolvers. He glanced up, feeling sudden guilt. His father was watching him. He eased the book under the table and rested it on his knees. After the blessing was asked, he ate. He scooped up peas and swallowed fat meat without chewing. Buttermilk helped to wash it down. He did not want to mention money before his father. He would do much better by cornering his mother when she was alone. He looked at his father uneasily out of the edge of his eye.

"Boy, how come yuh don quit foolin wid tha book n eat yo suppah."

"Yessuh."

"How yuh n ol man Hawkins gittin erlong?"

"Shuh?"

"Can't yuh hear. Why don yuh listen? Ah ast yuh how wuz yuh n ol man Hawkins gittin erlong?"

"Oh, swell, Pa. Ah plows mo lan than anybody over there."

"Waal, yuh oughta keep yo min on whut yuh doin."

"Yessuh."

He poured his plate full of molasses and sopped at it slowly with a dunk of cornbread. When all but his mother had left the kitchen he still sat and looked again at the guns in the catalogue. Lawd, ef Ah only had the pretty one! He could almost feel the slickness of the weapon with his fingers. If he had a gun like that he would polish it and keep it shining so it would never rust. N Ahd keep it loaded, by Gawd!

"Ma?"

"Hunh?"

"Ol man Hawkins give yuh mah money yit?"

"Yeah, but ain no usa yuh thinin bout thowin nona it erway. Ahm keepin tha money sos yuh kin have cloes t go to school this winter."

He rose and went to her side with the open catalogue in his palms. She was washing dishes, her head bent low over a pan. Shyly he raised the open book. When he spoke his voice was husky, faint.

"Ma, Gawd knows Ah wans one of these."

"One of whut?" she asked, not raising her eyes.

"One of these," he said again, not daring even to point. She glanced up at the page, then at him with wide eyes.

"Nigger, is yuh gone plum crazy?"

"Aw, Ma—"

"Git outta here! Don't yuh talk t me bout no gun! Yuh a fool!"

"Ma, Ah kin buy one fer two dollahs."

"Not ef Ah knows it yuh ain!"

"But yuh promised one more—"

"Ah don care whut Ah promised! Yuh ain nothing but a boy yit!"

"Ma, ef yuh lemme buy one Ahll never ast yuh fer nothing no mo."

"Ah tol yuh t git outta here! Yuh ain gonna toucha penny of tha money fer no gun! Thas how come Ah has Mistah Hawkins pay yo wages t me, cause Ah knows yuh ain got no sense."

"But Ma, we needa gun. Pa ain got no gun. We needa gun in the house. Yuh kin never tell whut might happen."

"Now don yuh try to maka fool outta me, boy! Ef we did hava gun yuh wouldn't have it!"

He laid the catalogue down and slipped his arm around her waist. "Ah, Ma, Ah done worked hard alls summer n ain ast yuh fer nothing, is Ah, now?"

"That whut yuh spose t do!"

"But Ma. Ah wants a gun. Yuh kin lemme have two dollah outa mah money. Please Ma. I kin give it to Pa. . . . Please, Ma! Ah loves yuh, Ma."

When she spoke her voice came soft and low.

"What yuh wan wida gun, Dave? Yuh don need no gun. Yuhll git in trouble. N ef yo Pa just thought Ah letyuh have money t buy a gun he'd hava fit."

"Ahll hide it, Ma. It ain but two dollahs."

"Lawd, chil, whuts wrong wid yuh?"

"Ain nothing wrong, Ma. Ahm almos a man now. Ah wants a gun."

"Who gonna sell yuh a gun?"

"Ol Joe at the sto."

"N it don cost but two dollahs?"

"Thas all, Ma. Just two dollahs. Please, Ma."

She was stacking the plates away; her hands moved slowly, reflectively. Dave kept an anxious silence. Finally she turned to him.

"Ahll let yuh git the gun ef yuh promise me one thing."

"Whuts tha, Ma?"

"Yuh bring it straight back t me, yuh hear? It'll be fer Pa."

"Yessum! Lemme go now, Ma."

She stooped, turned slightly to one side, raised the hem of her dress, rolled down the top of her stocking, and came up with a slender wad of bills.

"Here," she said. "Lawd knows yuh don need no gun. But yer Pa does. Yuh bring it right back t me, yuh hear. Ahma put it up. Now ef yuh don, Ahma have yuh Pa lick yuh so hard yuh won ferget it."

"Yessum."

He took the money, ran down the steps, and across the yard.

"Dave! Yuuuuuuh Daaaaaave!"

He heard, but he was not going to stop now. "Naw, Lawd!"

The first movement he made the following morning was to reach under his pillow for the gun. In the gray light of dawn he held it loosely, feeling a sense of power. Could killa man wida gun like this. Kill anybody, black or white. And if he were holding this gun in his hand nobody could run over him; they would have to respect him. It was a big gun, with a long barrel and a heavy handle. He raised and lowered it in his hand, marveling at its weight.

He had not come straight home with it as his mother had asked; instead he had stayed out in the fields, holding the weapon in his hand, aiming it now and then at some imaginary foe. But he had not fired it; he had been afraid that his father might hear. Also he was not sure he knew how to fire it.

To avoid surrendering the pistol he had not come into the house until he knew that all were asleep. When his mother had tiptoed to his bedside late that night and demanded the gun, he had first played 'possum; then he had told her that the gun was hidden outdoors, that he would bring it to her in the morning. Now he lay turning it slowly in his hands. He broke it, took out the cartridges, felt them, and then put them back.

He slid out of bed, got a long strip of old flannel from a trunk, wrapped the gun in it, and tied it to his naked thigh while it was still loaded. He did not go in to breakfast. Even though it was not yet daylight, he started for Jim Hawkins's plantation. Just as the sun was rising he reached the barns where the mules and plows were kept.

"Hey! That you, Dave?"

He turned. Jim Hawkins stood eyeing him suspiciously.

"What're yuh doing here so early?"

"Ah didn't know Ah wuz gittin up so early, Mistah Hawkins. Ah wuz fixing hitch up of Jenny n take her t the fiels."

"Good. Since you're here so early, how about plowing that stretch down by the woods?"

"Suits me, Mistah Hawkins."

"O.K. Go to it!"

He hitched Jenny to a plow and started across the fields. Hot dog! This was just what he wanted. If he could get down by the woods, he could shoot his gun and nobody would hear. He walked behind the plow, hearing the traces creaking, feeling the gun tied tight to his thigh.

When he reached the woods, he plowed two whole rows before he decided to take out the gun. Finally he stopped, looked in all directions, then untied the gun and held it in his hand. He turned to the mule and smiled.

"Know whut this is, Jenny? Naw, yuh wouldn't know! Yuhs just ol mule! Anyhow, this is a gun, n it kin shoot, by Gawd!"

He held the gun at arm's length. Whut t hell, Ahma shoot this thing! He looked at Jenny again.

"Lissen here, Jenny! When Ah pull this ol trigger Ah don wan yuh t run n acka fool now."

Jenny stood with head down, her short ears pricked straight. Dave walked off about twenty feet, held the gun far out from him, at arm's length, and turned his head. Hell, he told himself, Ah ain afraid. The gun felt loose in his fingers; he waved it wildly for a moment. Then he shut his eyes and tightened his forefinger. Bloom! The report half-deafened him and he thought his right hand was torn from his arm. He heard Jenny whinnying and galloping over the field, and he found himself on his knees squeezing his fingers hard between his legs. His hand was numb; he jammed it into his mouth, trying to warm it, trying to stop the pain. The gun lay at his feet. He did not quite know what had happened. He stood up and stared at the gun as though it were a living thing. He gritted his teeth and kicked the gun. Yuh almos broke mah arm! He turned to look for Jenny; she was far over the fields, tossing her head and kicking wildly.

"Hol on there, ol mule!"

When he caught up with her she stood trembling, walling her big white eyes at him. The plow was far away; the traces had broken. Then Dave stopped short, looking, not believing. Jenny was bleeding. Her left side was red and wet with blood. He went closer. Lawd, have mercy! Wondah did Ah shoot this mule? He grabbed for Jenny's mane. She flinched, snorted, whirled, tossing her head.

"Hol on now! Hol on."

Then he saw the hole in Jenny's side, right between the ribs. It was round, wet, red. A crimson stream streaked down the front leg, flowing fast. Good Gawd! Ah wuzn't shootin at tha mule. He felt panic. He knew he had to stop that blood, or Jenny would bleed to death. He had never seen so much blood in all his life. He chased the mule for half a mile, trying to catch her. Finally she stopped, breathing hard, stumpy tail half arched. He caught her mane and led her back to where the plow and gun lay. Then he stooped and grabbed handfuls of damp black earth and tried to plug the bullet hole. Jenny shuddered, whinnied, and broke from him.

"Hol on! Hol on now!"

He tried to plug it again, but blood came anyhow. His fingers were hot and sticky. He rubbed dirt into his palms, trying to dry them. Then again he attempted to plug the bullet hole, but Jenny shied away, kicking her heels high. He stood helpless. He had to do something. He ran at Jenny; she dodged him. He watched a red stream of blood flow down Jenny's leg and form a bright pool at her feet.

"Jenny . . . Jenny . . ." he called weakly.

His lips trembled! She's bleeding t death! He looked in the direction of home, wanting to go back, wanting to get help. But he saw the pistol lying in the damp black clay. He had a queer feeling that if he only did something, this would not be; Jenny would not be there bleeding to death.

When he went to her this time, she did not move. She stood with sleepy, dreamy eyes; and when he touched her she gave a low-pitched whinny and knelt to the ground, her front knees slopping in blood.

"Jenny . . . Jenny . . ." he whispered.

For a long time she held her neck erect; then her head sank, slowly. Her ribs swelled with a mighty heave and she went over.

Dave's stomach felt empty, very empty. He picked up the gun and held it gingerly between his thumb and forefinger. He buried it at the foot of a tree. He took a stick and tried to cover the pool of blood with dirt—but what was the use? There was Jenny lying with her mouth open and her eyes walled and glassy. He could not tell Jim Hawkins he had shot his mule. But he had to tell him something. Yeah, Ahll tell em Jenny started gittin wil n fell on the joint of the plow. . . . But that would hardly happen to a mule. He walked across the field slowly, head down.

It was sunset. Two of Jim Hawkins's men were over near the edge of the woods digging a hole in which to bury Jenny. Dave was surrounded by a knot of people; all of them were looking down at the dead mule.

"I don't see how in the world it happened," said Jim Hawkins for the tenth time.

The crowd parted and Dave's mother, father, and small brother pushed into the center.

"Where Dave?" his mother called.

"There he is," said Jim Hawkins.

His mother grabbed him.

"Whut happened, Dave? Whut yuh done?"

"Nothing."

"C'mon, boy, talk," his father said.

Dave took a deep breath and told the story he knew nobody believed.

"Waal," he drawled. "Ah brung ol Jenny down here sos Ah could do mah plowin. Ah plowed bout two rows, just like yuh see." He stopped and pointed at the long rows of upturned earth. "Then something musta been wrong wid ol Jenny. She wouldn't ack right a-tall. She started snortin n kickin her heels. Ah tried to hol her, but she pulled erway, rearin n goin on. Then when the point of the plow was stickin up in the air, she swung erroun n twisted herself back on it. . . . She stuck herself n started t bleed. N fo Ah could do anything, she wuz dead."

"Did you ever hear of anything like that in all your life?" asked Jim Hawkins.

There were white and black standing in the crowd. They murmured. Dave's mother came close to him and looked hard into his face.

"Tell the truth, Dave," she said.

"Looks like a bullet hole ter me," said one man.

"Dave, whut yuh do wid the gun?" his mother asked.

The crowd surged in, looking at him. He jammed his hands into his pockets, shook his head slowly from left to right, and backed away. His eyes were wide and painful.

"Did he hava gun?" asked Jim Hawkins.

"By Gawd, Ah tol yuh tha wuz a gunwound," said a man, slapping his thigh.

His father caught his shoulders and shook him till his teeth rattled.

"Tell whut happened, yuh rascal! Tell whut . . ."

Dave looked at Jenny's stiff legs and began to cry.

"Whut yuh do wid tha gun?" his mother asked.

"Come on and tell the truth," said Hawkins. "Ain't nobody going to hurt you. . . ."

His mother crowded close to him.

"Did yuh shoot that mule, Dave?"

Dave cried, seeing blurred white and black faces.

"Ahh ddinnt gggo tt sshoooot hher. . . . Ah ssswear off Gawd Ahh ddint. . . . Ah wuz a-tryin t sssee ef the ol gggun would sshoot—"

"Where yuh git the gun from?" his father asked.

"Ah got it from Joe, at the sto."

"Where yuh git the money?"

"Ma give it t me."

"He kept worryin me, Bob. . . . Ah had t. . . . Ah tol im t bring the gun right back t me. . . . It was fer yuh, the gun."

"But how yuh happen to shoot that mule?" asked Jim Hawkins.

"Ah wuznt shootin at the mule, Mistah Hawkins. The gun jumped when Ah pulled the trigger . . . N for Ah knowed anything Jenny wuz there a-bleedin."

Somebody in the crowd laughed. Jim Hawkins walked close to Dave and looked into his face.

"Well, looks like you have bought you a mule, Dave."

"Ah swear for Gawd, Ah didn't go t kill the mule, Mistah Hawkins!"

"But you killed her!"

All the crowd was laughing now. They stood on tiptoe and poked heads over one another's shoulders.

"Well, boy, looks like yuh done bought a dead mule! Hahaha!"

"Ain that ershame."

"Hohohohoho."

Dave stood, head down, twisting his feet in the dirt.

"Well, you needn't worry about it, Bob," said Jim Hawkins to Dave's father. "Just let the boy keep on working and pay me two dollars a month."

"Whut yuh wan fer yo mule, Mistah Hawkins?"

Jim Hawkins screwed up his eyes.

"Fifty dollars."

"Whut yuh do wid tha gun?" Dave's father demanded.

Dave said nothing.

"Yuh wan me t take a tree lim n beat yuh till yuh talk!"

"Nawsuh!"

"Whut yuh do wid it?"

"Ah thowed it erway."

"Where?"

"Ah . . . Ah thowed it in the creek."

"Waal, c mon home. N firs thing in the mawnin git to tha creek n fin the gun."

"Yessuh."

"Whut yuh pay fer it?"

"Two dollahs."

"Take tha gun n git yo money back n carry it t Mistah Hawkins, yuh hear? N don fergit Ahma lam you black bottom good fer this! Now march yosef on home, suh!"

Dave turned and walked slowly. He heard people laughing. Dave glared, his eyes welling with tears. Hot anger bubbled in him. Then he swallowed and stumbled on.

That night Dave did not sleep. He was glad that he had gotten out of killing the mule so easily, but he was hurt. Something hot seemed to turn over inside him each time he remembered how they had laughed. He tossed on his bed, feeling his hard pillow. N Pa says he's gonna beat me. . . . He remembered other beatings, and his back quivered. Naw, naw, Ah sho don wan im t beat me tha way no mo. . . . Dam em all! Nobody ever gave him anything. All he did was work. They treat me lika mule. . . . N then they beat me. . . . He gritted his teeth. N Ma had t tell on me.

Well, if he had to, he would take old man Hawkins that two dollars. But that meant selling the gun. And he wanted to keep that gun. Fifty dollahs fer a dead mule.

He turned over, thinking how he had fired the gun. He had an itch to fire it again. Ef other men kin shoota gun, by Gawd, Ah kin! He was still listening. Mebbe they all sleepin now. . . . The house was still. He heard the soft breathing of his brother. Yes, now! He would go down an get that gun and see if he could fire it! He eased out of bed and slipped into overalls.

The moon was bright. He ran almost all the way to the edge of the woods. He stumbled over the ground, looking for the spot where he had buried the gun. Yeah, here it is. Like a hungry dog scratching for a bone he pawed it up. He puffed his black cheeks and blew dirt from the trigger and barrel. He broke it and found four cartridges unshot. He looked around; the fields were filled with silence and moonlight. He clutched the gun stiff and hard in his fingers. But as soon as he wanted to pull the trigger, he shut his eyes and turned his head. Naw, Ah can't shoot wid mah eyes closed n mah head turned. With effort he held his eyes open; then he squeezed. Blooooom! He was stiff, not breathing. The gun was still in his hands. Dammit, he'd done it! He fired again. Bloooom! He smiled. Bloooom! Blooooom! Click, click. There! It was empty. If anybody could shoot a gun, he could. He put the gun into his hip pocket and started across the fields.

When he reached the top of a ridge he stood straight and proud in the moonlight, looking at Jim Hawkins's big white house, feeling the gun sagging in his pocket. Lawd, ef Ah had jus one mo bullet Ahd taka shot at tha house. Ahd like t scare ol man Hawkins jussa little. . . . Jussa enough t let im know Dave Sanders is a man.

To his left the road curved, running to the tracks of the Illinois Central. He jerked his head, listening. From far off came a faint hoooof-hoooof; hoooof-hoooof; hoooof-hoooof. . . . That's number eight. He took a swift look at Jim Hawkins's white house; he thought of Pa, of Ma, of his little brother, and the boys. He thought of the dead mule and heard hooof-hooof; hooof-hooof; hooof-hooof. . . . He stood rigid. Two dollahs a mont. Les see now . . . Tha means itll take bout two years. Shucks! Ahll be dam! He started down the road, toward the tracks. Yeah, here she comes! He stood beside the track and held himself stiffly. Here she comes, erroun the ben. . . . C mon, yuh slow poke! C mon! He had his hand on his gun; something quivered in his stomach. Then the train thundered past, the gray and brown boxcars rumbling and clinking. He gripped the gun tightly; then he jerked his hand out of his pocket. Ah betcha Bill wouldn't do it! Ah betcha. . . . The cars slid past, steel grinding upon steel. Ahm riding yuh ternight so hep me Gawd! He was hot all over. He hesitated just a moment; then he grabbed, pulled atop of a car, and lay flat. He felt his pocket; the gun was still there. Ahead the long rails were glinting in moonlight, stretching away, away to somewhere, somewhere where he could be a man. . . .

Theme Questions

1. Dave is "almos' a man"—or is he? Analyze incidents in the story that indicate this conflict within the character. Evaluate whether Dave is more man than boy or vice versa.

2. Ignorance and rebellion are basic to the characterization of Dave. In what actions does Wright reveal these traits? Find the thoughts, sound images, or feelings that show the repressed hostility under the surface action.

3. Discuss the setting of the story. What is revealed about the standard of living, the way of life, the education, the opportunities, and so on of the various characters of which Dave is just one? In this light what is the significance of the end of the story? Can you predict Dave's future?

4. The gun is the symbol of maturity to Dave. Trace references to the gun and analyze their symbolic value. Substitute the word "woman" for gun and analyze what the story reveals.

... also by Richard Wright   *Native Son*
                                     Black Boy
                                     The Outsider

Advice is free and therefore generously given. It is not always so generously received; even free gifts are sometimes unwanted. Yet adults love to advise youth. Here are four such examples: two classic, one not very well known and one by Shakespeare that is familiar to the whole English speaking world, and two that are contemporary. It will be readily seen that twentieth-century advice is not only different, but that the paternal tone of Fearing and Comfort is a far cry from that of Shakespeare's Polonius.

from "Hamlet," Act I, Scene 3

William Shakespeare

Polonius speaks to Laertes who is about to return to school in Paris.

POLONIUS.   Yet here, Laertes! aboard, aboard, for shame!
The wind sits in the shoulder of your sail,
And you are stay'd for. There, my blessing with thee!
And these few precepts in thy memory
Look thou character. Give thy thoughts no tongue,
Nor any unproportion'd thought his act.
Be thou familiar, but by no means vulgar;
The friends thou hast, and their adoption tried,
Grapple them to thy soul with hoops of steel:
But do not dull thy palm with entertainment
Of each new-hatch'd, unfledg'd comrade. Beware
Of entrance to a quarrel, but being in,
Bear 't that th' opposed may beware of thee.
Give every man thine ear, but few thy voice;
Take each man's censure, but reserve thy judgment.
Costly thy habit as thy purse can buy,
But not express'd in fancy; rich, not gaudy;
For the apparel oft proclaims the man,
And they in France of the best rank and station
Are most select and generous, chief in that.
Neither a borrower, nor a lender be;
For loan oft loses both itself and friend,
And borrowing dulls the edge of husbandry.
This above all—to thine own self be true,
And it must follow, as the night the day,
Thou canst not then be false to any man.
Farewell. My blessing season this in thee!

Advice to a Girl

Thomas Campion

> Never love unless you can
> Bear with all the faults of man!
> Men sometimes will jealous be
> Though but little cause they see,
> And hang the head as discontent,
> And speak what straight they will repent.
>
> Men, that but one Saint adore,
> Make a show of love to more;
> Beauty must be scorned in none,
> Though but truly served in one:
> For what is courtship but disguise?
> True hearts may have dissembling eyes.
>
> Men, when their affairs require,
> Must awhile themselves retire;
> Sometimes hunt, and sometimes hawk,
> And not ever sit and talk:—
> If these and such-like you can bear,
> Then like and love, and never fear!

Any Man's Advice to His Son

Kenneth Fearing

> If you have lost the radio beam, then guide yourself by the sun or
>   the stars.
> (By the North Star at night, and in daytime by the compass and
>   the sun.)
> Should the sky be overcast and there are neither stars nor a sun,
>   then steer by dead reckoning.
> If the wind and direction and speed are not known, then trust to
>   your wits and your luck.

From *New and Selected Poems* by Kenneth Fearing. Copyright © 1956 by Kenneth Fearing. Reprinted by permission of Indiana University Press.

Do you follow me? Do you understand? Or is this too difficult to
   learn?
But you must and you will, it is important that you do,
Because there may be troubles even greater than these that I have
   said.

Because, remember this: Trust no man fully.
Remember: If you must shoot at another man squeeze, do not jerk
   the trigger. Otherwise you may miss and die, yourself, at the
   hand of some other man's son.
And remember: In all this world there is nothing so easily squan-
   dered, or once gone, so completely lost as life.

I tell you this because I remember you when you were small,
And because I remember all your monstrous infant boasts and lies,
And the way you smiled, and how you ran and climbed, as no one
   else quite did, and how you fell and were bruised,
And because there is no other person, anywhere on earth, who
   remembers these things as clearly as I do now.

Notes for My Son

(From "The Song of Lazarus": VI)

Alex Comfort

Remember when you hear them beginning to say Freedom
Look carefully—see who it is that they want you to butcher.

Remember, when you say that the old trick would not have fooled
   you for a moment,
That every time it is the trick which seems new.

Remember that you will have to put in irons
Your better nature, if it will desert to them.

Remember, remember their faces—watch them carefully:
For every step you take is on somebody's body

And every cherry you plant for them is a gibbet,
And every furrow you turn for them is a grave.

Remember, the smell of burning will not sicken you
If they persuade you that it will thaw the world

Beware. The blood of a child does not smell so bitter
If you have shed it with a high moral purpose.

So that because the woodcutter disobeyed
They will not burn her today or any day

So that for lack of a joiner's obedience
The crucifixion will not now take place

So that when they come to sell you their bloody corruption
You will gather the spit of your chest
And plant it in their faces.

Theme Questions

1. Whose advice are you most willing to take? Why?

2. Compare the advice and the tone of the four poems. Is it possible to determine which adult is the most loving or the most concerned for the welfare of the youth?

As parents advise the young, youths learn to use the advice: what to accept, what to reject, what to ignore. Jim Jones of "The Man Jones" is probably more naive than the average college freshman, but he still learns a way to handle his well-meaning but nevertheless interfering mother. It is doubtful that she would applaud his technique, but the reader may.

The Man Jones

Frances Gray Patton

James Manigault Jones (who kept quiet about his middle name and was known to his college acquaintances as Jim or, when they were feeling high-flown and literary, as Eternity) paid a visit to Wendell Dormitory during the short interval between his lunch and his two-o'clock zoology-lab period. He carried a bunch of jonquils bought from a street-corner peddler—a poor, crop-legged man with hard-leather pads on his kneecaps—and as he entered the building he felt suddenly furtive, partly because he thought he must look foolish clutching those "flowers that bloom in the spring, tra-la" and partly because he suspected he was out of bounds. He hesitated in the vestibule, of half a mind to toss the jonquils in the trash can and retreat before anybody saw him. But he rose above that timid impulse. He started for the stairs, trying not to notice how his footsteps echoed in the empty corridor.

Early that morning, Jim and the rest of the boys had cleared out of Wendell, the main freshman dormitory at Amity College; in their wake, a crew of charwomen had arrived to make Wendell fit to receive a host of delicate visitors—the girls who were coming to the prom. The women had worked with a furious thoroughness that suggested contempt for the gross habits of the dormitory's regular inmates, scrubbing and polishing as if the place were far dirtier than it actually was. Now, in the purged, anomalous atmosphere, Jim had a fleeting illusion of being somewhere else. All this—the odors of soap and wax and furniture oil, the drone of a vacuum sweeper, and the rhythmic slipslap of a wet mop on the stairs—was like spring cleaning week at home. He caught himself listening for his mother to call, "Is that you, Mannie Boy? Will you take the kitchen screens in the back yard and squirt the hose on them before you settle down?" He frowned. He was too easily reminded of home, he thought, and it was abnormal to see a resemblance between anything here at Amity—this suave Eastern college, this "civilized oasis" —and Apex City, Georgia.

He picked his way up the stairs, walking on his toes to avoid tracking the still damp marble. On the first landing, he saw a stringy woman lift a pail of water and begin toiling toward the second floor.

"Here. Let me have that," Jim said. He snatched the bucket from the woman's hand and ran lightly up the half flight. "This where you want it, Ma'am?" (He could have kicked himself for letting that "Ma'am" slip out.)

The woman nodded. "That was real nice of you," she said. "They's not many students as thoughtful as that. Thank you." Her sallow, equine face grew soft with the expression of maternal approval that older women, to Jim's discomfiture, were likely to bestow upon him.

"Thank you, SIR!"

"You bet," said Jim.

"A bokay for your lady?"

"These?" Jim said. "Oh, they're just something I bought from a cripple"—he was miserably certain that the scrubwoman knew he had bought them because he'd remembered how his mother put fresh flowers in the guest room—"and now I've got to do something with 'em."

"That was a Christian act," the woman said. "And they'll make your room look like a home away from home."

"I figured they'd brighten it up," Jim said. "It's pretty austere, you know." He yearned to get away—to make sure the room was all right, to indulge in lonely fantasies about the marvelous girl who was soon to occupy it—but he didn't know how to. It seemed rude to leave while the woman wanted to talk.

"The little things in life make the big difference," she said. "You tell your mamma for me she raised a true Southern gentleman."

Jim felt himself blush, and knew that his heightened color gave him a heightened bloom of youth and innocence. He was a long-legged boy, with curly brown hair and pink cheeks. He looked like some mother's darling—which, indeed, he was—but, with a smile he hoped was a leer, he said, "She'll be surprised to hear THAT!"

"She prob'ly knows," the woman said. "I guess there ain't much a mother's heart don't know about her son." She plunged her mop into her pail, swished it, and plopped it down with a wet, slimy sound. "You don't happen to be Jones, do you? Room 202?"

"The man in person," said Jim.

"A special delivery come for you. I slipped it under your door."

"A special delivery? For ME?" Jim's bowels constricted. The letter, he was agonizingly sure, could be from no one but Barbara. From Barbara, breaking her date for the dance. And it seemed to him that he wasn't really surprised—that all week he had known such a letter was bound to come.

"I hope you ain't stood up," the woman said, leaning on her mop and regarding Jim with mournful eyes. "With the bokay and all, that would be a crime."

Her sympathy was a mirror. In it Jim saw reflected the image of what he feared was his true self. Not an Amity man—cool, civilized, capable of taking such things as freshman proms and the vagaries of girls with cynical undismay—but a skinny kid from the Bible Belt. A nice Sunday-school boy with yellow flowers in his fist. A boy who addressed a scrubwoman as "Ma'am" and blubbered into her bucket when somebody "went and hurt his Southern pride." In that drowning moment of self-realization, all that sustained Jim was the conviction, recently acquired from converse with a junior who was majoring in psychology, that self-realization, per se, was good. To view oneself objectively, ruthlessly—it was only thus that one gained insight into one's motivations and detached them from false values formed in infancy or even *in utero*. But to become aware of one's own hideous ignominy was one thing; to show it to a woman with a mop was another.

Jim cocked his left eyebrow—a muscular discipline that he practiced constantly. "There are plenty more fish in the sea," he said. His remark lacked urbanity, he knew—it was a disgruntled boast that one heard frequently in the Owl Drugstore in Apex City—but it had to serve. With a magnificent try at nonchalance, he sauntered down the long, quiet hall to Room 202.

Jim had met Barbara a week before, when he attended a dance at Hanna Benson, a small but reputedly sophisticated college for women. He had attended the function, with heavy misgivings, on the bid of a girl named Earline Fitch—a girl who had grown up next door to him and who had beaten him out by a slim academic margin for the position of high-school valedictorian. He had nothing against Earline—he was even fond of her, in an old-time's-sake sort of way—but he did not care to establish a public connection with her here in the East.

Earline was a big, bouncy, uncomplicated girl who poked you in the ribs to make sure you got the point of her jokes. She had a passion for food, and a passion, very like in character, for what she called ideas. "I can't get the McCarthy problem off my chest," she would declare, her carrying voice soaring above the sound of the juke box at the Owl. "I can't bear to think he honestly represents the deep-down spiritual calibre of the average American." At a moonlight picnic, when the other couples had wandered off into the shade of the pine woods, she would remain sitting in full lunar glare beside Jim (somehow, he was usually paired off with Earline) and would say, less softly than the whippoorwills, "Now take salvation through faith—here's my slant on it . . ." Her strong white teeth would glisten just as they did when they were about to seize upon a king-sized hamburger, succulent with chopped pickle and mustard. Worse still, she called Jim—and would always call him—by the humiliating abbreviation of his middle name. She called him Mannie.

Jim's immediate impulse had been to decline the invitation with emphasis. In the end, however, he had decided to accept it for two cogent, if disparate, reasons. First, he had wished not to embarrass his mother, who was a close friend of Mrs. Fitch's; second, he was aware that at Amity, where Earline's qualities were mercifully unknown, it wouldn't sound bad to say he had a date up at Benson. So he had gone to the dance, frozen-faced and wary, and there he had met the girl whom he'd always known he was fated to meet someday. (Jim, for all his determination to treat himself ruthlessly, nursed no morbid doubts as to Fate's tender preoccupation with his felicity.) He had assumed that the meeting would occur at some distant point in time when, as a key man in the diplomatic service, a novelist on safari in Africa, or perhaps, a psychiatrist long since beyond astonishment, he would be more than equal to it. Certainly he had never considered Earline Fitch as a probable instrument of destiny. But Fate moved in her own sweet way!

The visit to Benson had not begun auspiciously. The train had run late, and Jim had procured his supper from a vendor. (A sorry meal it had been, consisting of a carton of milk and a dry sandwich; its sole virtue, Jim had thought morosely, was that it saved him from having to watch Earline eat.) Arriving, hungry and pessimistic, he'd had just time to change his clothes in the village's one dinky hotel before joining Earline at her dormitory.

"Mannie Jones! You're a sight for sore eyes!" Earline cried, bursting into the reception room almost immediately after he had sat down to wait for her. She had on a ballooning sky-blue taffeta dress (the one in which she had delivered the valedictory), and it made her appear larger than life and crude-colored, like the blonde on the Holsum Bakery calendar in the Joneses' kitchen. Showing her teeth, she advanced across the carpet. Jim stepped back and bumped into a floor lamp.

"That's right! Break up the furniture!" Earline exclaimed, catching the lamp before it toppled. She grasped Jim's hand and ground its bones together. "Gee! Seeing you makes me feel like I'm back in good old Apex City!"

Jim retrieved his hand. "You're looking fit," he said.

"I keep fit," Earline said. "I'm on the house hockey team and I never skip my daily dozens at the gym. Notice my tummy." She slapped it. "Flat as a board. *Mens sana in corpore sano!*"

"Good going," said Jim.

"Listen, Mannie," Earline said. "I'm sick about tonight. This is an old-fashioned card dance, and I gave four numbers to Jane Sadler, one of the keenest girls in our class. She's here on a Religious Ed. scholarship, like me."

"She is?" said Jim.

"You and Jane would have hit it off like ham and eggs. I told her how you were an Eagle Scout and how you'd won the Kiwanis medal for your oration on crime prevention, and she was wild to meet you. But this morning she woke up all broken out!"

"Too bad," said Jim.

"Well, not too bad, one way you look at it," Earline said knowledgeably. "It's German measles, and, of course, it's good to get that over with before you get pregnant."

"I guess it is," Jim agreed quickly. Hoping to forestall a detailed lecture upon obstetrical hazards, he added gallantly, "Anyhow, it gives me four more dances with you."

"Well, no, it doesn't," Earline said. "I'd already promised those four to some other folks for their dates. So I got Jane's roommate, Barbara Davis, to pinch-hit."

"Much wrong with Barbara?"

"Not much," Earline said. "But she's not your type. Not very eager, you know. She wasn't even planning to come tonight. Said she preferred dances on men's campuses, where she had no responsibility! Though I must admit she was nice about filling in for Jane."

Jim's spirits, though scarcely bleeding for the loss of the eager Jane, were depressed by this juggling of partners. It was typical of the confusion—the absence of savoir-faire—that he had expected from Earline.

"Shall we shove off?" Earline said. "On with the dance, let joy be unrefined!" She jabbed her elbow into Jim's ribs. "Huh, Mannie?"

Jim made no attempt to smile. "Where do I call a cab?" he inquired.

Earline hooted. "What kind of golddigger do you take me for? A walk in the nippy air will tune up our blood pressure."

Before long, fox-trotting with Earline in the crowded ballroom, Jim understood why she had wanted a preliminary workout. Earline was a person in whom physical exercise excited the instinct for competition.

"I believe you're winded," she said to Jim when the orchestra had stopped playing. "Relax!"

"Shall we sit the next one out?" Jim asked.

"Oh, the next belongs to Barbara," she told him. "Here she is, Johnny-on-the-spot, to claim you now." She grabbed Jim by the arm and spun him around. "Barbara Davis. Mannie Jones."

Barbara was a slightly built girl, five feet three or so in height, with quiet, regular features, a pale complexion, and very soft, shiny brown hair, which hung just clear of her shoulders. In broad day, with his faculties collected, Jim would have thought her pretty; in the dim light of festivity, dizzy from Earline's whirls and gallops, he saw her as the pure incarnate principle of beauty. She stood so still. She was so undemanding. Her lips were curved in a half smile, amiable but aloof. Everything about her—her fragile white shoulders, the hollow at the base of her clavicle, the way she tilted her head, and even her dress, which was made of some foamy black stuff with pink shimmering through it—seemed serene and poised, and veiled in the filmy mystery of dream. She was, in brief, notably unlike Earline Fitch.

Barbara did not struggle for supremacy in the dance. Leaning on Jim's chest ("Light as a leaf on the wind," he thought), she seemed to float with him to the time of the music. She did not chatter, but by dint of direct questioning Jim learned something about her. She was from New York—"the city, not the suburbs." (Jim sneered with disdain at commuters' families, skulking in New Jersey.) She would like to live in Paris someday—or maybe Rome or Vienna. She guessed she was a gypsy at heart. (Jim decided definitely on foreign diplomacy instead of medicine.) She had never been to Amity (her tone implied familiarity with Yale, Princeton, Dartmouth, and the Service Academies), but she understood it was steeped in tradition. A civilized oasis, she said.

"Would you come down to my class prom next Friday?" Jim asked. He was shocked by the temerity of his question, blurted out bluntly, with no civilized prelude.

Barbara said why, yes, she'd love to come if he really meant it. "Only," she added, "You'll have to tell me your name. I can't very well call you what Earline did when she introduced us!" She began to laugh, noiselessly but uncontrollably, so that she was obliged, for a moment, to hide her face against his waistcoat.

"What did she call me?" asked Jim with death in his heart.

"She called you 'the man Jones'!" Barbara told him. She choked, and began to laugh again. "That's what she said—'Barbara Davis. The man Jones'!"

"Is that what she said? I never listen to poor Earline," said Jim. "My name's Jim."

"I like Jim," Barbara said. "It's a virile name. Last summer, I saw this revival of an old movie called 'Lord Jim.' It was a scream in parts— you know how those old movies are—but Ronald Colman was wonderful. I knew you reminded me of somebody."

And now, Jim thought as he approached Room 202, Barbara wasn't coming! Well, why should she? Why should a girl with the Ivy League at her feet climb on the smelly local train they called the Hedgehopper and ride for three hours, stopping at every wide place in the road, to attend a freshman dance with a boy from the upcountry of Georgia? It was out of sheer kindness—the reluctance to give pain—that she'd agreed to come in the first place. (He had read somewhere that beautiful women were invariably kind, frequently to their undoing!) Her letter would be kind, too. It would say that she had a cold, or a quiz to study for, or maybe that her family wanted her home for some special party at the Stork Club or "21."

He was not angry with Barbara. She was remote from human anger, like a classic myth. He was angry, and disgusted, with himself. He recalled several rich phrases in which he had described the girl's charms to his friends, and several optimistic hints as to the favorable light in which she regarded him. He remembered the government bond that his uncle had sent him on his eighteenth birthday, which he'd cashed to defray the expenses of the weekend; the new white dinner coat hanging in his locker at the gym; the orchid, selected and paid for, at the florist's; the table for two reserved at the Stromboli Tavern and the tip he'd added to the cover charge as tacit insurance against the management's querying his age when he ordered drinks. The thought of all that elaborate preparation for what should have been, to a young man of reasonable sang-froid, a routine occasion was mortifying to Jim. Like the charwoman's pity, it flayed him. It put his sentiment for Barbara into a mawkish category, along with his uncomfortable memories of the time he had stayed after school and cleaned the blackboards in order to be alone with a buxom teacher named Miss Myrtle Stubbs. (He had picked jonquils for Miss Myrtle—early February ones that bloomed in the sheltered corner of the dining-room ell—and his mother had fitted a lace-paper doily around their stems to make them look like a valentine.) Jim winced. He opened the door.

The letter lay on a strip of bare floor between sill and rug. Against the dark wood, the white envelope looked as bleak as an old, bleached bone. But as Jim, sweating forced himself to stoop for it he saw that it could scarcely contain a message of doom. It was postmarked Apex City and addressed, in the sloping, Palmer-method hand of his mother, to Mr. J. Manigault Jones!

Relief did not come to Jim by degrees, as it comes to timeworn people who must absorb it gradually into veins long torpid with chronic anxiety. It hit him full force, flooding him with a lovely, sanguine warmth. (He had a nebulous vision of Barbara. She sat, leaning toward him, at a small table illumined by a single candle. Something glittered, like a spangle of stars, in her hair. As she gazed languorously at him above a crystal cocktail glass, the orchid he'd sent her rose and fell on her breast. He saw himself, in his white coat, guiding her through an intricate maze of dancers; over the shoulders of their commonplace partners his jealous classmates eyed him with respect.) He tossed the letter, unopened, upon the dresser. Humming a few bars from "Some Enchanted Evening," he went into the adjoining bathroom, where he arranged the jonquils in his toothbrush glass.

He returned to the bedroom. He set the flowers upon the night table beside "War and Peace," a volume of poems by Ogden Nash, and the current issue of Holiday—an assortment that spelled, he felt, a catholic and unimpeachable taste in literature. He stood back and surveyed the room. It was a single room, narrow and utilitarian. Without the Varga girls that he'd removed from the walls, lest they strike Barbara as a display of naivete, it had, Jim fancied, a monkish aspect. But it was clean. Its bed was smoothly made. Its general effect could be called civilized.

Jim tried to imagine how that room—that celibate cell—would look after the dance. He conjured up a vague, intoxicating impression of diaphanous garments flung over a chair and of a girl's gently curving form swelling the covers on the bed. The girl's face was indistinct, but her hair made a shadowy mist on the pillow, and one shoulder— bare except for a wisp of black lace—was visible above the blanket. "Are you warm enough?" Jim whispered.

The scene changed. Years had passed. Jim sat in a closed compartment on a train that sped through the wine country of France. He was hard and lean. His eyes were shrewd. In his briefcase reposed the record—in code, of course—of an invetigation that would point the way to international peace for a generation. His papers were complete save for one scrap of information. One missing link. And he would get that. He always got what he wanted.

Or did he? Had he? He was a lonely man.

The door of the compartment opened. A cold thrill shot along Jim's nerves, but his hand remained so steady that the long ash on the end of his cigar was undisturbed. Silently as a shadow, a woman entered the compartment. She was veiled, and wrapped in exotic furs. She tossed a fine linen handkerchief upon Jim's knee. Its monogram, Jim saw at a glance, provided the clue; it was the missing link.

"Do you not know me?" the woman asked. She spoke with the faint foreign accent of the expatriate, but the timbre of her voice was familiar. It took Jim back, back, back. Dance music. Spring. A handful of simple golden flowers. He laid down his cigar. He rose and lifted the veil that hid the face of his visitor. It was a face that showed the ravages of passion and danger, but its bones had stayed beautiful. Its lips were curved in the old half smile. "Well, Lord Jim," said Barbara. She closed the door. She snapped off the light. "We are no longer children, Lord Jim!"

The clock in the tower of Amity College Library struck the half hour.

"Whew!" Jim said. He moved to the looking glass above the dresser, half expecting to find his own face marked by the ravages of life. Observing that it was still round and sleek, he sucked in his cheeks to encourage in himself a lean-jawed look. Then, with a start of alarm, he saw his mother's neglected letter. Why had she sent it special delivery? Was something wrong at home?

He ripped open the envelope and drew out a folded sheet of paper, inscribed closely on both sides. A five-dollar bill—an old, soft bill that wouldn't crackle and advertise its presence—lay in the fold. "Gosh!" Jim said, with the feeling of unworthiness that his mother's small attentions always gave him. He pictured her fingers as they'd smoothed the bill and as, immediately afterward, they'd seized a pencil to jot down "$5" under "Miscellaneous" in a black leather account book. He read her letter.

"Dear Mannie," she began. Jim stiffened. He had told his mother, as tactfully as he could, that he deplored being called Mannie—that it sounded babyish, like "Sonny" or "Bud"—but she had never been willing to see his point. It was short for a distinguished name, she had argued. His Manigault ancestor had been a Huguenot, a man who had sacrificed advantage to principle. It was a name to revere. Take it easy, Jim advised himself. She's too old to learn new tricks. She means well. She sent you five dollars. He began again:

> DEAR MANNIE:
>   This is just a line to let you know I'm thinking of you on the eve of your first big college dance and that I'll be with you in spirit, enjoying the sound of revelry by night. Earline wrote her mother that you'd asked a mighty pretty Benson girl to be your partner. Naturally, I'm a trifle disappointed that you didn't ask Earline (Jim groaned), because I've always liked the way your wholesome friendship with her expressed itself in work as well as play. You were pals on the debating platform as well as in the swimming pool. And then it would have been polite after she made the first move. I'm afraid the Fitches may be wounded! (To hell with the Fitches, thought Jim.) Earline doesn't think this girl—Barbara, isn't she?— is quite your intellectual or spiritual equal, but then Earline can't judge for you ("You're damn right she can't!" said Jim out loud), and I know you could never be ensnared by mere physical appeal. I'm thankful we discussed the mating instinct long ago (I merely asked the girl to a dance, Jim thought indignantly), and I'll always cherish the recollection of the clear-eyed way you looked at me after we had everything straight and said, "Biology is as neat as algebra, isn't it?" I hope you'll never forget that, either.

Would that I could, thought Jim. The "frank discussion" to which his mother referred had taken place three years before, when he was only fifteen, but every wretched word of it haunted his memory. He had been setting out for a Hi-Y hay ride—Earline Fitch was his date— when his mother had urged him to sit down and have "an intimate little chat" with her. He recalled the scene objectively now—a plump, earnest woman in a Boston rocker, and a blob of a boy, himself, sitting pigeon-toed on the edge of a Victorian love seat—but not so objectively that he failed to recover a sense of being trapped. His hands, resting on his knees, had seemed limp and heavy and grossly oversized; his mother, in her determination not to whisper, had spoken more loudly than usual. She had begun by asking Jim if he had noticed that his voice was changing and if he recognized that change as Nature's way of telling him he was growing into manhood. She had gone on to say, in a booming voice, that she'd heard that some boys and girls, being uninstructed and confused by their budding instincts, didn't always conduct themselves sensibly in a truck full of hay—with the chaperon, no doubt, sitting up front with the driver. She wished Mannie to be forewarned, so that if the proximity of Earline's young body should give him a queer sensation, he would know what it was. He mustn't be frightened, though. The desire to mate was a healthy, holy thing, so long as it was controlled.

Glassy-eyed with chagrin, Jim had known that he had to say something—and something in his mother's vein—before he could escape. With the algebraic analogy he had bought his freedom. He was morally certain that his fatuous remark had been widely quoted in P.T.A. circles; also, it had effectively nipped Jim's incipient interest in higher mathematics.

> Forgive me for clucking (the letter continued). I know you're a man now and I want you to make your own independent decisions. Maybe you can ask Earline another time. I hope the enclosure will ease the strain on your allowance. With love always,
> Mama

Jim put the bill into his wallet. It would take more than five dollars, he reflected wryly, to ease his strain. Amity wasn't like Apex City, where a girl was satisfied with a drive-in movie and a bag of popcorn. But he'd eke out. He'd heard some of the fellows say you could sell your blood to the hospital for fifty bucks a quart.

The library clock struck the third quarter. Jim went into the bathroom. He tore his mother's letter into fine fragments and flushed it down the toilet.

Jauntily, he walked along the hall, descended the gleaming stairs, and left the building. The cleaning woman, in a brown hat and coat, was leaving too.

"You look like your news warn't so bad," she said.

"Everything's rosy," said Jim. "Just a spot of dough from home."

At the moment, he meant what he said. But as he loped down the path that led to the Zoology Building, Jim realized that the true substance of the letter had not gone down the drain. It stayed in his consciousness and smirked at him. Its moralistic baby talk—such expressions as "wholesome friendship" and "mere physical appeal"—reduced the daring of the imagination to childish grandiosity. He would never, he was now persuaded, seem distinguished to a girl like Barbara Davis. He would never smoke an expensive cigar as he was borne through the wine country of France, or do anything beyond the ordinary. He would finish college (possibly with a B average), serve his time in the Army, and go back to Apex City and sell real estate. He would marry a local girl. (But NOT Earline!) He would lead, like other men, a life "of quiet desperation."

Yet only a short time before, the future had been his particular peach. And his mother had put a blight on it!

Jim's parents had been middle-aged when he was born. His father had died shortly thereafter, leaving his son's upbringing to his widow. He could not have left it in more consecrated hands. Mrs. Jones was a wonderful mother. (All Apex City said so, and until recently Jim had not dreamed that anyone would question the consensus.) Self-reliance, she had claimed, was her desire for her son, and she had consistently refused to weaken that quality by acts of overprotection. Other toddlers, when they skinned their knees were gathered to maternal bosoms, there to howl against cosmic injustice; all little Jim got from Mrs. Jones was a cheerful "Upsy-daisy" and a stinging dab of iodine. Later, when problems of personal conduct arose, Jim was refused the support of hard-and-fast rules. On such matters as church attendance, playing marbles for keeps, and reading comic books, Jim was told to think things out and be guided by his conscience. (That his conscience generally led him down paths that Mrs. Jones approved had seemed a happy accident.) When he began, now and then, to take the car out at night, his mother never sat up for him. Turning in to the driveway after a Scout meeting or a school party, Jim often saw her lighted bedroom window go dark; next morning she would say, "I slept like a log, Mannie. I didn't hear you come in."

That transparent lie had always touched Jim, but when, in a nostalgic, confidential mood, he had related it to his friend the psychology major, he had regretted doing so.

"Why did she wish to deceive you?" the psychology major asked.

"To keep me from knowing she worried," Jim replied, surprised by his friend's obtuseness. To make me independent."

"Not to render your chains invisible? Not to deprive you of the incentive to rebel? the psychology major suggested.

"Ahhh, baloney!" Jim retorted. "I was just a kid. Naturally, she worried.

"If it was natural, why was she ashamed?"

"She wasn't ashamed," said Jim.

"No. Your insight tells you that much," the other student said, slowly and significantly. "She wasn't ashamed, but she was making god-dam sure you'd be ashamed if you ever stayed out late—tomcatting in the red clay hills of Georgia."

"For Christ's sake!" Jim scoffed, hoping the oath did not sound as unaccustomed as it was. "I told you I was just a kid."

"Well, unless you want to remain a kid, you'd better get wise. You're in danger. You'd better make your break while there's time. Ruthlessly."

"You don't know my mother," Jim told him.

"If she wanted me chained, why did she help me leave home? Why did she send me to college"—he checked himself; he had been about to say "up North," the way they did in Apex City—"in the East?"

"Any number of reasons. Guilt. Prestige." The psychology major shrugged. Then he whistled, as if in pain. "But, boy, the light going off in the upstairs window—that was practically Machiavellian!"

Jim had laughed. The notion of his innocent mother employing a fine Italian hand had been plain funny.

Now, beneath the budding elms of Amity, Jim was not inclined to mirth. His friend had not exaggerated. He was in danger. "Ah want y'all to make y'all's own independent decisions," he muttered between his teeth, with a contemptuous distortion of his mother's Southern accent and diction. "Maybe y'all kin ask Uhline another time!" He knew he had to act.

He cut across the sprouting turf of the quadrangle and went to the post office, where he bought a stamped airmail envelope. Then he went to the college snack bar. He bought a milk shake, took it to an empty booth, sat down, and opened his loose-leaf notebook. He furrowed his brow. (Anyone seeing him would think him too deeply absorbed in scholarship to brook interruption.) After a while, when his anger had crystallized into sentences, he took his fountain pen (a Lifetime Sheaffer that his mother had given him when he won the Kiwanis medal) and started writing.

MY DEAR MOTHER (he wrote, making his letters dark and vertical): Thank you for the enclosure. Your generosity was unnecessary but not unappreciated. The big dance, as you put it, does not seem overwhelming to me. I expect, however, that it will prove diverting. Miss Davis, who is to be my guest, is from a prominent family in New York City—not the suburbs. She is not intimate with Earline Fitch nor does she care to be. She would be amazed to know that she had been discussed by Mrs. Fitch. I shall have to ask you not to bandy the names of my friends around the neighborhood. Who I take to a dance is absolutely none of the

Fitches' business. It is the business of nobody but myself and the other party involved. After mature consideration, I trust you will see that at my age any other state of affairs would lack valid reality.

In the future please address your letters to James M. Jones. Here in the East pedigrees are taken for granted and unusual middle names are not impressive.

Aff'y.
Jim

Jim lit a cigarette. He pictured his mother reading his communication. She looked older than she had at Christmas, and lonelier, like a patient woman on a Mother's Day card. Her face wore a blank, puzzled expression.

I'd better soften it, Jim thought. He added a postscript: "I must be cruel in order to be kind."

But the quotation, apt as it was, didn't seem to help much. It would not console his mother; it would only persuade her that her son had gone crazy. Why, she was liable to get right into her car—the old green Chevrolet that Jim had learned to drive in—and come straight to Amity. He could see her driving down the main street, sitting very straight and wearing the fierce, dedicated expression that she always wore in the face of illness. "Could any of you gentlemen direct me to Wendell?" she would call out to a group of students on the sidewalk. "I'm looking for Mannie Jones."

Jim tore the sheet from his notebook, crumpled it into a ball, placed it in his ashtray, and struck a match to it. He would have to do the thing over again a different way, he thought, as he watched the little conflagration flare and die out. He must say exactly what he'd said, but in his mother's native language.

This time, Jim wrote slowly. Now and again, he paused, trying out phrases in his mind and often shuddering as he set them down on paper. Short though his letter was, its composition consumed the better part of two hours.

DEAR MAMA (he wrote): Pardon this notebook paper. I'm in the snack bar guzzling a malted to rebuild my tissues after a day of intellectual (?) labor. It was swell of you to send me the fiver and I can really use it! The prom is going to be terrific. We've got Buzz King's orchestra—Buzz used to play trombone with Guy Lombardo—and at intermission we'll have strawberry punch and homemade cookies served by the wives of the profs on the Freshman Advisory Council. My date is an awfully nice girl, a real slick chick, named Barbara Davis. She's from New York. The city, not the suburbs. She's a better dancer than Earline. She lets me lead.

And now I have to say something I reckon most mothers couldn't take. But you and I have always been frank so I know you won't be hurt: It's this, Mama. Please stop being inquisitive about my date-life. You see, I've reached a stage in my development where I need to achieve emotional independence. Even if I make mistakes. Do you remember how it was when I first started driving the car? Other guys came home and found their families sitting up for them, ready to put them through the third degree. But you never did. Gee, I felt proud when I found the house dark and you asleep. I knew you trusted me. Well, that's what I can use now, Mama. Not questions. Not advice. Just TRUST that's too big for words.

Jim read over what he had written. It was ghastly. It reminded him of articles concerning the problems of adolescence that appeared in the women's magazines, which his mother read and often left (by design, perhaps?) in the bathroom. It was no less priggish—and infinitely less polished—than what he had said before the Hi-Y hay ride. But, as he had been obliged to escape then, so he was obliged now. His mother would understand this letter. What was more, she would respect it. She would let him alone.

"Your loving son," Jim wrote. He sighed. He might as well go whole hog. "Manigault," he signed himself. Sadly, with the air of a poet forced to speak the vernacular of the masses, he folded the sheet of paper and put it into the stamped envelope, which he addressed and slid in his inside coat pocket.

A freshman stopped at the booth. "Missed you in lab," he said.

"I wasn't in the mood," said Jim.

"Hell, neither was I, but with this shindig tonight I couldn't afford a makeup. Sometimes I wonder if women are worth it."

"My ma sent me a little extra dough," said Jim.

The boy looked impressed. "My people have hearts of stone," he said. "Your girl come yet? Mine was due on the bus an hour ago but I guess she's wending her own sweet way to Wendell. She's my brother-in-law's kid sister."

"Mine's coming on the four-twenty," Jim said. "The Hedgehopper." As he spoke, he realized that, with the lab period over, it must be close to four. He rose, stretched, and feigned a yawn. "I'd better get along over to the depot."

Jim arrived at the station a few minutes before the train was due. In the waiting room, two of his classmates sat, half reclining, on the wooden bench. Their eyes were closed; their legs, looking boneless and bored, were thrust far into the public passageway. Jim considered taking a place beside them, but an unwelcome twinge of honesty deterred him. The fashionable ennui that to most of his friends (so he thought) was as natural as skin would never be more than a thin, protective glaze on him. It was safe to assume that neither of those boys had just written home begging his mother to trust him!

Jim went out onto the open-air platform and paced up and down. A switch engine was backing and filling on the track. The fireman lifted a hand in salute to Jim; Jim lifted a hand to the fireman as he'd done a hundred times, waiting at the grade crossing in the center of Apex City. He was glad that only a baggage porter observed his small-town gesture.

In the distance, a diesel engine grunted.

"There she blows," the porter said.

"On time, for a change," Jim said with an air of indifference. A bell clanged. The Hedgehopper, a comical little train composed of a converted steam engine and a short string of antiquated coaches, charged into the station and shook itself to a stop.

The two boys emerged from the waiting room. "Pawing the earth, Jones?" one of them said.

"That's right," said Jim. Panic chilled him. Suppose she hadn't come. But there she was, alighting from the last coach!

She wore a tan coat, and a long plaid scarf hung around her neck. She looked much younger than she had at Benson. She gave the curious impression, which Jim took as spurious, of being scared. But her hair was the same. Her hair and the way she stood—stiller than most girls, with her chin raised a little.

Jim hurried to her. "Hello, Barbara," he said. He had meant to say something cleverer than that.

"Hello, Jim," said Barbara. Her voice sounded relieved. She smiled in a broad, shy, delighted way that made her face look plump. "Lord Jim!"

"Were you afraid you wouldn't know me?"

"That you wouldn't know me!"

"Never fear," Jim said. "This your bag?"

"Yes," Barbara said. "Only—listen, Jim. It's utterly ridic, but I promised my mother I'd mail her this the second I got here." She handed Jim a postcard upon which the single word "Safe" was written in a dark, vertical, sarcastic-looking hand. "I can't imagine what dire thing she thought could happen to me on the Hedgehopper!"

"I guess people in cities get the habit of being cautious," Jim said. "Just wait where you are."

He sprinted to the railway post box. He dropped Barbara's card through the slot and was about to follow it with his own letter when he was pierced by a shaft of sweet and humorous tenderness for his mother. The manifestations of her nervous love that had sickened and seemed to threaten him earlier were now clothed in natural dignity. They were universal foibles, common to all parents—even to those who chose to dwell in the heart of a metropolis. He stuffed the letter back in his pocket.

He was filled with a heady and perfectly wonderful sense of buoyancy. The evening lay ahead, bright with orchids, with candle flame at the Stromboli, and with the agreeable envy of friends. Beyond the evening, the world—his peach—hung suspended from a golden bough, ripening, ready to drop at the proper moment into the palm of his outstretched hand.

Theme Questions

1. "The Man Jones" could be considered an exploration of self-trust. Examine Jim's final action in this light and show how the author weaves the concept of trust through the story.

2. Jim has a vision of himself, "Not an Amity man—cool, civilized, capable of taking such things as freshman proms and the vagaries of girls with cynical undismay—but a skinny kid from the Bible Belt. A nice Sunday-school boy with yellow flowers in his fist." In what ways does the story reveal the conflict in Jim between what he wants to be and what he thinks he is? Is his self-appraisal realistic? What is your evaluation of him?

3. Dissect Jim's two letters to his mother. In the first one how does he employ language to convey maturity? Does he succeed or fail? What attitude does he convey? In the second letter, how does the language reveal immaturity? Why does the letter revolt him?

4. Contrast the two girls—Barbara as the girl of Jim's dreams and Earline as the girl of his mother's dreams. Evaluate the probable accuracy or fairness of Jim's view of each girl.

5. What was your response to Mrs. Jones' letter? Why? Compose an "answer" of your own. Evaluate the maturity of "answering" a letter or ignoring it.

. . . also by Frances Gray Patton   *Good Morning, Miss Dove*
A Piece of Luck
The Finer Things of Life

Children also give advice to parents on occasion. Not infrequently, the parents are as pigheaded and rebellious in rejecting good council as they would claim their children to be, if the situations reversed.

From two great tragedies, Antigone *and* King Lear, *come two examples. In* Antigone, *Haemon warns his father, Creon, against being too stubborn or proud. He asks Creon to modify his harsh rule that Antigone must die for defiance of his law, because she is obeying the higher law of the gods. He urges Creon to accept the fact that even the wisest mortal can make a mistake.*

from "Antigone"

Sophocles

HAEMON. Father, the gods have given men good sense,
the only sure possession that we have.
I couldn't find the words in which to claim
that there was error in your late remarks.
Yet someone else might bring some further light.
Because I am your son I must keep watch
on all men's doing where it touches you,
their speech, and most of all, their discontents.
Your presence frightens any common man
from saying things you would not care to hear.
But in dark corners I have heard them say
how the whole town is grieving for this girl,
unjustly doomed, if ever woman was,
to die in shame for glorious action done.
She would not leave her fallen, slaughtered brother
there, as he lay, unburied, for the birds
and hungry dogs to make an end of him.
Isn't her real desert a golden prize?
This is the undercover speech in town.
Father, your welfare is my greatest good.
What loveliness in life for any child
outweighs a father's fortune and good fame?
And so a father feels his children's faring.

From *Sophocles I, Antigone.* Translated by Elizabeth Wyckoff. Copyright © 1954 by The University of Chicago Press. Reprinted by permission.

Then, do not have one mind, and one alone
that only your opinion can be right.
Whoever thinks that he alone is wise,
his eloquence, his mind, above the rest,
come the unfolding, shows his emptiness.
A man, though wise, should never be ashamed
of learning more, and must unbend his mind.
Have you not seen the trees beside the torrent,
the ones that bend them saving every leaf,
while the resistant perish root and branch?
And so the ship that will not slacken sail,
the sheet drawn tight, unyielding, overturns.
She ends the voyage with her keel on top.
No, yield your wrath, allow a change of stand.
Young as I am, if I may give advice,
I'd say it would be best if men were born
perfect in wisdom, but that failing this
(which often fails) it can be no dishonor
to learn from others when they speak good sense.

In Shakespeare's King Lear, *the foolish king forces his daughters to compete and to declare how much they love him, and rewards each one by dividing his fortune according to the size of the compliment. Regan and Goneril lie outrageously and are bountifully rewarded. Only Cordelia speaks the loving, but, for Lear, unpleasant truth, and is therefore rejected by her father.*

from "King Lear," Act I, Scene 1

William Shakespeare

LEAR.   Now, our joy,
   Although the last, not least, to whose young love
   The vines of France and milk of Burgundy
   Strive to be interested, what can you say to draw
   A third more opulent than your sisters? Speak.
COR.   Nothing, my lord.
LEAR.   Nothing!
COR.   Nothing.
LEAR.   Nothing will come of nothing. Speak again.
COR.   Unhappy that I am, I cannot heave
   My heart into my mouth. I love your Majesty
   According to my bond, no more nor less.
LEAR.   How, how, Cordelia! Mend your speech a little,
   Lest it may mar your fortunes.
COR.   Good my lord,
   You have begot me, bred me, loved me. I
   Return those duties back as are right fit,
   Obey you, love you, and most honor you.
   Why have my sisters husbands if they say
   They love you all? Haply, when I shall wed,
   That lord whose hand must take my plight shall carry
   Half my love with him, half my care and duty.
   Sure, I shall never marry like my sisters,
   To love my father all.
LEAR.   But goes thy heart with this?
COR.   Aye, good my lord.
LEAR.   So young, and so untender?
COR.   So young, my lord, and true.

LEAR.   Let it be so. Thy truth then be thy dower.
For, by the sacred radiance of the sun,
The mysteries of Hecate, and the night,
By all the operation of the orbs
From whom we do exist and cease to be,
Here I disclaim all my paternal care,
Propinquity, and property of blood,
And as a stranger to my heart and me
Hold thee from this forever.

Theme Questions

1. How do Haemon and Cordelia interpret the love, devotion, and loyalty that a child should show a parent? Why do the parents reject their views?

2. Is loyalty to a parent, as shown in each poem, essentially different or the same as loyalty to a country? To answer, explain how Haemon and Cordelia view loyalty.

For all youth there is need to break from or at least loosen parental ties. Some do it rebelliously; some do it gradually; some do it partially; some can never do it. James Joyce's understanding of youth is revealed in his greatest works. Here too, in this very short story, we are treated to Joyce's genius. Eveline faces her problem under the binds of duty and two different kinds of love.

Eveline

James Joyce

She sat at the window watching the evening invade the avenue. Her head was leaned against the window curtains and in her nostrils was the odour of dusty cretonne. She was tired.

Few people passed. The man out of the last house passed on his way home; she heard his footsteps clacking along the concrete pavement and afterwards crunching on the cinder path before the new red houses. One time there used to be a field there in which they used to play every evening with other people's children. Then a man from Belfast bought the field and built houses in it—not like their little brown houses but bright brick houses with shining roofs. The children of the avenue used to play together in that field—the Devines, the Waters, the Dunns, little Keogh the cripple, she and her brothers and sisters. Ernest, however, never played: he was too grown up. Her father used often to hunt them in out of the field with his blackthorn stick; but usually little Keogh used to keep *nix* and call out when he saw her father coming. Still they seemed to have been rather happy then. Her father was not so bad then; and besides, her mother was alive. That was a long time ago; she and her brothers and sisters were all grown up; her mother was dead. Tizzie Dunn was dead, too, and the Waters had gone back to England. Everything changes. Now she was going to go away like the others, to leave her home.

Home! She looked round the room, reviewing all its familiar objects which she had dusted once a week for so many years, wondering where on earth all the dust came from. Perhaps she would never see again those familiar objects from which she had never dreamed of being divided. And yet during all those years she had never found out the name of the priest whose yellowing photograph hung on the wall above the broken harmonium beside the coloured print of the promises made to Blessed Margaret Mary Alacoque. He had been a school friend of her father. Whenever he showed the photograph to a visitor her father used to pass it with a casual word:

"He is in Melbourne now."

She had consented to go away, to leave her home. Was that wise? She tried to weigh each side of the question. In her home anyway she had shelter and food; she had those whom she had known all her life about her. Of course she had to work hard, both in the house and at business. What would they say of her in the Stores when they found out that she had run away with a fellow? Say she was a fool, perhaps; and her place would be filled up by advertisement. Miss Gavan would be glad. She had always had an edge on her, especially whenever there were people listening.

"Miss Hill, don't you see these ladies are waiting?"

"Look lively, Miss Hill, please."

She would not cry many tears at leaving the Stores.

But in her new home, in a distant unknown country, it would not be like that. Then she would be married—she, Eveline. People would treat her with respect then. She would not be treated as her mother had been. Even now, though she was over nineteen, she sometimes felt herself in danger of her father's violence. She knew it was that that had given her the palpitations. When they were growing up he had never gone for her, like he used to go for Harry and Ernest, because she was a girl; but latterly he had begun to threaten her and say what he would do to her only for her dead mother's sake. And now she had nobody to protect her. Ernest was dead and Harry, who was in the church decorating business, was nearly always down somewhere in the country. Besides, the invariable squabble for money on Saturday nights had begun to weary her unspeakably. She always gave her entire wages—seven shillings —and Harry always sent up what he could but the trouble was to get any money from her father. He said she used to squander the money, that she had no head, that he wasn't going to give her his hard-earned money to throw about the streets, and much more, for he was usually fairly bad on Saturday night. In the end he would give her the money and ask her had she any intention of buying Sunday's dinner. Then she had to rush out as quickly as she could and do her marketing, hold-ing her black leather purse tightly in her hand as she elbowed her way through the crowds and returning home late under her load of pro-visions. She had hard work to keep the house together and to see that the two young children who had been left to her charge went to school regularly and got their meals regularly. It was hard work—a hard life—but now that she was about to leave it she did not find it a wholly undesirable life.

She was about to explore another life with Frank. Frank was very kind, manly, open-hearted. She was to go away with him by the night-boat to be his wife and to live with him in Buenos Ayres where he had a home waiting for her. How well she remembered the first time she had seen him; he was lodging in a house on the main road where she used to visit. It seemed a few weeks ago. He was standing at the gate, his peaked cap pushed back on his head and his hair tumbled forward over a face of bronze. Then they had come to know each other. He used to meet her outside the Stores every evening and see her home. He took her to see *The Bohemian Girl* and she felt elated as she sat in an unaccustomed part of the theatre with him. He was awfully fond of music and sang a little. People knew that they were courting and, when he sang about the lass that loves a sailor, she always felt pleasantly confused. He used to call her Poppens out of fun. First of all it had been an excitement for her to have a fellow and then she had begun to like him. He had tales of distant countries. He had started as a deck boy at a pound a month on a ship of the Allan Line going out to Canada. He told her the names of the ships he had been on and the names of the different services. He had sailed through the Straits of Magellan and he told her stories of the terrible Patagonians. He had fallen on his feet in Buenos Ayres, he said, and had come over to the old country just for a holiday. Of course, her father had found out the affair and had forbidden her to have anything to say to him.

"I know these sailor chaps," he said.

One day he had quarrelled with Frank and after that she had to meet her lover secretly.

The evening deepened in the avenue. The white of two letters in her lap grew indistinct. One was to Harry; the other was to her father. Ernest had been her favourite but she liked Harry too. Her father was becoming old lately, she noticed; he would miss her. Sometimes he could be very nice. Not long before, when she had been laid up for a day, he had read her out a ghost story and made toast for her at the fire. Another day, when their mother was alive, they had all gone for a picnic to the Hill of Howth. She remembered her father putting on her mother's bonnet to make the children laugh.

Her time was running out but she continued to sit by the window, leaning her head against the window curtain, inhaling the odour of dusty cretonne. Down far in the avenue she could hear a street organ playing. She knew the air. Strange that it should come that very night to remind her of the promise to her mother, her promise to keep the home

together as long as she could. She remembered the last night of her
mother's illness; she was again in the close dark room at the other side
of the hall and outside she heard a melancholy air of Italy. The organ-
player had been ordered to go away and given sixpence. She remembered
her father strutting back into the sickroom saying:

"Damned Italians! coming over here!"

As she mused the pitiful vision of her mother's life laid its spell
on the very quick of her being—that life of commonplace sacrifices
closing in final craziness. She trembled as she heard again her mother's
voice saying constantly with foolish insistence:

"Derevaun Seraun! Derevaun Seraun!"

She stood up in a sudden impulse of terror. Escape! She must escape! Frank would save her. He would give her life, perhaps love, too.
But she wanted to live. Why should she be unhappy? She had a right
to happiness. Frank would take her in his arms, fold her in his arms. He
would save her.

She stood among the swaying crowd in the station at the North
Wall. He held her hand and she knew that he was speaking to her, saying
something about the passage over and over again. The station was full
of soldiers with brown baggages. Through the wide doors of the
sheds she caught a glimpse of the black mass of the boat, lying in beside
the quay wall, with illumined portholes. She answered nothing. She felt
her cheek pale and cold and, out of a maze of distress, she prayed to
God to direct her, to show her what was her duty. The boat blew a
long mournful whistle into the mist. If she went, tomorrow she would
be on the sea with Frank, steaming towards Buenos Ayres. Their passage had been booked. Could she still draw back after all he had done
for her? Her distress awoke a nausea in her body and she kept moving
her lips in silent fervent prayer.

A bell clanged upon her heart. She felt him seize her hand:

"Come!"

All the seas of the world tumbled about her heart. He was drawing her into them: he would drown her. She gripped with both hands at
the iron railing.

"Come!"

No! No! No! It was impossible. Her hands clutched the iron in
frenzy. Amid the seas she sent a cry of anguish.

"Eveline! Evvy!"

He rushed beyond the barrier and called to her to follow. He was
shouted at to go on but he still called to her. She set her white face to
him, passive, like a helpless animal. Her eyes gave him no sign of love
or farewell or recognition.

Theme Questions

1. In many ways Joyce prepares us for Eveline's decision. Find as many indications as you can of her passivity and her ties with the past, which serve as foreshadowing and justification for her final action. Evaluate Joyce's consistency in his treatment of her.

2. Eveline is not torn simply between love and duty; her conflict is a little more complicated. Discuss the inclusion of the references to her mother. What are the various tyrannies or dominant forces that determine her life?

3. "It was hard work—a hard life—but now that she was about to leave it she did not find it a wholly undesirable life." Joyce places this sentence near the midpoint in the story. Evaluate it as a rationalization for Eveline and as irony for the author. What is your objective evaluation of the significance of the sentence?

. . . **also by James Joyce**   *The Dubliners*
Portrait of the Artist as a Young Man
Ulysses

PART TWO

EVALUATION

The Rebel

Mari E. Evans

> When I
> die
> I'm sure
> I will have a
> Big Funeral . . .
> Curiosity
> seekers . . .
> coming to see
>
> if I
> am really
> Dead . . .
> or just
> trying to make
> Trouble. . . .

The values of life usually embrace one's ethical, moral, and social beliefs. Those who inexplicably call themselves "hard-headed" realists with pride generally confuse values with money, and invariably scoff at idealists who insist on subordinating money to values. The dollar-oriented are, in most instances, alienated from others who try to live by love, perfectability, and brotherhood.

Yet, strangely, the realists are unable to ignore the others. They are drawn to idealists and to rebels, if only to denigrate, debase, or destroy them. These are the sentiments of "The Rebel" and Herbert Gold's allegory, "Susanna at the Beach."

Susanna at the Beach

Herbert Gold

First came the girl. Then one fat man idly floated beside a friend in the water, lolling on his back, spitting, his great trunk rolling in the pleasure of himself. He liked to watch the girl while taking his pleasure.

Finally there were the people on shore. These September loiterers, with thin hocks and thick, with waddling rumps in dank wool or tendoned ones in Hawaiian shorts, with itching faces in devotion to sun or a suave glistening under the equivocation of lotion, all of them squinted and winked and finally moved toward her. They strolled, they turned on their heels, or they merely leaned. They came limping over the hot sand like the good wizards in a story.

The girl over whom the old men watched was diving from the end of a breakwater into the oily, brackish, waste-ridden substance of Lake Erie at Cleveland, Ohio. Her arms, deeply tanned, worked firmly; and heated from within, she scrambled up the rocks in haste after her discipline. She had fled all the billboard schemes of the life of a pretty girl. Lips soft and half-parted for a grand design rather than a Lucky Strike, hands taking the measure of ambition rather than the bottle of Coca-Cola, she had come to perfect her diving in a worn black cotton bathing suit which was already too small after her summer's growth. They were simple exercises, but she wanted them to be perfect. She had an idea of how they should be.

The old men, shaking off the sand flies which had multiplied among the refuse so late in the season, looked jealously to the thin cloth which held this girl and to the water which sheathed her. The girl measured the angle of her imagination against the remembered sting of an imperfect arc. Clean! she had prayed, but her worried brow was reporting, *No, another flop.* The black cloth gleamed in the wet. The droplets of water peeled down her body like broken beads as she climbed to try it again. The smile at the corners of her mouth was a promise to herself: Well! This time, then. Even in the brief instant of her stretching, a crescent-shaped slope at one shoulder flashed dry in the sunlight.

This time she went in straight and slender with the will of perfection.

It was a Tuesday afternoon, and a day of rare Indian summer heat. Still, only the most faithful had returned to the beach: the athletic grandfathers, white-haired and withered, with an eye for the weather; a student with his American history textbook and the glaze of sun in his face meeting the doze of exposure to knowledge; the kids pretending to fish and the dead shad belly-up at the washline of water on the sand; the occasional amorous ones, asking riddles, fondling each other slyly, their pockets a-jingle with desire and streetcar fare; women from the industrial flats nearby, sitting in housedress to recall, complain, worry, and take a sleepy hour's leisure together. Mostly, however, beneath the roar and thump of road construction on the slope above them, almost in the shadow of the Terminal Tower to the east, there were the old men: the salesman sunning himself with neck reaching out and pants rolled above the knee so that by evening he can look "just like Miami Beach, better even"; the flat-thighed wanderer in a straw hat and red woolen trunks with a white canvas belt, his sinewy breasts hanging—he sat in a patch of seaweed to observe the diver and stroke the sand from between his toes; another, the big-bellied swimmer, now paddling and spewing water, shaggily emerged onto the pier in order to get nearer to the girl. His friend accompanied him. Hairy-chested loungers, old-time beaux, their bodies both wasted and swollen, they joined the rest of the men along the breakwater. They watched the girl still diving, still climbing; her deep breathing pressed the erect buds of her adolescence against sleek black cloth, she rocked once on her toes, and then off she sprang.

This girl used herself hard, used her lightness hard; and each man there, turning to her from the beach or the pier, thought it a pity. A waste—her sufficiency unto herself silenced and saddened them and made their arms hang tensely forward. Challenged, they turned up the cards of their own sorts of sufficiencies.

The fat swimmer, swirls of hair on his belly and back, was now switching himself with a green branch as he talked business with his friend. They both studied the girl, and their discussion grew lyrical. They talked business and public affairs. He was saying: "You're John-cue Smith, let's put it, you want to get married—"

"I know! Got the taxes to pay, the down payments, the terms—"

"Yes, that's what I mean, to get ahead in life. The installments."

"I got the cost of living these days, Freddy."

"You got the government."

"Yes, Freddy, I got the taxes, yes—"

"The essentials of life."

"Yes, yes, all of that, yes"—and they both shook their heads mournfully and let their mouths fall open while the tips of the girl's feet, propelled by her dive, wriggled above water as she swam.

"Like to bite off a piece of that one, eh Freddy?"

"I saw it first, me, you want to say I didn't?"

A policeman on horseback on the beach looked for purse-snatching, nuisance-making, or drunkenness. Overhead, a pontooned airplane swooped low and up. The traffic rushed past the stillness of sun and beach and water, while, out on the lake, a single leaning sailboat, a visitor from the Clifton Club, kept its distance.

Two women, equipped for conversation with quart bottles of cherry pop, their dresses pulled over their knees and their stockings rolled down to their ankles, agreed on questions of mortality, bereavement, and the pleasures of a city beach. They sat on a log stripped by water and shaded their eyes first toward the industrial flats from which they had emerged, then over the lake and into the horizon and beyond. "My mama she die when she eighty-four," said the tanned younger one. "Just like baby, like new kid, she need milk to drink."

"Yah," sighed her friend, a fat and weary woman with concentric rings of flesh about her eyes. "Look that American girlie on the board, what she think? She hurt herself like that."

"She not able my mother care for herself or nothing."

"I know, dear."

"She die like so—sssst—after long life. She work hard."

"I *know*, dear."

"It ain't right, is it?" She nodded once, decisively, and said, "My father he still strong and smoke big cigar I buy for him. He sleep with woman and give her money and everything. Ain't nice old man like that. He make eye at every young girl—"

"Bad young girlie," said the plump woman to the sand, the water, and the figure now climbing back onto the rocks.

The tanned one pulled at her dress and said, "That's why, here in this country, many people go off on roof for fall down. My children all go away to Detroit and *I* give money to my papa."

"No justice on earth, darling," said the sad plump one.

2

The girl, the fine diver, went off the rocks again, measuring only with a frown the interior demands of her lonely stunt, absent from the beach on the parapets of ambition. She had scraped the cotton suit on a rock. The small split showed an edge of white breast, the first hard growth of the departure from girlhood. Some of the idlers had gathered in silence on the breakwater to watch her. "You want to tell me no, Freddy? I'm telling *you* no," the fat swimmer insisted. She did not see them; she had nothing to say to them; her regard was absorbed by the patch of black water and the rules of her skill.

Back on the beach, another immature and pretty girl sat with her feet drawn under her on the sands. No one, not even Freddy, the fat swimmer's friend, gave more than a glance to this one, whose tanned plumpness in stylish kneelength shorts promised an eventual stylish willingness while her profile remained strict, suburban, and pure. Her mother, shriveled to creamed skin rather than casual flesh, squatted like the image of her age by her side, but this was not the reason that the free-ranging eyes of the beach passed over the daughter so lightly. The men sensed that she feared to lie on grass because of disease, dirt, and small animals, that she shuddered at the thought of diving into the tricky, steaming, polluted waters, that despite her prettiness she had put herself apart from the play of caprice, open-mouthed laughter, and the risks of pleasure. "Look at the girl on the pier, the one that's diving again," this cute creature said.

"She's headed for earache, that's for sure," her mother commented with satisfaction. "Maybe she doesn't read the paper and how the water's unsafe. Dangerous for bathing. Full of organisms."

"I'm getting hungry, Mother"—wrinkling her junior-miss nose and hugging herself as her favorite starlet did.

"I *said* we'd stop at the Howard Johnson's."

Meanwhile, the diver scrambled over the rocks, up onto the pier, took three or four mincing, dancing steps, and bent her knees for her renewed essay at a controlled style. Her wide temples glowed pinker and pinker with the blood under her skin and the impact of water. Her innocence—an innocence of lessons—was informed by the heat and by the pressure of her blood which brought her climbing, diving, repeating this gesture again and again past the heaped-up rock. Had she seen them and gone on, it would have spoken for an angry and stubborn pride; but her way was the way of habit, of grace, and of a passionate ignorance, a deep communion with belly-smash on the shore of Lake Erie at Cleveland.

The plump lady from the flats was disturbed. "My doctor say: 'Playsuit no stockings! Like that you have no more colds for wintertime. You have upper repertory affection,' Doctor Sczymanski say. Neighbor she look at playsuit, close mouth, she say: shame! What can I do, darling?"

"That American girl, *she* have no shame," remarked the tanned woman whose father smoked big cigars. "Everybody is look at her legs" —and they both fell into a musing silence, and looked.

The beach was silent while a skin of complicity tightened like the dry sun about them all. Gradually these visitors to the September sands moved toward the breakwater, each one marvelously hushed because, if they said nothing, it could be presumed to be their habit and their devotion, an abandon to mutism in the heat, a pious thing superior to their daily selves: and thus, if the rip in the girl's suit grew longer, it was not their place to warn her of it. Let each creature hunger for itself alone— Freddy poked his pal to mean this—and thus send only appetite in the pursuit of others. The veiny old men moved fastest.

Within a few moments the beach was almost deserted except for the couple busily twisting and tickling in their well-worn place. The girl sat up with a jerk, spreading sand in an abrupt movement of her thighs, while her friend grinned, saying, "I'm not connerdicting you." He pulled her down again.

3

The tear in the diver's suit widened; the gash in this black second skin showed, to the fat man, the whiteness of belly, and then, to Freddy's bemusement, the flexing folds of flesh. Just once Freddy saw her fingers feel for the rip, but her body's intelligence calculated on nothing but the demands of perfection, and the thought of care for that clothing which was outside desire did not move further than the impatient, rummaging hand. She did not glance at herself. Turned to her idea, fixed on some inner certainty, she closed the split with her fingers, then forgot it, then let go.

She dived and climbed without liability to the give of cloth or the alteration of her world which Freddy and the big-bellied swimmer brought. She scrambled up dripping, let her eyes roam absently over the tense strollers gathering on the rocks, and dived once more. The pale wetness of her flesh opened to them like a wound under the suit while the girl, if she thought of her body at all, thought only of her skill and of her rehearsals for its sake. She was secure (small splash and ripple) in the exercise of method. She was an expert.

"You trying to tell me no, Freddy?" Behind the fat swimmer and his friend, past the city beach on this September afternoon, the machinery of road construction throbbed and the insect hiss of an afternoon breeze occupied the trees on the slope leading up to the highway past the tables, the shelters, and the park restroom. Because his mouth was dry, the fat man pointed to the girl and whispered, "Lookit." He squeezed the muscles of his friend's arm, thumb and forefinger twanging, and then they both moved forward again. The heat and the effort brought shiny tears to his eyes and a dampness to his forehead. The thickness of his body in swimming trunks, sagging at the middle and the rear, bulging beneath, looked enormous in the sunlight and the intimacy of one leg's motion against the other.

Repetitious, formal, and oblivious, the girl's ambition seemed madness or a mad joke to the watchers. It pleased the fat man; it was a delight to him. He opened his mouth, like a swimmer, and put his tongue sideways to breathe more easily. Freddy—as to him—he could hardly believe it. He wanted to float up an inner tube and go out someplace to think about it.

When she climbed over the rocks once again, the rip widened almost audibly, and still she did not see that her suit was ready to hang in tatters. No one warned her—as we do not warn a madman that he is talking nonsense—but they sighed when she extended her arms for the dive. The fat man sighed. All of them leaned together now, men and women, sharing the girl and sharing each other, waiting for their world's confirmation against the challenge she brought it, an assurance of which they were in need before the return to autumn and the years rapid upon them. A whiteness of breast flashed out, its pink sprouting from the girl's body like a delicate thing nurtured in the dark. But the day was bright and the shadows short. Looking at this tender and abstracted girl, the old Polish woman shivered at her own memories of paleness, of resiliency, of pink colors. The fat man, too, partook of their communion, frowning darkly, the green branch switching at his flanks, his knees slightly bent. He pinched his friend instead of himself. Now, her hair flat on her head and the flush of pleasure high on her cheeks after the repeated slap of her forehead against water, the girl was diving in a diminished rhythm, worn out but blind to risk, finished but unable to stop. The moment when her breast and belly slipped by the surface was the fat man's favorite.

The diver, that object for the vindictive imaginations of old men and old women, seemed to pause to acknowledge their study of her, but saw nothing, saw nothing again, and went on. The fat man's eyelids had dropped. He was moved. As she climbed, dripping and critical, bewitched by mastery of her body, feeling, if the presence of the others had come through to her at all, only a reward of praise earned through the long summer, the fat man released his friend's arm to break the silence at last with a shrill whoop. Then the old Polish woman screamed, "You're nekked, girlie! *Nekked!*"

The fat man, his friend, the salesman, the student, many of them were now yelling their cheers at her. Poised for her dive, she must suddenly have seen them and seen herself in their sight. Her look was one of incredulity. Her eyes turned from herself to their shouting, gaping, heavy-tongued mouths and back to the loose cloth dangling from straps. She did not speak. She turned her face from them. Its stern and peaceful determination hardly altered. Then suddenly the extended arms flashed down: she ran, she did not dive, she jumped and rolled into the oily water. Despite this folding upon herself, their eyes searched out a glimpse of sunlit flesh, white and pink and tender. While the crowd applauded, the student shouted, "She wants to drown herself," and leaped into the water.

"I'll get her! Me too! *Me!*"

The young man reached for her hair and only touched it before she wrenched free. She doubled under, holding herself, and then she was swimming. The crowd was roaring. Four, five, six of the men had pushed to the edge of the breakwater. The girl kicked forward and swam with short, quick, sure strokes, straight out into the lake, while a cluster of young men and old, their smiles strict in pursuit, tumbled down the rocks to be first to catch her. The fat man, paddling furiously, was ahead of Freddy. The righteousness of a mob's laughter urged them to be swift, but the girl was very strong, very skillful, gifted, and encumbered by nothing but her single thought.

Theme Questions

1. ". . . she had come to perfect her diving in a worn black cotton bathing suit which was already too small after her summer's growth. They were simple exercises, but she wanted them to be perfect. She had an idea of how they should be." Using these sentences as a base, analyze the story for plot and theme. What elements of characterization of Susanna are offered? What information is given to reveal that her effort is doomed?

2. Analyze the people on the beach—Freddy, his friend, the two fat women, and the pretty girl. In what ways do they serve as reflections of society as a whole? In what ways are they antagonists to Susanna?

3. Discuss Gold's artistry, particularly as he uses it to reveal Susanna's innocence and purity against the grossness or corruption of society, indicated by the beach scene and the lake itself.

4. "Susanna at the Beach" is related to the Bible tale of "Susanna and the Elders." Compare and contrast the two.

5. Analyze the conversations of the people on the beach. What do they reveal about their lives and their values? Why does the old

Polish woman's screams, "You're nekked, girlie! *NEKKED!*" have such an impact?

. . . also by Herbert Gold   *Love and Like*
Fathers
Salt

Idealists and/or perfectionists are, as already indicated, sometimes disparaged and ridiculed, but sometimes they are encouraged and lauded. Frank Horne speaks of an athlete, but his words carry import beyond a track event. Miller Williams' protagonist is more likely to be found in a protest rally than a stadium.

from "More Letters Found Near a Suicide"

Frank Horne

> *To James:*
> Do you remember
> How you won
> That last race . . . ?
> How you flung your body
> At the start . . .
> How your spikes
> Ripped the cinders
> In the stretch . . .
> How you catapulted
> Through the tape . . .
> Do you remember . . . ?
> Don't you think
> I lurched with you
> Out of those starting holes . . . ?
> Don't you think
> My sinews tightened
> At those first
> Few strides . . .
> And when you flew into the stretch
> Was not all my thrill
> Of a thousand races
> In your blood . . . ?
> At your final drive
> Through the finish line
> Did not my shout

Tell of the
Triumphant ecstasy
Of victory . . . ?
Live
As I have taught you
To run, Boy—
It's a short dash
Dig your starting holes
Deep and firm
Lurch out of them
Into the straightaway
With all the power
That is in you
Look straight ahead
To the finish line
Think only of the goal
Run straight
Run high
Run hard
Save nothing
And finish
With an ecstatic burst
That carries you
Hurtling
Through the tape
To victory. . . .

To an Idealist Sitting In

Miller Williams

Prophet, prophet, go back to the hay.
The sheep were always running away
and the harlot never lay with the man she loves.
Poor dreamer of dust and dungeon
the laws are with you and the cause is lost.
Calvin cooked Servetus in a wrong wind
Vanzetti lost his fish and old age
and Joan who was loved by half of France
died virgin

but there's too little tyranny here to burn you.
In Tennessee you will only win and grow old.
Go be the clerk you look like.
Take my sister to bed. Give her a son.
Tell him when he's twenty and reads books
what sins are not as simple as he thinks
and the welfare worker
who cares for men like god
cannot love a man she knows the name of.

Theme Questions

1. Compare the theme of "To James" with Housman's theme in "To an Athlete Dying Young" or with Williams' theme in "To an Idealist Sitting In."

2. Is striving for physical perfection, like perfecting a dive or breaking a world's record, analogous to striving for a perfect political world? Why or why not?

Conformity is often comforting but dull; nonconformity is often more exciting but hazardous. Poets, whose chosen art form makes them nonconformists, usually speak for the nonconformist, but in many different ways. Two different views are presented here in these poems by Vachel Lindsay and A. E. Housman.

The Leaden-Eyed*

Vachel Lindsay

Let not young souls be smothered out before
They do quaint deeds and fully flaunt their pride.
It is the world's one crime its babes grow dull,
Its poor are ox-like, limp and leaden-eyed.

Not that they starve, but starve so dreamlessly,
Not that they sow, but that they seldom reap,
Not that they serve, but have no gods to serve,
Not that they die, but that they die like sheep.

Oh Who Is That Young Sinner**

A. E. Housman

Oh who is that young sinner with the handcuffs on his wrists?
And what has he been after that they groan and shake their fists?
And wherefore is he wearing such a conscience-stricken air?
Oh they're taking him to prison for the color of his hair.

'Tis a shame to human nature, such a head of hair as his;
In the good old time 'twas hanging for the color that it is;
Though hanging isn't bad enough and flaying would be fair
For the nameless and abominable color of his hair.

Oh a deal of pains he's taken and a pretty price he's paid
To hide his poll or dye it of a mentionable shade;
But they've pulled the beggar's hat off for the world to see and stare,
And they're taking him to justice for the color of his hair.

Now 'tis oakum for his fingers and the treadmill for his feet,
And the quarry-gang on Portland in the cold and in the heat,
And between his spells of labor in the time he has to spare
He can curse the God that made him for the color of his hair.

Theme Question

1. What are the implied difficulties in the life of the conformist? of
the nonconformist? How do you know from the language of the
poems?

The setting for "Debbie Go Home" is the Union of South Africa, where apartheid, or complete racial separation, is practiced. The "coloreds" mentioned in the story are the people of mixed race who, for a while, were treated differently and somewhat better than the pure African tribes people; the coloreds were given some freedom, which was gradually taken away from them.

Except for a few local historical references, such as the one described, the story is universal. It is certainly pertinent to the United States.

Debbie Go Home

Alan Paton

It was too late to do anything or hide anything. There was the front gate clicking and Jim de Villiers walking up the path, one hour before his time. The room was strewn with paper and pins, and there was Janie in the new white dress, that cost more than any dress had ever cost in that house, or in most other houses that they knew.

Janie was in a panic because she saw her father walking up the front path, an hour before his time. She was a docile child, and obeyed her father in almost everything. Now she and her mother was deceiving him, and they were going to be caught in the act. She wanted to run, hide, cry, anything but stand there and wait.

Mrs. de Villiers saw that her daughter was in a panic, wringing her hands and wanting to run and hide. "Stand still," she said sharply. "It was my doing, and I'll take the medicine. And don't talk unless your father orders you to."

Then Jim de Villiers opened the front door that led him immediately into the combined living, dining, sitting room of the small house. He was angry at once. It didn't look good to see your daughter in a panic because you got home unexpectedly. It didn't look good to see your wife standing on guard, assuming already that you were going to attack her and her daughter. It didn't look good anyhow to see that you had stumbled on a secret that wasn't meant for you. What if one of his friends had been with him? That would have been a fine thing to see.

He put down his hat and his lunch tin, and then he looked at the

"Debbie Go Home" is reprinted with the permission of Charles Scribner's Sons from *Tales from a Troubled Land* by Alan Paton. Copyright © 1961 Alan Paton.

scene, daughter being fitted by mother into a dress of some stuff all shining and silver. Then because no one would speak, he had to say, "What's all this about?"

"It's a dress, Jim," said his wife. Some other time he could have laughed, not now, with the whole thing hanging over him. But she didn't wait for him to laugh or not to laugh. She went on as though she had learned a speech in the minute that it took him from the gate to the door.

"It's the first Debutantes' Ball," she said, "and it's going to be next month in the City Hall. Our girls are going to be received by the Administrator and his wife. I didn't think you'd like it, Jim, so I thought we wouldn't tell you."

"Why didn't you think I wouldn't like it?" he asked, purposely obtuse, "I've nothing against a ball."

She didn't answer him, so he said, "who's organising it?"

"The Parkside Mothers' Club, Jim."

De Villiers sat down. "The Parkside Mothers' Club, eh? But what about the Parkside fathers? Are you making fools of them all?"

"They don't hold your views, Jim."

"They don't," he agreed. "If they did, we shouldn't be outcasts in the country where we were born."

He returned to his attack. "Why did you think I'd be against the ball?" he asked.

He watched her stonily, and he looked at his daughter too, but she didn't look at him.

"Shall I tell you why?" he said, and when she didn't answer, he said again, "shall I tell you why?" So that she replied unwillingly "yes, you tell me why."

He went to the job with satisfaction.

"You've got some high white folks to receive our girls," he said. "They'll smile at them and shake their hands, and the Administrator will talk a lot of shit about the brotherhood of man and the sisterhood of women. But if one of our girls went to his house next week, it would be to the back door."

He looked at his daughter and said to her angrily, "haven't you got any pride? Why can't you be what you are, instead of what the white people think you ought to be? They don't think you're good enough to shake hands with them, but for the sake of this brotherhood shit you're allowed to shake hands with the Administrator. I suppose you're proud of that."

He continued to look at Janie, but she would not look at him.

"Talk to me, Jim," said his wife pleadingly, "I got her into this."

The girl came to life.

"You didn't," she said. "I wanted to be presented from the time I first heard."

"Shut your bloody mouth," her father shouted at her. "You don't belong to the Parkside Mothers' Club, do you?"

He turned to his wife. "I'll talk to you," he said. "You want our girls to be received by the Administrator, do you? Received into what? Into a world where they take away your vote and your house. Do you need a white Administrator to do that? How can a white man receive you into our kind of world? And why the hell should he?"

His anger was overpowering him and he stood up.

"Who made him Administrator?" he shouted. "The Government, the same bloody Government that took away our votes and our houses, and can make me a black man tomorrow if they feel like it. So you get their man to come and receive our daughters at a ball?"

He rounded on his daughter.

"Wait till your brother gets back from the university," he said. "Tell him you're going to a Debutantes' Ball, and a white man is going to welcome you into the shitting world that he and his friends have made for you. What do you think he'll have to say?"

He put his head in his hands in such a way that his wife called out "Jim, Jim," and took a step towards him.

"Don't touch me," he said. It's you who's driving me mad, licking the hand that whips us. Making me ashamed of all coloured people."

Mother and daughter watched him anxiously, but he suddenly pulled himself together.

"Where did you get the money for the dress?" he asked. "From what I give you?"

"No, Jim. I sewed for it."

"How much was it?"

"Four pounds."

He spoke to his daughter. "Take it off," he said, "and never put it on again." He sat down again, trembling a little.

"Go to your room and take it off," said her mother, "and stay there till you're called."

When her daughter had gone she said, "Jim, go and lie down."

"Lie down? What for?"

"You're sick."

"Yes, I'm sick all right, of all this belly-creeping to the same people that take away our rights."

She shook her head at him.

"Why are you home early?" she asked.

She knew him well. He could never hide anything, it all showed in his face. Something was badly wrong. When something was wrong, all the heart went out of him.

"There's trouble at the factory," she said.

He put his head in his hands again, this time covering his face. She went and stood by him, and said to him, "have they put you off?"

He shook his head. "Not yet," he said.

"When will they put you off?"

"We don't know. It's not certain yet."

"What's the matter? Is the market bad?"

"No."

"Jim, I can't hear you, speaking through your hands like that." She took his hands away from his face, and knelt down by him, holding them.

"Are they dissatisfied, Jim?"

"No."

"Do they say you're too old?"

"No."

Baffled, she searched his face. He had brought bad news, but he couldn't tell.

"Jim, you must tell me. I must know."

Then it came, seeming to tear at him as it came out.

"It's a new law," he said hoarsely. "A new law. The Industrial Conciliation Act."

"What does it say, Jim?"

"It says the Minister can reserve any occupation. So we may have to go. We, we. The Coloured men."

She jumped to her feet. "The wickedness," she said. "O the wickedness!"

She had no more to say, nor he, until she asked him again, "Why did you come home early, Jim?"

"I was sick," he said. "Just plain sick. I seemed to bring up all the food I ever ate. The boss said, what's the matter, Jim? I said it just made me sick to hear there was such a law."

"The wickedness," she said. "O the wickedness!"

"The boss said, Jim, it's not my fault. I said to him, you're white, aren't you? So he went away."

Suddenly he shouted at her.

"I suppose you think I did wrong. I suppose you think I should of got down on my belly and licked his hand."

"No, Jim, I would never have wanted that."

"But you want your daughter to shake their hands, and curtsy to them, and be received into their bloody world!"

"That's why!" she said. "There's many a hard thing coming to her as well. I'd like her to have one night, in a nice dress and the coloured lights, dancing before the Administrator in the City Hall. We get kicks aplenty. I wanted her to have a boost. And for one night the young men will be wearing gloves, and bowing to her as gentlemanly as you like, not pawing at her in some dark yard."

"It was good enough for us," he said.

"You never pawed at me," she said. "But don't you want it to be better for her? Don't you want her to begin where you left off?"

"Where I left off?" he asked. "Where did I leave off? With a law that took away my job, and a law that took away my vote, and a law that's going to take away my house, all because I've a coloured skin?" Can't you see it's going to be worse for her?"

"That may be," she said. "That's more reason I want her to have just this one night. Jim, go and lie down. I'll bring you a cup of tea."

He got to his feet.

"All right, I'll go," he said. Then perhaps he thought he was being too obedient. He said, "you go and comfort the debutante."

He went into their bedroom and shut the door, and she sat down and put her head in her hands too, not so much hopelessly because she was never hopeless, but because she couldn't see a way out of this hopeless mess. She sat there thinking for a long time, till a voice said to her, "what's got you down, ma?"

"Nothing's got me down," she said, "not yet. Johnny, how long have you been home?"

"Quite a time," said Johnny, "quite a time."

He was a gum-chewing nonchalant, and one of the militant students at the university.

"How many things have you heard?" she asked, "One or two?"

"Two."

"What are they?"

"The lost job," he said. "And the lost ball."

"And the lost mother," she said, "who doesn't know what to do. But it's your father I worry about."

"He hopes too much," said Johnny. "He knows what the world is like, yet he goes on hoping. And when the blow comes, it knocks him down."

"Don't you hope?" she asked.

"I hope?" he said. He laughed with worldly wisdom. "I hope for nothing," he said fiercely, "nothing, nothing, nothing. I hope for nothing that I won't get my own way." He laughed again. "You ought to be pleased that I'm that way," he said. "What does the Bible say? Blessed is he who hopes for nothing for he shall not be disappointed."

The Bible doesn't say that," she said.

He shrugged his shoulders.

"How would I know? But even if the Bible doesn't say it, it's God's own truth."

"Johnny, you've got to help. You can think what you like, believe what you like. But you've got to help me to get Janie to that Ball."

His face turned ugly.

"To be received by the Administrator," he said. "Not me."

"I know what you say," she said. "That he's white. I know he's white too. But the night of the Ball he's the Administrator, he's not white any more, he's got no colour."

"He's always got colour for me," said Johnny, "a dirty stinking white. And I'll help no sister of mine to shake his hand. Can you see the sense of it? It's not the ordinary people we're allowed to shake hands with, only the big shots. How does that make sense to you?"

"It makes sense to me," she said pleadingly. "He's the Administrator, he belongs to us all." She waved him quiet. "Give me a chance to speak," she said, "I know we didn't elect him or appoint him," she said, "but in a way he's above all colour. But that's not my argument, Johnny. . . ."

"I know your argument," he said. "You want her to have one night, one night of magic and romance. You want her to go in a shining silver dress, like the Duchess of Musgrave Road." He parodied her argument without pity. "She'll get kicks, poor little girl, and they'll take something more away from her when she grows up, and they'll call her a tottie and think that she'd sell herself for a bottle of gin, but this one night—just this one night—let them treat her like a queen."

The boy was pouring it out hot and strong, till he looked at his mother, and saw that she had put her head in her hands again. He lost his enthusiasm at once, and said to her "Why should I help you for that?"

She didn't lift her head, but she said to him, "because I'm your mother, because it's your mother wants this one thing, this one harmless thing."

There was a knock at the door, and she said to him in a whisper, "I can't face a visitor, make some excuse." Then he saw that she was afraid of weeping. He opened the door, and went out quickly, but in a minute he was back. His mother was wiping her eyes, and she said to him, "who was it?"

"Someone wanting the Tomlinsons," he said.

He stood and looked at her, and remembered a thousand acts of love. He went to her and said, "don't cry, ma, I'll do it for you. This once, and never again."

"I shan't want it again," she said. "Only this once."

He threw up his eyes to heaven piously. "Only this once," he said in a false high voice, "let her be treated like a queen."

She blew her nose and laughed.

"Tell your father, I'm making the tea," she said. "I hope this won't get you into trouble with the Unity Movement, Johnny."

"That would no doubt cause you grief and pain," he said.

"I can't say that," she said, "but I don't want trouble for you."

"I'll look after myself," he said, chewing his gum.

He went to his parents' bedroom and knocked on the door. His father said "come in," and there he was lying on the bed.

"Have a cigarette, dad."

"Thanks, Johnny, don't mind if I do."

"Smoke while you can," advised his son cynically. "Ma's told me about the job. Has it got you down?"

"Yes, son," said his father apologetically. "For the time it's got me down."

"It's because you hope for the best and fear for the worst," said his son. "I expect the worst, so when it comes, I don't take it hard."

"You were lucky," said his father defensively. "I was brought up in a world where we always hoped for the best. But you live in a time when no false hopes are left. I was a Smuts man, don't forget."

"Smuts," said Johnny contemptuously. "Who was Smuts?"

"Johnny," said his father, "you see me down now, but I want to be up tomorrow. I want to speak at the union meeting. Will you help me with a speech?"

"A hard speech?"

Jim de Villiers considered it.

"I want a fighting speech," he said. "I want to stand up for our rights, but I don't want to blackguard the whites. I don't want trouble, Johnny."

"You don't, eh? Then why don't you let Janie go to the Ball?"

Jim looked at his son. "I don't get you," he said. "Are you wanting Janie to go to the Ball?"

Johnny chewed his gum. "I don't want her to go to the Ball," he said carelessly. "But her going to the Ball is the price of a speech."

His father sat up on the bed. "Do I hear you right?" he asked.

"You hear me right," said Johnny. "It's the price for a fighting speech, free of all hatred, bitterness, resentment, full of shit about freedom and the rights of man. No one will give you a better."

"Why are you doing this, Johnny?"

Johnny chewed his gum. "Because Ma said to me, I'm your mother," he said. "And your mother wants your sister to have a night as a queen."

He looked at his father with expressionless eyes.

His father said, "I don't understand you, Johnny."

"You don't have to understand me," said Johnny. "You just have to tell me, is she going to the Ball?"

"I don't understand you, Johnny. It was mainly because of you that I said she couldn't go."

"Now it'll be mainly because of me that you'll say she can go," said Johnny.

Jim de Villiers lay down again. "You beat me," he said.

"I beat lots of people," said his son. "Just tell me, can she go, so I can get on with the speech."

"All right, she can go," he said, "on one condition. Tell me how you justify it."

"Rock-bottom necessity," said Johnny. "If I boycott American food, and I'm dying of hunger, and everywhere round me is American food, then I eat American food."

"You eat American food so you can go on boycotting it," said de Villiers.

Johnny smiled against his will. "You're getting better," he said. "Listen, Dad, I can't study in a house of weeping women."

"Was your mother weeping?"

"As near as she gets."

"Son, don't tell her we bargained for it."

"O.K. I won't. See you again."

He went to his room which was no more than a bit of enclosed verandah, and sat down at his small table to think about the speech on freedom and the rights of man. Then on second thoughts he got up, and hauled some posters out from under his bed and put them against the wall where they could be seen. They were all headed DEBUTANTES BALL. One said, DEBBIE GO HOME, and another, ornamented with a bar of music, asked WHO STOLE MY VOTE AWAY? The third one was his own, but his friends thought it was too learned, for it said: WELCOME, SPICK LITTLE LICKSPITTLE. When he had put them up, he sat down at the table, but his thoughts were not on the speech, they were on his mother's entrance.

Then she burst in, with her eyes shining, and she would have embraced him if she had not suddenly seen the new decorations.

"I suppose you came to thank me," he said.

"I did."

She sat down in the other chair, and looked at the posters.

"You can't do that now," she said.

"Why not?"

"You can't," she said. "You can't give with one hand and take away with the other."

"I gave you your share," he said hotly. "That's my share there."

"You can't do it," she said. "If you take your share, mine's worth nothing. Do you think that's fair?"

"I can't help it," he said. "We fixed this up long before I knew you wanted Janie to go." When she said nothing, he went on, "what we're doing is an important thing. You can't just stop because your sister's going to a ball."

"I understand what you're doing," she said. "I understand what you want, you and your friends. But don't you ever let up? Don't you ever have mercy on anyone?"

"Mercy," he said, with a sudden flight of fancy, "it's like a door of a cage. Open it once, and everything's gone."

"Do you know Hazel's going to the Ball?" she asked.

"Yes," he said defiantly.

"What about Fred?" she asked. "Is he acting the same way as you?"

"Yes."

"The world's mad," she said. She stood up and rubbed her brow with the back of her hand. "Brother against sister, husband against wife. You know what Christ said?"

He looked at her with annoyance. She took an unfair advantage of him by talking religion. He could sneer at white people's religion, but not at hers.

"Go your own way," she said. "But let me teach you one thing about giving. When you give, give with your whole heart. Don't keep half of it back."

She went out and closed his door. As all his attention had been on her entrance, now it was on her exit. He heard no doors opening, no voices speaking. The house was quite silent. When he could stand it no more, he followed her, and found her sitting in the living-room, in the evening dark.

"What are you doing?" he asked.

She answered him in a matter-of-fact voice. That was her way, that was why you had to live your life with her to know what she was.

"I'm thinking it out," she said.

She didn't ask for help, he knew she wouldn't ask for any. A spiritless husband, a day-dreaming daughter, a tough son, they weren't much use to her.

"If it'll help you," he said, "I won't let Janie see me."

She considered his proposition. "How will you do that?" she asked. "You know where the cars will stop, outside the main foyer. Where will you be, inside or out?"

"Wouldn't you like to know?" he asked. "All I'm saying is, I won't let Janie see me."

"Is Fred doing the same for Hazel?" she asked.

He could not help admiring her cleverness.

"That's Fred's business," he said.

She got up and he saw that she was intending to kiss him, so he waved her away.

"Don't thank me too much," he said harshly.

"She'll see all the others."

But she kissed him all the same.

"Give the kiss to Fred," she said. "Now I'll go and tell Janie the news."

At Janie's door she turned and gave him a smile.

"You'd better get on with your father's speech," she said.

Theme Questions

1. Who is the protagonist—Johnny or his mother or both? Is the story primarily a family conflict or a racial conflict? Does the race issue transcend the usual de Villiers' family problems or does it intensify them? Examine both conflicts carefully before developing your answer.

2. Mr. de Villiers says, "I don't understand you, Johnny." In what ways does he fail to understand his son? Why? What is the critical issue of his father's "fighting speech"? How is this indicative of the differences between father and son?

3. Each member of the family seems to stand symbolically for a segment of opinion on racial questions. Analyze the personality of each and relate each to its group counterpart.

4. The story deals with accommodation and hope. In what ways do the family members accommodate one another to solve their problem? What are the hopes of the various characters?

5. "It was too late to do anything or hide anything." Interpret this sentence as it might pertain to the plot, the political situation in South Africa, and the author's viewpoint as expressed by his theme and tone.

. . . **also by Alan Paton**   *Tales from a Troubled Land*
Cry the Beloved Country
Too Late the Phalarope

A Moment Please

Samuel Allen

When I gaze at the sun
    I walked to the subway booth
    for change for a dime.
and know that this great earth
    Two adolescent girls stood there
    alive with eagerness to know
is but a fragment from it thrown
    all in their new found world
    there was for them to know
in heat and flame a billion years ago,
    they looked at me and brightly asked
    "Are you Arabian?"
that then this world was lifeless
    I smiled and cautiously
    —for one grows cautious—
    shook my head.
as, a billion hence,
    "Egyptian?"
it shall again be,
    Again I smiled and shook my head
    and walked away.
what moment is it that I am betrayed,
    I've gone but seven paces now
oppressed, cast down,
    and from behind comes swift the sneer

or warm with love or triumph?
  "Or Nigger?"

  A moment, please
What is it that to fury I am roused?
  for still it takes a moment
What meaning for me
  and now
in this homeless clan
  I'll turn
the dupe of space
  and smile
the toy of time?
  and nod my head.

Tableau

Countee Cullen

> Locked arm in arm they cross the way,
>   The black boy and the white,
> The golden splendor of the day,
>   The sable pride of night.
>
> From lowered blinds the dark folk stare,
>   And here the fair folk talk,
> Indignant that these two should dare
>   In unison to walk.
>
> Oblivious to look and word
>   They pass, and see no wonder
> That lightning brilliant as a sword
>   Should blaze the path of thunder.

Junior Addict

Langston Hughes

The little boy
who sticks a needle in his arm
and seeks an out in other worldly dreams,
who seeks an out in eyes that droop
and ears that close to Harlem screams,
cannot know, of course
(and has no way to understand)
a sunrise that he cannot see
beginning in some other land—
but destined sure to flood—and soon—
the very room in which he leaves
his needle and his spoon,
the very room in which today the air
is heavy with the drug
of his despair.

    (Yet little can
    tomorrow's sunshine give
    to one who will not live.)

Quick, sunrise, come—
Before the mushroom bomb
Pollutes his stinking air
With better death
Than is his living here,
With viler drugs
Than bring today's release
In poison from the fallout
Of our peace.

    "It's easier to get dope
    than it is to get a job."

Yes, easier to get dope
than to get a job—
daytime or nightime job,
teen-age, pre-draft,
pre-lifetime job.

Quick, sunrise, come!
Sunrise out of Africa,
Quick, come!
Sunrise, please come!
Come! Come!

Theme Questions

1. What statement does each poem make about prejudice and its impact on both black and white?
2. Discuss the poems in terms of their complexity of form and statement. Is there a relationship? How does the form relate to the theme of each?

Questions and doubts about God and religion are usually troublesome as they involve both personal guilt and a rejection of one's family's traditions. Furthermore, alternatives of atheism or agnosticism are often seen as a kind of no-man's land. Nevertheless, at least once in every lifetime, most people do lose faith, although probably not in quite the same way as the narrator of V. S. Pritchett's "The Saint."

The Saint

V. S. Pritchett

When I was seventeen years old I lost my religious faith. It had been unsteady for some time and then, very suddenly, it went as the result of an incident in a punt on the river outside the town where we lived. My uncle, with whom I was obliged to stay for long periods of my life, had started a small furniture-making business in the town. He was always in difficulties about money, but he was convinced that in some way God would help him. And this happened. An investor arrived who belonged to a sect called the Church of the Last Purification, of Toronto, Canada. Could we imagine, this man asked, a good and omnipotent God allowing his children to be short of money? We had to admit we could not imagine this. The man paid some capital into my uncle's business and we were converted. Our family were the first Purifiers—as they were called—in the town. Soon a congregation of fifty or more were meeting every Sunday in a room at the Corn Exchange.

At once we found ourselves isolated and hated people. Everyone made jokes about us. We had to stand together because we were sometimes dragged into the courts. What the unconverted could not forgive in us was first that we believed in successful prayer and, secondly, that our revelation came from Toronto. The success of our prayers had a simple foundation. We regarded it as "Error"—our name for Evil—to believe the evidence of our senses and if we had influenza or consumption, or had lost our money or were unemployed, we denied the reality of these things, saying that since God could not have made them they therefore did not exist. It was exhilarating to look at our congregation and to know that what the vulgar would call miracles were performed among us, almost as a matter of routine, every day. Not very big miracles, perhaps; but up in London and out in Toronto, we knew that deafness and blindness, cancer and insanity, the great scourges, were constantly vanishing before the prayers of the more advanced Purifiers.

"What!" said my schoolmaster, an Irishman with eyes like broken glass and a sniff of irritability in the bristles of his nose. "What! Do you have the impudence to tell me that if you fell off the top floor of this building and smashed your head in, you would say you hadn't fallen and were not injured?"

I was a small boy and very afraid of everybody, but not when it was a question of my religion. I was used to the kind of conundrum the Irishman had set. It was useless to argue, though our religion had already developed an interesting casuistry.

"I *would* say so," I replied with coldness and some vanity. "And my head would not be smashed."

"You would not say so," answered the Irishman. "You would not say so." His eyes sparkled with pure pleasure. "You'd be dead."

The boys laughed, but they looked at me with admiration.

Then I do not know how or why, I began to see a difficulty. Without warning and as if I had gone into my bedroom at night and had found a gross ape seated in my bed and thereafter following me about with his grunts and his fleas and a look, relentless and ancient, scored on his brown face, I was faced with the problem which prowls at the centre of all religious faith. I was faced by the difficulty of the origin of evil. Evil was an illusion, we were taught. But even illusions have an origin. The Purifiers denied this.

I consulted my uncle. Trade was bad at the time and this made his faith abrupt. He frowned as I spoke.

"When did you brush your coat last?" he said. "You're getting slovenly about your appearance. If you spent more time studying books"—that is to say, the Purification literature—"and less with your hands in your pockets and playing about with boats on the river, you wouldn't be letting Error in."

All dogmas have their jargon; my uncle as a business man loved the trade terms of the Purification. "Don't let Error in," was a favorite one. The whole point about the Purification, he said, was that it was scientific and therefore exact; in consequence it was sheer weakness to admit discussion. Indeed, betrayal. He unpinched his pince-nez, stirred his tea and indicated I must submit or change the subject. Preferably the latter. I saw, to my alarm, that my arguments had defeated my uncle. Faith and doubt pulled like strings round my throat.

"You don't mean to say you don't believe that what our Lord said was true?" my aunt asked nervously, following me out of the room. "Your uncle does, dear."

I could not answer. I went out of the house and down the main street to the river where the punts were stuck like insects in the summery flash of the reach. Life was a dream, I thought; no, a nightmare, for the ape was beside me.

I was still in this state, half sulking and half exalted, when Mr. Hubert Timberlake came to the town. He was one of the important people from the headquarters of our Church and he had come to give an address on the Purification at the Corn Exchange. Posters announcing this were everywhere. Mr. Timberlake was to spend Sunday afternoon with us. It was unbelievable that a man so eminent would actually sit in our dining-room, use our knives and forks, and eat our food. Every imperfection in our home and our characters would jump out at him. The Truth had been revealed to man with scientific accuracy —an accuracy we could all test by experiment—and the future course of human development on earth was laid down, finally. And here in Mr. Timberlake was a man who had not merely performed many miracles— even, it was said with proper reserve, having twice raised the dead—but who had actually been to Toronto, our headquarters, where this great and revolutionary revelation had first been given.

"This is my nephew," my uncle said, introducing me. "He lives with us. He thinks he thinks, Mr. Timberlake, but I tell him he only thinks he does. Ha, ha." My uncle was a humorous man when he was with the great. "He's always on the river," my uncle continued. "I tell him he's got water on the brain. I've been telling Mr. Timberlake about you, my boy."

A hand as soft as the best quality chamois leather took mine. I saw a wide upright man in a double-breasted navy blue suit. He had a pink square head with very small ears and one of those torpid, enamelled smiles which were said by our enemies to be too common in our sect.

"Why, isn't that just fine?" said Mr. Timberlake who, owing to his contacts with Toronto, spoke with an American accent. "What say we tell your uncle it's funny he thinks he's funny."

The eyes of Mr. Timberlake were direct and colourless. He had the look of a retired merchant captain who had become decontaminated from the sea and had reformed and made money. His defence of me had made me his at once. My doubts vanished. Whatever Mr. Timberlake believed must be true and as I listened to him at lunch, I thought there could be no finer life than his.

"I expect Mr. Timberlake's tired after his address," said my aunt.

"Tired?" exclaimed my uncle, brilliant with indignation. "How can Mr. Timberlake be tired? Don't let Error in!"

For in our faith the merely inconvenient was just as illusory as a great catastrophe would have been, if you wished to be strict, and Mr. Timberlake's presence made us very strict.

I noticed then that, after their broad smiles, Mr. Timberlake's lips had the habit of setting into a long depressed sarcastic curve.

"I guess," he drawled, "I guess the Almighty must have been tired sometimes, for it says He relaxed on the seventh day. Say, do you know what I'd like to do this afternoon," he said, turning to me. "While your uncle and aunt are sleeping off this meal let's you and me go on the river and get water on the brain. I'll show you how to punt."

Mr. Timberlake, I saw to my disappointment, was out to show he understood the young. I saw he was planning a "quiet talk" with me about my problems.

"There are too many people on the river on Sundays," said my uncle uneasily.

"Oh, I like a crowd," said Mr. Timberlake, giving my uncle a tough look. "This is the day of rest, you know." He had had my uncle gobbling up every bit of gossip from the sacred city of Toronto all the morning.

My uncle and aunt were incredulous that a man like Mr. Timberlake should go out among the blazers and gramophones of the river on a Sunday afternoon. In any other member of our Church they would have thought this sinful.

"Waal, what say?" said Mr. Timberlake. I could only murmur.

"That's fixed," said Mr. Timberlake. And on came the smile as simple, vivid and unanswerable as the smile on an advertisement. "Isn't that just fine!"

Mr. Timberlake went upstairs to wash his hands. My uncle was deeply offended and shocked, but he could say nothing. He unpinched his glasses.

"A very wonderful man," he said. "So human," he apologized.

"My boy," my uncle said. "This is going to be an experience for you. Hubert Timberlake was making a thousand a year in the insurance business ten years ago. Then he heard of the Purification. He threw everything up, just like that. He gave up his job and took up the work. It was a struggle, he told me so himself this morning. 'Many's the time,' he said to me this morning, 'when I wondered where my next meal was coming from.' But the way was shown. He came down from Worcester to London and in two years he was making fifteen hundred a year out of his practice."

To heal the sick by prayer according to the tenets of the Church of the Last Purification was Mr. Timberlake's profession.

My uncle lowered his eyes. With his glasses off the lids were small and uneasy. He lowered his voice too.

"I have told him about your little trouble," my uncle said quietly, with emotion. I was burned with shame. My uncle looked up and stuck out his chin confidently.

"He just smiled," my uncle said. "That's all."

Then we waited for Mr. Timberlake to come down.

I put on white flannels and soon I was walking down to the river with Mr. Timberlake. I felt that I was going with him under false pretences; for he would begin explaining to me the origin of evil and I would have to pretend politely that he was converting me when, already, at the first sight of him, I had believed. A stone bridge, whose two arches were like an owlish pair of eyes gazing up the reach, was close to the landing-stage. I thought what a pity it was the flannelled men and the sunburned girls there did not know I was getting a ticket for *the* Mr. Timberlake who had been speaking in the town that very morning. I looked round for him and when I saw him I was a little startled. He was standing at the edge of the water looking at it with an expression of empty incomprehension. Among the white crowds his air of brisk efficiency had dulled. He looked middle-aged, out of place and insignificant. But the smile switched on when he saw me.

"Ready?" he called. "Fine!"

I had the feeling that inside him there must be a gramophone record going round and round, stopping at that word.

He stepped into the punt and took charge.

"Now I just want you to paddle us over to the far bank," he said, "and then I'll show you how to punt."

Everything Mr. Timberlake said still seemed unreal to me. The fact that he was sitting in a punt, of all commonplace material things, was incredible. That he should propose to pole us up the river was terrifying. Suppose he fell into the river? At once I checked the thought. A leader of our Church under the direct guidance of God could not possibly fall into a river.

The stream is wide and deep in this reach, but on the southern bank there is a manageable depth and a hard bottom. Over the clay banks the willows hang, making their basket-work print of sun and shadow on the water, while under the gliding boats lie cloudy, chloride caverns. The hoop-like branches of the trees bend down until their tips touch the water like fingers making musical sounds. Ahead in midstream, on a day sunny as this one was, there is a path of strong light which is hard to look at unless you half close your eyes and down this path on the crowded Sundays, go the launches with their parasols and their pennants; and also the rowing boats with their beetle-leg oars, which seem to dig the sunlight out of the water as they rise. Upstream one goes, on and on between the gardens and then between fields kept for grazing. On the afternoon when Mr. Timberlake and I went out to settle the question of the origin of evil, the meadows were packed densely with buttercups.

"Now," said Mr. Timberlake decisively when I had paddled to the other side. "Now I'll take her."

He got over the seat into the well at the stern.

"I'll just get you clear of the trees," I said.

"Give me the pole," said Mr. Timberlake, standing up on the little platform and making a squeak with his boots as he did so. "Thank you, sir. I haven't done this for eighteen years but I can tell you, brother, in those days I was considered some poler."

He looked around and let the pole slide down through his hands. Then he gave the first difficult push. The punt rocked pleasantly and we moved forward. I sat facing him, paddle in hand, to check any inward drift of the punt.

"How's that, you guys?" said Mr. Timberlake, looking round at our eddies and drawing in the pole. The delightful water swished down it.

"Fine," I said. Deferentially I had caught the word.

He went on to his second and his third strokes, taking too much water on his sleeve, perhaps, and uncertain in his steering, which I corrected, but he was doing well.

"It comes back to me," he said. "How am I doing?"

"Just keep her out from the trees," I said.

"The trees?" he said.

"The willows," I said.

"I'll do it now," he said. "How's that? Not quite enough? Well, how's this?"

"Another one," I said. "The current runs strong this side."

"What? More trees?" he said. He was getting hot.

"We can shoot out past them," I said. "I'll ease over with the paddle."

Mr. Timberlake did not like this suggestion.

"No, don't do that. I can manage it," he said. I did not want to offend one of the leaders of our Church, so I put the paddle down; but I felt I ought to have taken him farther along away from the irritation of the trees.

"Of course," I said. "We could go under them. It might be nice."

"I think," said Mr. Timberlake, "that would be a very good idea."

He lunged hard on the pole and took us towards the next archway of willow branches.

"We may have to duck a bit, that's all," I said.

"Oh, I can push the branches up," said Mr. Timberlake.

"It is better to duck," I said.

We were gliding now quickly towards the arch, in fact I was already under it.

"I think I should duck," I said. "Just bend down for this one."

"What makes the trees lean over the water like this?" asked Mr. Timberlake. "Weeping willows—I'll give you a thought there. Now Error likes to make us dwell on sorrow. Why not call them *laughing* willows?" discoursed Mr. Timberlake as the branch passed over my head.

"Duck," I said.

"Where? I don't see them," said Mr. Timberlake turning round.

"No, your head," I said. "The branch," I called.

"Oh, the branch. This one?" said Mr. Timberlake, finding a branch just against his chest, and he put out a hand to lift it. It is not easy to lift a willow branch and Mr. Timberlake was surprised. He stepped back as it gently and firmly leaned against him. He leaned back and pushed from his feet. And he pushed too far. The boat went on, I saw Mr. Timberlake's boots leave the stern as he took an unthoughtful step backwards. He made a last-minute grasp at a stronger and higher branch, and then, there he hung a yard above the water, round as a blue damson that is ripe and ready, waiting only for a touch to make it fall. Too late with the paddle and shot ahead by the force of his thrust, I could not save him.

For a full minute I did not believe what I saw; indeed our religion taught us never to believe what we saw. Unbelieving I could not move. I gaped. The impossible had happened. Only a miracle, I found myself saying, could save him.

What was the most striking was the silence of Mr. Timberlake as he hung from the tree. I was lost between gazing at him and trying to get the punt out of the small branches of the tree. By the time I had got the punt out there were several yards of water between us and the soles of his boots were very near the water as the branch bent under his weight. Boats were passing at the time but no one seemed to notice us. I was glad about this. This was a private agony. A double chin had appeared on the face of Mr. Timberlake and his head was squeezed between his shoulders and his hanging arms. I saw him blink and look up at the sky. His eyelids were pale like a chicken's. He was tidy and dignified as he hung there, the hat was not displaced and the top button of his coat was done up. He had a blue silk handkerchief in his breast pocket. So unperturbed and genteel he seemed that as the tips of his shoes came nearer and nearer to the water, I became alarmed. He could perform what are called miracles. He would be thinking at this moment that only in an erroneous and illusory sense was he hanging from the branch of the tree over six feet of water. He was probably praying one of the closely reasoned prayers of our faith which were more like conversations with Euclid than appeals to God. The calm of his face suggested this. Was he, I asked myself, within sight of the main road, the town Recreation Ground and the landing-stage crowded with people, was he about to re-enact a well-known miracle? I hoped that he was not. I prayed that he was not. I prayed with all my will that Mr. Timberlake would not walk upon the water. It was my prayer and not his that was answered.

I saw the shoes dip, water rise above his ankles and up his socks. He

tried to move his grip now to a yet higher branch—he did not succeed
—and in making this effort his coat and waist-coat rose and parted from
his trousers. One seam of shirt with its pant-loops and brace-taps broke
like a crack across the middle of Mr. Timberlake. It was like a fatal
flaw in a statue, an earthquake crack which made the monumental
mortal. The last Greeks must have felt as I felt then, when they saw a
crack across the middle of some statue of Apollo. It was at this moment
I realized that the final revelation about man and society on earth
had come to nobody and that Mr. Timberlake knew nothing at all about
the origin of evil.

All this takes long to describe, but it happened in a few seconds as I
paddled towards him. I was too late to get his feet on the boat and
the only thing to do was to let him sink until his hands were nearer the
level of the punt and then to get him to change hand-holds. Then I
would paddle him ashore. I did this. Amputated by the water, first a
torso, then a bust, then a mere head and shoulders, Mr. Timberlake,
I noticed, looked sad and lonely as he sank. He was a declining dogma.
As the water lapped his collar—for he hesitated to let go of the branch
to hold the punt—I saw a small triangle of deprecation and pathos
between his nose and the corners of his mouth. The head resting on the
platter of water had the sneer of calamity on it, such as one sees in the
pictures of a beheaded saint.

"Hold on to the punt, Mr. Timberlake," I said urgently. "Hold on
to the punt."

He did so.

"Push from behind," he directed in a dry businesslike voice. They
were his first words. I obeyed him. Carefully I paddled him towards the
bank. He turned and, with a splash, climbed ashore. There he stood, raising his arms and looking at the water running down his swollen suit
and making a puddle at his feet.

"Say," said Mr. Timberlake coldly, "we let some Error in that
time."

How much he must have hated our family.

"I am sorry, Mr. Timberlake," I said. "I am most awfully sorry.
I should have paddled. It was my fault. I'll get you home at once. Let
me wring out your coat and waist-coat. You'll catch your death . . ."

I stopped. I had nearly blasphemed. I had nearly suggested that
Mr. Timberlake had fallen into the water and that to a man of his age
that might be dangerous.

Mr. Timberlake corrected me. His voice was impersonal, addressing the laws of human existence, rather than myself.

"If God made water it would be ridiculous to suggest He made it
capable of harming His creatures. Wouldn't it?"

"Yes," I murmured hypocritically.

"O.K.," said Mr. Timberlake. "Let's go."

"I'll soon get you across," I said.

"No," he said. "I mean let's go on. We're not going to let a little thing like this spoil a beautiful afternoon. Where were we going? You spoke of a pretty landing-place farther on. Let's go there."

"But I must take you home. You can't sit there soaked to the skin. It will spoil your clothes."

"Now, now," said Mr. Timberlake. "Do as I say. Go on."

There was nothing to be done with him. I held the punt into the bank and he stepped in. He sat like a bursting and sodden bolster in front of me while I paddled. We had lost the pole of course.

For a long time I could hardly look at Mr. Timberlake. He was taking the line that nothing had happened and this put me at a disadvantage. I knew something considerable had happened. That glaze, which so many of the members of our sect had on their faces and persons, their minds and manners, had been washed off. There was no gleam for me from Mr. Timberlake.

"What's the house over there?" he asked. He was making conversation. I had steered into the middle of the river to get him into the strong sun. I saw steam rise from him.

I took courage and studied him. He was a man, I realized, in poor physical condition, unexercised and sedentary. Now the gleam had left him one saw the veined empurpled skin of the stoutish man with a poor heart. I remember he had said at lunch:

"A young woman I know said, 'Isn't it wonderful. I can walk thirty miles a day without being in the least tired.' I said, 'I don't see that bodily indulgence is anything a member of the Church of the Last Purification should boast about.' "

Yes, there was something flaccid, passive and slack about Mr. Timberlake. Bunched in swollen clothes, he refused to take them off. It occurred to me, as he looked with boredom at the water, the passing boats and the country, that he had not been in the country before. That it was something he had agreed to do but wanted to get over quickly. He was totally uninterested. By his questions—what is that church? Are there any fish in this river? Is that a wireless or a gramophone?—I understood that Mr. Timberlake was formally acknowledging a world he did not live in. It was too interesting, too eventful a world. His spirit, inert and preoccupied, was elsewhere in an eventless and immaterial habitation. He was a dull man, duller than any man I have ever known; but his dullness was a sort of earthly deposit left by a being whose diluted mind was far away in the effervescence of metaphysical matters. There was a slightly pettish look on his face as (to himself, of course) he declared he was not wet and that he would not have a heart attack or catch pneumonia.

Mr. Timberlake spoke little. Sometimes he squeezed water out of his sleeve. He shivered a little. He watched his steam. I had planned when we set out to go up as far as the lock but now the thought of another two miles of this responsibility was too much. I pretended I wanted to go only as far as the bend which we were approaching, where one of the richest buttercup meadows was. I mentioned this to him. He turned and looked with boredom at the field. Slowly we came to the bank.

We tied up the punt and we landed.

"Fine," said Mr. Timberlake. He stood at the edge of the meadow, just as he had stood at the landing-stage—lost, stupefied, uncomprehending.

"Nice to stretch our legs," I said. I led the way into the deep flowers. So dense were the buttercups there was hardly any green. Presently I sat down. Mr. Timberlake looked at me and sat down also. Then I turned to him with a last try at persuasion. Respectability, I was sure, was his trouble.

"No one will see us," I said. "This is out of sight of the river. Take off your coat and trousers and wring them out."

Mr. Timberlake replied firmly:

"I am satisfied to remain as I am.

"What is this flower?" he asked to change the subject.

"Buttercup," I said.

"Of course," he replied.

I could do nothing with him. I lay down full length in the sun; and, observing this and thinking to please me, Mr. Timberlake did the same. He must have supposed that this was what I had come out in the boat to do. It was only human. He had come out with me, I saw, to show me that he was only human.

But as we lay there I saw the steam still rising. I had had enough.

"A bit hot," I said getting up.

He got up at once.

"Do you want to sit in the shade?" he asked politely.

"No," I said. "Would you like to?"

"No," he said. "I was thinking of you."

"Let's go back," I said. We both stood up and I let him pass in front of me. When I looked at him again I stopped dead. Mr. Timberlake was no longer a man in a navy blue suit. He was blue no longer. He was transfigured. He was yellow. He was covered with buttercup pollen, a fine yellow paste of it made by the damp, from head to foot.

"Your suit," I said.

He looked at it. He raised his thin eyebrows a little, but he did not smile or make any comment.

The man is a saint, I thought. As saintly as any of those gold-leaf figures in the churches of Sicily. Golden he sat in the punt; golden he sat for the next hour as I paddled him down the river. Golden and bored. Golden, as we landed at the town and as we walked up the street back to my uncle's house. There he refused to change his clothes or to sit by a fire. He kept an eye on the time for his train back to London. By no word did he acknowledge the disasters or the beauties of the world. If they were printed upon him, they were printed upon a husk.

Sixteen years have passed since I dropped Mr. Timberlake in the river and since the sight of his pant-loops destroyed my faith. I have not seen him since, and today I heard that he was dead. He was fifty-seven. His mother, a very old lady with whom he had lived all his life, went into his bedroom when he was getting ready for church and found him lying on the floor in his shirt-sleeves. A stiff collar with the tie half inserted was in one hand. Five minutes before, she told the doctor, she had been speaking to him.

The doctor who looked at the heavy body lying on the single bed saw a middle-aged man, wide rather than stout and with an extraordinary box-like thick-jawed face. He had got fat, my uncle told me, in later years. The heavy liver-coloured cheeks were like the chaps of a hound. Heart disease, it was plain, was the cause of the death of Mr. Timberlake. In death the face was lax, even coarse and degenerate. It was a miracle, the doctor said, that he had lived so long. Any time during the last twenty years the smallest shock might have killed him.

I thought of our afternoon on the river. I thought of him hanging from the tree. I thought of him, indifferent and golden in the meadow. I understood why he had made for himself a protective, sedentary blandness, an automatic smile, a collection of phrases. He kept them on like the coat after his ducking. And I understood why—though I had feared it all the time we were on the river—I understood why he did not talk to me about the origin of evil. He was honest. The ape was with us. The ape that merely followed me was already inside Mr. Timberlake eating out his heart.

Theme Questions

1. Was Mr. Timberlake a saint, or is the title ironic? Check the story carefully for the narrator's evalution in order to defend your answer properly.

2. References are made to "the ape." What does "the ape" represent to the narrator? Why is he troubled by "the ape"? What was

Mr. Timberlake's "ape"? Why does the narrator's respect for Mr. Timberlake develop in later years?

3. Discuss "The Saint" as a satire, not only against the "Purifiers" but against any religion. What are the main criticisms implied or stated by the narrator?

4. The humor of the story is both situational and stylistic. What are the techniques used to make the story funny?

... **also by V. S. Pritchett**   *The Sailor, Sense of Humor and Other Stories*
When My Girl Comes Home
Blind Love and Other Stories

Religion seeks to develop reverence, but it sometimes produces irreverence. More unusual than either is the kind of irreverent reverence of "The Saint" or of the two poems that follow. X. J. Kennedy's "First Confession" and Vassar Miller's "Letters to a Young Girl Considering a Religious Vocation." Man's perspective on life is in balance when life's most serious concerns can be viewed with humor and skepticism.

First Confession

X. J. Kennedy

Blood thudded in my ears, I scuffed,
　　Steps stubborn, to the telltale booth
Beyond whose curtained portal coughed
　　The robed repositor of truth.

The slat shot back. The universe
　　Bowed down his cratered dome to hear
Enumerated my each curse,
　　The sip snitched from my old man's beer,

My sloth pride envy lechery,
　　The dime held back from Peter's Pence
With which I'd bribed my girl to pee
　　That I might spy her instruments.

Hovering scale pans when I'd done
　　Settled their balance slow as silt
While in the restless dark I burned
　　Bright as a brimstone in my guilt

Until as one feeds birds he doled
　　Seven Our Fathers and a Hail
Which I to double-scrub my soul
　　Intoned twice at the altar rail

Where Sunday in seraphic light
    I knelt, as full as grace as most,
And stuck my tongue out at the priest:
    A fresh roost for the Holy Ghost.

Letters to a Young Girl Considering a Religious Vocation

Vassar Miller

    I
    I hope that you are certain,
    for if you are not, you will be
    a baby playing with matches
    and may burn up your whole world.
    Soon you will find
    that the cross is less often of wood
    than of air, that the nails are the winds
    whistling through the holes in your heart.
    Since the cross is implied
    in the shape of everybody,
    do not say I presume
    who wear no habit
    but the habit of every day.
    Where else but here have I learned
    how well we do
    to get through our lives alive!
    So, I could wish for you
    that there, where you are supposed to die,
    you do not finish as merely
    an extended death-gasp.
    It would be a matter for weeping
    were we to stand side by side
    and not to be told apart
    when dissected down to our cinders
    that used to be souls.

    II
    After our applause,
    harmless enough in itself,
    after our envy,

not really malignant,
after our praise,
which, though it cannot carry you far,
cannot wreck you,
if you are determined to go—
may all of this cease
in a hush that is more than their echo
of a whining importunity
whereto you grimace and gesture
and writhe and gyrate
and wriggle and jump
in the postures of peace;
more than their elongation
of the shadow cast by a crone
clapping her toothless gums
stealing the name of silence.

Theme Questions

1. What do the two poets imply as their speaker's attitudes toward religion and the religious life? Are these attitudes applicable only to the Catholic clergy or may they be generalized for all faiths? Why?

2. Analyze the language of each poem, especially for all words that pertain to religion. What does the analysis reveal?

*In an age of Univac, shopping plazas, the drive-in and moon travel,
modern man doesn't often think of chivalry or the "grand gesture."
Long ago, it is told, Walter Raleigh spread his cloak for Queen Elizabeth to walk on so she would not soil her feet in a muddy puddle. This
was not history's last chivalric gesture if the narrator's act in "A & P"
is granted its proper status.*

A & P

John Updike

In walks these three girls in nothing but bathing suits. I'm in the
third checkout slot, with my back to the door, so I don't see them until
they're over by the bread. The one that caught my eye first was the one
in the plaid green two-piece. She was a chunky kid, with a good tan
and a sweet broad soft-looking can with those two crescents of white
just under it, where the sun never seems to hit, at the top of the backs
of her legs. I stood there with my hand on a box of HiHo crackers
trying to remember if I rang it up or not. I ring it up again and the
customer starts giving me hell. She's one of these cash-register-watchers,
a witch about fifty with rouge on her cheekbones and no eyebrows,
and I know it made her day to trip me up. She'd been watching cash reg-
isters for fifty years and probably never seen a mistake before.

By the time I got her feathers smoothed and her goodies into a bag
—she gives me a little snort in passing, if she'd been born at the right
time they would have burned her over in Salem—by the time I get her
on her way the girls had circled around the bread and were coming
back, without a pushcart, back my way along the counters, in the aisle
between the checkouts and the Special bins. They didn't even have
shoes on. There was this chunky one, with the two-piece—it was bright
green and the seams on the bra were still sharp and her belly was still
pretty pale so I guessed she just got it (the suit)—there was this one,
with one of those chubby berry-faces, the lips all bunched together under
her nose, this one, and a tall one, with black hair that hadn't quite frizzed
right, and one of these sunburns right across under the eyes, and a

chin that was too long—you know, the kind of girl other girls think is very "striking" and "attractive" but never quite makes it, as they very well know, which is why they like her so much—and then the third one, that wasn't quite so tall. She was the queen. She kind of led them, the other two peeking around and making their shoulders round. She didn't look around, not this queen, she just walked straight on slowly, on these long white prima-donna legs. She came down a little hard on her heels, as if she didn't walk in her bare feet that much, putting down her heels and then letting the weight move along to her toes as if she was testing the floor with every step, putting a little deliberate extra action into it. You never know for sure how girls' minds work (do you really think it's a mind in there or just a little buzz like a bee in a glass jar?) but you got the idea she had talked the other two into coming in here with her, and now she was showing them how to do it, walk slow and hold yourself straight.

She had on a kind of dirty-pink—beige maybe, I don't know—bathing suit with a little nubble all over it and, what got me, the straps were down. They were off her shoulders looped loose around the cool tops of her arms, and I guess as a result the suit had slipped a little on her, so all around the top of the cloth there was this shining rim. If it hadn't been there you wouldn't have known there could have been anything whiter than those shoulders. With the straps pushed off, there was nothing between the top of the suit and the top of her head except just *her*, this clean bare plane of the top of her chest down from the shoulder bones like a dented sheet of metal tilted in the light. I mean, it was more than pretty.

She had sort of oaky hair that the sun and salt had bleached, done up in a bun that was unravelling, and a kind of prim face. Walking into the A & P with your straps down, I suppose it's the only kind of face you *can* have. She held her head so high her neck, coming up out of those white shoulders, looked kind of stretched, but I didn't mind. The longer her neck was, the more of her there was.

She must have felt in the corner of her eye me and over my shoulder Stokesie in the second slot watching, but she didn't tip. Not this queen. She kept her eyes moving across the racks, and stopped, and turned so slow it made my stomach rub the inside of my apron, and buzzed to the other two, who kind of huddled against her for relief, and then they all three of them went up the cat-and-dog-food-breakfast-cereal-macaroni-rice-raisins-seasonings-spreads-spaghetti-soft-drinks-crackers-and-cookies aisle. From the third slot I look straight up this aisle to the meat counter, and I watched them all the way. The fat one with the tan sort of fumbled with the cookies, but on second thought she put the package back. The sheep pushing their carts down the aisle—the girls were walking against the usual traffic (not that we have one-way signs or anything)—were pretty hilarious. You could see them, when Queenie's white shoulders dawned on them, kind of jerk, or hop, or hiccup, but their eyes snapped back to their own baskets and on they pushed. I bet you could set off dynamite in an A & P and the people would by and large keep reaching and checking oatmeal off their lists and muttering "Let me see, there was a third thing, began with A, asparagus, no, ah, yes, applesauce!" or whatever it is they do mutter. But there was no doubt, this jiggled them. A few houseslaves in pin curlers even looked around after pushing their carts past to make sure what they had seen was correct.

You know, it's one thing to have a girl in a bathing suit down on the beach, where what with the glare nobody can look at each other much anyway, and another thing in the cool of the A & P, under the fluorescent lights, against all those stacked packages, with her feet paddling along naked over our checkerboard green-and-cream rubber-tile floor.

"Oh Daddy," Stokesie said beside me. "I feel so faint."

"Darling," I said. "Hold me tight." Stokesie's married, with two babies chalked up on his fuselage already, but as far as I can tell that's the only difference. He's twenty-two, and I was nineteen this April.

"Is it done?" he asks, the responsible married man finding his voice. I forgot to say he thinks he's going to be manager some sunny day, maybe in 1990 when it's called the Great Alexandrov and Petrooshki Tea Company or something.

What he meant was, our town is five miles from a beach, with a big summer colony out on the Point, but we're right in the middle of town, and the women generally put on a shirt or shorts or something before they get out of the car into the street. And anyway these are usually women with six children and varicose veins mapping their legs and nobody, including them, could care less. As I say, we're right in the middle of town, and if you stand at our front doors you can see two banks and the Congregational church and the newspaper store and three real-estate offices and about twenty-seven old freeloaders tearing up Central Street because the sewer broke again. It's not as if we're on the Cape; we're north of Boston and there's people in this town haven't seen the ocean for twenty years.

The girls had reached the meat counter and were asking McMahon something. He pointed, they pointed, and they shuffled out of sight behind a pyramid of Diet Delight peaches. All that was left for us to see was old McMahon patting his mouth and looking after them sizing up their joints. Poor kids, I began to feel sorry for them, they couldn't help it.

Now here comes the sad part of the story, at least my family says it's sad, but I don't think it's so sad myself. The store's pretty empty, it being Thursday afternoon, so there was nothing much to do except lean on the register and wait for the girls to show up again. The whole store was like a pinball machine and I didn't know which tunnel they'd come out of. After a while they come around out of the far aisle, around the light bulbs, records at discount of the Caribbean Six or Tony Martin Sings or some such gunk you wonder they waste the wax on, sixpacks of candy bars, and plastic toys done up in cellophane that fall apart when a kid looks at them anyway. Around they come, Queenie still leading the way, and holding a little gray jar in her hand. Slots Three through Seven are unmanned and I could see her wondering between Stokes and me, but Stokesie with his usual luck draws an old party in baggy gray pants who stumbles up with four giant cans of pineapple juice (what do these bums *do* with all that pineapple juice? I've often asked myself) so the girls come to me. Queenie puts down the jar and I take it into my fingers icy cold. Kingfish Fancy Herring Snacks in Pure Sour Cream: 49¢. Now her hands are empty, not a ring or a bracelet, bare as God made them, and I wonder where the money's coming from. Still with that prim look she lifts a folded dollar bill out of the hollow at the center of her nubbled pink top. The jar went heavy in my hand. Really, I thought that was so cute.

Then everybody's luck begins to run out. Lengel comes in from haggling with a truck full of cabbages on the lot and is about to scuttle into that door marked MANAGER behind which he hides all day when the girls touch his eye. Lengel's pretty dreary, teaches Sunday School and the rest, but he doesn't miss that much. He comes over and says, "Girls, this isn't the beach."

Queenie blushes, though maybe it's just a brush of sunburn I was noticing for the first time, now that she was so close. "My mother asked me to pick up a jar of herring snacks." Her voice kind of startled me, the way voices do when you see the people first, coming out so flat and dumb yet kind of tony, too, the way it ticked over "pick up" and "snacks." All of a sudden I slid right down her voice into her living room. Her father and the other men were standing around in ice-cream coats and bow ties and the women were in sandals picking up herring snacks on toothpicks off a big glass plate and they were all holding drinks the color of water with olives and sprigs of mint in them. When my parents have somebody over they get lemonade and if it's a real racy affair Schlitz in tall glasses with "They'll Do It Every Time" cartoons stencilled on.

"That's all right," Lengel said. "But this isn't the beach." His repeating this struck me as funny, as if it had just occurred to him, and he had been thinking all these years the A & P was a great big dune and he was the head lifeguard. He didn't like my smiling—as I say he doesn't miss much—but he concentrates on giving the girls that sad Sunday-school-superintendent stare.

Queenie's blush is no sunburn now, and the plump one in plaid, that I liked better from the back—a really sweet can—pipes up, "We weren't doing any shopping. We just came in for the one thing."

"That makes no difference," Lengel tells her, and I could see from the way his eyes went that he hadn't noticed she was wearing a two-piece before. "We want you decently dressed when you come in here."

"We *are* decent," Queenie says suddenly, her lower lip pushing, getting sore now that she remembers her place, a place from which the crowd that runs the A & P must look pretty crummy. Fancy Herring Snacks flashed in her very blue eyes.

"Girls, I don't want to argue with you. After this come in here with your shoulders covered. It's our policy." He turns his back. That's policy for you. Policy is what the kingpins want. What the others want is juvenile delinquency.

All this while, the customers had been showing up with their carts but, you know, sheep, seeing a scene, they had all bunched up on Stokesie, who shook open a paper bag as gently as peeling a peach, not wanting to miss a word. I could feel in the silence everybody getting nervous, most of all Lengel, who asks me, "Sammy, have you rung up their purchase?"

I thought and said "No" but it wasn't about that I was thinking. I go through the punches, 4, 9, GROC, TOT—it's more complicated than you think, and after you do it often enough, it begins to make a little song, that you hear words to, in my case "Hello (*bing*) there, you (*gung*) hap-py *pee*-pul (*splat*)!"—the *splat* being the drawer flying out. I uncrease the bill, tenderly as you may imagine, it just having come from between the two smoothest scoops of vanilla I had ever known were there, and pass a half and a penny into her narrow pink palm, and nestle the herrings in a bag and twist its neck and hand it over, all the time thinking.

The girls, and who'd blame them, are in a hurry to get out, so I say "I quit" to Lengel quick enough for them to hear, hoping they'll stop and watch me, their unsuspected hero. They keep right on going, into the electric eye; the door flies open and they flicker across the lot to their car, Queenie and Plaid and Big Tall Goony-Goony (not that as raw material she was so bad), leaving me with Lengel and a kink in his eyebrow.

"Did you say something, Sammy?"

"I said I quit."

"I thought you did."

"You didn't have to embarrass them."

"It was they who were embarrassing us."

I started to say something that came out "Fiddle-de-doo." It's a saying of my grandmother's, and I know she would have been pleased.

"I don't think you know what you're saying," Lengel said.

"I know you don't," I said. "But I do." I pull the bow at the back of my apron and start shrugging it off my shoulders. A couple customers that had been heading for my slot begin to knock against each other, like scared pigs in a chute.

Lengel sighs and begins to look very patient and old and gray. He's been a friend of my parents for years. "Sammy, you don't want to do this to your Mom and Dad," he tells me. It's true, I don't. But it seems to me that once you begin a gesture it's fatal not to go through with it. I fold the apron, "Sammy" stitched in red on the pocket, and put it on the counter, and drop the bow tie on top of it. The bow tie is theirs, if you've ever wondered. "You'll feel this for the rest of your life," Lengel says, and I know that's true, too, but remembering how he made that pretty girl blush makes me so scrunchy inside I punch the No Sale tab and the machine whirs "pee-pul" and the drawer splats out. One advantage to this scene taking place in summer, I can follow this up with a clean exit, there's no fumbling around getting your coat and galoshes, I just saunter into the electric eye in my white shirt that my mother ironed the night before, and the door heaves itself open, and outside the sunshine is skating around on the asphalt.

I look around for my girls, but they're gone, of course. There wasn't anybody but some young married screaming with her children about some candy they didn't get by the door of a powder-blue Falcon station wagon. Looking back in the big windows, over the bags of peat moss and aluminum lawn furniture stacked on the pavement, I could see Lengel in my place in the slot, checking the sheep through. His face was dark gray and his back stiff, as if he'd just had an injection of iron, and my stomach kind of fell as I felt how hard the world was going to be to me hereafter.

Theme Questions

1. "She had . . . a kind of prim face. Walking into the A & P with your straps down, I suppose it's the only kind of face you can have." Discuss the context and the full significance of the quotation. Analyze or characterize "Queenie."

2. "Policy is what the kingpins want. What the others want is juvenile delinquency." This is Sammy's evaluation. Discuss this as it relates to the conflict of values between the manager and Sammy, and as it pertains to ideas and attitudes of the portion of society that each represents.   .

3. "A & P" offers several comments on American life. Note the references to the customers and the store's staff, particularly the manager. From these and the details given about the store's layout and stock, deduce Updike's comment on the United States.

4. With whom do you identify: Sammy, the manager, or Queenie? Why? With whom does Updike's sympathy lie?

. . . **also by John Updike**   *Rabbit Run*
                                Pigeon Feathers
                                The Centaur

In every age man has praised woman—if not for her beauty, for her charm; if not for her virtue, for her lack of it.

To believe in flattery is one thing; to wish for its elimination is another. Yeats and Summers admire two young women, while Wallace Stevens indicates that the male is just as susceptible to flattery as the female.

For Anne Gregory

William Butler Yeats

'Never shall a young man,
Thrown into despair
By those great honey-coloured
Ramparts at your ear,
Love you for yourself alone
And not your yellow hair.'

'But I can get a hair-dye
And set such colour there,
Brown, or black, or carrot,
That young men in despair
May love me for myself alone
And not my yellow hair.'

'I heard an old religious man
But yesternight declare
That he had found a text to prove
That only God, my dear,
Could love you for yourself alone
And not your yellow hair.'

Girl with the Top Down*

Hollis Summers

She moves in her jeweled barge down the bright street
Her lips parted as if she smiled a word
Like *sin*. Her gold hair floats in the reluctant air
Which does not want to admit her passing. She
Is no more overwhelming than an actress
Dancing naked in Cinemascope
Accompanied by drums and sweated applause.

At the intersection she glides to a gentle pause;
The traffic light blushes at its carnal hope,
And turns an immediate envious green. Pitiless
She proceeds. She probably does not see
The other girl who is always standing there
Waiting for a bus, smiling as if she preferred
Waiting virtuous in the sun on her own two feet.

The Plot against the Giant**

Wallace Stevens

First Girl
When this yokel comes maundering,
Whetting his hacker,
I shall run before him,
Diffusing the civilest odors
Out of geraniums and unsmelled flowers.
It will check him.

Second Girl
I shall run before him,
Arching cloths besprinkled with colors

* From *The Walks near Athens* by Hollis Summers. Copyright by Hollis Summers. Reprinted by permission.
** Copyright 1923 and renewed 1951 by Wallace Stevens. Reprinted from *The Collected Poems of Wallace Stevens* by permission of Alfred A. Knopf, Inc.

As small as fish-eggs.
The threads
Will abash him.

Third Girl
Oh, la . . . le pauvre!
I shall run before him,
With a curious puffing.
He will bend his ear then.
I shall whisper
Heavenly labials in a world of gutturals.
It will undo him.

Theme Questions

1. In the three poems, what are the devices or temptations the five girls offer for the admiration or "undoing" of the male?

2. Who is the speaker of each poem? What is his attitude toward his subject? What effect does knowledge of the speaker have on the content of the poem?

PART THREE

ENCOUNTER

Covenant

Tennessee Williams

If you are happy, I will give you an apple,
if you are anxious, I will twist your arm,
and if you permit me, I will be glad to hold you
close to my heart forever and do you no harm.

If I am happy, will you give me an apple?
If I am anxious, you may twist my arm.
And if you would like to, I would like you to hold me
close to your heart forever and do me no harm.

This is a bargain, only two can make it.
This is a covenant offered with desperate calm,
it being uncertain that lovers can drive out demons
with the gift of an apple or the twist of an arm.

Tennessee Williams, *In the Winter of Cities.* Copyright © 1964 by Tennessee Williams. Reprinted by permission of New Directions Publishing Corporation.

First love is often the sweetest, most tender, and most heartbreaking of all—partly because it is love, partly because it is the first. The first encounter with love reawakens our sense of childhood wonder. Hands and lips bring new sensations and invite new sensations.

The modern poet John Logan, using "old-fashioned" blank verse, and the ever contemporary William Shakespeare illustrate first encounter in "The Picnic" and the meeting of Romeo and Juliet.

The Picnic

John Logan

It is the picnic with Ruth in the spring.
Ruth was third on my list of seven girls
But the first two were gone (Betty) or else
Had someone (Ellen has accepted Doug).
Indian Gully the last day of school;
Girls make the lunches for the boys too.
I wrote a note to Ruth in algebra class
Day before the test. She smiled, and nodded.
We left the cars and walked through the young corn
The shoots green as paint and the leaves like tongues
Trembling. Beyond the fence where we stood
Some wild strawberry flowered by an elm tree
And Jack-in-the-pulpit was olive ripe.
A blackbird fled as I crossed, and showed
A spot of gold or red under its quick wing.
I held the wire for Ruth and watched the whip
Of her long, striped skirt as she followed.
Three freckles blossomed on her thin, white back
Underneath the loop where the blouse buttoned.
We went for our lunch away from the rest,
Stretched in the new grass, our heads close
Over unknown things wrapped up in wax papers.
Ruth tried for the same, I forget what it was,
And our hands were together. She laughed,
And a breeze caught the edge of her little

Collar and the edge of her brown, loose hair
That touched my cheek. I turned my face in-
to the gentle fall. I saw how sweet it smelled.
She didn't move her head or take her hand.
I felt a soft caving in my stomach
As at the top of the highest slide
When I had been a child, but was not afraid,
And did not know why my eyes moved with wet
As I brushed her cheek with my lips and brushed
Her lips with my own lips. She said to me
Jack, Jack, different than I had ever heard,
Because she wasn't calling me, I think,
Or telling me. She used my name to
Talk in another way I wanted to know.
She laughed again and then she took her hand;
I gave her what we both had touched—can't
Remember what it was, and we ate the lunch.
Afterward we walked in the small, cool creek
Our shoes off, her skirt hitched, and she smiling,
My pants rolled, and then we climbed up the high
Side of Indian Gully and looked
Where we had been, our hands together again.
It was then some bright thing came in my eyes,
Starting at the back of them and flowing
Suddenly through my head and down my arms
And stomach and my bare legs that seemed not
To stop in feet, not to feel the red earth
Of the Gully, as though we hung in a
Touch of birds. There was a word in my throat
With the feeling and I knew the first time
What it meant and I said, it's beautiful.
Yes, she said, and I felt the sound and word
In my hand join the sound and word in hers
As in one name said, or in one cupped hand.
We put back on our shoes and socks and we
Sat in the grass awhile, crosslegged, under
A blowing tree, not saying anything.
And Ruth played with shells she found in the creek,
As I watched. Her small wrist which was so sweet
To me turned by her breast and the shells dropped
Green, white, blue, easily into her lap,
Passing light through themselves. She gave the pale
Shells to me, and got up and touched her hips
With her light hands, and we walked down slowly
To play the school games with the others.

from "Romeo and Juliet," Act I, Scene 5

"If I profane with my unworthiest hand"

William Shakespeare

ROMEO   If I profane with my unworthiest hand
   This holy shrine, the gentle fine is this,
   My lips, two blushing pilgrims, ready stand
   To smooth that rough touch with a tender kiss.
JULIET   Good pilgrim, you do wrong your hand too much,
   Which mannerly devotion shows in this;
   For saints have hands that pilgrims' hands do touch,
   And palm to palm is holy palmers' kiss.
ROMEO   Have not saints lips, and holy palmers too?
JULIET   Aye, pilgrim, lips that they must use in prayer.
ROMEO   Oh then, dear saint, let lips do what hands do.
   Then pray. Grant thou lest faith turn to despair.
JULIET   Saints do not move, though grant for prayers' sake.
ROMEO   Then move not while my prayer's effect I take.

Theme Questions

1. In these two dissimilar poems, find the similarities of experience. In what other ways are the poems alike? In what ways are they unlike?

2. Read the whole scene in "Romeo and Juliet" from which the sonnet is taken. With the full context in mind, compare the two poems.

Yuri Kazakov is a contemporary Russian writer. In this rather long story, he recalls the shyness and joys of first love, but he goes further. Here is not only the wonder and exhilaration of love, but also the anguish and bewilderment that is part of breaking up.

The Blue and the Green

Yuri Kazakov

"Lilya," she says in a deep throaty voice and gives me a small warm hand.

I take her hand carefully, squeeze it and let it go. At the same time I mumble my name. It seems I'd forgotten the possibility that I'd have to pronounce my own name. The hand I've just relinquished is lovely and pale in the darkness. "What an extraordinarily lovely hand!" I think ecstatically.

We're standing in a dark courtyard. There are so many windows in this dark square yard: there are pale blue windows, green, pink, and plain white windows. From a blue window on the second floor music can be heard. There they've turned on the radio and I hear jazz. I like jazz a lot, not to dance to—I don't know how to dance—I like to listen to good jazz. Some don't like it, but I do. I don't know, maybe that's bad. I'm standing and I'm listening to jazz coming down from the second floor, from the blue window. That's evidently an excellent radio they have.

After she says her name, there's a long silence. I know she's waiting for me to do something. Maybe she thinks I'll start talking, say something funny, maybe she's waiting for a first word from me, some kind of question so she can start talking. But I'm quiet, I'm entirely in the power of that extraordinary rhythm and the silvery sound of the trumpet. How nice that music is playing and I don't have to say anything!

Finally we go off. We come out onto a lighted street. There are four of us: my friend and a girl, Lilya and I. We're going to the movies. It's the first time I've been to a movie with a girl, it's the first time I've met her, and she gave me her hand and told me her name. A wonderful name—pronounced in a throaty voice! And here we are side by side, complete strangers to each other and yet friends somehow. There's no music to protect me any more. My friend drops behind with his girl. Panicky, I slow down, but they go even slower. I know he's doing it on purpose. That's not nice of him—to leave us alone. I never expected such treachery from him!

What can I say to her? What does she like? I sneak a look at her sideways: shining eyes, which reflect the light, dark, probably very coarse hair, thick eyebrows which are run together and give her the sternest look, but her cheeks are strained as if she were trying to keep from laughing. What is there to say to her anyway?

"You like Moscow?" she asks suddenly, and looks at me sternly. I start at the sound of her deep voice. Does anyone else have a voice like that?

I don't say anything for a while, getting my breath. Finally I collect my strength. Yes of course I like Moscow. I like the Arbat region especially. But I like other streets too. Then I shut up again.

We get to Arbat Square. I put my hands in my pockets and start to whistle. Let her think that knowing her isn't all that interesting to me. After all, I can go home, I live right near by, and I'm not obliged to go to the movies and feel bad because she looks as if she's trying not to laugh at me.

But we go to the movies anyway. There's still fifteen minutes before the showing. We stand in the foyer and listen to a singer, but it's hard to hear her, there are a lot of people around and they're all talking. The only ones listening and applauding are the ones in front, but behind everyone is eating ice cream and candy and talking. Deciding that you listen to a singer properly or not at all, I start looking at the pictures on the walls. I've never paid any attention to them before, but now I'm very interested. I'm thinking about the artists that did them. It wasn't such a bad idea to hang those pictures. It's nice that they're hanging there.

Lilya looks at me with shining gray eyes. She's so pretty! She isn't really pretty though, it's just those shining eyes and pink cheeks. When she smiles she gets dimples and her eyebrows come apart and she doesn't look so stern. She has a clear high forehead. Only once in a while a frown appears on it. That's probably when she's thinking.

No! I can't stand here with her any longer. Why is she looking at me that way?

"I'm going to smoke—" I say abruptly and carelessly, and I go into the smoking lounge. There I sit down and breathe more easily. It's strange but when there's a lot of smoke in the room, when the air is practically black with smoke, I don't feel like smoking for some reason. I look around: there are many people standing and sitting around. Some are talking quietly, others smoke quickly in silence, inhaling deeply, throw away their cigarettes without finishing them and go out. Where are they hurrying to? It's interesting, if you smoke fast, a cigarette tastes bittersweet. It's better to smoke without hurrying, and to take small puffs. I look at the clock: still five minutes to the showing. No, I'm probably a dope. Other people get to know each other so easily, they talk and laugh. Terribly clever people can talk football or anything they like. They argue about cybernetics. I wouldn't talk about cybernetics with a girl for anything. Lilya is a hard person, I decide, she has coarse hair. I've got fine hair. That's probably why I'm sitting smoking when I don't feel like it at all. But I sit here anyway. What can I do in the foyer? Look at pictures some more? You know, they're bad pictures, and who knows why they hung them. It's a good thing I never noticed them before.

Finally the bell. I walk very slowly out of the smoking lounge, looking for Lilya in the crowd. Without looking at each other, we go in and sit down. Then they turn out the lights and start the film.

When we come out of the movie, my friend has disappeared completely. This makes me give up trying to think about anything at all. I just walk and don't say anything. There's almost no one on the street. Cars shoot past me. Our footsteps reverberate off the walls and can be heard way off in the distance.

So we get to her house. We stop again in the courtyard. It's late and not all the windows are lighted now, it's darker than it was two hours ago. Many of the white and pink windows have gone out, but the green ones are still burning. There's a light on in the blue window on the second floor but no more music to be heard. We stand for a while without saying anything at all. Lilya is behaving strangely; she looks up, looking at the windows as if she were counting them; she's almost turned her back on me. Then she starts to fix her hair. Then I say carelessly, just sort of by the way, that we ought to meet tomorrow. I'm very glad it's dark in the courtyard and she can't see my ears burning.

She agrees to meet me. I can come to her place, her window is on the street. She is on vacation, her family has gone to the country, and she's a bit bored. She'd love to go out.

I wonder if it's proper to shake her hand goodbye. She gives me her narrow hand herself, pale in the darkness, and again I feel how warm and trusting she is.

2

The next day I go to her house in the afternoon. This time there are lots of kids in the yard. Two of them have bicycles. They're going somewhere or have they just arrived maybe? The rest are just standing around. It seems to me they're looking at me, knowing perfectly well why I've come. I simply can't go into the courtyard, so I go up to her window on the street. I look in the window and cough.

"You home, Lilya?" I ask loudly. I ask it very loudly and my voice doesn't shake. That's absolutely amazing that my voice didn't break!

Yes, she's home. She has a girl friend with her. They're arguing about something interesting and I've got to settle the argument.

"Come quickly!" Lilya calls.

But I can't bear to go through the yard—I just can't.

"I'll come through the window!" I say decisively, and jump up. I jump up easily and gracefully, and only when I throw one leg over the windowsill do I notice the amazed amusement of the girl friend and Lilya's embarrassment. I guess right away that I've done something awkward, and freeze astride the windowsill: one leg in the room, the other in the street. I sit and look at Lilya.

"Well, climb in," Lilya says impatiently. Her eyebrows separate and her cheeks are getting red.

"I don't like to hang around inside in summer," I mutter, assuming a supercilious expression. "I'd better wait for you outside."

I jump down and go toward the gates. How they're laughing at me now! I know girls are all cruel and they never understand us. Why did I come here? Why do I play the clown? I'd better leave. If I run now I can get to the corner and turn before she comes out. Should I run or not? I think it over a minute: is this the moment? Then I turn and see Lilya suddenly. She and her friend are coming through the gates. She's looking at me, the laughter still hasn't gone out of her eyes, and her cheeks are dimpled.

I don't look at her friend. Why is she coming with us? What will I do with the two of them? I'm quiet and Lilya begins talking to her girl friend. They talk and I don't say anything. When we pass billboards I read them all attentively. Sometimes you can read billboards backwards, and you get funny guttural words. We get to the corner and the girl friend starts saying goodbye. I look at her gratefully. She's very pretty and intelligent.

The girl friend goes off and we go to Tverskii Boulevard. How many lovers have walked along Tverskii Boulevard! And now we're walking along it. True we're not in love yet. On the other hand maybe we are, I don't know. We're walking far enough apart. About a yard from each other. The linden trees have already blossomed. There are lots of flowers in the flower beds. They have no smell at all and probably no one knows what they're called.

We talk a lot. There's just no stopping us. We're talking about ourselves and our friends, we jump from subject to subject and forget what we were talking about a minute before. But that doesn't bother us, we've got a lot of time, a long, long night ahead and we can remember anything we've forgotten. It's even better to remember later on, at night.

Suddenly I notice her dress has come undone. She has on a marvelous dress. I've never seen one like it on anyone—tiny little buttons run from the collar to the waist. Now some of those buttons are undone and she hasn't noticed. But she can't go along the street in an unfastened dress! How can I tell her? Maybe I should start buttoning it myself? Make some funny remark and start buttoning as if it were an everyday matter. That would be nice! No, I can't do that, that's simply impossible. So I turn away, wait for a pause in the conversation and say that she's unfastened. Right away she's quiet. And I look at a great big sign hanging from the roofs. It says that everyone can win 100,000 rubles. A very optimistic sign. We should win sometime!

Then I light a cigarette. I make it last a long time. In general it's a good idea to smoke in difficult situations. It helps a lot. Then I look at her timidly. Her dress is buttoned, her cheeks are on fire, her eyes are dark and stern. She looks at me, looks as if I had changed greatly or had found out something important about her. Now we're walking a little closer to each other.

The hours pass, and we're still walking, talking, and walking. You can walk around Moscow endlessly. We go to Pushkin Square, from Pushkin Square to Trubnaya Square, from there we walk along Neglinaya Street to the Bolshoi Theater, then to Stone Bridge. I'm ready to walk forever. I ask if *she's* tired though. No, she's not tired, it's very interesting. The street lamps go on. The sky, awaiting darkness, falls, the stars grow bigger. Then the sun gently begins to set. Lovers walk along the boulevards clinging to each other. There's a couple on every bench. I look at them enviously and wonder if Lilya and I will ever sit like that.

There's absolutely no one in the streets but policemen. They all look at us. Several cough significantly as we go past. They probably want to say something but they don't. Lilya bends her head and hurries past. That seems funny to me for some reason. Now we're walking side by side. Her hand brushes against mine sometimes. It's just the smallest brush, but I feel it.

We part in her dark quiet courtyard. Everyone is sleeping, not a single window is lighted. We lower our voices to a whisper but our words still come out loud and it seems to me that someone is listening.

I get home at three. Only then do I feel my legs shaking. How tired she must be! I turn on the lamp and start to read. I'm reading *Castle Browdi* which Lilya gave me. It's a remarkable book. All the time I'm reading it for some reason I see Lilya's face. Then I close my eyes and hear her sweet throaty voice. I find a long dark hair between the pages. It's her hair—she must have read *The Castle*. Why did I think she had coarse hair? It's a soft silky hair. I fold it carefully and put it in the encyclopedia. I'll find a better place to hide it later.

It's quite light and I can't read any more. I lie down and look out the window. We live high up, on the seventh floor. We can see the roofs of many houses from our windows. In the distance, where the sun comes up in the summer, the star on top of the Kremlin Tower is visible. You can only see one star. I love to look at that star. At night when it's quiet in Moscow I listen to the Kremlin chimes. It's very nice to listen at night. I lie there, I look at the stars and I think about Lilya.

3

A week later my mother and I went up north. I had been dreaming about this trip since spring. But now life in the country had taken on special sense and meaning for me.

I went straight to the woods, the real, wild woods. I felt like an explorer. I had a gun—it was given to me when I finished the ninth class—and I went hunting. I could go out all by myself and never get bored. Sometimes I would stop and sit down to watch the wide river, the low autumn sky. August. It's often bad weather in August. But good weather or bad, I would leave home early and go to the woods. There I would hunt or gather mushrooms or just walk around the clearings looking at the white camomile flowers which grow a lot around there. There's not too much to do in the woods. If you sit quietly by a lake, ducks will fly up and drop down with a hiss right beside you. They'll just sit there at first, stretching their necks out straight, and then they'll begin to dive and splash and swim around. I'd follow them with my eyes, without turning my head.

Then the sun would come from behind a cloud, and break through the leaves over my head, sending trembling golden fingers down deep into the water. You could see the long stems of the water lilies and large fish swimming around in the stems. When they hit a sunspot, they'd stop cold, not a fin moving, as if they were sunning or sleeping. I had the queer sensation as I watched them of freezing up myself, and everything seemed a dream.

There's not too much to do in the woods. You can simply lie there, listening to the pine trees howl, and think about Lilya. You can even talk to her. I talked to her about hunting, about the woods and the lake, about the wonderful smell of gunsmoke, and she would always understand, though women usually don't like or understand hunting.

Sometimes I wouldn't go home until dark. I'd be a bit scared crossing the fields. Even with a loaded gun, I still looked around nervously. It was very dark. Owls would fly around in circles over my head. I could see them but I couldn't hear how many because I couldn't hear their wingbeats. Once I took a shot at them, and for a long time afterwards an owl flew around and around the clearing, hooting in the darkness.

After a month I returned to Moscow. I went straight from the station, just stopping off to leave my bags at home, to see Lilya. It was evening, her window was lighted, that meant she was home. I went up to the window, crawled under the scaffolding—they were remodeling her building—and looked through the curtain.

She was sitting alone at the table, reading by the table lamp. Her face was thoughtful. She turned the page, leaned on her elbows, raised her eyes and looked at the lamp, winding a lock of hair around her finger. What dark eyes! How could I have thought they were gray? They were dark, almost black. I stood there under the scaffolding, and it smelled of pine and plaster. The smell of pine was a distant echo of hunting, a reminder of everything I'd left in the north. Footsteps behind me. People going somewhere in a hurry, stepping loudly along the pavement. With their own thoughts and loves and lives. Moscow overwhelmed me. I had forgotten its noise, its lights, its smells, its crowds. And I reflected with quiet joy that, in an enormous city, it was good to have someone to love.

"Lilya!" I called softly.

She jumped, her eyebrows jumped. Then she got up, came to the window, raised the curtain, and leaned toward me. Her eyes were dark and delighted.

"Alyosha!" she said slowly. Two scarcely noticeable dimples appeared on her cheeks. "Alyosha! Is that you? Is it really you? I'm coming right out. You want to go for a walk? I want to. I'm coming right out."

I got out from under the scaffold, crossed the street and watched her window. There, the light went out, a short minute, and Lilya's figure appeared in the dark space between the gates. She saw me at once and ran across the street. She grabbed my hands and held them in hers a long time. She seemed browner and thinner. Her eyes were bigger. I could hear her heart thumping and her broken breathing.

"Let's go!" she said at last. And I suddenly realized that she'd been speaking to me in the familiar. I felt like sitting down or leaning against something—my legs were so weak. Even after the most exhausting hunt, they'd never shaken so hard.

But I felt uncomfortable walking beside her. I'd only dropped in to see her for a minute. I was so badly dressed. I had come straight from the train, in my old ski pants and boots. My pants were burned in several spots, because I had slept in them out hunting. When you sleep by the fire, you often burn your pants and jacket. No, I couldn't take a walk with her.

"What nonsense!" she said, unconcerned, and pulled me by the hand. She had to talk to me. She'd been all alone, her girl friends had all gone away, her parents were in the country, she was frightfully bored waiting for me all that time. What difference did my pants make? And why didn't I write? Maybe I liked making other people suffer?

And there we were again, walking around Moscow. It was a crazy night somehow. It began to rain. We ducked into an empty doorway, breathing hard from running, and watched the street. Water ran loudly down the drainpipes, the sidewalks glistened, the passing cars were wet all over, and sent red and white lines of light creeping over the wet pavement toward us. Then the rain stopped, we came out, laughing and jumping over the puddles. But it started to rain again with renewed vigor and we ducked back under. Drops of rain sparkled in her hair. And when she looked at me her eyes shone even brighter.

"You thought about me?" she asked. "I thought about you almost the whole time, not that I wanted to. I don't know why I did myself. You know, we don't know each other very well. Isn't that true? I read a book and wondered if you'd like it. Were your ears red? They say that if you think about someone a lot, that person's ears will get red. I didn't even go to the Bolshoi. My mama gave me a ticket, but I didn't go. Do you like opera?"

"Sure! Maybe I'll become a singer. They tell me I have a good bass."

"Alyosha! Are you a bass? Sing for me, please? Sing softly, and no one but me will hear."

I refused at first. Then I sang anyway. I sang romances and arias and I didn't even notice that it had stopped raining, and that people on the widewalk were looking at us. Lilya didn't notice either. She looked at me and her eyes shone.

4

It's terrible being young. Life goes quickly, you're seventeen or eighteen already and you haven't done anything. It's still unclear whether or not you have any talent. And you want such tremendous things out of life! You want to write poems that the whole country will learn by heart. Or to compose a heroic symphony and come out to conduct the orchestra, dressed in a tuxedo, pale, your hair in your face, with Lilya— and this was essential—sitting in the parterre! What could I do? What could I do so that life would not pass in vain, to make each day a day of battle and victory? The thought tortured and tormented me, I wasn't a hero, I wasn't an explorer. Was I capable of heroic feats? Was I capable of hard work, did I have the strength to accomplish great deeds? The worst thing is that no one understands. They all look, and pat your head as if you were a ten-year-old boy! Only Lilya, Lilya alone understood me, only with her could I be completely open.

We'd been in school a long time: she was in the ninth class, and I in the tenth. I decided to study swimming and become a soviet champion, then a world champion. I took lessons at the pool. The crawl— that seemed to be the best style, the most dashing style. I liked it very much. At night I liked to dream.

There's a brief moment in winter when the snow on the rooftops and the sky turn dark blue, purple even, at twilight. I would stand at the window, looking at the purple snow, breathing the light frosty air and dreaming of distant expeditions, unknown countries, unclimbed mountains. I would be hungry, I would grow a red beard, I'd be sunburned or frostbitten, I would even die, but I would disclose one more of nature's secrets. That would be the life! If only I could get on an expedition!

I began going around to the industrial firms and administrative offices. There are a lot of them in Moscow and they all have mysterious-sounding names. Yes, there were expeditions going out. To Central Asia, to the Urals, up north. Yes, they needed men. My training? Oh, none. That was too bad, but they could do nothing to help in that case. I had to be trained. Could I go as a laborer? They hire laborers on the spot. Goodbye and good luck!

And so I went back to school and prepared my lessons. So what, it was the fault of the circumstances. All right, I'd finish the tenth class and enter the institute and become an engineer or a teacher. But in me they were losing a great explorer.

December came. I spent all my free time with Lilya. I loved her more than ever. I didn't know love could be so limitless. But it can. Every month Lilya became dearer to me, there was no sacrifice I wouldn't have made for her. She would often call me on the telephone. We'd talk for a long time, and after hanging up I just couldn't get back to my books. Then the heavy snowstorms and cold set in. My mother planned to go to the country but didn't have a warm scarf. My aunt, who lives in the suburbs, had a heavy, old-fashioned shawl. I was to go and get it.

I left on Sunday morning. But instead of going to the station, I dropped in on Lilya. We were skating, and warmed up at the Tretyakov Gallery. The Tretyakov is very warm in winter, and there are benches where you can sit and talk. We walked around, looking at the pictures. I love Serov's "Girl with the Pears" especially. The girl looks a lot like Lilya. Lilya blushed and laughed when I told her this. Sometimes we'd get to whispering and looking at each other so hard we'd forget all about the pictures. Meanwhile it was getting dark fast. The Tretyakov would be closing soon, and as we went out into the cold, I suddenly remembered that I was supposed to go for the shawl. I was scared, and told Lilya. Well, so what, that was just fine, we could go now.

And so we went, happy not to have to separate. We got out on a

platform buried in snow and took a path through a field. Ahead and behind us were the dark figures of people, coming like us from the electric train. We could hear them laughing and talking, and we could see
the glowing tips of their cigarettes. Once someone threw away a lighted
cigarette butt, which was still burning as we approached, encircled by a
ring of pink snow. We didn't step on it, we let it burn in the darkness.
Then we crossed the frozen river, the wooden bridge creaking over our
heads. It was very cold. We passed through the dark woods. Beside us
the fir trees and pines were completely black. It was much darker than
in the fields. The windows in several cabins sent out yellow bands of
light on the snow. Many cabins were standing dark and lonely: there
was probably no one living there in winter. There was the strong smell
of birch buds and clean snow that you never get in Moscow.

Finally we reached my aunt's house. For some reason it seemed
impossible to go in there with Lilya.

"Lilya, will you wait for me a minute?" I asked her uncertainly.
"I'll be very fast."

"All right," she agreed. "Only don't be long. I'm frozen. My feet are
frozen. And my face. And you flatter yourself that I'm glad I came
with you! Just don't be long, all right?"

I went off, leaving her all alone in the dark clearing. I didn't feel
very good about it.

My aunt and my cousin were surprised and delighted. Why was I so
late? How I'd grown! Quite a little man. I would spend the night of
course?

"How's your mama?"

"Very well, thank you."

"Your papa working?"

"Yes, papa's working."

"Everything the same there? How's your uncle?"

Heavens, a thousand questions! My cousin looked at the train
schedule. The next train went back at eleven. I must take off my coat
and have some tea. Then I must let them look at me and tell about everything. After all, I hadn't been there for a whole year—and that's a long
time.

They made me take my coat off. The stove was going, the lamp
burning brightly under its print lampshade. The grandfather clock struck.
It was very warm and I would have loved some tea. But Lilya was
waiting for me in the dark clearing.

Finally I said, "Excuse me, but I'm in a hurry. The fact is, I'm not
alone. A friend is waiting outside."

How they scolded me! I was a completely unmannered person. Was
it really possible to leave someone outside in this cold? My cousin ran out
into the garden, and I could hear the crunch of her feet under the win-

dows. A little while later the snow crunched again and my cousin brought Lilya into the room. She was completely white. They took off her coat and put her near the stove. She had tall warm boots on.

We warmed up a bit and then sat down to tea. Lilya was crimson from the warmth and her embarrassment. She didn't raise her eyes from her cup, but from time to time looked at me terribly seriously. Her dimpled cheeks were holding something back. I knew the meaning of that and was very happy. I drank five glasses of tea.

Then we got up. It was time to go. We got dressed and they gave me the shawl. Then they changed their minds, and made Lilya take off her coat, wrap the shawl around her head and shoulders, and then put on her coat again. She looked very fat and the shawl almost entirely covered her face, except for her shining eyes.

We went outside and couldn't see anything at first. Lilya held on to me very tight. As we got away from the house, we began to make out the path. Lilya suddenly began to laugh. She even fell down twice, she was laughing so hard, and I had to pick her up and brush her off.

"What a face you made!" she said, barely able to get the words out. "You looked like an ostrich when they brought me in!"

I roared with laughter.

"Alyosha!" she said, suddenly terrified. "They might hold us up!"

"Who's they?"

"Anyone . . . Bandits . . . They might kill us."

"Nonsense," I said loudly.

A little too loudly perhaps. And I suddenly began to feel the cold. It seemed to have gotten colder while we were drinking tea and talking.

"Nonsense," I repeated. "There's no one around."

"But what if there is all of a sudden?" Lily asked quickly, looking around.

"You scared?" she asked in a loud voice.

"No, although . . . Are you?"

"I'm terribly scared! They'll rob us for sure! I have a presentiment."

"You believe in them?"

"I do. By the way, I'm still glad I came."

"Really?"

"Really. Even if they rob us and kill us, I won't be sorry. And you? Would you die for me?"

I didn't answer. I just squeezed her hand harder. If only something would happen so I could prove my love!

"Alyosha . . ."

"Yes?"

"I want to ask you something. Only don't look at me. Don't you dare look at my face! So, what did I want to ask? Turn away!"

"All right, I've turned away. You look at where we're going. Or else we'll stumble."

"That's nothing. I've got the shawl on. I don't mind falling."

"So?"

"Have you ever kissed anyone, Alyosha?"

"No, I never kissed anyone. Why?"

"Absolutely never?"

"Well, once, but that was when I was in the first class. I kissed some little girl. I don't remember what she was called."

"Really? You don't remember her name?"

"No, I don't."

"Then it doesn't count. You were still a little boy."

"Yes, I was."

"Alyosha, do you want to kiss me?"

I stumbled, and started watching the path more attentively. "When? Now?" I asked.

"No, no. If we get to the station without being killed, then I'll kiss you."

I didn't answer. It didn't seem so cold. I couldn't even feel it. My cheeks were burning. It was hot. Were we walking that fast?

"Alyosha."

"Yes?"

"I've never kissed anyone."

I looked at the stars without replying. Then I looked ahead at the haze of yellow light over Moscow. It was fifteen miles to Moscow but the haze was still visible. Life was wonderful after all!

"Kissing is probably a shameful thing. Were you ashamed?"

"I don't remember, it was so long ago—I don't think I was particularly ashamed."

"Yes, but that was a long time ago. It's probably shameful."

We'd already reached the field. This time the field was empty and we were all alone. Not a soul to be seen ahead or behind. No one throwing lighted cigarettes into the snow. Only the loud crunch of our feet. Suddenly there was a glow up ahead, a pale glow, like a candle from far off. It flared, flickered a moment, and went out. Then it flared again, closer this time. We watched it and finally realized that it was an electric lamp. Then we made out some small black figures, coming from the station. Maybe they'd just arrived on the train? No, the train couldn't have come, we hadn't heard a sound.

"There they are," Lilya said, pressing closer to me. "I knew it. Now they'll kill us. Those are the bandits."

What could I say? I didn't say anything. We were slowly getting nearer. I looked and counted the black figures—six men. I felt around in my pocket for my key, and I suddenly felt a hot wave of courage and excitement. I was going to fight them off! I coughed nervously, my heart beating wildly. They were talking loudly, but when they were twenty feet away, they fell silent.

"I'd better kiss you now," Lilya said sadly. "It's too bad . . ."

We met at last in the middle of the empty field. The six men stopped and lit their lamp, its weak reddish light passing over the snow to fall on us. We squinted. They looked at us in silence. Two of them were wearing their coats open. One hurriedly finished a cigarette and spat in the snow. I waited for the first blow to fall, or a yell. There was no yell. We passed each other.

"That girl wasn't bad," someone remarked regretfully. "Hey, boy, don't be scared. We'll make it."

"Were you scared?" Lilya asked a little later.

"No, just about you."

"About me?" She slowed down and gave me a strange, sideways glance. "I wasn't one drop afraid! I was just sorry about the shawl."

We said no more until we reached the station. At the station Lilya stood on tiptoe and broke off a pine twig, bringing down a flutter of snow, and put it in her pocket. Then we went up on the platform. No one else was there. There was one lamp burning in the ticket office and the snow on the platform glistened like salt. We began stamping our feet—it was cold. Suddenly Lilya walked away and leaned against the rail. I stood at the very edge of the platform, over the rails, craning my neck, trying to see the lights of the train.

"Alyosha," Lilya called. Her voice sounded strange.

I went to her. My legs were shaking. I was afraid suddenly.

"Hold me, Alyosha," said Lilya. "I'm frozen."

I put my arms around her and hugged her, my face practically touching hers, and I saw her eyes up close for the first time. Her eyelashes were covered with frost, as was the hair that had crept out from under the shawl. What a frightened look in those big eyes! The snow crunched under our feet. We were standing still, but the snow was crunching nonetheless. Suddenly there was a sharp crack of wind behind us. It rolled over the signboards, with a sound like ice cracking in the river, and died out somewhere at the end of the platform. Why didn't we say anything? We just didn't feel like it.

Lilya's lips moved. Her eyes were completely black.

"Why don't you kiss me?" she asked in a faint voice. The steam of our breath blended together. I looked at her lips. They moved and parted. I bent over and gave them a long kiss, and the world silently began to spin. I saw as she kissed me that she loved me.

So we kissed for the first time. Then we stood motionless, her cold cheek pressed against my face. I looked over her shoulders into the dark winter woods behind the platform. I felt her warm childish breath on my face and I listened to the quick beat of her heart as she was probably listening to mine. Then she moved and caught her breath. I bent and found her lips and kissed her again. This time she closed her eyes.

There was a low whistle in the distance, and a dazzling flash of light. The train was coming. A minute later we entered the warm, lighted car, slamming the door behind us, and sat down on the warm wooden bench. There were very few people in the car. Lilya was quiet and looked out the window the whole way, although the glass was frosted over and there was absolutely nothing to see.

5

It's probably impossible to pick out the exact moment when love comes to you. I can't decide when I fell in love with Lilya. Maybe when I was wandering alone in the north? Or maybe during the kiss on the platform? Or when she gave me her hand the first time and sweetly told me her name, Lilya? I don't know. I only know that at one point I couldn't get along without her. My whole life divided into two parts: before Lilya and since. How did I live and what was the point without her? I didn't even want to think about it, the way I didn't want to think about the death of people close to me.

Our winter passed wonderfully. Everything, everything belonged to us: the past and future, joy and all of life to the last breath. What a happy time, what days we had, what giddiness!

But in the spring I began to notice something. No, nothing specific, I just had the painful sense that there was something new coming. It would have been hard to say what it was. It just turned out that our characters were different. She didn't seem to like my funny looks any more, she laughed at my dreams, laughed cruelly, and sometimes we quarreled. Then . . . Then, everything went downhill, faster and faster, worse and worse. More and more often she wouldn't be home, more and more often our conversations were unnaturally gay and stupid. I felt her getting farther and farther away from me.

How many seventeen-year-old girls there are in the world. But when you're in love you know just one, you look just one in the eyes, see their sparkle, their depth, their wetness; only her voice moves you to tears. It's only her hands you're afraid to kiss. She talks to you, listens to you, laughs, is silent, and you see that you're the only one she needs. That she lives because of you and for you, that she loves you alone, as you love her.

But you notice with horror that her eyes that used to give off their warmth, their sparkle, their life just for you, are now indifferent, withdrawn, and she has withdrawn to such a distance that you can't find her, a distance from which she won't return. Your most holy aspirations, your proudest, most secret dreams, are not for her and you yourself in the complexity and beauty of your soul are not for her. You chase her, you reach and strain, but everything's gone, everything's wrong. She has escaped and withdrawn somewhere into her own wonderful unique world and you aren't to be admitted. You're a sinner—heaven is not for you. What despair, regret and pain grip you! You're ravaged, deceived, humiliated and unhappy. Everything is gone and you're standing there with empty hands, ready to fall down and cry out to some unknown god about your pain and helplessness. But when you fall and cry out, she looks at you with fear and wonder and pity in her eyes—with everything except what you need; you don't receive the one look you want; her love, her life are no longer yours. You could become a hero, a genius, someone who'd be the pride of the nation, but you still would never get that one look. How unbearable and painful it is to be alive!

And so it was spring. Sun and light, blue skies, the linden trees on the boulevards were becoming fragrant. Everyone was cheerful, and full of high spirits, preparing for the First of May. So was I. I was given a hundred rubles for the holiday, and was therefore the richest of men! Three free days. Three days to spend with Lilya—if only she weren't studying for exams then! No, I wasn't going to go anywhere, I didn't need company, just her. It had been so long since we'd been together.

But she couldn't be with me. She had to go see a sick uncle in the country. Her uncle was sick and bored and wanted to spend the holiday in the family circle. So they were going, she and her parents. Excellent plan! Very good to spend the holidays in the country. But I'd wanted so much to be with her. Maybe the second of May?

Second? She thought a minute, wrinkling up her forehead and blushing slightly. Yes, she could probably get away. Of course she wanted to! We certainly hadn't been together in a long time. So, the night of the second then, at the Telegraph Building on Gorky Street.

I was standing at the Telegraph Building at the appointed hour. So many people everywhere! There was a globe hanging over my head. It was still daylight, but the globe was already lighted—blue with yellow continents—and was swaying slightly. There was a blaze of fireworks, golden wheels, blue and green sparklers. In the light of the fireworks everyone's face looked beautiful. I had a hundred rubles in my pocket. I hadn't spent them the day before, I still had them. But there wasn't much we could do on the second. We could go to the park or to a movie. I waited patiently. Everyone else was scurrying about, but I was amazingly calm.

Crowds of people were walking in the middle of the street. So many boys and girls, all singing, shouting, and playing accordions. There were flags on all the houses, slogans, lights. They were singing and I wanted to sing too, because I have a good voice. I'm a bass. I once dreamed of becoming a singer. I once dreamed a lot of things.

Suddenly I saw Lilya. She was coming toward me, climbing the steps, and everyone was looking at her, she was so pretty. I'd never seen her so pretty. My heart began to pound. She looked around at

everyone, her eyes running over their faces, looking for someone, looking for me. I took a step toward her, just one, and suddenly a sharp
pain struck me in the chest, and my mouth went dry. She wasn't alone!
A boy in a cap was with her, and looking at me. He was good-looking,
that boy, and he was holding her hand.

"Hello, Alyosha," said Lilya. Her voice trembled a little and she
looked embarrassed. Not much embarrassed, just a little bit. "Have you
been waiting long? I guess we're late . . ."

She looked at the large clock under the globe and frowned. Then
she turned her head and looked at the boy. Her neck was lovely as she
looked at him. Did she look at me that way?

"Let me introduce you . . ."

We shook hands. His grip was firm and sure.

"You know, Alyosha, our date today didn't work out. We're on
our way to the Bolshoi. Do you mind?"

"No, I don't mind."

"Will you walk along with us for a while? I guess you have nothing to do now."

"Sure, I will. I really haven't anything else to do."

We mixed in with the crowd and moved down toward Okhotny
Row. Why did I go? What should I have done? Everyone around us was
singing. Playing accordions. Loudspeakers thundering out on the house-
tops. I had a hundred rubles in my pocket. A crackling, brand-new
hundred-ruble note. Why was I going? And where?

"Well, how's your uncle?" I asked.

"Uncle? Which uncle? Oh, you mean about yesterday?" She bit
her lip and took a quick look at the boy.

"He's better. We had a good celebration, very gay. We danced.
And you? Did you have a good time?"

"Me? Very good."

"I'm glad."

We turned toward the theater. We were walking along in a row,
all three of us. Only, I wasn't holding her hand. That goodlooking boy
was. She wasn't with me, she was with him. A thousand miles away.
Why did my throat tickle? And my eyes sting? Was I coming down with
something? We got to the Bolshoi and stopped. We were silent. There was
absolutely nothing to say. I saw the boy squeeze her elbow.

"Well, we'll be off. Be seeing you!" said Lilya and smiled at me.
Such a guilty, and at the same time such an absent smile!

I took her hand. It was still a nice hand. They turned and walked
off slowly toward the columns. I stood looking after them. She'd grown a
lot in that last year. She was seventeen already. She was slender. When
did I first become aware of her figure? Oh yes, in the black space between
the gates when I came back from the north. That was when I was first
struck by her figure. And I had loved her in the Hall of Columns and at

the Conservatory. Then at the dance . . . a marvelous winter dance! Now she was going off without even looking back. She always used to look back. Sometimes she would even come back, give me a long look, and ask, "What was it you wanted to say to me?"

"Nothing," I'd answer, glad that she'd come back.

She'd look around quickly. "Kiss me," she'd say.

And she'd smell of the cold as I kissed her, standing in a square or on a street corner. She loved those fleeting kisses on the street.

"What do they know about it?" she'd say about the people who would see us kissing. "They don't know anything. We might be brother and sister. Right?"

But this time she didn't look back. I was standing and people were passing me, as if I were a thing, or a column. There was the sound of laughter. People were walking in twos and threes and whole groups— no one was alone. A street on a holiday is an unbearable place to be alone. The other people who were alone were probably sitting at home. I stood looking. Lilya and the boy had already disappeared through the lighted entrance. All evening long they would listen to the opera, enjoying being near each other. I would have flown into the violet sky if those four winged horses in front of the Bolshoi had only known how. And I had a hundred rubles in my pocket. A brand-new note which I hadn't spent on the First of May.

6

A year passed. The world wasn't destroyed, life didn't come to an end. I almost forgot about Lilya. I did forget her. Rather, I tried not to think about her. Why should I? Once I ran into her on the street. True, my spine froze, but I controlled myself. I'd lost all interest in her life. I didn't ask what she was doing and she didn't ask about me. Although a lot new had happened to me in that time. A year—you know, that's a lot!

I was studying at the institute. Studying hard, with no distractions, no dates. I was doing a lot of public service work, and working on my swimming. I was first rate already. I'd finally mastered the crawl, the most dashing of all styles. But then, that's not important.

And then I received a letter from her. It was spring again. May, gentle May, and my heart was light. I love spring. I had passed my exams and was now a second-year student. And then, this letter from her. She wrote that she was getting married. She went on to say that she was going to the north with her husband and asked me to come see her off. She called me "sweet" and signed the letter, "Your old, old friend."

I sat for a long time looking at the wallpaper. We have very pretty wallpaper, ingeniously drawn. I love to look at it. Of course I'd see her off if that was what she wanted. Why not? She wasn't my enemy, she'd done me no wrong. I'd see her off, all the more because everything was forgotten; there was a lot more to life. You can't remember everything that happened a year ago.

And so I was at the station on the day and the hour she wrote in her letter. For a long time I couldn't find her on the platform, and when I finally did I was so startled that I jumped. She was standing in a bright-colored dress with bare arms and her face and arms were already slightly burned. Her arms were still lovely. But her face had changed, it had become the face of a woman. She wasn't a girl any more—no, not a girl. She was standing with her family and her husband, that same boy. They were talking loudly and laughing, but I noticed that Lilya was looking around impatiently, waiting for me.

I went up to her. She took my hand.

"I'll just be a minute," she said to her husband, with a sweet smile.

Her husband waved to me with an affable look. Yes, he remembered me. He shook hands magnanimously. Then Lilya and I walked away.

"Well, I'm grown up and going away. This is goodbye, Moscow," she said sadly, looking at the station tower. "I'm glad you came. It's strange to see you though. You've grown a lot. How are you?"

"Fine," I answered, trying to smile. But I didn't achieve a smile, my face had gone wooden for some reason. Lilya looked at me attentively, her forehead broken by a frown. That was always her way when she was thinking.

"What's the matter?" she asked.

"Nothing. I'm just glad for you. Have you been married long?"

"A week. It's such happiness."

"Yes, it's happiness."

Lilya laughed. "How do you know? But you're making a strange face."

"It just seems I am. It's the sun. And I'm a little tired, I'm taking exams, you know. German."

" 'Damned German'?" she laughed. "Remember, how I helped you?"

"Yes, I remember." I moved my lips into a smile.

"Listen, Alyosha, what's wrong?" she asked, alarmed, moving closer. And I saw her beautiful face up close again. It had lost something. Yes, she had changed, she was quite strange to me now. Whether she was better or not I couldn't decide.

"You're hiding something," she said reproachfully. "You didn't used to!"

"No, you're mistaken," I said firmly. "It's just that I didn't sleep much last night."

She looked at the clock. Then she looked around. Her husband waved to her.

"I'm coming!" she called to him and took my hand again. "You know, I'm so happy! Be happy for me! We're going to work up north. Remember how you told me about the north? Are you happy for me?"

Why, why did she have to ask me that! Suddenly she started to laugh.

"You know, I just remembered. Remember the winter we kissed on the platform? I kissed you and you were shaking so hard the platform creaked. You had such a stupid look!"

She laughed. Then she looked at me with those gay, gray eyes. During the day her eyes were gray. They only seemed dark at night. There were dimples in her cheeks.

"What fools we were!" she said lightly and looked affectionately at her husband.

"Yes," I agreed. "We were fools."

"No, not fools, that's not right. We were just stupid kids. Don't you think?"

"Yes, we were stupid kids."

The green light had gone on up ahead. Lilya went to her car. They were waiting for her.

"Well, goodbye," she said. "No, be seeing you! I'll write you for sure."

"Good."

I knew she wouldn't. Why should she? She knew it too. She looked at me sideways and flushed a little.

"I'm glad you came to see me off. And without flowers of course! You never gave me a single flower!"

"No, I never gave you anything . . ."

She dropped my hand, took her husband's arm and they climbed up on the train. We stood below on the platform. Her parents asked me something, but I didn't understand a thing. Up ahead the engine gave a long low whistle. The cars moved. It was amazing how gently they moved! Everyone smiled, waving handkerchiefs and hats, calling, running alongside the train. Two or three accordions were being played in various places, and in one car they were singing loudly. Students probably. Lilya was already a long way off. She was holding on to her husband's shoulder with one hand, and waving to us with the other. Even from afar you could see how lovely her arms were. And you could see how happy her smile was.

The train passed. I lit a cigarette, stuffed my hands in my pockets and moved off in the crowd toward the square. I clenched the cigarette in my teeth and looked at the silver paint on the lampposts. In the sunlight they were so bright they hurt my eyes. I looked down. Now I could admit it: the whole year I had had hope. Now everything was finished. So I was happy for her, really I was, happy! Only there was a pain in my heart for some reason.

An ordinary occurrence, a girl gets married—it happens all the time. Girls getting married—that's a good thing. It's just too bad not to be able to cry. The last time I cried I was fifteen years old. I was now twenty. My heart was in my throat and climbing still higher—pretty soon I'd be chewing on it and still I couldn't cry. It's a very good thing—girls getting married.

I came out on the square, the face of the clock on Kazan Station jumped out at me. It has strange figures instead of numbers—I couldn't make them out. I went into a soda fountain. At first I asked for a soda, and then I changed my mind and ordered plain water. It's hard to drink soda when your heart's in your throat. I picked up the cold glass, and took the water in my mouth, but I couldn't swallow. I swallowed some finally, in one gulp. I felt a little better, I thought.

Then I went down into the subway. Something had happened to my face. I noticed that people were staring. At home, I thought for a while about Lilya. Then I began to study the patterns in the wallpaper again. If you look at them you can see many curious things. You can see jungles and elephants with wounded trunks. Or strange cloaks and berets. Or the faces of friends. But not Lilya's face.

She was probably passing that platform where we first kissed right now. Only now the platform was surrounded by green. Would she look at it? Would she think of me? But why should she look at it? She'd be looking at her husband, loving him. He's very good-looking, her husband.

7

There's nothing constant in this world but sorrow. Life doesn't stop. No, life never stops, it just absorbs your soul and all your sorrows, your little human sorrows, dissipate like smoke by comparison. Such is the excellent construction of the world.

Now I'm finishing the institute. My youth is over, gone far, far off, forever. And that's good: I'm grown up and can do anything I want, no one pats me on the head like a boy. I'll be going up north soon. I don't know why, but something calls me north. Probably because I went hunting and was happy there. I've forgotten Lilya completely, so many years have passed! It would be very hard to live if you didn't forget. No, happily, a lot has been forgotten. She has never written of course. I don't know where she is; I don't even want to know. I don't think about her at all. My life is good. It's true I haven't become a poet, or a musician, but we can't all be poets. Sports, conferences, vocational training, exams, all have kept me very busy. I haven't had a free moment. I have learned to dance, and have gotten to know a lot of pretty and bright girls. I go out with them and fall in love with some of them, and they fall in love with me.

But sometimes I dream about Lilya. She comes to me in my dream and I hear her voice, her sweet laughter, I touch her hand and talk to her, about what I don't know. Sometimes she's sad and glum, sometimes joyful and her dimples flash, so small that a stranger wouldn't notice them. And I cheer up and laugh and feel young and bashful, as if I were seventeen again and in love for the first time in my life.

When I wake up the next morning I go to my lectures at the institute, preside at the trade union meeting, speak at the meeting of the Young Communists. But the day goes badly for me for some reason, and I want to be alone and sit somewhere with my eyes closed.

It doesn't happen often—four times a year maybe. But then, those dreams. Those dreams, those uninvited dreams.

I don't want them. I love it when I dream about music. They say if you sleep on your right side, you stop dreaming. I've started sleeping on my right side. I'm going to sleep soundly and wake up happy in the morning. Life is an excellent thing after all!

But oh God, I don't want dreams!

Theme Questions

1. Although she is sixteen and Alyosha is seventeen at the beginning of the story, Lilya always appears to be older than Alyosha. Why? What actions indicate that their romance won't last?

2. The personal point of view restricts the story so that we never really know what motivates Lilya. Furthermore, some of Alyosha's comments may or may not be ironic. With these limitations in mind and using the evidence that the story provides, characterize Lilya as she might be perceived by a less subjective viewer than the narrator. For instance, is she cruel? Is she playing with him? Is he perhaps a bit of a fool?

3. Alyosha is possibly the most painfully shy boy the reader has ever met. Trace his growth from his almost speechless first date to his untrue statement, "I've forgotten Lilya completely, so many years have passed!"

4. Dreams figure throughout the story—daydreams, night dreams and nightmares. The romance itself sometimes has a dream-like quality. Analyze the story from this perspective. How do dreams relate to the structuring of the plot?

5. The symbols of the story are chiefly those of color—blue, green, the gray and/or black of Lilya's eyes and the emphasis on bright lights. Interpret the colors as they relate to the narrative.

Also by Yuri Kazakov   *Going to Town and Other Stories*

Love brings exuberance, a marvelous gaiety, a heightened sensitivity to joy with the loved one. Miss Millay's poem recalls a wonderful date, and Robert Burns almost sings of his Jean. But Archibald MacLeish, not to be outdone in his admiration, nevertheless adds a sober note.

Recuerdo

Edna St. Vincent Millay

We were very tired, we were very merry—
We had gone back and forth all night on the ferry.
It was bare and bright, and smelled like a stable—
But we looked into a fire, we leaned across a table,
We lay on a hill-top underneath the moon;
And the whistles kept blowing, and the dawn came soon.

We were very tired, we were very merry—
We had gone back and forth all night on the ferry;
And you ate an apple, and I ate a pear,
From a dozen of each we had bought somewhere:
And the sky went wan, and the wind came cold,
And the sun rose dripping, a bucketful of gold.

We were very tired, we were very merry,
We had gone back and forth all night on the ferry.
We hailed, "Good morrow, mother!" to a shawl-covered head,
And bought a morning paper, which neither of us read;
And she wept, "God bless you!" for the apples and pears,
And we gave her all our money but our subway fares.

From *Collected Poems*, Harper & Row. Copyright 1922, 1928, 1950, 1955 by Edna St. Vincent Millay and Norma Millay Ellis.

I Love My Jean

Robert Burns

Of a' the airts the wind can blaw
  I dearly like the west,
For there the bonnie lassie lives,
  The lassie I lo'e best:
There wild woods grow, an' rivers row,
  An' monie a hill between;
But day and night my fancy's flight
  Is ever wi' my Jean.

I see her in the dewy flow'rs,
  I hear her sweet and fair;
I see her in the tunefu' birds,
  I hear her charm the air:
There's not a bonnie flow'r that springs
  By fountain, shaw, or green,
There's not a bonnie bird that sings,
  But minds me o' my Jean.

"Not Marble nor the Gilded Monuments"

Archibald MacLeish

The praisers of women in their proud and beautiful poems
Naming the grave mouth and the hair and the eyes
Boasted those they loved should be forever remembered
These were lies

The words sound but the face in the Istrian sun is forgotten
The poet speaks but to her dead ears no more
The sleek throat is gone—and the breast that was troubled to listen
Shadow from door

From *Collected Poems* by Archibald MacLeish. Reprinted by permission of the publisher, Houghton Mifflin Company.

Therefore I will not praise your knees nor your fine walking
Telling you men shall remember your name as long
As lips move or breath is spent or the iron of English
Rings from a tongue

I shall say you were young and your arms straight and your mouth
    scarlet
I shall say you will die and none will remember you
Your arms change and none remember the swish of your garments
Nor the click of your shoe

Not with my hand's strength not with difficult labor
Springing the obstinate words to the bones of your breast
And the stubborn line to your young stride and the breath to your
    breathing
And the beat to your haste
Shall I prevail on the hearts of unborn men to remember

(What is a dead girl but a shadowy ghost
Or a dead man's voice but a distant and vain affirmation
Like dream words most)

Therefore I will not speak of the undying glory of women
I will say you were young and straight and your skin fair
And you stood in the door and the sun was a shadow of leaves on
    your shoulders
And a leaf on your hair

I will not speak of the famous beauty of dead women
I will say the shape of a leaf lay once on your hair
Till the world ends and the eyes are out and the mouths broken
Look! It is there!

Theme Questions

1. What poetic devices are used to make the Burns and Millay poems sing? How does technique reinforce the gaiety of the themes? Compare both with the more intricate MacLeish poem.

2. Read Shakespeare's Sonnet LV. Compare MacLeish's query, stated chiefly in the parenthetical statement of stanza six, with Shakespeare's statement. Discuss the basic difference in their viewpoints.

Love may be chemistry, but it is also compatibility. People are often drawn to one another for reasons they can't explain. Time passes and differences appear. At first they are overlooked, but after a while they can no longer be set aside. F. Scott Fitzgerald brings a girl from the hot South to the cold North where, unexpectedly, even her love freezes in "The Ice Palace."

The Ice Palace

F. Scott Fitzgerald

The sunlight dripped over the house like golden paint over an art jar, and the freckling shadows here and there only intensified the rigor of the bath of light. The Butterworth and Larkin houses flanking were intrenched behind great stodgy trees; only the Happer house took the full sun, and all day long faced the dusty road-street with a tolerant kindly patience. This was the city of Tarleton in southernmost Georgia, September afternoon.

Up in her bedroom window Sally Carrol Happer rested her nineteen-year-old chin on a fifty-two-year-old sill and watched Clark Darrow's ancient Ford turn the corner. The car was hot—being partly metallic it retained all the heat it absorbed or evolved—and Clark Darrow sitting bolt upright at the wheel wore a pained, strained expression as though he considered himself a spare part, and rather likely to break. He laboriously crossed two dust ruts, the wheels squeaking indignantly at the encounter, and then with a terrifying expression he gave the steering-gear a final wrench and deposited self and car approximately in front of the Happer steps. There was a plaintive heaving sound, a death-rattle, followed by a short silence; and then the air was rent by a startling whistle.

Sally Carrol gazed down sleepily. She started to yawn, but finding this quite impossible unless she raised her chin from the window-sill, changed her mind and continued silently to regard the car, whose owner sat brilliantly if perfunctorily at attention as he waited for an answer to his signal. After a moment the whistle once more split the dusty air.

"Good mawnin'."

With difficulty Clark twisted his tall body round and bent a distorted glance on the window.

" 'Tain't mawnin', Sally Carrol."

"Isn't it, sure enough?"

"What you doin'?"

"Eatin' 'n apple."

"Come on go swimmin'—want to?"

"Reckon so."

"How 'bout hurryin' up?"

"Sure enough."

Sally Carrol sighed voluminously and raised herself with profound inertia from the floor, where she had been occupied in alternately destroying parts of a green apple and painting paper dolls for her younger sister. She approached a mirror, regarded her expression with a pleased and pleasant languor, dabbed two spots of rouge on her lips and a grain of powder on her nose, and covered her bobbed corn-colored hair with a rose-littered sunbonnet. Then she kicked over the painting water, said, "Oh, damn!"—but let it lay—and left the room.

"How you, Clark?" she inquired a minute later as she slipped nimbly over the side of the car.

"Mighty fine, Sally Carrol."

"Where we go swimmin'?"

"Out to Walley's Pool. Told Marylyn we'd call by an' get her an' Joe Ewing."

Clark was dark and lean, and when on foot was rather inclined to stoop. His eyes were ominous and his expression somewhat petulant except when startlingly illuminated by one of his frequent smiles. Clark had "a income"—just enough to keep himself in ease and his car in gasoline—and he had spent the two years since he graduated from Georgia Tech in dozing round the lazy streets of his home town, discussing how he could best invest his capital for an immediate fortune.

Hanging round he found not at all difficult; a crowd of little girls had grown up beautifully, the amazing Sally Carrol foremost among them; and they enjoyed being swum with and danced with and made love to in the flower-filled summery evenings—and they all liked Clark immensely. When feminine company palled there were half a dozen other youths who were always just about to do something, and meanwhile were quite willing to join him in a few holes of golf, or a game of billiards, or the consumption of a quart of "hard yella licker." Every once in a while one of these contemporaries made a farewell round of calls before going up to New York or Philadelphia or Pittsburgh to go into business, but mostly they just stayed round in this languid paradise of dreamy skies and firefly evenings and noisy niggery street fairs—and especially of gracious, soft-voiced girls, who were brought up on memories instead of money.

The Ford having been excited into a sort of restless resentful life Clark and Sally Carrol rolled and rattled down Valley Avenue into Jefferson Street, where the dust road became a pavement; along opiate Millicent Place, where there were half a dozen prosperous, substantial mansions; and on into the down-town section. Driving was perilous here, for it was shopping time; the population idled casually across the streets and a drove of low-moaning oxen were being urged along in front of a placid street-car; even the shops seemed only yawning their doors and blinking their windows in the sunshine before retiring into a state of utter and finite coma.

"Sally Carrol," said Clark suddenly, "it a fact that you're engaged?"

She looked at him quickly.

"Where'd you hear that?"

"Sure enough, you engaged?"

" 'At's a nice question!"

"Girl told me you were engaged to a Yankee you met up in Asheville last summer."

Sally Carrol sighed.

"Never saw such an old town for rumors."

"Don't marry a Yankee, Sally Carrol. We need you round here."

Sally Carrol was silent a moment.

"Clark," she demanded suddenly, "who on earth shall I marry?"

"I offer my services."

"Honey, you couldn't support a wife," she answered cheerfully. "Anyway, I know you too well to fall in love with you."

" 'At doesn't mean you ought to marry a Yankee," he persisted.

"S'pose I love him?"

He shook his head.

"You couldn't. He'd be a lot different from us, every way."

He broke off as he halted the car in front of a rambling, dilapidated house. Marylyn Wade and Joe Ewing appeared in the doorway.

" 'Lo, Sally Carrol."

"Hi!"

"How you-all?"

"Sally Carrol," demanded Marylyn as they started off again, "you engaged?"

"Lawdy, where'd all this start? Can't I look at a man 'thout everybody in town engagin' me to him?"

Clark stared straight in front of him at a bolt on the clattering windshield.

"Sally Carrol," he said with a curious intensity, "don't you like us?"

"What?"

"Us down here?"

"Why, Clark, you know I do. I adore all you boys."

"Then why you gettin' engaged to a Yankee?"

"Clark, I don't know. I'm not sure what I'll do, but—well, I want to go places and see people. I want my mind to grow. I want to live where things happen on a big scale."

"What you mean?"

"Oh, Clark, I love you, and I love Joe here, and Ben Arrot, and you-all, but you'll—you'll—"

"We'll all be failures?"

"Yes. I don't mean only money failures, but just sort of—of ineffectual and sad, and—oh, how can I tell you?"

"You mean because we stay here in Tarleton?"

"Yes, Clark; and because you like it and never want to change things or think or go ahead."

He nodded and she reached over and pressed his hand.

"Clark," she said softly, "I wouldn't change you for the world. You're sweet the way you are. The things that'll make you fail I'll love always—the living in the past, the lazy days and nights you have, and all your carelessness and generosity."

"But you're goin' away?"

"Yes—because I couldn't ever marry you. You've a place in my heart no one else ever could have, but tied down here I'd get restless. I'd feel I was—wastin' myself. There's two sides to me, you see. There's the sleepy old side you love; an' there's a sort of energy—the feelin' that makes me do wild things. That's the part of me that may be useful somewhere, that'll last when I'm not beautiful any more."

She broke off with characteristic suddenness and sighed, "Oh, sweet cooky!" as her mood changed.

Half closing her eyes and tipping back her head till it rested on the seat-back she let the savory breeze fan her eyes and ripple the fluffy curls of her bobbed hair. They were in the country now, hurrying between tangled growths of bright-green coppice and grass and tall trees that sent sprays of foliage to hang a cool welcome over the road. Here and there they passed a battered Negro cabin, its oldest white-haired inhabitant smoking a corncob pipe beside the door, and half a dozen scantily clothed pickaninnies parading tattered dolls on the wild-grown grass in front. Farther out were lazy cotton-fields, where even the workers seemed intangible shadows lent by the sun to the earth, not for toil, but to while away some age-old tradition in the golden September fields. And round the drowsy picturesqueness, over the trees and shacks and muddy rivers, flowed the heat, never hostile, only comforting, like a great warm nourishing bosom for the infant earth.

"Sally Carrol, we're here!"

"Poor chile's soun' asleep."

"Honey, you dead at last outa sheer laziness?"

"Water, Sally Carrol! Cool water waitin' for you!"

Her eyes opened sleepily.

"Hi!" she murmured, smiling.

II

In November Harry Bellamy, tall, broad, and brisk, came down from his Northern city to spend four days. His intention was to settle a matter that had been hanging fire since he and Sally Carrol had met in Asheville, North Carolina, in midsummer. The settlement took only a quiet afternoon and an evening in front of a glowing open fire, for Harry Bellamy had everything she wanted; and, besides, she loved him— loved him with that side of her she kept especially for loving. Sally Carrol had several rather clearly defined sides.

On his last afternoon they walked, and she found their steps tending half-unconsciously toward one of her favorite haunts, the cemetery. When it came in sight, gray-white and golden-green under the cheerful late sun, she paused, irresolute, by the iron gate.

"Are you mournful by nature, Harry?" she asked with a faint smile.

"Mournful? Not I."

"Then let's go in here. It depresses some folks, but I like it."

They passed through the gateway and followed a path that led through a wavy valley of graves—dusty-gray and mouldy for the fifties; quaintly carved with flowers and jars for the seventies; ornate and hideous for the nineties, with fat marble cherubs lying in sodden sleep on stone pillows, and great impossible growths of nameless granite flowers. Occasionally they saw a kneeling figure with tributary flowers, but over most of the graves lay silence and withered leaves with only the fragrance that their own shadowy memories could waken in living minds.

They reached the top of a hill where they were fronted by a tall, round head-stone, freckled with dark spots of damp and half grown over with vines.

"Margery Lee," she read; "1844–1873. Wasn't she nice? She died when she was twenty-nine. Dear Margery Lee," she added softly. "Can't you see her, Harry?"

"Yes, Sally Carrol."

He felt a little hand insert itself into his.

"She was dark, I think; and she always wore her hair with a ribbon in it, and gorgeous hoop-skirts of alice blue and old rose."

"Yes."

"Oh, she was sweet, Harry! And she was the sort of girl born to stand on a wide, pillared porch and welcome folks in. I think perhaps a lot of men went away to war meanin' to come back to her; but maybe none of 'em ever did."

He stooped down close to the stone, hunting for any record of marriage.

"There's nothing here to show."

"Of course not. How could there be anything there better than just 'Margery Lee,' and that eloquent date?"

She drew close to him and an unexpected lump came into his throat as her yellow hair brushed his cheek.

"You see how she was, don't you, Harry?"

"I see," he agreed gently. "I see through your precious eyes. You're beautiful now, so I know she must have been."

Silent and close they stood, and he could feel her shoulders trembling a little. An ambling breeze swept up the hill and stirred the brim of her floppidy hat.

"Let's go down there!"

She was pointing to a flat stretch on the other side of the hill where along the green turf were a thousand grayish-white crosses stretching in endless, ordered rows like the stacked arms of a battalion.

"Those are the Confederate dead," said Sally Carrol simply.

They walked along and read the inscriptions, always only a name and a date, sometimes quite indecipherable.

"The last row is the saddest—see, 'way over there. Every cross has just a date on it, and the word 'Unknown.' "

She looked at him and her eyes brimmed with tears.

"I can't tell you how real it is to me, darling—if you don't know."

"How you feel about it is beautiful to me."

"No, no, it's not me, it's them—that old time that I've tried to have live in me. These were just men, unimportant evidently or they wouldn't have been 'unknown'; but they died for the most beautiful thing in the world—the dead South. You see," she continued, her voice still husky, her eyes glistening with tears, "people have these dreams they fasten onto things, and I've always grown up with that dream. It was so easy because it was all dead and there weren't any disillusions comin' to me. I've tried in a way to live up to those past standards of noblesse oblige—there's just the last remnants of it, you know, like the roses of an old garden dying all round us—streaks of strange courtliness and chivalry in some of these boys an' stories I used to hear from a Confederate soldier who lived next door, and a few old darkies. Oh, Harry, there was something, there was something! I couldn't ever make you understand, but it was there."

"I understand," he assured her again quietly.

Sally Carrol smiled and dried her eyes on the tip of a handkerchief protruding from his breast pocket.

"You don't feel depressed, do you, lover? Even when I cry I'm happy here, and I get a sort of strength from it."

Hand in hand they turned and walked slowly away. Finding soft grass she drew him down to a seat beside her with their backs against the remnants of a low broken wall.

"Wish those three old women would clear out," he complained. "I want to kiss you, Sally Carrol."

"Me, too."

They waited impatiently for the three bent figures to move off, and then she kissed him until the sky seemed to fade out and all her smiles and tears to vanish in an ecstasy of eternal seconds.

Afterward they walked slowly back together, while on the corners twilight played at somnolent black-and-white checkers with the end of day.

"You'll be up about mid-January," he said, "and you've got to stay a month at least. It'll be slick. There's a winter carnival on, and if you've never really seen snow it'll be like fairy-land to you. There'll be skating and skiing and tobogganing and sleigh-riding, and all sorts of torchlight parades on snow-shoes. They haven't had one for years, so they're going to make it a knock-out."

"Will I be cold, Harry?" she asked suddenly.

"You certainly won't. You may freeze your nose, but you won't be shivery cold. It's hard and dry, you know."

"I guess I'm a summer child. I don't like any cold I've never seen."

She broke off and they were both silent for a minute.

"Sally Carrol," he said very slowly, "what do you say to—March?"

"I say I love you."

"March?"

"March, Harry."

III

All night in the Pullman it was very cold. She rang for the porter to ask for another blanket, and when he couldn't give her one she tried vainly, by squeezing down into the bottom of her berth and doubling back the bedclothes, to snatch a few hours' sleep. She wanted to look her best in the morning.

She rose at six and sliding uncomfortably into her clothes stumbled up to the diner for a cup of coffee. The snow had filtered into the vestibules and covered the floor with a slippery coating. It was intriguing, this cold, it crept in everywhere. Her breath was quite visible and she blew into the air with a naïve enjoyment. Seated in the diner she stared out the window at white hills and valleys and scattered pines whose every branch was a green platter for a cold feast of snow. Sometimes a solitary farmhouse would fly by, ugly and bleak and lone on the white waste; and with each one she had an instant of chill compassion for the souls shut in there waiting for spring.

As she left the diner and swayed back into the Pullman she experienced a surging rush of energy and wondered if she was feeeling the bracing air of which Harry had spoken. This was the North, the North— her land now!

> "Then blow, ye winds, heigho!
>   A-roving I will go,"

she chanted exultantly to herself.

"What's 'at?" inquired the porter politely.

"I said: 'Brush me off.' "

The long wires of the telegraph-poles doubled; two tracks ran up beside the train—three—four; came a succession of white-roofed houses, a glimpse of a trolley-car with frosted windows, streets—more streets— the city.

She stood for a dazed moment in the frosty station before she saw three fur-bundled figures descending upon her.

"There she is!"

"Oh, Sally Carrol!"

Sally Carrol dropped her bag.

"Hi!"

A faintly familiar icy-cold face kissed her, and then she was in a group of faces all apparently emitting great clouds of heavy smoke; she was shaking hands. There were Gordon, a short, eager man of thirty who looked like an amateur knocked-about model for Harry, and his wife, Myra, a listless lady with flaxen hair under a fur automobile cap. Almost immediately Sally Carrol thought of her as vaguely Scandinavian. A cheerful chauffeur adopted her bag, and amid ricochets of half-phrases, exclamations, and perfunctory listless "my dears" from Myra, they swept each other from the station.

Then they were in a sedan bound through a crooked succession of snowy streets where dozens of little boys were hitching sleds behind grocery wagons and automobiles.

"Oh," cried Sally Carrol, "I want to do that! Can we, Harry?"

"That's for kids. But we might—"

"It looks like such a circus!" she said regretfully.

Home was a rambling frame house set on a white lap of snow, and there she met a big, gray-haired man of whom she approved, and a lady who was like an egg, and who kissed her—these were Harry's parents.

There was a breathless indescribable hour crammed full of half-sentences, hot water, bacon and eggs and confusion; and after that she was alone with Harry in the library, asking him if she dared smoke.

It was a large room with a Madonna over the fireplace and rows upon rows of books in covers of light gold and dark gold and shiny red. All the chairs had little lace squares where one's head should rest, the couch was just comfortable, the books looked as if they had been read—some—and Sally Carrol had an instantaneous vision of the battered old library at home, with her father's huge medical books, and the oil-paintings of her three great-uncles, and the old couch that had been mended up for forty-five years and was still luxurious to dream in. This room struck her as being neither attractive nor particularly otherwise. It was simply a room with a lot of fairly expensive things in it that all looked about fifteen years old.

"What do you think of it up here?" demanded Harry eagerly. "Does it surprise you? Is it what you expected, I mean?"

"You are, Harry," she said quietly, and reached out her arms to him.

But after a brief kiss he seemed anxious to extort enthusiasm from her.

"The town, I mean. Do you like it? Can you feel the pep in the air?"

"Oh, Harry," she laughed, "you'll have to give me time. You can't just fling questions at me."

She puffed at her cigarette with a sigh of contentment.

"One thing I want to ask you," he began rather apologetically; "you Southerners put quite an emphasis on family, and all that—not that it isn't quite all right, but you'll find it a little different here. I mean —you'll notice a lot of things that'll seem to you sort of vulgar display at first, Sally Carrol; but just remember that this is a three-generation town. Everybody has a father, and about half of us have grandfathers. Back of that we don't go."

"Of course," she murmured.

"Our grandfathers, you see, founded the place, and a lot of them had to take some pretty queer jobs while they were doing the founding. For instance, there's one woman who at present is about the social model for the town; well, her father was the first public ash man— things like that."

"Why," said Sally Carrol, puzzled, "did you s'pose I was goin' to make remarks about people?"

"Not at all," interrupted Harry; "and I'm not apologizing for any one either. It's just that—well, a Southern girl came up here last summer and said some unfortunate things, and—oh, I just thought I'd tell you."

Sally Carrol felt suddenly indignant—as though she had been un-justly spanked—but Harry evidently considered the subject closed, for he went on with a great surge of enthusiasm.

"It's carnival time, you know. First in ten years. And there's an ice palace they're building now that's the first they've had since eighty-five. Built out of blocks of the clearest ice they could find—on a tremendous scale."

She rose and walking to the window pushed aside the heavy Turkish portières and looked out.

"Oh!" she cried suddenly. "There's two little boys makin' a snow man! Harry, do you reckon I can go out an' help 'em?"

"You dream! Come here and kiss me."

She left the window rather reluctantly.

"I don't guess this is a very kissable climate, is it? I mean, it makes you so you don't want to sit round, doesn't it?"

"We're not going to. I've got a vacation for the first week you're here, and there's a dinner-dance to-night."

"Oh, Harry," she confessed, subsiding in a heap, half in his lap, half in the pillows, "I sure do feel confused. I haven't got an idea whether I'll like it or not, an' I don't know what people expect, or anythin'. You'll have to tell me, honey."

"I'll tell you," he said softly, "if you'll just tell me you're glad to be here."

"Glad—just awful glad!" she whispered, insinuating herself into his arms in her own peculiar way. "Where you are is home for me, Harry."

And as she said this she had the feeling for almost the first time in her life that she was acting a part.

That night, amid the gleaming candles of a dinner-party, where the men seemed to do most of the talking while the girls sat in a haughty and expensive aloofness, even Harry's presence on her left failed to make her feel at home.

"They're a good-looking crowd, don't you think?" he demanded. "Just look round. There's Spud Hubbard, tackle at Princeton last year, and Junie Morton—he and the red-haired fellow next to him were both Yale hockey captains; Junie was in my class. Why, the best athletes in the world come from these States round here. This is a man's country, I tell you. Look at John J. Fishburn!"

"Who's he?" asked Sally Carrol innocently.

"Don't you know?"

"I've heard the name."

"Greatest wheat man in the Northwest, and one of the greatest financiers in the country."

She turned suddenly to a voice on her right.

"I guess they forgot to introduce us. My name's Roger Patton."

"My name is Sally Carrol Happer," she said graciously.

"Yes, I know. Harry told me you were coming."

"You a relative?"

"No, I'm a professor."

"Oh," she laughed.

"At the university. You're from the South, aren't you?"

"Yes; Tarleton, Georgia."

She liked him immediately—a reddish-brown mustache under watery blue eyes that had something in them that these other eyes lacked, some quality of appreciation. They exchanged stray sentences through dinner, and she made up her mind to see him again.

After coffee she was introduced to numerous good-looking young men who danced with conscious precision and seemed to take it for granted that she wanted to talk about nothing except Harry.

"Heavens," she thought, "they talk as if my being engaged made me older than they are—as if I'd tell their mothers on them!"

In the South an engaged girl, even a young married woman, expected the same amount of half-affectionate badinage and flattery that would be accorded a débutante, but here all that seemed banned. One young man, after getting well started on the subject of Sally Carrol's eyes, and how they had allured him ever since she entered the room, went into a violent confusion when he found she was visiting the Bellamys—was Harry's fiancée. He seemed to feel as though he had made some risqué and inexcusable blunder, became immediately formal, and left her at the first opportunity.

She was rather glad when Roger Patton cut in on her and suggested that they sit out a while.

"Well," he inquired, blinking cheerily, "how's Carmen from the South?"

"Mighty fine. How's—how's Dangerous Dan McGrew? Sorry, but he's the only Northerner I know much about."

He seemed to enjoy that.

"Of course," he confessed, "as a professor of literature I'm not supposed to have read Dangerous Dan McGrew."

"Are you a native?"

"No, I'm a Philadelphian. Imported from Harvard to teach French. But I've been here ten years."

"Nine years, three hundred an' sixty-four days longer than me."

"Like it here?"

"Uh-huh. Sure do!"

"Really?"

"Well, why not? Don't I look as if I were havin' a good time?"

"I saw you look out the window a minute ago—and shiver."

"Just my imagination," laughed Sally Carrol. "I'm used to havin' everythin' quiet outside, an' sometimes I look out an' see a flurry of snow, an' it's just as if somethin' dead was movin'."

He nodded appreciatively.

"Ever been North before?"

"Spent two Julys in Asheville, North Carolina."

"Nice-looking crowd, aren't they?" suggested Patton, indicating the swirling floor.

Sally Carrol started. This had been Harry's remark.

"Sure are! They're—canine."

"What?"

She flushed.

"I'm sorry; that sounded worse than I meant it. You see I always think of people as feline or canine, irrespective of sex."

"Which are you?"

"I'm feline. So are you. So are most Southern men an' most of these girls here."

"What's Harry?"

"Harry's canine distinctly. All the men I've met to-night seem to be canine."

"What does 'canine' imply? A certain conscious masculinity as opposed to subtlety?"

"Reckon so. I never analyzed it—only I just look at people an' say 'canine' or 'feline' right off. It's right absurd, I guess."

"Not at all. I'm interested. I used to have a theory about these people. I think they're freezing up."

"What?"

"I think they're growing like Swedes—Ibsenesque, you know. Very gradually getting gloomy and melancholy. It's these long winters. Ever read any Ibsen?"

She shook her head.

"Well, you find in his characters a certain brooding rigidity. They're righteous, narrow, and cheerless, without infinite possibilities for great sorrow or joy."

"Without smiles or tears?"

"Exactly. That's my theory. You see there are thousands of Swedes up here. They come, I imagine, because the climate is very much like their own, and there's been a gradual mingling. They're probably not half a dozen here to-night, but—we've had four Swedish governors. Am I boring you?"

"I'm mighty interested."

"Your future sister-in-law is half Swedish. Personally I like her, but my theory is that Swedes react rather badly on us as a whole. Scandinavians, you know, have the largest suicide rate in the world."

"Why do you live here if it's so depressing?"

"Oh, it doesn't get me. I'm pretty well cloistered, and I suppose books mean more than people to me anyway."

"But writers all speak about the South being tragic. You know—Spanish señoritas, black hair and daggers an' haunting music."

He shook his head.

"No, the Northern races are the tragic races—they don't indulge in the cheering luxury of tears."

Sally Carrol thought of her graveyard. She supposed that that was vaguely what she had meant when she said it didn't depress her.

"The Italians are about the gayest people in the world—but it's a dull subject," he broke off. "Anyway, I want to tell you you're marrying a pretty fine man."

Sally Carrol was moved by an impulse of confidence.

"I know. I'm the sort of person who wants to be taken care of after a certain point, and I feel sure I will be."

"Shall we dance? You know," he continued as they rose, "it's encouraging to find a girl who knows what she's marrying for. Nine-tenths of them think of it as a sort of walking into a moving-picture sunset."

She laughed, and liked him immensely.

Two hours later on the way home she nestled near Harry in the back seat.

"Oh, Harry," she whispered, "it's so co-old!"

"But it's warm in here, darling girl."

"But outside it's cold; and oh, that howling wind!"

She buried her face deep in his fur coat and trembled involuntarily as his cold lips kissed the tip of her ear.

IV

The first week of her visit passed in a whirl. She had her promised toboggan-ride at the back of an automobile through a chill January twilight. Swathed in furs she put in a morning tobogganing on the country-club hill; even tried skiing, to sail through the air for a glorious moment and then land in a tangled laughing bundle on a soft snowdrift. She liked all the winter sports, except an afternoon spent snowshoeing over a glaring plain under pale yellow sunshine, but she soon realized that these things were for children—that she was being humored and that the enjoyment round her was only a reflection of her own.

At first the Bellamy family puzzled her. The men were reliable and she liked them; to Mr. Bellamy especially, with his iron-gray hair and energetic dignity, she took an immediate fancy, once she found that he was born in Kentucky; this made of him a link between the old life and the new. But toward the women she felt a definite hostility. Myra, her future sister-in-law, seemed the essence of spiritless conventionality.

Her conversation was so utterly devoid of personality that Sally Carrol, who came from a country where a certain amount of charm and assurance could be taken for granted in the women, was inclined to despise her.

"If those women aren't beautiful," she thought, "they're nothing. They just fade out when you look at them. They're glorified domestics. Men are the centre of every mixed group."

Lastly there was Mrs. Bellamy, whom Sally Carrol detested. The first day's impression of an egg had been confirmed—an egg with a cracked, veiny voice and such an ungracious dumpiness of carriage that Sally Carrol felt that if she once fell she would surely scramble. In addition, Mrs. Bellamy seemed to typify the town in being innately hostile to strangers. She called Sally Carrol "Sally," and could not be persuaded that the double name was anything more than a tedious ridiculous nickname. To Sally Carrol this shortening of her name was like presenting her to the public half clothed. She loved "Sally Carrol"; she loathed "Sally." She knew also that Harry's mother disapproved of her bobbed hair; and she had never dared smoke down-stairs after that first day when Mrs. Bellamy had come into the library sniffing violently.

Of all the men she met she preferred Roger Patton, who was a frequent visitor at the house. He never again alluded to the Ibsenesque tendency of the populace, but when he came in one day and found her curled upon the sofa bent over "Peer Gynt" he laughed and told her to forget what he'd said—that it was all rot.

And then one afternoon in her second week she and Harry hovered on the edge of a dangerously steep quarrel. She considered that he precipitated it entirely, though the Serbia in the case was an unknown man who had not had his trousers pressed.

They had been walking homeward between mounds of high-piled snow and under a sun which Sally Carrol scarcely recognized. They passed a little girl done up in gray wool until she resembled a small Teddy bear, and Sally Carrol could not resist a gasp of maternal appreciation.

"Look! Harry!"

"What?"

"That little girl—did you see her face?"

"Yes, why?"

"It was red as a little strawberry. Oh, she was cute!"

"Why, your own face is almost as red as that already! Everybody's healthy here. We're out in the cold as soon as we're old enough to walk. Wonderful climate!"

She looked at him and had to agree. He was mighty healthy-looking; so was his brother. And she had noticed the new red in her own cheeks that very morning.

Suddenly their glances were caught and held, and they stared for a moment at the street-corner ahead of them. A man was standing there, his knees bent, his eyes gazing upward with a tense expression as though he were about to make a leap toward the chilly sky. And then they both exploded into a shout of laughter, for coming closer they discovered it had been a ludicrous momentary illusion produced by the extreme bagginess of the man's trousers.

"Reckon that's one on us," she laughed.

"He must be a Southerner, judging by those trousers," suggested Harry mischievously.

"Why, Harry!"

Her surprised look must have irritated him.

"Those damn Southerners!"

Sally Carrol's eyes flashed.

"Don't call 'em that!"

"I'm sorry, dear," said Harry, malignantly apologetic, "but you know what I think of them. They're sort of—sort of degenerates—not at all like the old Southerners. They've lived so long down there with all the colored people that they've gotten lazy and shiftless."

"Hush your mouth, Harry!" she cried angrily. "They're not! They may be lazy—anybody would be in that climate—but they're my best friends, an' I don't want to hear 'em criticised in any such sweepin' way. Some of 'em are the finest men in the world."

"Oh, I know. They're all right when they come North to college, but of all the hangdog, ill-dressed, slovenly lot I ever saw, a bunch of small-town Southerners are the worst!"

Sally Carrol was clinching her gloved hands and biting her lip furiously.

"Why," continued Harry, "there was one in my class at New Haven, and we all thought that at last we'd found the true type of Southern aristocrat, but it turned out that he wasn't an aristocrat at all—just the son of a Northern carpetbagger, who owned about all the cotton round Mobile."

"A Southerner wouldn't talk the way you're talking now," she said evenly.

"They haven't the energy!"

"Or the somethin' else."

"I'm sorry, Sally Carrol, but I've heard you say yourself that you'd never marry—"

"That's quite different. I told you I wouldn't want to tie my life to any of the boys that are round Tarleton now, but I never made any sweepin' generalities."

They walked along in silence.

"I probably spread it on a bit thick, Sally Carrol. I'm sorry."

She nodded but made no answer. Five minutes later as they stood in the hallway she suddenly threw her arms round him.

"Oh, Harry," she cried, her eyes brimming with tears, "let's get married next week. I'm afraid of having fusses like that. I'm afraid, Harry. It wouldn't be that way if we were married."

But Harry, being in the wrong, was still irritated.

"That'd be idiotic. We decided on March."

The tears in Sally Carrol's eyes faded; her expression hardened slightly.

"Very well—I suppose I shouldn't have said that."

Harry melted.

"Dear little nut!" he cried. "Come and kiss me and let's forget."

That very night at the end of a vaudeville performance the orchestra played "Dixie" and Sally Carrol felt something stronger and more enduring than her tears and smiles of the day brim up inside her. She leaned forward gripping the arms of her chair until her face grew crimson.

"Sort of get you, dear?" whispered Harry.

But she did not hear him. To the spirited throb of the violins and the inspiring beat of the kettledrums her own old ghosts were marching by and on into the darkness, and as fifes whistled and sighed in the low encore they seemed so nearly out of sight that she could have waved good-by.

> "Away, away,
>   Away down South in Dixie!
>   Away, away,
>   Away down South in Dixie!"

V

It was a particularly cold night. A sudden thaw had nearly cleared the streets the day before, but now they were traversed again with a powdery wraith of loose snow that travelled in wavy lines before the feet of the wind, and filled the lower air with a fine-particled mist. There was no sky—only a dark, ominous tent that draped in the tops of the streets and was in reality a vast approaching army of snowflakes— while over it all, chilling away the comfort from the brown-and-green glow of lighted windows and muffling the steady trot of the horse pulling their sleigh, interminably washed the north wind. It was a dismal town after all, she thought—dismal.

Sometimes at night it had seemed to her as though no one lived here—they had all gone long ago—leaving lighted houses to be covered in time by tombing heaps of sleet. Oh, if there should be snow on her grave! To be beneath great piles of it all winter long, where even her headstone would be a light shadow against light shadows. Her grave—a grave that should be flower-strewn and washed with sun and rain.

She thought again of those isolated country houses that her train had passed, and of the life there the long winter through—the ceaseless glare through the windows, the crust forming on the soft drifts of snow, finally the slow, cheerless melting, and the harsh spring of which Roger Patton had told her. Her spring—to lose it forever—with its lilacs and the lazy sweetness it stirred in her heart. She was laying away that spring—afterward she would lay away that sweetness.

With a gradual insistence the storm broke. Sally Carrol felt a film of flakes melt quickly on her eyelashes, and Harry reached over a furry arm and drew down her complicated flannel cap. Then the small flakes came in skirmish-line, and the horse bent his neck patiently as a transparency of white appeared momentarily on his coat.

"Oh, he's cold, Harry," she said quickly.

"Who? The horse? Oh, no, he isn't. He likes it!"

After another ten minutes they turned a corner and came in sight of their destination. On a tall hill outlined in vivid glaring green against the wintry sky stood the ice palace. It was three stories in the air, with battlements and embrasures and narrow icicled windows, and the innumerable electric lights inside made a gorgeous transparency of the great central hall. Sally Carrol clutched Harry's hand under the fur robe.

"It's beautiful!" he cried excitedly. "My golly, it's beautiful, isn't it! They haven't had one here since eighty-five!"

Somehow the notion of there not having been one since eighty-five oppressed her. Ice was a ghost, and this mansion of it was surely peopled by those shades of the eighties, with pale faces and blurred snow-filled hair.

"Come on, dear," said Harry.

She followed him out of the sleigh and waited while he hitched the horse. A party of four—Gordon, Myra, Roger Patton, and another girl—drew up beside them with a mighty jingle of bells. There were quite a crowd already, bundled in fur or sheepskin, shouting and calling to each other as they moved through the snow, which was now so thick that people could scarcely be distinguished a few yards away.

"It's a hundred and seventy feet tall," Harry was saying to a muffled figure beside him as they trudged toward the entrance; "covers six thousand square yards."

She caught snatches of conversation: "One main hall"—"walls twenty to forty inches thick"—"and the ice cave has almost a mile of—"—"this Canuck who built it—"

They found their way inside, and dazed by the magic of the great crystal walls Sally Carrol found herself repeating over and over two lines from "Kubla Khan":

> "It was a miracle of rare device,
> A sunny pleasure-dome with caves of ice!"

In the great glittering cavern with the dark shut out she took a seat on a wooden bench, and the evening's oppression lifted. Harry was right—it was beautiful; and her gaze travelled the smooth surface of the walls, the blocks for which had been selected for their purity and clearness to obtain this opalescent, translucent effect.

"Look! Here we go—oh, boy!" cried Harry.

A band in a far corner struck up "Hail, Hail, the Gang's All Here!" which echoed over to them in wild muddled acoustics, and then the lights suddenly went out; silence seemed to flow down the icy sides and sweep over them. Sally Carrol could still see her white breath in the darkness, and a dim row of pale faces over on the other side.

The music eased to a sighing complaint, and from outside drifted in the full-throated resonant chant of the marching clubs. It grew louder like some paean of a viking tribe traversing an ancient wild; it swelled— they were coming nearer; then a row of torches appeared, and another and another, and keeping time with their moccasined feet a long column of gray-mackinawed figures swept in, snowshoes slung at their shoulders, torches soaring and flickering as their voices rose along the great walls.

The gray column ended and another followed, the light streaming luridly this time over red toboggan caps and flaming crimson mackinaws, and as they entered they took up the refrain; then came a long platoon of blue and white, of green, of white, of brown and yellow.

"Those white ones are the Wacouta Club," whispered Harry eagerly. "Those are the men you've met round at dances."

The volume of the voices grew; the great cavern was a phantasmagoria of torches waving in great banks of fire, of colors and the rhythm of soft-leather steps. The leading column turned and halted, platoon deployed in front of platoon until the whole procession made a solid flag of flame, and then from thousands of voices burst a mighty shout that filled the air like a crash of thunder, and sent the torches wavering. It was magnificent, it was tremendous! To Sally Carrol it was the North offering sacrifice on some mighty altar to the gray pagan God of Snow. As the shout died the band struck up again and there came more singing, and then long reverberating cheers by each club. She sat very quiet listening while the staccato cries rent the stillness; and then she started, for there was a volley of explosion, and great clouds of smoke went up here and there through the cavern—the flash-light photographers at work—and the council was over. With the band at their head the clubs formed in column once more, took up their chant, and began to march out.

"Come on!" shouted Harry. "We want to see the labyrinths downstairs before they turn the lights off!"

They all rose and started toward the chute—Harry and Sally Carrol in the lead, her little mitten buried in his big fur gantlet. At the bottom of the chute was a long empty room of ice, with the ceiling so low that they had to stoop—and their hands were parted. Before she realized what he intended Harry had darted down one of the half-dozen glittering passages that opened into the room and was only a vague receding blot against the green shimmer.

"Harry!" she called.

"Come on!" he cried back.

She looked round the empty chamber; the rest of the party had evidently decided to go home, were already outside somewhere in the blundering snow. She hesitated and then darted in after Harry.

"Harry!" she shouted.

She had reached a turning-point thirty feet down; she heard a faint muffled answer far to the left, and with a touch of panic fled toward it. She passed another turning, two more yawning alleys.

"Harry!"

No answer. She started to run straight forward, and then turned like lightning and sped back the way she had come, enveloped in a sudden icy terror.

She reached a turn—was it here?—took the left and came to what should have been the outlet into the long, low room, but it was only another glittering passage with darkness at the end. She called again but the walls gave back a flat, lifeless echo with no reverberations. Retracing her steps she turned another corner, this time following a wide passage. It was like the green lane between the parted waters of the Red Sea, like a damp vault connecting empty tombs.

She slipped a little now as she walked, for ice had formed on the bottom of her overshoes; she had to run her gloves along the half-slippery, half-sticky walls to keep her balance.

"Harry!"

Still no answer. The sound she made bounced mockingly down to the end of the passage.

Then on an instant the lights went out, and she was in complete darkness. She gave a small, frightened cry, and sank down into a cold little heap on the ice. She felt her left knee do something as she fell, but she scarcely noticed it as some deep terror far greater than any fear of being lost settled upon her. She was alone with this presence that came out of the North, the dreary loneliness that rose from ice-bound whalers in the Arctic seas, from smokeless, trackless wastes where were strewn the whitened bones of adventure. It was an icy breath of death; it was rolling down low across the land to clutch at her.

With a furious, despairing energy she rose again and started blindly down the darkness. She must get out. She might be lost in here for days, freeze to death and lie embedded in the ice like corpses she had read of, kept perfectly preserved until the melting of a glacier. Harry probably thought she had left with the others—he had gone by now; no one would know until late next day. She reached pitifully for the wall. Forty inches thick, they had said—forty inches thick!

"Oh!"

On both sides of her along the walls she felt things creeping, damp souls that haunted this palace, this town, this North.

"Oh, send somebody—send somebody!" she cried aloud.

Clark Darrow—he would understand; or Joe Ewing; she couldn't be left here to wander forever—to be frozen, heart, body, and soul. This her—this Sally Carrol! Why, she was a happy thing. She was a happy little girl. She liked warmth and summer and Dixie. These things were foreign—foreign.

"You're not crying," something said aloud. "You'll never cry any more. Your tears would just freeze; all tears freeze up here!"

She sprawled full length on the ice.

"Oh, God!" she faltered.

A long single file of minutes went by, and with a great weariness she felt her eyes closing. Then some one seemed to sit down near her and take her face in warm, soft hands. She looked up gratefully.

"Why, it's Margery Lee," she crooned softly to herself. "I knew you'd come." It really was Margery Lee, and she was just as Sally Carrol had known she would be, with a young, white brow, and wide, welcoming eyes, and a hoop-skirt of some soft material that was quite comforting to rest on.

"Margery Lee."

It was getting darker now and darker—all those tombstones ought to be repainted, sure enough, only that would spoil 'em, of course. Still, you ought to be able to see 'em.

Then after a succession of moments that went fast and then slow, but seemed to be ultimately resolving themselves into a multitude of blurred rays converging toward a pale-yellow sun, she heard a great cracking noise break her new-found stillness.

It was the sun, it was a light; a torch, and a torch beyond that, and another one, and voices; a face took flesh below the torch, heavy arms raised her, and she felt something on her cheek—it felt wet. Some one had seized her and was rubbing her face with snow. How ridiculous—with snow!

"Sally Carrol! Sally Carrol!"

It was Dangerous Dan McGrew; and two other faces she didn't know.

"Child, child! We've been looking for you two hours! Harry's half-crazy!"

Things came rushing back into place—the singing, the torches, the great shout of the marching clubs. She squirmed in Patton's arms and gave a long low cry.

"Oh, I want to get out of here! I'm going back home. Take me home"—her voice rose to a scream that sent a chill to Harry's heart as he came racing down the next passage—"to-morrow!" she cried with delirious, unrestrained passion—"To-morrow! To-morrow! To-morrow!"

VI

The wealth of golden sunlight poured a quite enervating yet oddly comforting heat over the house where day long it faced the dusty stretch of road. Two birds were making a great to-do in a cool spot found among the branches of a tree next door, and down the street a colored woman was announcing herself melodiously as a purveyor of strawberries. It was April afternoon.

Sally Carrol Happer, resting her chin on her arm, and her arm on an old window-seat gazed sleepily down over the spangled dust whence the heat waves were rising for the first time this spring. She was watching a very ancient Ford turn a perilous corner and rattle and groan to a jolting stop at the end of the walk. She made no sound, and in a minute a strident familiar whistle rent the air. Sally Carrol smiled and blinked.

"Good mawnin'."

A head appeared tortuously from under the car-top below.

" 'Tain't mawnin', Sally Carrol."

"Sure enough!" she said in affected surprise. "I guess maybe not."

"What you doin'?"

"Eatin' green peach. 'Spect to die any minute."

Clark twisted himself a last impossible notch to get a view of her face.

"Water's warm as a kettle steam, Sally Carrol. Wanta go swimmin'?"

"Hate to move," sighed Sally Carrol lazily, "but I reckon so."

Theme Questions

1. "Sally Carrol had several rather clearly defined sides." Did she? or did she merely think she did? Consider her desires, her sentimentality, her maturity, and her illusions (delusions?) about herself, and describe Sally Carrol. What does her return to the South indicate?

2. What are the forces of death that underlie "The Ice Palace?" How are they related to the incompatibility of Sally Carrol and Harry?

3. How does Roger Patton serve as a foil character for both Sally Carroll and Harry. Is it of any significance that he is a professor, an Easterner, something of a bigot, and Sally's rescuer?

4. Setting is crucial to the plot of "The Ice Palace." Analyze the setting descriptions, particularly the opening paragraph and the ice palace. How does the setting function in the plot structure for foreshadowing, climax, and dénouement?

5. If the story is read as ironic commentary and not as romance, it reveals strong criticism of several segments of American life. What are these criticisms?

. . . also by F. Scott Fitzgerald   *Babylon Revisited and Other Stories*
This Side of Paradise
The Great Gatsby

There are few girls alive who have not received the basic advice of the next three poems. It seems that the same things have been said for centuries since Herrick wrote in the 1600s. But if the basic advice is the same, there are variations that the passing centuries and changing philosophies have dictated. Ransom and cummings, both of the twentieth century, present views that are more ominous than Herrick's.

To the Virgins, To Make Much of Time

Robert Herrick

Gather ye rosebuds while ye may,
   Old time is still a-flying,
And this same flower that smiles to-day,
   To-morrow will be dying.

The glorious lamp of heaven, the sun,
   The higher he's a-getting,
The sooner will his race be run,
   And nearer he's to setting.

That age is best which is the first,
   When youth and blood are warmer;
But being spent, the worse, and worst
   Times still succeed the former.

Then be not coy, but use your time,
   And while ye may, go marry;
For having lost but once your prime,
   You may for ever tarry.

Blue Girls*

John Crowe Ransom

Twirling your blue skirts, travelling the sward
Under the towers of your seminary,
Go listen to your teachers old and contrary
Without believing a word.

Tie the white fillets then about your hair
And think no more of what will come to pass
Than bluebirds that go walking on the grass
And chattering on the air.

Practise your beauty, blue girls, before it fail;
And I will cry with my loud lips and publish
Beauty which all our power shall never establish,
It is so frail.

For I could tell you a story which is true;
I know a lady with a terrible tongue,
Blear eyes fallen from blue,
All her perfections tarnished—yet it is not long
Since she was lovelier than any of you.

a pretty a day**

e. e. cummings

a pretty a day
(and every fades)
is here and away
(but born are maids

to flower an hour
in all,all)

o yes to flower
until so blithe
a doer a wooer
some limber and lithe
some very fine mower
a tall;tall

some jerry so very
(and nellie and fan)
some handsomest harry
(and sally and nan
they tremble and cower
so pale:pale)

for betty was born
to never say nay
but lucy could learn
and lily could pray
and fewer were shyer
than doll. doll

Theme Question

1. While all the poets operate from the same premise, their con-
clusions and attitudes vary markedly. Compare the three poems and
discuss the likenesses and differences.

Unrequited love is often a source of comedy, but it is usually not funny for the participants. For the unloved one, it is usually painful, especially when there has been a betrayal. With modern chemistry at work, the precise problem of Turgenev's Akulina does not occur so often today. But chemistry has not solved the problem of the false lovers, the insincere Viktors.

The Rendezvous

Ivan Turgenev

I was sitting in a birch-wood one autumn, about the middle of September. Ever since morning a fine drizzle had been falling, giving way now and again to warm sunshine: it was fluky weather. One moment the sky would be all overcast with puffy white clouds, at another it would suddenly clear in places for a moment, and, through the rift, the azure would appear, clear and smiling, like the glance of a brilliant eye. I sat and looked about me and listened. The leaves were whispering faintly over my head: you could have told the time of year from their whisper alone. It was not the gay, laughing shiver of spring, nor the soft murmur, the long discourse of summer, nor the cold, frightened rustling of late autumn, but a scarcely perceptible, drowsy converse. A little breeze was just stirring among the treetops. The interior of the wood, drenched with rain, kept changing its appearance as the sun shone out or went in behind the clouds: sometimes it was all ablaze, as if everything there was smiling: the slender boles of the scattered birches suddenly took on the fresh brilliance of white silk, the tiny leaves on the ground gleamed and blazed with purple and gold, and the handsome stems of the tall, curly bracken, already tinged with their autumn hue, the hue of overripe grapes, stood out luminously before me in an infinite, crisscrossed maze; then suddenly the whole scene took on a faint shade of blue: in an instant, the bright colours went out, the birches stood blankly white as new-fallen snow, not yet touched by the cold light of the winter sun; and furtively, slyly, the finest of drizzles began to spray and whisper through the wood. The leaves of the birches were almost all of them still green, though of a marked pallor; only here and there stood a single young one, quite red or quite gold, and it was a sight to see how brightly it flared up when the sun's rays suddenly found their way to it, slipping and dappling through the thick net of fine branches, all newly washed in sparkling rain. There was not a sound from the birds: they were all snuggled down and keeping quiet; just occasionally the laughing voice of the tit-mouse rang out like a tiny steel bell. Before coming to a halt in this birch-wood, my dog and I had passed through a tall spinney of poplars. I confess that I am not overfond of this tree—the poplar—with its pale lilac-coloured trunk and the grey-green, metallic foliage which it lifts up as high as it can and throws out in a trembling fan into the air; I dislike the perpetual shaking of its untidy round leaves, fixed so awkwardly on their long stems. The poplar is good only on certain summer evenings when, standing out sharply from amidst the low brushwood, it faces straight into the glowing rays of the setting sun, and blazes and shines, suffused from root to summit with an even, yellowish purple—or on a clear windy day, when the whole tree ripples and murmurs under the blue sky, and every leaf is as if seized with a longing to break loose and fly off far away into the distance. But for the most part I am no lover of this tree, and so I didn't pause for rest in the poplar-spinney, but went on to the birch-wood, curled myself up under a tree whose branches began close to the ground and so could give me shelter from the rain, and, after admiring the scene around me, fell into the unbroken and tranquil sleep which is known only to the hunter.

I cannot say for how long I slept, but, when I opened my eyes, the whole inside of the wood was filled with sunlight, and in all directions, through joyfully murmuring foliage, the sky appeared, bright blue and sparkling; the clouds had vanished, chased by a newly-risen breeze; the weather had cleared, and you could feel in the air that special dry freshness which, filling the heart with a sense of well-being, nearly always presages a calm bright evening after a day of rain. I was preparing to get up and try my luck again, when suddenly my eyes came to rest on a motionless human figure. I peered at it: it was a young peasant-girl. She was sitting twenty yeards away from me, her head sunk in reflection, and both hands dropped on her knees; in one hand, which was half-open, a thick bunch of wild flowers lay, and every time she breathed it slipped quietly farther down on to her check skirt. A clean white blouse, buttoned at the front and wrists, lay in short, soft folds around her body; two rows of thick yellow beads fell from her neck on to her breast. She was quite pretty. Dense fair hair, of a fine ash colour, emerged in two carefully-brushed half-circles from beneath a narrow head-band, worn right down on her forehead, which was white as ivory; the rest of her face was faintly sunburnt, with that golden tan which comes only to a fine skin. I couldn't see her eyes—she did not raise them; but I saw clearly her fine, arched brows, her long eyelashes: they were wet, and, on one of her cheeks, the sun caught the drying streak of a tear that had stopped just at the side of her palish lips. It was a charming head; even a somewhat thick round nose didn't spoil it. I liked especially the expression of her face. It was so simple and gentle, so sad, so full of a childlike bewilderment in the presence of a private sorrow. Evidently she was waiting for someone; there was a faint crackling in the wood; she lifted her head at once and looked around; in the translucent shadow I could see the swift flash of her eyes, large, bright and timid, like a doe's. For a few moments she listened, without moving her wide-open eyes from the place whence the faint sound had come, sighed, quietly turned her head, bent down even lower and began slowly to arrange her flowers. Her eyelids reddened, her lips trembled with grief, and a fresh tear rolled out from beneath her thick lashes, halting and sparkling brilliantly on her cheek. Quite a while passed like this. The poor girl never stirred—only now and then a cheerless gesture of her hands—and listened and listened . . . Again there was a noise in the wood—she started. The noise continued, grew clearer, approached, and at last swift decisive steps could be heard. She sat up and seemed to be afraid; her attentive gaze wavered, kindled with anticipation. Soon a man's figure appeared through the undergrowth. She stared, blushed suddenly, burst into a joyous, blissful smile, made as if to get up, and at once sank back again, turned pale, became embarrassed, and only raised her trembling, almost imploring look to the new arrival when he had already come to a halt beside her.

I looked at him curiously from my hiding-place. I confess that the impression he made on me was disagreeable. By all appearances he must have been the spoiled valet of a rich young master. His clothes displayed a pretension to good taste and a dandyish negligence; he wore a short, bronze-coloured overcoat, probably off his master's shoulders, buttoned right up, a pink cravat with lilac ends, and a black gold-laced velvet cap rammed right down on his forehead. The rounded collar of his white shirt pushed up mercilessly against his ears and cut into his cheeks, and starched cuffs covered his whole hand down to his curving red fingers, which were adorned with silver and gold rings with forget-me-nots in turquoise. His face, ruddy, fresh, cheeky, was one of those which, so far as my observation goes, exasperate men and, unfortunately, very often appeal to women. He was clearly trying to give his coarse features an expression of contempt and boredom; he kept narrowing his milky-grey eyes, which were anyway tiny enough, making wry faces, dropping the corners of his lips, yawning constrainedly and with a careless, but not quite easy nonchalance, adjusting his reddish, nattily-brushed temples, or fingering the yellow hairs which bristled from his thick upper lip—in a word, he was intolerably affected. His affectation began from the moment he caught sight of the young peasant-girl waiting for him; he came up to her slowly, with a lounging gait, halted, worked his shoulders, plunged both hands into the pockets of his overcoat, and, hardly bestowing on the poor girl so much as a cursory, indifferent glance, sank down on the grass.

"Why," he began, still looking far away into the distance, fidgeting his leg and yawning, "been here long?"

The girl could not answer him immediately.

"Yes, Viktor Alexandrich," she said at last, in a hardly audible voice.

"Oh!" He took off his cap, passed his hand majestically over his thick, tightly-curled hair, which began practically at his eyebrows, and, looking round with dignity, scrupulously covered his precious head again. "I nearly forgot altogether. Besides, there was the rain, you see!" He yawned again. "Lots of work: you can't keep your eye on everything, with him scolding you into the bargain. We leave to-morrow . . ."

"To-morrow?" the girl brought out, turning a frightened gaze upon him.

"To-morrow . . . There, there, there, for goodness' sake!" he interjected hurriedly and with irritation, seeing that she had started to tremble all over and had quietly dropped her head. "For goodness' sake, Akulina, don't cry. You know I can't bear it." And he wrinkled his snub nose. "Or else I'll go away at once. It's too stupid-grizzling!"

"No, no, I won't," said Akulina hurriedly, swallowing her tears with an effort. "So you're leaving to-morrow?" she added after a short silence. "When will God grant us to see each other again, Viktor Alexandrich?"

"We'll see each other again all right. If not next year—then later. I think the master wants to go to Petersburg and get a Government job," he went on, pronouncing the words negligently and slightly through his nose, "but it's possible that we shall go abroad."

"You'll forget me, Viktor Alexandrich," said Akulina sorrowfully.

"No, why should I? I won't forget you: but just you be sensible; don't do silly things, do what your father tells you . . . I won't forget you—no-o." And he stretched calmly and yawned again.

"Don't forget me, Viktor Alexandrich," she went on, in an imploring voice. "I do love you so much, there's nothing I wouldn't do for you. . . . You tell me to obey my father . . . but how can I obey him?. . ."

"Well?" He pronounced the word as if from his stomach, lying on his back, with his hands folded beneath his head.

"But how can I, Viktor Alexandrich—you know very well . . ." She paused. Viktor played with his steel watch-chain.

"You're no fool, Akulina," he began at length, "so you mustn't talk nonsense. I've got your interests at heart, d'you see? Of course, you're no fool, you're not just an ordinary peasant-girl, as it were; your mother wasn't always a peasant, either. All the same, you've got no education—so you ought to do as you're told."

"But I'm scared, Viktor Alexandrich."

"Pooh, what nonsense, my dear; what is there to be scared about? What have you got there?" he added, moving closer to her. "Flowers?"

"Yes," answered Akulina sadly. "This I picked from a wild costmary," she went on, with somewhat more animation, "it's good for calves. This one's marigold—good against the scrofula. Then look at this wonderful flower; such a wonderful flower as I've never seen in all my days. These are forget-me-nots, and this one's called mother's darling. And these are for you," she added, taking out, from below the yellow costmary, a small bunch of blue cornflowers bound with a slender grass. "Would you like them?"

Viktor lazily stretched out a hand, took the flowers, smelt them indifferently, and began to turn them over between his fingers, looking up meanwhile, meditative and aloof. Akulina gazed at him . . . In her sad glance there was so much tender devotion, reverent submissiveness and love. She was afraid of him, she didn't dare cry, she was saying good-bye to him, admiring him for the last time: while he lay, sprawling like a sultan, and suffered her adoration with magnanimous patience and condescension. I confess that I looked indignantly at his red face, in which, through the pretence of contemptuous indifference, a contented, surfeited egoism peeped out. Akulina was so lovely at that moment: her whole soul bared itself trustfully, passionately, to him, and strove in all humility to approach him, while he . . . he dropped the cornflowers in the grass, brought out from the side pocket of his coat a little round glass in a bronze frame and proceeded to squeeze it into his eye; but, try as he might to hold it in, with screwed-up brow, raised cheek, even with his nose—the glass kept falling out and dropping into his hand.

"What's that?" asked Akulina at length, in astonishment.

"A lorgnette," he answered, with dignity.

"What for?"

"To see better with."

"Let me look."

Viktor scowled, but gave her the glass.

"Look out, don't break it."

"Don't worry, I won't break it." She put it shyly up to her eye. "I can't see anything," she observed innocently.

"But your eye—you must screw up your eye," he rejoined in the voice of a dissatisfied instructor. She screwed up the eye in front of which she was holding the glass. "Not that one, not that one, stupid! The other one!" exclaimed Viktor and, without allowing her to correct her mistake, took the lorgnette away from her.

Akulina flushed, laughed faintly and turned away.

"It's not meant for the likes of us, I can see," she said.

"It certainly isn't!"

The poor girl was silent and sighed deeply.

"Oh, Viktor Alexandrich, it'll be so hard for us, without you," she said suddenly.

Viktor wiped the lorgnette with his coat-tail and put it back in his pocket.

"Yes, yes," he said at length; "it'll be hard for you at first, certainly." He patted her condescendingly on the shoulder; she gently took his hand from her shoulder and shyly kissed it. "Well, yes, you're certainly a good girl," he went on, smiling complacently; "but there's nothing for it, is there now? The master and I can't stay here; it'll soon be winter now, and winter in the country—you know it yourself—is sheer misery. While, in Petersburg! There are such marvellous sights there, such as you could never imagine, you stupid, not even in a dream. The houses, the streets, the society, the education—simply amazing! . . ." Akulina listened to him with consuming attention, her lips slightly parted, like a child's. "But anyway," he added, turning over on the ground, "what's the good of my telling you all this? It's something that you can never understand."

"Why not, Viktor Alexandrich? I've understood; I've understood it all."

"There you go!"

Akulina lowered her head.

"There was a time once when you didn't talk to me like this, Viktor Alexandrich," she said, without looking up.

"Once? . . . once! There you are! . . . Once!" he observed, with a hint of indignation.

They were both silent.

"Well, it's time I was going," said Viktor, who had already propped himself up on his elbow. . . .

"Wait a little longer," said Akulina imploringly.

"What for? . . . I've already said good-bye to you."

"Wait," repeated Akulina.

Viktor lay back again and started to whistle. Akulina still kept her eyes fixed on him. I could see that she was growing more and more agitated: her lips twitched, her pale cheeks were faintly flushed.

"Viktor Alexandrich," she began, at length, chokingly. "It's wrong of you . . . it's wrong, before God, it is."

"What's wrong?" he rejoined, scowling, and he lifted himself slightly and turned his head towards her.

"It's wrong, Viktor Alexandrich. You might at least have had a kind word for me when you're saying good-bye; you might have had a word for me, poor little orphan that I am . . ."

"What can I say to you?"

"I don't know; it's you who should know, Viktor Alexandrich. Here you are, leaving, and not so much as a word . . . What have I done to deserve it?"

"What a funny girl you are! What else can I do?"

"Only a word . . ."

"Always the same thing," he said crossly, and got up.

"Don't be angry, Viktor Alexandrich," she added hastily, hardly holding in her tears.

"I'm not angry, you're just such a fool . . . What d'you want? I can't marry you—can I now? So what else d'you want? What is it?" He looked blank, as if waiting for an answer, and spread out his fingers.

"Nothing . . . I want nothing," she answered, stammering, and only just daring to stretch her trembling hands out towards him; "Just a word, to say good-bye . . ."

And her tears started streaming down.

"There it is, she's started to cry," said Viktor coldly, tilting his cap forward over his eyes.

"I want nothing," she went on, gulping and covering her face with both hands; "but what will it be like for me at home now, what'll it be like? What will become of me, poor wretch that I am? They'll marry me off to someone I don't love . . . poor, wretched me."

"Sing away, sing away," muttered Viktor in a low voice, shifting his position.

"He might have said a word, just one even . . . 'Akulina,' he might have said, 'I . . .' "

Sudden heart-rending sobs prevented her from finishing—she buried her face in the grass and burst into bitter, bitter tears . . . Her whole body shook spasmodically, she raised her head . . . Her long pent-up grief had at last found a way out. Viktor stood over her, stood, shrugged his shoulders, turned and strode away.

A few moments passed . . . She grew quiet, lifted her head, jumped up, looked round, and threw up her arms: she made as if to run after him, but her legs failed her, and she fell on her knees . . . I could stand it no longer and rushed towards her—but the moment she saw me, goodness knows where she got her strength from, she rose with a faint cry and vanished behind the trees, leaving the flowers scattered on the ground.

I stopped, picked up the bunch of cornflowers and walked out of the wood into the field. The sun stood low in the pale, clear sky, and its rays seemed to have faded and grown cold: they had no radiance; it was an even, almost watery light they distilled. There was only half an hour to nightfall, but the sunset had hardly begun to glow. A gusty wind blew headlong towards me over the parched yellow stubble; tiny, shrivelled leaves, whirling swiftly up before it, flew past across the road, along the edge of the wood; the side of it that abutted like a wall on the field was all shivering and sparkling with a fine glitter that had clarity but no brilliance; on the reddish grass, on blades and straws, everywhere, in glittering festoons, lay countless autumn spiders' webs. I stopped . . . sadness overcame me; behind the crisp yet cheerless smile of languishing nature, I thought I sensed the gloom and dread of approaching winter. High above me, cutting the air with sharp, heavy wing-strokes, flew a cautious raven: he looked at me with a sideways turn of his head, shot upwards and disappeared, croaking abruptly, behind the wood; a big flock of pigeons, flying gaily from the threshing-floor, suddenly formed up into a pillar and settled swiftly on the field—sure sign of autumn! On the other side of the bare hill, someone was driving by in a loud-rattling, empty cart.

I returned home; but it was some time before poor Akulina's image went out of my head, and I still have her cornflowers, faded long since.

Theme Questions

1. Who is the protagonist, the narrator or Akulina? Is there a double protagonist? Defend your answer. Why did the narrator save Akulina's flowers "faded long since?"

2. ". . . the expression of her face . . . was so simple and gentle, so sad, so full of childlike bewilderment in the presence of a private sorrow" describes how the narrator first views Akulina. What signs are there that the "private sorrow" may be pregnancy? Is there another explanation for her great grief?

3. The narrator intrudes his comments throughout the story— particularly in his descriptions of Akulina and Viktor. Examine the language of the story: how is it loaded so that the reader will agree with the narrator's sentiments? In what ways does the narrator justify Akulina's attraction to Viktor?

4. How does the setting aid the plot, set the mood, underlie the theme, and give the story unity? What symbols can be found in the long descriptive passages. How may they be interpreted?

. . . also by Ivan Turgenev   *Hunting Sketches* or *A Sportsman's Notebook*
Fathers and Sons
Virgin Soil

Not all "fallen maidens" are woeful waifs like Akulina. Some even bloom in their new condition, or so D. H. Lawrence and Thomas Hardy would have us believe. Lawrence's "maiden" seems to be a girl of no little determination, while Hardy's appears positively to enjoy the fact that she is a "fallen" woman who is "ruined."

A Youth Mowing

D. H. Lawrence

There are four men mowing down by the Isar;
I can hear the swish of the scythe-strokes, four
Sharp breaths taken; yea, and I
Am sorry for what's in store.

The first man out of the four that's mowing
Is mine, I claim him once and for all;
Though it's sorry I am, on his young feet, knowing
None of the trouble he's led to stall.

As he sees me bring the dinner, he lifts
His head as proud as a deer that looks
Shoulder-deep out of the corn; and wipes
His scythe-blade bright, unhooks

The scythe-stone and over the stubble to me.
Lad, thou hast gotten a child in me,
Laddie, a man thou'lt ha'e to be,
Yea, though I'm sorry for thee.

From *The Complete Poems of D. H. Lawrence, Volume I* edited by Vivian de Sola Pinto and F. Warren Roberts. All rights reserved. Reprinted by permission of the Viking Press, Inc.

The Ruined Maid

Thomas Hardy

"O 'Melia, my dear, this does everything crown!
Who could have supposed I should meet you in Town?
And whence such fair garments, such prosperi—ty?"—
"O didn't you know I'd been ruined?" said she.

—"You left us in tatters, without shoes or socks,
Tired of digging potatoes, and spudding up docks;
And now you've gay bracelets and bright feathers three!"—
"Yes: that's how we dress when we're ruined," said she.

—"At home in the barton you said 'thee' and 'thou',
And 'thik oon', and 'theäs oon', and 't 'other'; but now
Your talking quite fits 'ee for high compa—ny!"—
"Some polish is gained with one's ruin," said she.

—"Your hands were like paws then, your face blue and bleak
But now I'm bewitched by your delicate cheek,
And your little gloves fit as on any la—dy!"—
"We never do work when we're ruined," says she.

—"You used to call home-life a hag-ridden dream,
And you'd sigh, and you'd sock; but at present you seem
To know not of megrims or melancho—ly!"—
"True. One's pretty lively when ruined," said she.

—"I wish I had feathers, a fine, sweeping gown,
And a delicate face, and could strut about Town!"—
"My dear—a raw country girl, such as you be,
Cannot quite expect that. You ain't ruined," said she.

A broken romance is usually followed by a period of hurt, bewilderment, and guilt. Part of the adjustment is the necessity of picking up the pieces of oneself. Nick Adams in the protagonist of many Hemingway stories, including "The Killers" and "The Battler." In "The Three Day Blow" Nick almost literally gets his message of adjustment blowin' in the wind.

The Three-Day Blow

Ernest Hemingway

The rain stopped as Nick turned into the road that went up through the orchard. The fruit had been picked and the fall wind blew through the bare trees. Nick stopped and picked up a Wagner apple from beside the road, shiny in the brown grass from the rain. He put the apple in the pocket of his Mackinaw coat.

The road came out of the orchard on to the top of the hill. There was the cottage, the porch bare, smoke coming from the chimney. In back was the garage, the chicken coop and the second-growth timber like a hedge against the woods behind. The big trees swayed far over in the wind as he watched. It was the first of the autumn storms.

As Nick crossed the open field above the orchard the door of the cottage opened and Bill came out. He stood on the porch looking out.

"Well, Wemedge," he said.

"Hey, Bill," Nick said, coming up the steps.

They stood together looking out across the country, down over the orchard, beyond the road, across the lower fields and the woods of the point to the lake. The wind was blowing straight down the lake. They could see the surf along Ten Mile point.

"She's blowing," Nick said.

"She'll blow like that for three days," Bill said.

"Is your dad in?" Nick asked.

"No. He's out with the gun. Come on in."

Nick went inside the cottage. There was a big fire in the fireplace. The wind made it roar. Bill shut the door.

"Have a drink?" he said.

He went out to the kitchen and came back with two glasses and a pitcher of water. Nick reached the whisky bottle from the shelf above the fireplace.

"All right?" he said.

"Good," said Bill.

They sat in front of the fire and drank the Irish whisky and water.

"It's got a swell, smoky taste," Nick said, and looked at the fire through the glass.

"That's the peat," Bill said.

"You can't get peat into liquor," Nick said.

"That doesn't make any difference," Bill said.

"You ever seen any peat?" Nick asked.

"No," said Bill.

"Neither have I," Nick said.

His shoes, stretched out on the hearth, began to steam in front of the fire.

"Better take your shoes off," Bill said.

"I haven't got any socks on."

"Take them off and dry them and I'll get you some," Bill said. He went upstairs into the loft and Nick heard him walking about overhead. Upstairs was open under the roof and was where Bill and his father and he, Nick, sometimes slept. In back was a dressing room. They moved the cots back out of the rain and covered them with rubber blankets.

Bill came down with a pair of heavy wool socks.

"It's getting too late to go around without socks," he said.

"I hate to start them again," Nick said. He pulled the socks on and slumped back in the chair, putting his feet up on the screen in front of the fire.

"You'll dent in the screen," Bill said. Nick swung his feet over to the side of the fireplace.

"Got anything to read?" he asked.

"Only the paper."

"What did the Cards do?"

"Dropped a double header to the Giants."

"That ought to cinch it for them."

"It's a gift," Bill said. "As long as McGraw can buy every good ball player in the league there's nothing to it."

"He can't buy them all," Nick said.

"He buys all the ones he wants," Bill said. "Or he makes them discontented so they have to trade them to him."

"Like Heinie Zim," Nick agreed.

"That bonehead will do him a lot of good."

Bill stood up.

"He can hit," Nick offered. The heat from the fire was baking his legs.

"He's a sweet fielder, too," Bill said. "But he loses ball games."

"Maybe that's what McGraw wants him for," Nick suggested.

"Maybe," Bill agreed.

"There's always more to it than we know about," Nick said.

"Of course. But we've got pretty good dope for being so far away."

"Like how much better you can pick them if you don't see the horses."

"That's it."

Bill reached down the whisky bottle. His big hand went all the way around it. He poured the whisky into the glass Nick held out.

"How much water?"

"Just the same."

He sat down on the floor beside Nick's chair.

"It's good when the fall storms come, isn't it?" Nick said.

"It's swell."

"It's the best time of year," Nick said.

"Wouldn't it be hell to be in town?" Bill said.

"I'd like to see the World Series," Nick said.

"Well, they're always in New York or Philadelphia now," Bill said. "That doesn't do us any good."

"I wonder if the Cards will ever win a pennant?"

"Not in our lifetime," Bill said.

"Gee, they'd go crazy," Nick said.

"Do you remember when they got going that once before they had the train wreck?"

"Boy!" Nick said, remembering.

Bill reached over to the table under the window for the book that lay there, face down, where he had put it when he went to the door. He held his glass in one hand and the book in the other, leaning back against Nick's chair.

"What are you reading?"

" 'Richard Feverel.' "

"I couldn't get into it."

"It's all right," Bill said. "It ain't a bad book, Wemedge."

"What else have you got I haven't read?" Nick asked.

"Did you read the 'Forest Lovers'?"

"Yup. That's the one where they go to bed every night with the naked sword between them."

"That's a good book, Wemedge."

"It's a swell book. What I couldn't ever understand was what good the sword would do. It would have to stay edge up all the time because if it went over flat you could roll right over it and it wouldn't make any trouble."

"It's a symbol," Bill said.

"Sure," said Nick, "but it isn't practical."

"Did you ever read 'Fortitude?' "

"It's fine," Nick said. "That's a real book. That's where his old man is after him all the time. Have you got any more by Walpole?"

" 'The Dark Forest,' " Bill said. "It's about Russia."

"What does he know about Russia?" Nick asked.

"I don't know. You can't ever tell about those guys. Maybe he was there when he was a boy. He's got a lot of dope on it."

"I'd like to meet him," Nick said.

"I'd like to meet Chesterton," Bill said.

"I wish he was here now," Nick said. "We'd take him fishing to the 'Voix tomorrow."

"I wonder if he'd like to go fishing," Bill said.

"Sure," said Nick. "He must be about the best guy there is. Do you remember the 'Flying Inn'?"

> " 'If an angel out of heaven
>   Gives you something else to drink,
>   Thank him for his kind intentions;
>   Go and pour them down the sink.' "

"That's right," said Nick. "I guess he's a better guy than Walpole."

"Oh, he's a better guy, all right," Bill said.

"But Walpole's a better writer."

"I don't know," Nick said. "Chesterton's a classic."

"Walpole's a classic, too," Bill insisted.

"I wish we had them both here," Nick said. "We'd take them both fishing to the 'Voix tomorrow."

"Let's get drunk," Bill said.

"All right," Nick agreed.

"My old man won't care," Bill said.

"Are you sure?" said Nick.

"I know it," Bill said.

"I'm a little drunk now," Nick said.

"You aren't drunk," Bill said.

He got up from the floor and reached for the whisky bottle. Nick held out his glass. His eyes fixed on it while Bill poured.

Bill poured the glass half full of whisky.

"Put in your own water," he said. "There's just one more shot."

"Got any more?" Nick asked.

"There's plenty more but dad only likes me to drink what's open."

"Sure," said Nick.

"He says opening bottles is what makes drunkards," Bill explained.

"That's right," said Nick. He was impressed. He had never thought of that before. He had always thought it was solitary drinking that made drunkards.

"How is your dad?" he asked respectfully.

"He's all right," Bill said. "He gets a little wild sometimes."

"He's a swell guy," Nick said. He poured water into his glass out of the pitcher. It mixed slowly with the whisky. There was more whisky than water.

"You bet your life he is," Bill said.

"My old man's all right," Nick said.

"You're damn right he is," said Bill.

"He claims he's never taken a drink in his life," Nick said, as though announcing a scientific fact.

"Well, he's a doctor. My old man's a painter. That's different."

"He's missed a lot," Nick said sadly.

"You can't tell," Bill said. "Everything's got its compensations."

"He says he's missed a lot himself," Nick confessed.

"Well, dad's had a tough time," Bill said.

"It all evens up," Nick said.

They sat looking into the fire and thinking of this profound truth.

"I'll get a chunk from the back porch," Nick said. He had noticed while looking into the fire that the fire was dying down. Also he wished to show he could hold his liquor and be practical. Even if his father had never touched a drop Bill was not going to get him drunk before he himself was drunk.

"Bring one of the big beech chunks," Bill said. He was also being consciously practical.

Nick came in with the log through the kitchen and in passing knocked a pan off the kitchen table. He laid the log down and picked up the pan. It had contained dried apricots, soaking in water. He carefully picked up all the apricots off the floor, some of them had gone under the stove, and put them back in the pan. He dipped some more water onto them from the pail by the table. He felt quite proud of himself. He had been thoroughly practical.

He came in carrying the log and Bill got up from the chair and helped him put it on the fire.

"That's a swell log," Nick said.

"I'd been saving it for the bad weather," Bill said. "A log like that will burn all night."

"There'll be coals left to start the fire in the morning," Nick said.

"That's right," Bill agreed. They were conducting the conversation on a high plane.

"Let's have another drink," Nick said.

"I think there's another bottle open in the locker," Bill said.

He kneeled down in the corner in front of the locker and brought out a square-faced bottle.

"It's Scotch," he said.

"I'll get some more water," Nick said. He went out into the kitchen again. He filled the pitcher with the dipper dipping cold spring water from the pail. On his way back to the living room he passed a mirror in the dining room and looked in it. His face looked strange. He smiled at the face in the mirror and it grinned back at him. He winked at it and went on. It was not his face but it didn't make any difference.

Bill had poured out the drinks.

"That's an awfully big shot," Nick said.

"Not for us, Wemedge," Bill said.

"What'll we drink to?" Nick asked, holding up the glass.

"Let's drink to fishing," Bill said.

"All right," Nick said. "Gentlemen, I give you fishing."

"All fishing," Bill said. "Everywhere."

"Fishing," Nick said. "That's what we drink to."

"It's better than baseball," Bill said.

"There isn't any comparison," said Nick. "How did we ever get talking about baseball?"

"It was a mistake," Bill said. "Baseball is a game for louts."

They drank all that was in their glasses.

"Now let's drink to Chesterton."

"And Walpole," Nick interposed.

Nick poured out the liquor. Bill poured in the water. They looked at each other. They felt very fine.

"Gentlemen," Bill said, "I give you Chesterton and Walpole."

"Exactly, gentlemen," Nick said.

They drank. Bill filled up the glasses. They sat down in the big chairs in front of the fire.

"You were very wise, Wemedge," Bill said.

"What do you mean?" asked Nick.

"To bust off that Marge business," Bill said.

"I guess so," said Nick.

"It was the only thing to do. If you hadn't, by now you'd be back home working trying to get enough money to get married."

Nick said nothing.

"Once a man's married he's absolutely bitched," Bill went on. "He hasn't got anything more. Nothing. Not a damn thing. He's done for. You've seen the guys that get married."

Nick said nothing.

"You can tell them," Bill said. "They get this sort of fat married look. They're done for."

"Sure," said Nick.

"It was probably bad busting it off," Bill said. "But you always fall for somebody else and then it's all right. Fall for them but don't let the ruin you."

"Yes," said Nick.

"If you'd have married her you would have had to marry the whole family. Remember her mother and that guy she married."

Nick nodded.

"Imagine having them around the house all the time and going to Sunday dinners at their house, and having them over to dinner and her telling Marge all the time what to do and how to act."

Nick sat quiet.

"You came out of it damned well," Bill said. "Now she can marry somebody of her own sort and settle down and be happy. You can't mix oil and water and you can't mix that sort of thing any more than if I'd marry Ida that works for Strattons. She'd probably like it, too."

Nick said nothing. The liquor had all died out of him and left him alone. Bill wasn't there. He wasn't sitting in front of the fire or going fishing tomorrow with Bill and his dad or anything. He wasn't drunk. It was all gone. All he knew was that he had once had Marjorie and that he had lost her. She was gone and he had sent her away. That was all that mattered. He might never see her again. Probably he never would. It was all gone, finished.

"Let's have another drink," Nick said.

Bill poured it out. Nick splashed in a little water.

"If you'd gone on that way we wouldn't be here now," Bill said.

That was true. His original plan had been to go down home and get a job. Then he had planned to stay in Charlevoix all winter so he could be near Marge. Now he did not know what he was going to do.

"Probably we wouldn't even be going fishing tomorrow," Bill said. "You had the right dope, all right."

"I couldn't help it," Nick said.

"I know. That's the way it works out," Bill said.

"All of a sudden everything was over," Nick said. "I don't know why it was. I couldn't help it. Just like when the three-day blows come now and rip all the leaves off the trees."

"Well, it's over. That's the point," Bill said.

"It was my fault," Nick said.

"It doesn't make any difference whose fault it was," Bill said.

"No, I suppose not," Nick said.

The big thing was that Marjorie was gone and that probably he would never see her again. He had talked to her about how they would go to Italy together and the fun they would have. Places they would be together. It was all gone now. Something gone out of him.

"So long as it's over that's all that matters," Bill said. "I tell you, Wemedge, I was worried while it was going on. You played it right. I understand her mother is sore as hell. She told a lot of people you were engaged."

"We weren't engaged," Nick said.

"It was all around that you were."

"I can't help it," Nick said. "We weren't."

"Weren't you going to get married?" Bill asked.

"Yes. But we weren't engaged," Nick said.

"What's the difference?" Bill asked judicially.

"I don't know. There's a difference."

"I don't see it," said Bill.

"All right," said Nick. "Let's get drunk."

"All right," Bill said. "Let's get really drunk."

"Let's get drunk and then go swimming," Nick said.

He drank off his glass.

"I'm sorry as hell about her but what could I do?" he said. "You know what her mother was like!"

"She was terrible," Bill said.

"All of a sudden it was over," Nick said. "I oughtn't to talk about it."

"You aren't," Bill said. "I talked about it and now I'm through. We won't ever speak about it again. You don't want to think about it. You might get back into it again."

Nick had not thought about that. It had seemed so absolute. That was a thought. That made him feel better.

"Sure," he said. "There's always that danger."

He felt happy now. There was not anything that was irrevocable. He might go into town Saturday night. Today was Thursday.

"There's always a chance," he said.

"You'll have to watch yourself," Bill said.

"I'll watch myself," he said.

He felt happy. Nothing was finished. Nothing was ever lost. He would go into town on Saturday. He felt lighter, as he had felt before Bill started to talk about it. There was always a way out.

"Let's take the guns and go down to the point and look for your dad," Nick said.

"All right."

Bill took down the two shotguns from the rack on the wall. He opened a box of shells. Nick put on his Mackinaw coat and his shoes. His shoes were stiff from the drying. He was still quite drunk but his head was clear.

"How do you feel?" Nick asked.

"Swell. I've just got a good edge on." Bill was buttoning up his sweater.

"There's no use getting drunk."

"No. We ought to get outdoors."

They stepped out the door. The wind was blowing a gale.

"The birds will lie right down in the grass with this," Nick said.

They struck down toward the orchard.

"I saw a woodcock this morning," Bill said.

"Maybe we'll jump him," Nick said.

"You can't shoot in this wind," Bill said.

Outside now the Marge business was no longer so tragic. It was not even very important. The wind blew everything like that away.

"It's coming right off the big lake," Nick said.

Against the wind they heard the thud of a shotgun.

"That's dad," Bill said. "He's down in the swamp."

"Let's cut down that way," Nick said.

"Let's cut across the lower meadow and see if we jump anything," Bill said.

"All right," Nick said.

None of it was important now. The wind blew it out of his head. Still he could always go into town Saturday night. It was a good thing to have in reserve.

Theme Questions

1. What is the three-day blow? What is the "Marge business"? In what ways does one come to stand for the other? How does Nick resolve his conflict?

2. In Hemingway's very spare style, Nick and Bill reveal themselves chiefly through their conversation. What is given about their backgrounds, their interests, and their problems? What, in addition, may the reader infer either from the tone and quality of their conversation or from what is *not* said?

3. Bill states a basic Hemingway attitude, "You don't want to think about it." to Nick. What is its significance to both Bill and Nick? What is its significance beyond the context of the story?

4. What symbolic inferences can be drawn from the boys' need to get drunk, their repeated references to hunting and swimming, and the three day blow?

. . . **also by Ernest Hemingway**   *In Our Time*
The Sun Also Rises
A Farewell to Arms
For Whom the Bell Tolls

Here are two more young lovers having troubles with their girls, who seem to be rather wayward and capricious. Suckling's poem offers some sensible advice from an older man. Robinson's young lovers act out their problem in a dramatic ballad. Robinson leaves it to the reader to figure out the why's and wherefore's of this quarrel.

Why So Pale and Wan, Fond Lover?

Sir John Suckling

> Why so pale and wan, fond lover?
>   Prithee, why so pale?
> Will, when looking well can't move her,
>   Looking ill prevail?
>   Prithee, why so pale?
>
> Why so dull and mute, young sinner?
>   Prithee, why so mute?
> Will, when speaking well can't win her,
>   Saying nothing do't?
>   Prithee, why so mute?
>
> Quit, quit, for shame! this will not move:
>   This cannot take her.
> If of herself she will not love,
>   Nothing can make her:
>   The devil take her!

John Gorham

Edwin Arlington Robinson

"Tell me what you're doing over here, John Gorham,
Sighing hard and seeming to be sorry when you're not;
Make me laugh or let me go now, for long faces in the moonlight
Are a sign for me to say again a word that you forgot."—

"I'm over here to tell you what the moon already
May have said or maybe shouted ever since a year ago;
I'm over here to tell you what you are, Jane Wayland,
And to make you rather sorry, I should say, for being so."—

"Tell me what you're saying to me now, John Gorham,
Or you'll never see as much of me as ribbons any more;
I'll vanish in as many ways as I have toes and fingers,
And you'll not follow far for one where flocks have been before."—

"I'm sorry now you never saw the flocks, Jane Wayland,
But you're the one to make of them as many as you need.
And then about the vanishing. It's I who mean to vanish;
And when I'm here no longer you'll be done with me indeed."—

"That's a way to tell me what I am, John Gorham!
How am I to know myself until I make you smile?
Try to look as if the moon were making faces at you,
And a little more as if you meant to stay a little while."—

"You are what it is that over rose-blown gardens
Makes a pretty flutter for a season in the sun;
You are what it is that with a mouse, Jane Wayland,
Catches him and lets him go and eats him up for fun."—

"Sure I never took you for a mouse, John Gorham;
All you say is easy, but so far from being true
That I wish you wouldn't ever be again the one to think so;
For it isn't cats and butterflies that I would be to you."—

"All your little animals are in one picture—
One I've had before me since a year ago to-night;
And the picture where they live will be of you, Jane Wayland,
Till you find a way to kill them or to keep them out of sight."—

"Won't you ever see me as I am, John Gorham,
Leaving out the foolishness and all I never meant?
Somewhere in me there's a woman, if you know the way to find her.
Will you like me any better if I prove it and repent?"—

"I doubt if I shall ever have the time, Jane Wayland;
And I dare say all this moonlight lying round us might as well
Fall for nothing on the shards of broken urns that are forgotten,
As on two that have no longer much of anything to tell."

Theme Questions

1. Would John Gorham benefit from Suckling's advice or Nick's experience? In what ways?

2. Which lover, Nick, John or Suckling's young man, is in the most enviable position? Which is in the least? Why?

In popular romance, boy usually happily gets girl. In the romantic fiction of Hawthorne, however, love is more usually associated with death. Yet Hawthorne's old romantic and fanciful tales are truer than the modern ones in many ways. His explorations of the human heart and his mistrust of cold intellect have transcended time, as in "Rappaccini's Daughter."

Rappaccini's Daughter

Nathaniel Hawthorne

A young man, named Giovanni Guasconti, came, very long ago, from the more southern region of Italy, to pursue his studies at the University of Padua. Giovanni, who had but a scanty supply of gold ducats in his pocket, took lodgings in a high and gloomy chamber of an old edifice which looked not unworthy to have been the palace of a Paduan noble, and which, in fact, exhibited over its entrance the armorial bearings of a family long since extinct. The young stranger, who was not unstudied in the great poem of his country, recollected that one of the ancestors of this family, and perhaps an occupant of this very mansion, had been pictured by Dante as a partaker of the immortal agonies of his Inferno. These reminiscences and associations, together with the tendency to heartbreak natural to a young man for the first time out of his native sphere, caused Giovanni to sigh heavily as he looked around the desolate and ill-furnished apartment.

"Holy Virgin, signor!" cried old Dame Lisabetta, who, won by the youth's remarkable beauty of person, was kindly endeavoring to give the chamber a habitable air, "what a sigh was that to come out of a young man's heart! Do you find this old mansion gloomy? For the love of Heaven, then, put your head out of the window, and you will see as bright sunshine as you have left in Naples."

Guasconti mechanically did as the old woman advised, but could not quite agree with her that the Paduan sunshine was as cheerful as that of southern Italy. Such as it was, however, it fell upon a garden beneath the window and expended its fostering influences on a variety of plants, which seemed to have been cultivated with exceeding care.

"Does this garden belong to the house?" asked Giovanni.

"Heaven forbid, signor, unless it were fruitful of better pot herbs than any that grow there now," answered old Lisabetta. "No; that garden is cultivated by the old hands of Signor Giacomo Rappaccini, the famous doctor, who, I warrant him, has been heard of as far as Naples. It is said that he distils these plants into medicines that are as potent as a charm. Oftentimes you may see the signor doctor at work, and perchance the signora, his daughter, too, gathering the strange flowers that grow in the garden."

The old woman had now done what she could for the aspect of the chamber; and, commending the young man to the protection of the saints, took her departure.

Giovanni still found no better occupation than to look down into the garden beneath his window. From its appearance, he judged it to be one of those botanic gardens which were of earlier date in Padua than elsewhere in Italy or in the world. Or, not improbably, it might once have been the pleasure-place of an opulent family; for there was the ruin of a marble fountain, in the centre, sculptured with rare art, but so woefully shattered that it was impossible to trace the original design from the chaos of remaining fragments. The water, however, continued to gush and sparkle into the sunbeams as cheerfully as ever. A little gurgling sound ascended to the young man's window, and made him feel as if the fountain were an immortal spirit that sung its song unceasingly and without heeding the vicissitudes around it, while one century imbodied it in marble and another scattered the perishable garniture on the soil. All about the pool into which the water subsided grew various plants, that seemed to require a plentiful supply of moisture for the nourishment of gigantic leaves, and, in some instances, flowers gorgeously magnificent. There was one shrub in particular, set in a marble vase in the midst of the pool, that bore a profusion of purple blossoms, each of which had the lustre and richness of a gem; and the whole together made a show so resplendent that it seemed enough to illuminate the garden, even had there been no sunshine. Every portion of the soil was peopled with plants and herbs, which, if less beautiful, still bore tokens of assiduous care, as if all had their individual virtues, known to the scientific mind that fostered them. Some were placed in urns, rich with old carving, and others in common garden pots; some crept serpent-like along the ground or climbed on high, using whatever means of ascent was offered them. One plant had wreathed itself round a statue of Vertumnus, which was thus quite veiled and shrouded in a drapery of hanging foliage, so happily arranged that it might have served a sculptor for a study.

While Giovanni stood at the window he heard a rustling behind a screen of leaves, and became aware that a person was at work in the garden. His figure soon emerged into view, and showed itself to be that of no common laborer, but a tall, emaciated, sallow, and sickly-looking

man, dressed in a scholar's garb of black. He was beyond the middle
term of life, with gray hair, a thin, gray beard, and a face singularly
marked with intellect and cultivation, but which could never, even in his
more youthful days, have expressed much warmth of heart.

Nothing could exceed the intentness with which this scientific gardener examined every shrub which grew in his path: it seemed as if he
was looking into their inmost nature, making observations in regard
to their creative essence, and discovering why one leaf grew in this
shape and another in that, and wherefore such and such flowers differed
among themselves in hue and perfume. Nevertheless, in spite of this
deep intelligence on his part, there was no approach to intimacy between himself and these vegetable existences. On the contrary, he avoided
their actual touch or the direct inhaling of their odors with a caution
that impressed Giovanni most disagreeably; for the man's demeanor was
that of one walking among malignant influences, such as savage beasts,
or deadly snakes, or evil spirits, which, should he allow them one moment of license, would wreak upon him some terrible fatality. It was
strangely frightful to the young man's imagination to see this air of in-
security in a person cultivating a garden, that most simple and innocent
of human toils, and which had been alike the joy and labor of the un-
fallen parents of the race. Was this garden, then, the Eden of the present world? And this man, with such a perception of harm in what his
own hands caused to grow,—was he the Adam?

The distrustful gardener, while plucking away the dead leaves or
pruning the two luxuriant growth of the shrubs, defended his hands with
a pair of thick gloves. Nor were these his only armor. When, in his
walk through the garden, he came to the magnificent plant that hung its
purple gems beside the marble fountain, he placed a kink of mask over
his mouth and nostrils, as if all this beauty did but conceal a deadlier
malice; but, finding his task still too dangerous, he drew back, removed
the mask, and called loudly, but in the infirm voice of a person affected
with inward disease,—

"Beatrice! Beatrice!"

"Here am I, my father. What would you?" cried a rich and youthful voice from the window of the opposite house—a voice as rich as a
tropical sunset, and which made Giovanni, though he knew not why,
think of deep hues of purple or crimson and of perfumes heavily de-
lectable. "Are you in the garden?"

"Yes, Beatrice," answered the gardener, "and I need your help."

Soon there emerged from under a sculptured portal the figure of a
young girl, arrayed with as much richness of taste as the most splendid
of the flowers, beautiful as the day, and with a bloom so deep and
vivid that one shade more would have been too much. She looked re-
dundant with life, health, and energy; all of which attributes were bound

down and compressed, as it were, and girdled tensely, in their luxuriance, by her virgin zone. Yet Giovanni's fancy must have grown morbid while he looked down into the garden; for the impression which the fair stranger made upon him was as if here were another flower, the human sister of those vegetable ones, as beautiful as they, more beautiful than the richest of them, but still to be touched only with a glove, not to be approached without a mask. As Beatrice came down the garden path, it was observable that she handled and inhaled the odor of several of the plants which her father had most sedulously avoided.

"Here, Beatrice," said the latter, "see how many needful offices require to be done to our chief treasure. Yet, shattered as I am, my life might pay the penalty of approaching it so closely as circumstances demand. Henceforth, I fear, this plant must be consigned to your sole charge."

"And gladly will I undertake it," cried again the rich tones of the young lady, as she bent towards the magnificent plant and opened her arms as if to embrace it. "Yes, my sister, my splendor, it shall be Beatrice's task to nurse and serve thee; and thou shalt reward her with thy kisses and perfumed breath, which to her is as the breath of life."

Then, with all the tenderness in her manner that was so strikingly expressed in her words, she busied herself with such attentions as the plant seemed to require; and Giovanni, at his lofty window, rubbed his eyes and almost doubted whether it were a girl tending her favorite flower, or one sister performing the duties of affection to another. The scene soon terminated. Whether Dr. Rappaccini had finished his labors in the garden, or that his watchful eye had caught the stranger's face, he now took his daughter's arm and retired. Night was already closing in; oppressive exhalations seemed to proceed from the plants and steal upward past the open window; and Giovanni, closing the lattice, went to his couch and dreamed of a rich flower and beautiful girl. Flower and maiden were different, and yet the same, and fraught with some strange peril in either shape.

But there is an influence in the light of morning that tends to rectify whatever errors of fancy, or even of judgment, we may have incurred during the sun's decline, or among the shadows of the night, or in the less wholesome glow of moonshine. Giovanni's first movement, on starting from sleep, was to throw open the window and gaze down into the garden which his dreams had made so fertile of mysteries. He was surprised and a little ashamed to find how real and matter-of-fact an affair it proved to be, in the first rays of the sun which gilded the dewdrops that hung upon leaf and blossom, and, while giving a brighter beauty to each rare flower, brought everything within the limits of ordinary experience. The young man rejoiced that, in the heart of the barren city, he had the privilege of overlooking this spot of lovely and luxuriant vegetation. It would serve, he said to himself, as a symbolic language to keep him in communion with Nature. Neither the sickly and thoughtworn Dr. Giacomo Rappaccini, it is true, nor his brilliant daughter, were now visible; so that Giovanni could not determine how much of the singularity which he attributed to both was due to their own qualities and how much to his wonder-working fancy; but he was inclined to take a most rational view of the whole matter.

In the course of the day he paid his respects to Signor Pietro Baglioni, professor of medicine in the university, a physician of eminent repute, to whom Giovanni had brought a letter of introduction. The professor was an elderly personage, apparently of genial nature, and habits that might almost be called jovial. He kept the young man to dinner, and made himself very agreeable by the freedom and liveliness of his conversation, especially when warmed by a flask or two of Tuscan wine. Giovanni, conceiving that men of science, inhabitants of the same city, must needs be on familiar terms with one another, took an opportunity to mention the name of Dr. Rappaccini. But the professor did not respond with so much cordiality as he had anticipated.

"Ill would it become a teacher of the divine art of medicine," said Professor Pietro Baglioni, in answer to a question of Giovanni, "to withhold due and well-considered praise of a physician so eminently skilled as Rappaccini; but, on the other hand, I should answer it but scantily to my conscience were I to permit a worthy youth like yourself, Signor Giovanni, the son of an ancient friend, to imbibe erroneous ideas respecting a man who might hereafter chance to hold your life and death in his hands. The truth is, our worshipful Dr. Rappaccini has as much science as any member of the faculty—with perhaps one single exception— in Padua, or all Italy; but there are certain grave objections to his professional character."

"And what are they?" asked the young man.

"Has my friend Giovanni any disease of body or heart, that he is so inquisitive about physicians?" said the professor, with a smile. "But as for Rappaccini, it is said of him—and I, who know the man well, can answer for its truth—that he cares infinitely more for science than for mankind. His patients are interesting to him only as subjects for some new experiment. He would sacrifice human life, his own among the rest, or whatever else was dearest to him, for the sake of adding so much as a grain of mustard seed to the great heap of his accumulated knowledge."

"Methinks he is an awful man indeed," remarked Guasconti, mentally recalling the cold and purely intellectual aspect of Rappaccini. "And yet, worshipful professor, is it not a noble spirit? Are there many men capable of so spiritual a love of science?"

"God forbid," answered the professor, somewhat testily; "at least, unless they take sounder views of the healing art than those adopted by

Rappaccini. It is his theory that all medicinal virtues are comprised within those substances which we term vegetable poisons. These he cultivates with his own hands, and is said even to have produced new varieties of poison, more horribly deleterious than Nature, without the assistance of this learned person, would ever have plagued the world withal. That the signor doctor does less mischief than might be expected with such dangerous substances is undeniable. Now and then, it must be owned, he has effected, or seemed to effect, a marvellous cure; but, to tell you my private mind, Signor Giovanni, he should receive little credit for such instances of success,—they being probably the work of chance,—but should be held strictly accountable for his failures, which may justly be considered his own work."

The youth might have taken Baglioni's opinions with many grains of allowance had he known that there was a professional warfare of long continuance between him and Dr. Rappaccini, in which the latter was generally thought to have gained the advantage. If the reader be inclined to judge for himself, we refer him to certain black-letter tracts on both sides, preserved in the medical department of the University of Padua.

"I know not, most learned professor," returned Giovanni, after musing on what had been said of Rappaccini's exclusive zeal for science,—"I know not how dearly this physician may love his art; but surely there is one object more dear to him. He has a daughter."

"Aha!" cried the professor, with a laugh. "So now our friend Giovanni's secret is out. You have heard of this daughter, whom all the young men in Padua are wild about, though not half a dozen have ever had the good hap to see her face. I know little of the Signora Beatrice save that Rappaccini is said to have instructed her deeply in his science, and that, young and beautiful as fame reports her, she is already qualified to fill a professor's chair. Perchance her father destines her for mine! Other absurd rumors there be, not worth talking about or listening to. So now, Signor Giovanni, drink off your glass of lachryma."

Guasconti returned to his lodgings somewhat heated with the wine he had quaffed, and which caused his brain to swim with strange fantasies in reference to Dr. Rappaccini and the beautiful Beatrice. On his way, happening to pass by a florist's, he bought a fresh bouquet of flowers.

Ascending to his chamber, he seated himself near the window, but within the shadow thrown by the depth of the wall, so that he could look down into the garden with little risk of being discovered. All beneath his eye was a solitude. The strange plants were basking in the sunshine, and now and then nodding gently to one another, as if in acknowledgement of sympathy and kindred. In the midst, by the shattered fountain, grew the magnificent shrub, with its purple gems clustering all over it; they glowed in the air, and gleamed back again out of the depths of the pool, which thus seemed to overflow with colored radiance from the rich reflection that was steeped in it. At first, as we have said, the garden was a solitude. Soon, however,—as Giovanni had half hoped, half feared, would be the case,—a figure appeared beneath the antique sculptured portal, and came down between the rows of plants, inhaling their various perfumes as if she were one of those beings of old classic fable that lived upon sweet odors. On again beholding Beatrice, the young man was even startled to perceive how much her beauty exceeded his recollection of it; so brilliant, so vivid, was its character, that she glowed amid the sunlight, and, as Giovanni whispered to himself, positively illuminated the more shadowy intervals of the garden path. Her face being now more revealed than on the former occasion, he was struck by its expression of simplicity and sweetness,—qualities that had not entered into his idea of her character, and which made him ask anew what manner of mortal she might be. Nor did he fail again to observe, or imagine, an analogy between the beautiful girl and the gorgeous shrub that hung its gemlike flowers over the fountain,—a resemblance which Beatrice seemed to have indulged a fantastic humor in heightening, both by the arrangement of her dress and the selection of its hues.

Approaching the shrub, she threw open her arms, as with a passionate ardor, and drew its branches into an intimate embrace—so intimate that her features were hidden in its leafy bosom and her glistening ringlets all intermingled with the flowers.

"Give me thy breath, my sister," exclaimed Beatrice; "for I am faint with common air. And give me this flower of thine, which I separate with gentlest fingers from the stem and place it close beside my heart."

With these words the beautiful daughter of Rappaccini plucked one of the richest blossoms of the shrub, and was about to fasten it in her bosom. But now, unless Giovanni's draughts of wine had bewildered his senses, a singular incident occurred. A small orange-colored reptile, of the lizard or chameleon species, chanced to be creeping along the path, just at the feet of Beatrice. It appeared to Giovanni,—but, at the distance from which he gazed, he could scarcely have seen anything so minute,—it appeared to him, however, that a drop or two of moisture from the broken stem of the flower descended upon the lizard's head. For an instant the reptile contorted itself violently, and then lay motionless in the sunshine. Beatrice observed this remarkable phenomenon, and crossed herself, sadly, but without surprise; nor did she therefore hesitate to arrange the fatal flower in her bosom. There it blushed, and almost glimmered with the dazzling effect of a precious stone, adding to her dress and aspect the one appropriate charm which nothing else in the world could have supplied. But Giovanni, out of the shadow of his window, bent forward and shrank back, and murmured and trembled.

"Am I awake? Have I my senses?" said he to himself. "What is this being? Beautiful shall I call her, or inexpressibly terrible?"

Beatrice now strayed carelessly through the garden, approaching closer beneath Giovanni's window, so that he was compelled to thrust his head quite out of its concealment in order to gratify the intense and painful curiosity which she excited. At this moment there came a beautiful insect over the garden wall; it had, perhaps, wandered through the city, and found no flowers or verdure among those antique haunts of men until the heavy perfumes of Dr. Rappaccini's shrubs had lured it from afar. Without alighting on the flowers, this winged brightness seemed to be attracted by Beatrice, and lingered in the air and fluttered about her head. Now, here it could not be but that Giovanni Guasconti's eyes deceived him. Be that as it might, he fancied that, while Beatrice was gazing at the insect with childish delight, it grew faint and fell at her feet; its bright wings shivered; it was dead—from no cause that he could discern, unless it were the atmosphere of her breath. Again Beatrice crossed herself and sighed heavily as she bent over the dead insect.

An impulsive movement of Giovanni drew her eyes to the window. There she beheld the beautiful head of the young man—rather a Grecian than an Italian head, with fair, regular features, and a glistening of gold among his ringlets—gazing down upon her like a being that hovered in mid air. Scarcely knowing what he did, Giovanni threw down the bouquet which he had hitherto held in his hand.

"Signora," said he, "there are pure and healthful flowers. Wear them for the sake of Giovanni Guasconti."

"Thanks, signor," replied Beatrice, with her rich voice, that came forth as it were like a gush of music, and with a mirthful expression half childish and half woman-like. "I accept your gift, and would fain recompense it with this precious purple flower; but if I toss it into the air it will not reach you. So Signor Guasconti must even content himself with my thanks."

She lifted the bouquet from the ground, and then, as if inwardly ashamed at having stepped aside from her maidenly reserve to respond to a stranger's greeting, passed swiftly homeward through the garden. But few as the moments were, it seemed to Giovanni, when she was on the point of vanishing beneath the sculptured portal, that his beautiful bouquet was already beginning to wither in her grasp. It was an idle thought; there could be no possibility of distinguishing a faded flower from a fresh one at so great a distance.

For many days after this incident the young man avoided the window that looked into Dr. Rappaccini's garden, as if something ugly and monstrous would have blasted his eyesight had he been betrayed into a glance. He felt conscious of having put himself, to a certain extent, within the influence of an unintelligible power by the communication which he had opened with Beatrice. The wisest course would have been, if his heart were in any real danger, to quit his lodgings and Padua itself at once; the next wiser, to have accustomed himself, as far as possible, to the familiar and daylight view of Beatrice—thus bringing her rigidly and systematically within the limits of ordinary experience. Least of all, while avoiding her sight, ought Giovanni to have remained so near this extraordinary being that the proximity and possibility even of intercourse should give a kind of substance and reality to the wild vagaries which his imagination ran riot continually in producing. Guasconti had not a deep heart—or, at all events, its depths were not sounded now; but he had a quick fancy, and an ardent southern temperament, which rose every instant to a higher fever pitch. Whether or no Beatrice possessed those terrible attributes, that fatal breath, the affinity with those so beautiful and deadly flowers which were indicated by what Giovanni had witnessed, she had at least instilled a fierce and subtle poison into his system. It was not love, although her rich beauty was a madness to him; nor horror, even while he fancied her spirit to be imbued with the same baneful essence that seemed to pervade her physical frame; but a wild offspring of both love and horror that had each parent in it, and burned like one and shivered like the other. Giovanni knew not what to dread; still less did he know what to hope; yet hope and dread kept a continual warfare in his breast, alternately vanquishing one another and starting up afresh to renew the contest. Blessed are all simple emotions, be they dark or bright! It is the lurid intermixture of the two that produces the illuminating blaze of the infernal regions.

Sometimes he endeavored to assuage the fever of his spirit by a rapid walk through the streets of Padua or beyond its gates: his footsteps kept time with the throbbings of his brain, so that the walk was apt to accelerate itself to a race. One day he found himself arrested; his arm was seized by a portly personage, who had turned back on recognizing the young man and expended much breath in overtaking him.

"Signor Giovanni! Stay, my young friend!" cried he. "Have you forgotten me! That might well be the case if I were as much altered as yourself."

It was Baglioni, whom Giovanni had avoided ever since their first meeting, from a doubt that the professor's sagacity would look too deeply into his secrets. Endeavoring to recover himself, he stared forth wildly from his inner world into the outer one and spoke like a man in a dream.

"Yes; I am Giovanni Guasconti. You are Professor Pietro Baglioni. Now let me pass!"

"Not yet, not yet, Signor Giovanni Guasconti," said the professor, smiling, but at the same time scrutinizing the youth with an earnest glance. "What! did I grow up side by side with your father? and shall his son pass me like a stranger in these old streets of Padua? Stand still, Signor Giovanni; for we must have a word or two before we part."

"Speedily, then, most worshipful professor, speedily," said Giovanni, with feverish impatience. "Does not your worship see that I am in haste?"

Now, while he was speaking there came a man in black along the street, stooping and moving feebly like a person in inferior health. His face was all overspread with a most sickly and sallow hue, but yet so pervaded with an expression of piercing and active intellect that an observer might easily have overlooked the merely physical attributes and have seen only this wonderful energy. As he passed, this person exchanged a cold and distant salutation with Baglioni, but fixed his eyes upon Giovanni with an intentness that seemed to bring out whatever was within him worthy of notice. Nevertheless, there was a peculiar quietness in the look, as if taking merely a speculative, not a human, interest in the young man.

"It is Dr. Rappaccini!" whispered the professor when the stranger had passed. "Has he ever seen your face before?"

"Not that I know," answered Giovanni, starting at the name.

"He *has* seen you! he must have seen you!" said Baglioni, hastily. "For some purpose or other, this man of science is making a study of you. I know that look of his! It is the same that coldly illuminates his face as he bends over a bird, a mouse, or a butterfly, which, in pursuance of some experiment, he has killed by the perfume of a flower; a look as deep as Nature itself, but without Nature's warmth of love. Signor Giovanni, I will stake my life upon it, you are the subject of one of Rappaccini's experiments!"

"Will you make a fool of me?" cried Giovanni, passionately. "*That*, signor professor, were an untoward experiment."

"Patience! patience!" replied the imperturbable professor. "I tell thee, my poor Giovanni, that Rappaccini has a scientific interest in thee. Thou has fallen into fearful hands! And the Signora Beatrice,—what part does she act in this mystery?"

But Guasconti, finding Baglioni's pertinacity intolerable, here broke away, and was gone before the professor could again seize his arm. He looked after the young man intently and shook his head.

"This must not be," said Baglioni to himself. "The youth is the son of my old friend, and shall not come to any harm from which the arcana of medical science can preserve him. Besides, it is too insufferable an impertinence in Rappaccini, thus to snatch the lad out of my own hands, as I may say, and make use of him for his infernal experiments. This daughter of his! It shall be looked to. Perchance, most learned Rappaccini, I may foil you where you little dream of it!"

Meanwhile Giovanni had pursued a circuitous route, and at length found himself at the door of his lodgings. As he crossed the threshold he was met by old Lisabetta, who smirked and smiled, and was evidently desirous to attract his attention; vainly, however, as the ebullition of his feelings had momentarily subsided into a cold and dull vacuity. He turned his eyes full upon the withered face that was puckering itself into a smile, but seemed to behold it not. The old dame, therefore, laid her grasp upon his cloak.

"Signor! signor!" whispered she, still with a smile over the whole breadth of her visage, so that it looked not unlike a grotesque carving in wood, darkened by centuries. "Listen, signor! There is a private entrance into the garden!"

"What do you say?" exclaimed Giovanni, turning quickly about, as if an inanimate thing should start into feverish life. "A private entrance into Dr. Rappaccini's garden?"

"Hush! hush! not so loud!" whispered Lisabetta, putting her hand over his mouth. "Yes; into the worshipful doctor's garden, where you may see all his fine shrubbery. Many a young man in Padua would give gold to be admitted among those flowers."

Giovanni put a piece of gold into her hand.

"Show me the way," said he.

A surmise, probably excited by his conversation with Baglioni, crossed his mind, that this interposition of old Lisabetta might perchance be connected with the intrigue, whatever were its nature, in which the professor seemed to suppose that Dr. Rappaccini was involving him. But such a suspicion, though it disturbed Giovanni, was inadequate to restrain him. The instant that he was aware of the possibility of approaching Beatrice, it seemed an absolute necessity of his existence to do so. It mattered not whether she were angel or demon; he was irrevocably within her sphere, and must obey the law that whirled him onward, in ever-lessening circles, towards a result which he did not attempt to foreshadow; and yet, strange to say, there came across him a sudden doubt whether this intense interest on his part were not delusory; whether it were really of so deep and positive a nature as to justify him in now thrusting himself into an incalculable position; whether it were not merely the fantasy of a young man's brain, only slightly or not at all connected with his heart.

He paused, hesitated, turned half about, but again went on. His withered guide led him along several obscure passages, and finally undid a door, through which, as it was opened, there came the sight and sound of rustling leaves, with the broken sunshine glimmering among them. Giovanni stepped forth, and, forcing himself through the entanglement of a shrub that wreathed its tendrils over the hidden entrance, stood beneath his own window in the open area of Dr. Rappaccini's garden.

How often is it the case that, when impossibilities have come to pass and dreams have condensed their misty substance into tangible realities, we find outselves calm, and even coldly self-possessed, amid circumstances which it would have been a delirium of joy or agony to anticipate! Fate delights to thwart us thus. Passion will choose his own time to rush upon the scene, and lingers sluggishly behind when an appropriate adjustment of events would seem to summon his appearance. So was it now with Giovanni. Day after day his pulses had throbbed with feverish blood at the improbable idea of an interview with Beatrice, and of standing with her, face to face, in this very garden, basking in the Oriental sunshine of her beauty, and snatching from her full gaze the mystery which he deemed the riddle of his own existence. But now there was a singular and untimely equanimity within his breast. He threw a glance around the garden to discover if Beatrice or her father were present, and, perceiving that he was alone, began a critical observation of the plants.

The aspect of one and all of them dissatisfied him; their gorgeousness seemed fierce, passionate, and even unnatural. There was hardly an individual shrub which a wanderer, straying by himself through a forest, would not have been startled to find growing wild, as if an unearthly face had glared at him out of the thicket. Several also would have shocked a delicate instinct by an appearance of artificialness indicating that there had been such commixture, and, as it were, adultery, of various vegetable species, that the production was no longer of God's making, but the monstrous offspring of man's depraved fancy, glowing with only an evil mockery of beauty. They were probably the result of experiment, which in one or two cases had succeeded in mingling plants individually lovely into a compound possessing the questionable and ominous character that distinguished the whole growth of the garden. In fine, Giovanni recognized but two or three plants in the collection, and those of a kind that he well knew to be poisonous. While busy with these contemplations he heard the rustling of a silken garment, and, turning, beheld Beatrice emerging from beneath the sculptured portal.

Giovanni had not considered with himself what should be his deportment; whether he should apologize for his intrusion into the garden, or assume that he was there with the privity at least, if not by the desire, of Dr. Rappaccini or his daughter; but Beatrice's manner placed him at his ease, though leaving him still in doubt by what agency he had gained admittance. She came lightly along the path and met him near the broken fountain. There was surprise in her face, but brightened by a simple and kind expression of pleasure.

"You are a connoisseur in flowers, signor," said Beatrice, with a smile, alluding to the bouquet which he had flung her from the window. "It is no marvel, therefore, if the sight of my father's rare collection has tempted you to take a nearer view. If he were here, he could tell you many strange and interesting facts as to the nature and habits of these shrubs; for he has spent a lifetime in such studies, and this garden is his world."

"And yourself, lady," observed Giovanni, "if fame says true,—you likewise are deeply skilled in the virtues indicated by these rich blossoms and these spicy perfumes. Would you deign to be my instructress, I should prove an apter scholar than if taught by Signor Rappaccini himself."

"Are there such idle rumors?" asked Beatrice, with the music of a pleasant laugh. "Do people say that I am skilled in my father's science of plants? What a jest is there! No; though I have grown up among these flowers, I know no more of them than their hues and perfume; and sometimes methinks I would fain rid myself of even that small knowledge. There are many flowers here, and those not the least brilliant, that shock and offend me when they meet my eye. But pray, signor, do not believe these stories about my science. Believe nothing of me save what you see with your own eyes."

"And must I believe all that I have seen with my own eyes?" asked Giovanni, pointedly, while the recollection of former scenes made him shrink. "No, signora; you demand too little of me. Bid me believe nothing save what comes from your own lips."

It would appear that Beatrice understood him. There came a deep flush to her cheek; but she looked full into Giovanni's eyes, and responded to his gaze of uneasy suspicion with a queenlike haughtiness.

"I do so bid you, signor," she replied. "Forget whatever you may have fancied in regard to me. If true to the outward senses, still it may be false in its essence; but the words of Beatrice Rappaccini's lips are true from the depths of the heart outward. Those you may believe."

A fervor glowed in her whole aspect and beamed upon Giovanni's consciousness like the light of truth itself; but while she spoke there was a fragrance in the atmosphere around her, rich and delightful, though evanescent, yet which the young man, from an indefinable reluctance, scarcely dared to draw into his lungs. It might be the odor of the flowers. Could it be Beatrice's breath which thus embalmed her words with a strange richness, as if by steeping them in her heart? A faintness passed like a shadow over Giovanni and flitted away; he seemed to gaze through the beautiful girl's eyes into her transparent soul, and felt no more doubt or fear.

The tinge of passion that had colored Beatrice's manner vanished; she became gay, and appeared to derive a pure delight from her communion with the youth not unlike what the maiden of a lonely island might have felt conversing with a voyager from the civilized world. Evidently her experience of life had been confined within the limits of that garden. She talked now about matters as simple as the daylight or sum-

mer clouds, and now asked questions in reference to the city, or Giovanni's distant home, his friends, his mother, and his sisters—questions
indicating such seclusion, and such lack of familiarity with modes and
forms, that Giovanni responded as if to an infant. Her spirit gushed out
before him like a fresh rill that was just catching its first glimpse of the
sunlight and wondering at the reflections of earth and sky which were
flung into its bosom. There came thoughts, too, from a deep source, and
fantasies of a gemlike brilliancy, as if diamonds and rubies sparkled upward among the bubbles of the fountain. Ever and anon there gleamed
across the young man's mind a sense of wonder that he should be walking side by side with the being who had so wrought upon his imagination,
whom he had idealized in such hues of terror, in whom he had positively witnessed such manifestations of dreadful attributes,—that he
should be conversing with Beatrice like a brother, and should find her
so human and so maidenlike. But such reflections were only momentary;
the effect of her character was too real not to make itself familiar at
once.

In this free intercourse they had strayed through the garden, and
now, after many turns among its avenues, were come to the shattered
fountain, beside which grew the magnificent shrub, with its treasury of
glowing blossoms. A fragrance was diffused from it which Giovanni recognized as identical with that which he had attributed to Beatrice's
breath, but incomparably more powerful. As her eyes fell upon it, Giovanni beheld her press her hand to her bosom as if her heart were
throbbing suddenly and painfully.

"For the first time in my life," murmured she, addressing the
shrub, "I had forgotten thee."

"I remember, Signora," said Giovanni, "that you once promised to
reward me with one of these living gems for the bouquet which I had
the happy boldness to fling to your feet. Permit me now to pluck it as a
memorial of this interview."

He made a step towards the shrub with extended hand; but Beatrice
darted forward, uttering a shriek that went through his heart like a
dagger. She caught his hand and drew it back with the whole force of
her slender figure. Giovanni felt her touch thrilling through his fibres.

"Touch it not!" exclaimed she, in a voice of agony. "Not for thy
life! It is fatal!"

Then, hiding her face, she fled from him and vanished beneath the
sculptured portal. As Giovanni followed her with his eyes, he beheld
the emaciated figure and pale intelligence of Dr. Rappaccini, who had
been watching the scene, he knew not how long, within the shadow of
the entrance.

No sooner was Guasconti alone in his chamber than the image of
Beatrice came back to his passionate musings, invested with all the witch-

ery that had been gathering around it ever since his first glimpse of her, and now likewise imbued with a tender warmth of girlish womanhood. She was human; her nature was endowed with all gentle and feminine qualities; she was worthiest to be worshipped; she was capable, surely, on her part, of the height and heroism of love. Those tokens which he had hitherto considered as proofs of a frightful peculiarity in her physical and moral system were now either forgotten, or, by the subtle sophistry of passion transmitted into a golden crown of enchantment, rendering Beatrice the more admirable by so much as she was the more unique. Whatever had looked ugly was now beautiful; or, if incapable of such a change, it stole away and hid itself among those shapeless half ideas which throng the dim region beyond the daylight of our perfect consciousness. Thus did he spend the night, nor fell asleep until the dawn had begun to awake the slumbering flowers in Dr. Rappaccini's garden, whither Giovanni's dreams doubtless led him. Up rose the sun in his due season, and, flinging his beams upon the young man's eyelids, awoke him to a sense of pain. When thoroughly aroused, he became sensible of a burning and tingling agony in his hand—in his right hand— the very hand which Beatrice had grasped in her own when he was on the point of plucking one of the gemlike flowers. On the back of that hand there was now a purple print like that of four small fingers, and the likeness of a slender thumb upon his wrist.

Oh, how stubbornly does love,—or even that cunning semblance of love which flourishes in the imagination, but strikes no depth of root into the heart,—how stubbornly does it hold its faith until the moment comes when it is doomed to vanish into thin mist! Giovanni wrapped a handkerchief about his hand and wondered what evil thing had stung him, and soon forgot his pain in a reverie of Beatrice.

After the first interview, a second was in the inevitable course of what we call fate. A third; a fourth; and a meeting with Beatrice in the garden was no longer an incident in Giovanni's daily life, but the whole space in which he might be said to live; for the anticipation and memory of that ecstatic hour made up the remainder. Nor was it otherwise with the daughter of Rappaccini. She watched for the youth's appearance, and flew to his side with confidence as unreserved as if they had been playmates from early infancy—as if they were such playmates still. If, by any unwonted chance, he failed to come at the appointed moment, she stood beneath the window and sent up the rich sweetness of her tones to float around him in his chamber and echo and reverberate throughout his heart: "Giovanni! Giovanni! Why tarriest thou? Come down!" And down he hastened into that Eden of poisonous flowers.

But, with all this intimate familiarity, there was still a reserve in Beatrice's demeanor, so rigidly and invariably sustained that the idea of infringing it scarcely occurred to his imagination. By all appreciable signs, they loved; they had looked love with eyes that conveyed the holy secret from the depths of one soul into the depths of the other, as if it were too sacred to be whispered by the way; they had even spoken love in those gushes of passion when their spirits darted forth in articulated breath like tongues of long-hidden flame; and yet there had been no seal of lips, no clasp of hands, nor any slightest caress such as love claims and hallows. He had never touched one of the gleaming ringlets of her hair; her garment—so marked was the physical barrier between them—had never been waved against him by a breeze. On the few occasions when Giovanni had seemed tempted to overstep the limit, Beatrice grew so sad, so stern, and withal wore such a look of desolate separation, shuddering at itself, that not a spoken word was requisite to repel him. At such times he was startled at the horrible suspicions that rose, monster-like, out of the caverns of his heart and stared him in the face; his love grew thin and faint as the morning mist, his doubts alone had substance. But, when Beatrice's face brightened again after the momentary shadow, she was transformed at once from the mysterious, questionable being whom he had watched with so much awe and horror; she was now the beautiful and unsophisticated girl whom he felt his spirit knew with a certainty beyond all other knowledge.

A considerable time had now passed since Giovanni's last meeting with Baglioni. One morning, however, he was disagreeably surprised by a visit from the professor, whom he had scarcely thought of for whole weeks, and would willingly have forgotten still longer. Given up as he had long been to a pervading excitement, he could tolerate no companions except upon condition of their perfect sympathy with his present state of feeling. Such sympathy was not to be expected from Professor Baglioni.

The visitor chatted carelessly for a few moments about the gossip of the city and the university, and then took up another topic.

"I have been reading an old classic author lately," said he, "and met with a story that strangely interested me. Possibly you may remember it. It is of an Indian prince, who sent a beautiful woman as a present to Alexander the Great. She was as lovely as the dawn and gorgeous as the sunset; but what especially distinguished her was a certain rich perfume in her breath—richer than a garden of Persian roses. Alexander, as was natural to a youthful conqueror, fell in love at first sight with this magnificent stranger; but a certain sage physician, happening to be present, discovered a terrible secret in regard to her."

"And what was that?" asked Giovanni, turning his eyes downward to avoid those of the professor.

"That this lovely woman," continued Baglioni, with emphasis, "had been nourished with poisons from her birth upward, until her whole nature was so imbued with them that she herself had become the deadliest poison in existence. Poison was her element of life. With that rich perfume of her breath she blasted the very air. Her love would have been poison—her embrace death. Is not this a marvellous tale?"

"A childish fable," answered Giovanni, nervously starting from his chair. "I marvel how your worship finds time to read such nonsense among your graver studies."

"By the by," said the professor, looking uneasily about him, "what singular fragrance is this in your apartment? Is it the perfume of your gloves? It is faint, but delicious; and yet, after all, by no means agreeable. Were I to breathe it long, methinks it would make me ill. It is like the breath of a flower; but I see no flowers in the chamber."

"Nor are there any," replied Giovanni, who had turned pale as the professor spoke; "nor, I think, is there any fragrance except in your worship's imagination. Odors, being a sort of element combined of the sensual and the spiritual, are apt to deceive us in this manner. The recollection of a perfume, the bare idea of it, may easily be mistaken for a present reality."

"Ay; but my sober imagination does not often play such tricks," said Baglioni; "and, were I to fancy any kind of odor, it would be that of some vile apothecary drug, wherewith my fingers are likely enough to be imbued. Our worshipful friend Rappaccini, as I have heard, tinctures his medicaments with odors richer than those of Araby. Doubtless, likewise, the fair and learned Signora Beatrice would minister to her patients with draughts as sweet as a maiden's breath; but woe to him that sips them!"

Giovanni's face evinced many contending emotions. The tone in which the professor alluded to the pure and lovely daughter of Rappaccini was a torture to his soul; and yet the intimation of a view of her character, opposite to his own, gave instantaneous distinctness to a thousand dim suspicions, which now grinned at him like so many demons. But he strove hard to quell them and to respond to Baglioni with a true lover's perfect faith.

"Signor professor," said he, "you were my father's friend; perchance, too, it is your purpose to act a friendly part towards his son. I would fain feel nothing towards you save respect and deference; but I pray you to observe, signor, that there is one subject on which we must not speak. You know not the Signora Beatrice. You cannot, therefore, estimate the wrong—the blasphemy, I may even say—that is offered to her character by a light or injurious word."

"Giovanni! my poor Giovanni!" answered the professor, with a calm expression of pity, "I know this wretched girl far better than yourself. You shall hear the truth in respect to the poisoner Rappaccini and his poisonous daughter; yes, poisonous as she is beautiful. Listen; for, even should you do violence to my gray hairs, it shall not silence me. That old fable of the Indian woman has become a truth by the deep and deadly science of Rappaccini and in the person of the lovely Beatrice."

Giovanni groaned and hid his face.

"Her father," continued Baglioni, "was not restrained by natural affection from offering up his child in this horrible manner as the victim of his insane zeal for science; for, let us do him justice, he is as true a man of science as ever distilled his own heart in an alembic. What, then, will be your fate? Beyond a doubt you are selected as the material of some new experiment. Perhaps the result is to be death; perhaps a fate more awful still. Rappaccini, with what he calls the interest of science before his eyes, will hesitate at nothing."

"It is a dream," muttered Giovanni to himself; "surely it is a dream."

"But," resumed the professor, "be of good cheer, son of my friend. It is not yet too late for the rescue. Possibly we may even succeed in bringing back this miserable child within the limits of ordinary nature, from which her father's madness has estranged her. Behold this little silver vase! It was wrought by the hands of the renowned Benvenuto Cellini, and is well worthy to be a love gift to the fairest dame in Italy. But its contents are invaluable. One little sip of this antidote would have rendered the most virulent poisons of the Borgias innocuous. Doubt not that it will be as efficacious against those of Rappaccini. Bestow the vase, and the precious liquid within it, on your Beatrice, and hopefully await the result."

Baglioni laid a small, exquisitely wrought silver vial on the table and withdrew, leaving what he had said to produce its effect upon the young man's mind.

"We will thwart Rappaccini yet," thought he, chuckling to himself, as he descended the stairs; "but, let us confess the truth of him, he is a wonderful man—a wonderful man indeed; a vile empiric, however, in his practice, and therefore not to be tolerated by those who respect the good old rules of the medical profession."

Throughout Giovanni's whole acquaintance with Beatrice, he had occasionally, as we have said, been haunted by dark surmises as to her character; yet so thoroughly had she made herself felt by him as a simple, natural, most affectionate, and guileless creature, that the image now held up by Professor Baglioni looked as strange and incredible as if it were not in accordance with his own original conception. True, there were ugly recollections connected with his first glimpses of the beautiful girl; he could not quite forget the bouquet that withered in her grasp, and the insect that perished amid the sunny air, by no ostensible agency save the fragrance of her breath. These incidents, however, dissolving in the pure light of her character, had no longer the efficacy of facts, but were acknowledged as mistaken fantasies, by whatever testimony of the senses they might appear to be substantiated. There is something truer and more real than what we can see with the eyes and touch with the finger. On such better evidence had Giovanni founded his confidence in Beatrice, though rather by the necessary force of her high attributes than by any deep and generous faith on his part. But now his spirit was incapable of sustaining itself at the height to which the early enthusiasm of passion had exalted it; he fell down, grovelling among earthly doubts, and defiled therewith the pure whiteness of Beatrice's image. Not that he gave her up; he did but distrust. He resolved to institute some decisive test that should satisfy him, once for all, whether there were those dreadful peculiarities in her physical nature which could not be supposed to exist without some corresponding monstrosity of soul. His eyes, gazing down afar, might have deceived him as to the lizard, the insect, and the flowers; but if he could witness, at the distance of a few paces, the sudden blight of one fresh and healthful flower in Beatrice's hand, there would be room for no further question. With this idea he hastened to the florist's and purchased a bouquet that was still gemmed with the morning dew-drops.

It was now the customary hour of his daily interview with Beatrice. Before descending into the garden, Giovanni failed not to look at his figure in the mirror,—a vanity to be expected in a beautiful young man, yet, as displaying itself at that troubled and feverish moment, the token of a certain shallowness of feeling and insincerity of character. He did gaze, however, and said to himself that his features had never before possessed so rich a grace, nor his eyes such vivacity, nor his cheeks so warm a hue of superabundant life.

"At least," thought he, "her poison has not yet insinuated itself into my system. I am no flower to perish in her grasp."

With that thought he turned his eyes on the bouquet, which he had never once laid aside from his hand. A thrill of indefinable horror shot through his frame on perceiving that those dewy flowers were already beginning to droop; they wore the aspect of things that had been fresh and lovely yesterday. Giovanni grew white as marble, and stood motionless before the mirror, staring at his own reflection there as at the likeness of something frightful. He remembered Baglioni's remark about the fragrance that seemed to pervade the chamber. It must have been the poison in his breath! Then he shuddered—shuddered at himself. Recovering from his stupor, he began to watch with curious eye a spider that was busily at work hanging its web from the antique cornice of the apartment, crossing and recrossing the artful system of interwoven lines —as vigorous and active a spider as ever dangled from an old ceiling. Giovanni bent towards the insect, and emitted a deep, long breath. The spider suddenly ceased its toil; the web vibrated with a tremor originating in the body of the small artisan. Again Giovanni sent forth a breath, deeper, longer, and imbued with a venomous feeling out of his heart: he knew not whether he were wicked, or only desperate. The spider made a convulsive gripe with his limbs and hung dead across the window.

"Accursed! accursed!" muttered Giovanni, addressing himself. "Hast thou grown so poisonous that this deadly insect perishes by thy breath?"

At that moment a rich, sweet voice came floating up from the garden.

"Giovanni! Giovanni! It is past the hour! Why tarriest thou? Come down!"

"Yes," muttered Giovanni again. "She is the only being whom my breath may not slay! Would that it might!"

He rushed down, and in an instant was standing before the bright and loving eyes of Beatrice. A moment ago his wrath and despair had been so fierce that he could have desired nothing so much as to wither her by a glance; but with her actual presence there came influences which had too real an existence to be at once shaken off: recollections of the delicate and benign power of her feminine nature, which had so often enveloped him in a religious calm; recollections of many a holy and passionate outgush of her heart, when the pure fountain had been unsealed from its depths and made visible in its transparency to his mental eye; recollections which, had Giovanni known how to estimate them, would have assured him that all this ugly mystery was but an earthly illusion, and that, whatever mist of evil might seem to have gathered over her, the real Beatrice was a heavenly angel. Incapable as he was of such high faith, still her presence had not utterly lost its magic. Giovanni's rage was quelled into an aspect of sullen insensibility. Beatrice, with a quick spiritual sense, immediately felt that there was a gulf of blackness between them which neither he nor she could pass. They walked on together, sad and silent, and came thus to the marble fountain and to its pool of water on the ground, in the midst of which grew the shrub that bore gem-like blossoms. Giovanni was affrighted at the eager enjoyment—the appetite, as it were—with which he found himself inhaling the fragrance of the flowers.

"Beatrice," asked he, abruptly, "whence came this shrub?"

"My father created it," answered she, with simplicity.

"Created it! created it!" repeated Giovanni. "What mean you, Beatrice?"

"He is a man fearfully acquainted with the secrets of Nature," replied Beatrice; "and, at the hour when I first drew breath, this plant sprang from the soil, the offspring of his science, of his intellect, while I was but his earthly child. Approach it not!" continued she, observing with terror that Giovanni was drawing nearer to the shrub. "It has qualities that you little dream of. But I, dearest Giovanni,—I grew up and blossomed with the plant and was nourished with its breath. It was my sister, and I loved it with a human affection; for, alas!—hast thou not suspected it?—there was an awful doom."

Here Giovanni frowned so darkly upon her that Beatrice paused and trembled. But her faith in his tenderness reassured her, and made her blush that she had doubted for an instant.

"There was an awful doom," she continued, "the effect of my father's fatal love of science, which estranged me from all society of my kind. Until Heaven sent thee, dearest Giovanni, oh, how lonely was thy poor Beatrice!"

"Was it a hard doom?" asked Giovanni, fixing his eyes upon her.

"Only of late have I known how hard it was," answered she, tenderly. "Oh, yes; but my heart was torpid, and therefore quiet."

Giovanni's rage broke forth from his sullen gloom like a lightning flash out of a dark cloud.

"Accursed one!" cried he, with venomous scorn and anger. "And, finding thy solitude wearisome, thou has severed me likewise from all the warmth of life and enticed me into thy region of unspeakable horror!"

"Giovanni!" exclaimed Beatrice, turning her large bright eyes upon his face. The force of his words had not found its way into her mind; she was merely thunderstruck.

"Yes, poisonous thing!" repeated Giovanni, beside himself with passion. "Thou has done it! Thou hast blasted me! Thou hast filled my veins with poison! Thou hast made me as hateful, as ugly, as loathsome and deadly a creature as thyself—a world's wonder of hideous monstrosity! Now, if our breath be happily as fatal to ourselves as to all others, let us join our lips in one kiss of unutterable hatred, and so die!"

"What has befallen me?" murmured Beatrice, with a low moan out of her heart. "Holy Virgin, pity me, a poor heartbroken child!"

"Thou,—dost thou pray?" cried Giovanni, still with the same fiendish scorn. "Thy very prayers, as they come from thy lips, taint the atmosphere with death. Yes, yes; let us pray! Let us to church and dip our fingers in the holy water at the portal! They that come after us will perish as by a pestilence! Let us sign crosses in the air! It will be scattering curses abroad in the likeness of holy symbols!"

"Giovanni," said Beatrice, calmly, for her grief was beyond passion, "why dost thou join thyself with me thus in those terrible words? I, it is true, am the horrible thing thou namest me. But thou,—what hast thou to do, save with one other shudder at my hideous misery to go forth out of the garden and mingle with thy race, and forget that there ever crawled on earth such a monster as poor Beatrice?"

"Dost thou pretend ignorance?" asked Giovanni, scowling upon her. "Behold! this power have I gained from the pure daughter of Rappaccini."

There was a swarm of summer insects flitting through the air in search of the food promised by the flower odors of the fatal garden. They circled round Giovanni's head, and were evidently attracted towards him by the same influence which had drawn them for an instant within the sphere of several of the shrubs. He sent forth a breath among them, and smiled bitterly at Beatrice as at least a score of the insects fell dead upon the ground.

"I see it! I see it!" shrieked Beatrice. "It is my father's fatal science! No, no, Giovanni; it was not I! Never! never! I dreamed only to love thee and be with thee a little time, and so to let thee pass away, leaving but thine image in mine heart; for, Giovanni, believe it, though my body be nourished with poison, my spirit is God's creature, and craves love as its daily food. But my father,—he has united us in this fearful sympathy. Yes; spurn me, tread upon me, kill me! Oh, what is death after such words as thine? But it was not I. Not for a world of bliss would I have done it."

Giovanni's passion had exhausted itself in its outburst from his lips. There now came across him a sense, mournful, and not without tenderness, of the intimate and peculiar relationship between Beatrice and himself. They stood, as it were, in an utter solitude, which would be made none the less solitary by the densest throng of human life. Ought not, then, the desert of humanity around them to press this insulated pair closer together? If they should be cruel to one another, who was there to be kind to them? Besides, thought Giovanni, might there not still be a hope of his returning within the limits of ordinary nature, and leading Beatrice, the redeemed Beatrice, by the hand? O, weak, and selfish, and unworthy spirit, that could dream of an earthly union and earthly happiness as possible, after such deep love had been so bitterly wronged as was Beatrice's love by Giovanni's blighting words! No, no; there could be no such hope. She must pass heavily, with that broken heart, across the borders of Time—she must bathe her hurts in some fount of paradise, and forget her grief in the light of immortality, and *there* be well.

But Giovanni did not know it.

"Dear Beatrice," said he, approaching her, while she shrank away as always at his approach, but now with a different impulse, "dearest Beatrice, our fate is not yet so desperate. Behold! there is a medicine, potent, as a wise physician has assured me, and almost divine in its efficacy. It is composed of ingredients the most opposite to those by which thy awful father has brought this calamity upon thee and me. It is distilled of blessed herbs. Shall we not quaff it together, and thus be purified from evil?"

"Give it me!" said Beatrice, extending her hand to receive the little silver vial which Giovanni took from his bosom. She added, with a peculiar emphasis, "I will drink; but do thou await the result."

She put Baglioni's antidote to her lips; and, at the same moment, the figure of Rappaccini emerged from the portal and came slowly towards the marble fountain. As he drew near, the pale man of science seemed to gaze with a triumphant expression at the beautiful youth and maiden, as might an artist who should spend his life in achieving a picture or a group of statuary and finally be satisfied with his success. He paused; his bent form grew erect with conscious power; he spread out his hands over them in the attitude of a father imploring a blessing upon his children; but those were the same hands that had thrown poison into the stream of their lives. Giovanni trembled. Beatrice shuddered nervously, and pressed her hand upon her heart.

"My daughter," said Rappaccini, "thou art no longer lonely in the world. Pluck one of those precious gems from thy sister shrub and bid thy bridegroom wear it in his bosom. It will not harm him now. My science and the sympathy between thee and him have so wrought within his system that he now stands from common men, as thou dost, daughter of my pride and triumph, from ordinary women. Pass on, then, through the world, most dear to one another and dreadful to all besides!"

"My father," said Beatrice, feebly,—and still as she spoke she kept her hand upon her heart,—"wherefore didst thou inflict this miserable doom upon thy child?"

"Miserable!" exclaimed Rappaccini. "What mean you, foolish girl? Dost thou deam it misery to be endowed with marvellous gifts against which no power nor strength could avail an enemy—misery, to be able to quell the mightiest with a breath—misery, to be as terrible as thou art beautiful? Wouldst thou, then, have preferred the condition of a weak woman, exposed to all evil and capable of none?"

"I would fain have been loved, not feared," murmured Beatrice, sinking down upon the ground. "But now it matters not. I am going, father, where the evil which thou hast striven to mingle with my being will pass away like a dream—like the fragrance of these poisonous flowers, which will no longer taint my breath among the flowers of Eden. Farewell, Giovanni! Thy words of hatred are like lead within my heart; but they, too, will fall away as I ascend. Oh, was there not, from the first, more poison in thy nature than in mine?"

To Beatrice,—so radically had her earthly part been wrought upon by Rappaccini's skill,—as poison had been life, so the powerful antidote was death; and thus the poor victim of man's ingenuity and of thwarted nature, and of the fatality that attends all such efforts of perverted wisdom, perished there, at the feet of her father and Giovanni. Just at that moment Professor Pietro Baglioni looked forth from the window, and called loudly, in a tone of triumph mixed with horror, to the thunderstricken man of science,—

"Rappaccini! Rappaccini! and is *this* the upshot of your experiment!"

Theme Questions

1. Giovanni's feelings toward Beatrice show ambivalence. Trace the course of their romance, place emphasis on his psychological responses. Consider whether his giving Beatrice the elixir was a pure act of love for her salvation.

2. "Was this garden, then, the Eden of the present world? And this man, [Rappaccini] with such a perception of harm in what his own hands caused to grow,—was he the Adam?" Develop your answer to Hawthorne's question by considering the tale of the original Garden of Eden and comparing it to Hawthorne's very special one.

3. Baglioni disapproves of Rappaccini because he "cares infinitely more for science than for mankind." Discuss the criticism in the context of the story. What modern application does the criticism have?

4. The story is an allegory filled with ambiguity and irony. What are some of the ironies and ambiguities? In what ways is the story applicable to contemporary life?

. . . also by Nathaniel Hawthorne   *The Tanglewood Tales*
The Scarlet Letter
The House of the Seven Gables
The Marble Faun

There is something of an affinity between the two ancient ballads, "Lord Randal" and "Barbara Allen." Both tell dramatic tales of betrayal between lovers, although one is from the male's point of view and the other is from the female's. Both deal with murder—one with a stated motive, the other with a concealed one. One perhaps shows repentance.

The reader might speculate how much poems like these have contributed to the myth that the female is the deadlier of the species.

Lord Randal

"O where hae ye been, Lord Randal, my son?
O where hae ye been, my handsome young man?"
"I hae been to the wild wood; mother, make my bed soon,
For I'm weary wi hunting, and fain wald lie down."

"Where gat ye your dinner, Lord Randal, my son?
Where gat ye your dinner, my handsome young man?"
"I dined wi my true-love; mother, make my bed soon,
For I'm weary wi hunting, and fain wald lie down."

"What gat ye to your dinner, Lord Randal, my son?
What gat ye to your dinner, my handsome young man?"
"I gat eels boiled in broo; mother, make my bed soon,
For I'm weary wi hunting, and fain wald lie down."

"What became of your bloodhounds, Lord Randal, my son?
What became of your bloodhounds, my handsome young man?"
"O they swelld and they died; mother, make my bed soon,
For I'm weary wi hunting, and fain wald lie down."

"O I fear ye are poisond, Lord Randal, my son!
O I fear ye are poisond, by handsome young man!"
"O yes! I am poisond; mother, make my bed soon,
For I'm sick at the heart, and I fain wald lie down."

Barbara Allan

It was in and about the Martinmas time,
　When the green leaves were a falling,
That Sir John Graeme, in the West Country,
　Fell in love with Barbara Allan.

He sent his man down through the town,
　To the place where she was dwelling:
"O haste and come to my master dear,
　Gin ye be Barbara Allan."

O hooly, hooly rose she up,
　To the place where he was lying,
And when she drew the curtain by,
　"Young man, I think you're dying."

"O it's I'm sick, and very, very sick,
　And 't is a' for Barbara Allan:"
"O the better for me ye's never be,
　Tho your heart's blood were a spilling.

"O dinna ye mind, young man," said she,
　"When ye was in the tavern a drinking,
That ye made the healths gae round and round,
　And slighted Barbara Allan?"

He turnd his face unto the wall,
　And death was with him dealing:
"Adieu, adieu, my dear friends all,
　And be kind to Barbara Allan."

And slowly, slowly raise she up,
　And slowly, slowly left him,
And sighing said, she coud not stay,
　Since death of life had reft him,

She had not gane a mile but twa,
　When she heard the dead-bell ringing,
And every jow that the dead-bell geid,
　It cry'd, Woe to Barbara Allan!

"O mother, mother, make my bed!
    O make it saft and narrow!
Since my love died for me to-day,
    I'll die for him to-morrow."

*Modern psychologists may mutter "necrophilia" but no matter—
there are few more romantic statements about love and death than
that of Poe in his "Annabel Lee." And more readers are bona fide
romantics than bona fide psychologists. . . .*

Annabelle Lee

Edgar Allan Poe

It was many and many a year ago,
　In a kingdom by the sea,
That a maiden there lived whom you may know
　By the name of Annabel Lee;—
And this maiden she lived with no other thought
　Than to love and be loved by me.

She was a child and *I* was a child,
　In this kingdom by the sea,
But we loved with a love that was more than love—
　I and my Annabel Lee—
With a love that the wingéd seraphs of Heaven
　Coveted her and me.

And this was the reason that, long ago,
　In this kingdom by the sea,
A wind blew out of a cloud by night
　Chilling my Annabel Lee;
So that her highborn kinsmen came
　And bore her away from me,
To shut her up in a sepulchre
　In this kingdom by the sea.

The angels, not half so happy in Heaven,
　Went envying her and me:—
Yes! that was the reason (as all men know,
　In this kingdom by the sea)
That the wind came out of the cloud, chilling
　And killing my Annabel Lee.

But our love it was stronger by far than the love
   Of those who were older than we—
   Of many far wiser than we—
And neither the angels in Heaven above
   Nor the demons down under the sea,
Can ever dissever my soul from the soul
   Of the beautiful Annabel Lee:—

For the moon never beams without bringing me dreams
   Of the beautiful Annabel Lee;
And the stars never rise but I see the bright eyes
   Of the beautiful Annabel Lee;
And so, all the night-tide, I lie down by the side
Of my darling, my darling, my life and my bride,
   In her sepulchre there by the sea—
   In her tomb by the side of the sea.

Inevitably, all members of the human race must deal with death, whether it comes from illness, accident, or the victim's own hand. Encounters with death, especially for the young, raise the eternal, "Why?" Suicide especially raises this question. So often moralistically viewed as the act of a coward, it is more often an act of total despair as in "Paul's Case."

Paul's Case

Willa Cather

It was Paul's afternoon to appear before the faculty of the Pittsburgh High School to account for his various misdemeanors. He had been suspended a week ago, and his father had called at the Principal's office and confessed his perplexity about his son. Paul entered the faculty room suave and smiling. His clothes were a trifle outgrown, and the tan velvet on the collar of his open overcoat was frayed and worn; but for all that there was something of the dandy about him, and he wore an opal pin in his neatly knotted black four-in-hand, and a red carnation in his buttonhole. This latter adornment the faculty somehow felt was not properly significant of the contrite spirit befitting a boy under the ban of suspension.

Paul was tall for his age and very thin, with high, cramped shoulders and a narrow chest. His eyes were remarkable for a certain hysterical brilliancy, and he continually used them in a conscious, theatrical sort of way, peculiarly offensive in a boy. The pupils were abnormally large, as though he were addicted to belladonna, but there was a glassy glitter about them which that drug does not produce.

When questioned by the Principal as to why he was there, Paul stated, politely enough, that he wanted to come back to school. This was a lie, but Paul was quite accustomed to lying; found it, indeed, indispensable for overcoming friction. His teachers were asked to state their respective charges against him, which they did with such a rancor and aggrievedness as evinced that this was not a usual case. Disorder and impertinence were among the offenses named, yet each of his instruc-

Reprinted from *Youth and the Bright Medusa*, by Willa Cather, courtesy of Alfred A. Knopf, Inc.

tors felt that it was scarcely possible to put into words the real cause of the trouble, which lay in a sort of hysterically defiant manner of the boy's; in the contempt which they all knew he felt for them, and which he seemingly made not the least effort to conceal. Once, when he had been making a synopsis of a paragraph at the blackboard, his English teacher had stepped to his side and attempted to guide his hand. Paul had started back with a shudder and thrust his hands violently behind him. The astonished woman could scarcely have been more hurt and embarrassed had he struck at her. The insult was so involuntary and definitely personal as to be unforgettable. In one way and another, he had made all his teachers, men and women alike, conscious of the same feeling of physical aversion. In one class he habitually sat with his hand shading his eyes; in another he always looked out of the window during the recitation; in another he made a running commentary on the lecture, with humorous intent.

His teachers felt this afternoon that his whole attitude was symbolized by his shrug and his flippantly red carnation flower, and they fell upon him without mercy, his English teacher leading the pack. He stood through it smiling, his pale lips parted over his white teeth. (His lips were continually twitching, and he had a habit of raising his eyebrows that was contemptuous and irritating to the last degree.) Older boys than Paul had broken down and shed tears under that ordeal, but his set smile did not once desert him, and his only sign of discomfort was the nervous trembling of the fingers that toyed with the buttons of his overcoat, and an occasional jerking of the other hand which held his hat. Paul was always smiling, always glancing about him, seeming to feel that people might be watching him and trying to detect something. This conscious expression, since it was as far as possible from boyish mirthfulness, was usually attributed to insolence or "smartness."

As the inquisition proceeded, one of his instructors repeated an impertinent remark of the boy's, and the Principal asked him whether he thought that a courteous speech to make to a woman. Paul shrugged his shoulders slightly and his eyebrows twitched.

"I don't know," he replied. "I didn't mean to be polite or impolite, either. I guess it's a sort of way I have, of saying things regardless."

The Principal asked him whether he didn't think that a way it would be well to get rid of. Paul grinned and said he guessed so. When he was told that he could go, he bowed gracefully and went out. His bow was like a repetition of the scandalous red carnation.

His teachers were in despair, and his drawing master voiced the feeling of them all when he declared there was something about the boy which none of them understood. He added: "I don't really believe that smile of his comes altogether from insolence; there's something sort of haunted about it. The boy is not strong, for one thing. There is something wrong about the fellow."

The drawing master had come to realize that, in looking at Paul, one saw only his white teeth and the forced animation of his eyes. One warm afternoon the boy had gone to sleep at his drawing board, and his master had noted with amazement what a white, blue-veined face it was; drawn and wrinkled like an old man's about the eyes, the lips twitching even in his sleep.

His teachers left the building dissatisfied and unhappy; humiliated to have felt so vindictive toward a mere boy, to have uttered this feeling in cutting terms, and to have set each other on, as it were, in the gruesome game of intemperate reproach. One of them remembered having seen a miserable street cat set at bay by a ring of tormentors.

As for Paul, he ran down the hill whistling the Soldiers' Chorus from *Faust*, looking wildly behind him now and then to see whether some of his teachers were not there to witness his light-heartedness. As it was now late in the afternoon and Paul was on duty that evening as usher at Carnegie Hall, he decided that he would not go home to supper.

When he reached the concert hall the doors were not yet open. It was chilly outside, and he decided to go up into the picture gallery—always deserted at this hour—where there were some of Raffelli's gay studies of Paris streets and an airy blue Venetian scene or two that always exhilarated him. He was delighted to find no one in the gallery but the old guard, who sat in the corner, a newspaper on his knee, a black patch over one eye and the other closed. Paul possessed himself of the place and walked confidently up and down, whistling under his breath. After a while he sat down before a blue Rico and lost himself. When he bethought him to look at his watch, it was after seven o'clock, and he rose with a start and ran downstairs, making a face at Augustus Caesar, peering out from the cast-room, and an evil gesture at the Venus of Milo as he passed her on the stairway.

When Paul reached the ushers' dressing-room half a dozen boys were there already, and he began excitedly to tumble into his uniform. It was one of the few that at all approached fitting, and Paul thought it very becoming—though he knew the tight, straight coat accentuated his narrow chest, about which he was exceedingly sensitive. He was always excited while he dressed, twanging all over to the tuning of the strings and the preliminary flourishes of the horns in the music-room; but tonight he seemed quite beside himself, and he teased and plagued the boys until, telling him that he was crazy, they put him down on the floor and sat on him.

Somewhat calmed by his suppression, Paul dashed out to the front of the house to seat the early comers. He was a model usher. Gracious and smiling he ran up and down the aisles. Nothing was too much trouble for him; he carried messages and brought programs as though it were his greatest pleasure in life, and all the people in his section thought him a charming boy, feeling that he remembered and admired them. As the house filled, he grew more and more vivacious and animated, and the color came to his cheeks and lips. It was very much as though this were a great reception and Paul were the host. Just as the musicians came out to take their places, his English teacher arrived with checks for the seats which a prominent manufacturer had taken for the season. She betrayed some embarrassment when she handed Paul the tickets, and a *hauteur* which subsequently made her feel very foolish. Paul was startled for a moment, and had the feeling of wanting to put her out; what business had she here among all these fine people and gay colors? He looked her over and decided that she was not appropriately dressed and must be a fool to sit downstairs in such togs. The tickets had probably been sent her out of kindness, he reflected, as he put down a seat for her, and she had about as much right to sit there as he had.

When the symphony began Paul sank into one of the rear seats with a long sigh of relief, and lost himself as he had done before the Rico. It was not that symphonies, as such, meant anything in particular to Paul, but the first sigh of the instruments seemed to free some hilarious spirit within him; something that struggled there like the Genius in the bottle found by the Arab fisherman. He felt a sudden zest of life; the lights danced before his eyes and the concert hall blazed into unimaginable splendor. When the soprano soloist came on, Paul forgot even the nastiness of his teacher's being there, and gave himself up to the peculiar intoxication such personages always had for him. The soloist chanced to be a German woman, by no means in her first youth, and the mother of many children; but she wore a satin gown and a tiara, and she had that indefinable air of achievement, that world-shine upon her, which always blinded Paul to any possible defects.

After a concert was over, Paul was often irritable and wretched until he got to sleep,—and tonight he was even more than usually restless. He had the feeling of not being able to let down; of its being impossible to give up this delicious excitement which was the only thing that could be called living at all. During the last number he withdrew and, after hastily changing his clothes in the dressing-room, slipped out to the side door where the singer's carriage stood. Here he began pacing rapidly up and down the walk, waiting to see her come out.

Over yonder the Schenley, in its vacant stretch, loomed big and square through the fine rain, the windows of its twelve stories glowing like those of a lighted cardboard house under a Christmas tree. All the actors and singers of any importance stayed there when they were in the city, and a number of the big manufacturers of the place lived there in the winter. Paul had often hung about the hotel, watching the people go in and out, longing to enter and leave schoolmasters and dull care behind him forever.

At last the singer came out, accompanied by the conductor, who helped her into her carriage and closed the door with a cordial *auf wiedersehen*,—which set Paul to wondering whether she were not an old sweetheart of his. Paul followed the carriage over to the hotel, walking so rapidly as not to be far from the entrance when the singer alighted and disappeared behind the swinging glass doors which were opened by a Negro in a tall hat and a long coat. In the moment that the door was ajar, it seemed to Paul that he, too, entered. He seemed to feel himself go after her up the steps, into the warm, lighted building, into an exotic, a tropical world of shiny, glistening surfaces and basking ease. He reflected upon the mysterious dishes that were brought into the dining-room, the green bottles in buckets of ice, as he had seen them in the supper party pictures of the Sunday supplement. A quick gust of wind brought the rain down with sudden vehemence, and Paul was startled to find that he was still outide in the slush of the gravel driveway; that his boots were letting in the water and his scanty overcoat was clinging wet about him; that the lights in front of the concert hall were out, and that the rain was driving in sheets between him and the orange glow of the windows above him. There it was, what he wanted—tangibly before him, like the fairy world of a Christmas pantomime; as the rain beat in his face, Paul wondered whether he were destined always to shiver in the black night outside, looking up at it.

He turned and walked reluctantly toward the car tracks. The end had to come some time; his father in his night-clothes at the top of the stairs, explanations that did not explain, hastily improvised fictions that were forever tripping him up, his upstairs room and its horrible yellow wall paper, the creaking bureau with the greasy plush collar-box, and over his painted wooden bed the pictures of George Washington and John Calvin, and the framed motto, "Feed my Lambs," which had been worked in red worsted by his mother, whom Paul could not remember.

Half an hour later, Paul alighted from the Negley Avenue car and went slowly down one of the side streets off the main thoroughfare. It was a highly respectable street, where all the houses were exactly alike, and where business men of moderate means begot and reared large families of children, all of whom went to Sabbath-school and learned the shorter catechism, and were interested in arithmetic; all of whom were as exactly alike as their homes, and of a piece with the monotony in which they lived. Paul never went up Cordelia Street without a shudder of loathing. His home was next the house of the Cumberland minister. He approached it tonight with the nerveless sense of defeat, the hopeless feeling of sinking back forever into ugliness and commonness that he had always had when he came home. The moment he turned into

Cordelia Street he felt the waters close above his head. After each of these orgies of living, he experienced all the physical depression which follows a debauch; the loathing of respectable beds, of common food, of a house permeated by kitchen odors; a shuddering repulsion for the flavorless, colorless mass of everyday existence; a morbid desire for cool things and soft lights and fresh flowers.

The nearer he approached the house, the more absolutely unequal Paul felt to the sight of it all; his ugly sleeping chamber; the cold bathroom with the grimy zinc tub, the cracked mirror, the dripping spiggots; his father, at the top of the stairs, his hairy legs sticking out from his nightshirt, his feet thrust into carpet slippers. He was so much later than usual that there would certainly be inquiries and reproaches. Paul stopped short before the door. He felt that he could not be accosted by his father tonight; that he could not toss again on that miserable bed. He would not go in. He would tell his father that he had no car fare, and it was raining so hard he had gone home with one of the boys and stayed all night.

Meanwhile, he was wet and cold. He went around to the back of the house and tried one of the basement windows, found it open, raised it cautiously, and scrambled down the cellar wall to the floor. There he stood, holding his breath, terrified by the noise he had made; but the floor above him was silent, and there was no creak on the stairs. He found a soap-box, and carried it over to the soft ring of light that streamed from the furnace door, and sat down. He was horribly afraid of rats, so he did not try to sleep, but sat looking distrustfully at the dark, still terrified lest he might have awakened his father. In such reactions, after one of the experiences which made days and nights out of the dreary blanks of the calendar, when his senses were deadened, Paul's head was always singularly clear. Suppose his father had heard him getting in at the window and had come down and shot him for a burglar? Then, again, suppose his father had come down, pistol in hand, and he had cried out in time to save himself, and his father had been horrified to think how nearly he had killed him? Then, again, suppose a day should come when his father would remember that night, and wish there had been no warning cry to stay his hand? With this last supposition Paul entertained himself until daybreak.

The following Sunday was fine; the sodden November chill was broken by the last flash of autumnal summer. In the morning Paul had to go to church and Sabbath-school, as always. On seasonable Sunday afternoons the burghers of Cordelia Street usually sat out on their front "stoops," and talked to their neighbors on the next stoop, or called to those across the street in neighborly fashion. The men sat placidly on gay cushions placed upon the steps that led down to the sidewalk, while the women, in their Sunday "waists," sat in rockers on the cramped porches, pretending to be greatly   at their ease. The children played in the streets; there were so many of them that the place resembled the recreation grounds of a kindergarten. The men on the steps—all in their shirt sleeves, their vests unbuttoned—sat with their legs well apart, their stomachs comfortably protruding, and talked of the prices of things, or told anecdotes of the sagacity of their various chiefs and overlords. They occasionally looked over the multitude of squabbling children, listened affectionately to their high-pitched, nasal voices, smiling to see their own proclivities reproduced in their offspring, and interspersed their legends of the iron kings with remarks about their sons' progress at school, their grades in arithmetic, and the amounts they had saved in their toy banks. On this last Sunday of November, Paul sat all the afternoon on the lowest step of his stoop, staring into the street, while his sisters, in their rockers, were talking to the minister's daughters next door how many shirtwaists they had made in the last week, and how many waffles someone had eaten at the last church supper. When the weather was warm, and his father was in a particularly jovial frame of mind, the girls made lemonade, which was always brought out in a red-glass pitcher, ornamented with forget-me-nots in blue enamel. This the girls thought very fine, and the neighbors joked about the suspicious color of the pitcher.

Today Paul's father, on the top step, was talking to a young man who shifted a restless baby from knee to knee. He happened to be the young man who was daily held up to Paul as a model, and after whom it was his father's dearest hope that he would pattern. This young man was of a ruddy complexion, with a compressed, red mouth, and faded, nearsighted eyes, over which he wore thick spectacles, with gold bows that curved about his ears. He was clerk to one of the magnates of a great steel corporation, and was looked upon in Cordelia Street as a young man with a future. There was a story that, some five years ago—he was now barely twenty-six—he had been a trifle "dissipated," but in order to curb his appetites and save the loss of time and strength that a sowing of wild oats might have entailed, he had taken his chief's advice, oft reiterated to his employees, and at twenty-one had married the first woman whom he could persuade to share his fortunes. She happened to be an angular school mistress, much older than he, who also wore thick glasses, and who had now borne him four children, all nearsighted, like herself.

The young man was relating how his chief, now cruising in the Mediterranean, kept in touch with all the details of the business, arranging his office hours on his yacht just as though he were at home, and "knocking off work enough to keep two stenographers busy." His father told, in turn, the plan his corporation was considering, of putting in an electric railway plant at Cairo. Paul snapped his teeth; he had an awful apprehension that they might spoil it all before he got there. Yet he rather liked to hear these legends of the iron kings, that were told and retold on Sundays and holidays; these stories of palaces in Venice, yachts on the Mediterranean, and high play at Monte Carlo appealed to his fancy, and he was interested in the triumphs of cash boys who had become famous, though he had no mind for the cash-boy stage.

After supper was over, and he had helped to dry the dishes, Paul nervously asked his father whether he could go to George's to get some help in his geometry, and still more nervously asked for car fare. This latter request he had to repeat, as his father, on principle, did not like to hear requests for money, whether much or little. He asked Paul whether he could not go to some boy who lived nearer, and told him that he ought not to leave his school work until Sunday; but he gave him the dime. He was not a poor man, but he had a worthy ambition to come up in the world. His only reason for allowing Paul to usher was that he thought a boy ought to be earning a little.

Paul bounded upstairs, scrubbed the greasy odor of the dishwater from his hands with the ill-smelling soap he hated, and then shook over his fingers a few drops of violet water from the bottle he kept hidden in his drawer. He left the house with his geometry conspicuously under his arm, and the moment he got out of Cordelia Street and boarded a downtown car, he shook off the lethargy of two deadening days, and began to live again.

The leading juvenile of the permanent stock company which played at one of the downtown theaters was an acquaintance of Paul's, and the boy had been invited to drop in at the Sunday night rehearsals whenever he could. For more than a year Paul had spent every available moment loitering about Charley Edwards's dressing-room. He had won a place among Edwards's following not only because the young actor, who could not afford to employ a dresser, often found him useful, but because he recognized in Paul something akin to what churchmen term "vocation."

It was at the theater and at Carnegie Hall that Paul really lived; the rest was but a sleep and a forgetting. This was Paul's fairy tale, and it had for him all the allurement of a secret love. The moment he inhaled the gassy, painty, dusty odor behind the scenes, he breathed like a prisoner set free, and felt within him the possibility of doing or saying splendid, brilliant things. The moment the cracked orchestra beat out the overture from *Martha*, or jerked at the serenade from *Rigoletto*, all stupid and ugly things slid from him, and his senses were deliciously, yet delicately fired.

Perhaps it was because, in Paul's world, the natural nearly always wore the guise of ugliness, that a certain element of artificiality seemed to him necessary in beauty. Perhaps it was because his experience of life elsewhere was so full of Sabbath-school picnics, petty economies, whole-some advice as to how to succeed in life, and the unescapable odors of cooking that he found this existence so alluring, these smartly-clad men and women so attractive, that he was so moved by these starry apple orchards that bloomed perennially under the limelight.

It would be difficult to put it strongly enough how convincingly the stage entrance of that theater was for Paul the actual portal of Ro-mance. Certainly none of the company ever suspected it, least of all Charley Edwards. It was very like the old stories that used to float about London of fabulously rich Jews, who had subterranean halls, with palms, and fountains, and soft lamps and richly apparelled women who never saw the disenchanting light of London day. So, in the midst of that smoke-palled city, enamored of figures and grimy toil, Paul had his secret temple, his wishing-carpet, his bit of blue-and-white Mediter-ranean shore bathed in perpetual sunshine.

Several of Paul's teachers had a theory that his imagination had been perverted by garish fiction; but the truth was, he scarcely ever read at all. The books at home were not such as would either tempt or corrupt a youthful mind, and as for reading the novels that some of his friends urged upon him—well, he got what he wanted much more quickly from music; any sort of music, from an orchestra to a barrel organ. He needed only the spark, the indescribable thrill that made his imagination master of his senses, and he could make plots and pictures enough of his own. It was equally true that he was not stage-struck—not, at any rate, in the usual acceptation of that expression. He had no desire to become an actor, any more than he had to become a musician. He felt no necessity to do any of these things; what he wanted was to see, to be in the atmosphere, float on the wave of it, to be carried out, blue league after blue league, away from everything.

After a night behind the scenes, Paul found the school-room more than ever repulsive; the bare floors and naked walls; the prosy men who never wore frock coats, or violets in their buttonholes; the women with their dull gowns, shrill voices, and pitiful seriousness about preposi-tions that govern the dative. He could not bear to have the other pupils think, for a moment, that he took these people seriously; he must convey to them that he considered it all trivial, and was there only by way of a joke, anyway. He had autograph pictures of all the members of the stock company which he showed his classmates, telling them the most in-credible stories of his familiarity with these people, of his acquaintance with the soloists who came to Carnegie Hall, his suppers with them and the flowers he sent them. When these stories lost their effect, and his audience grew listless, he would bid all the boys good-by, announcing that he was going to travel for a while; going to Naples, to California, to Egypt. Then, next Monday, he would slip back, conscious and nervously smiling; his sister was ill, and he would have to defer his voyage until spring.

Matters went steadily worse with Paul at school. In the itch to let his instructors know how heartily he despised them, and how thoroughly he was appreciated elsewhere, he mentioned once or twice that he had no time to fool with theorems; adding—with a twitch of the eyebrows and a touch of that nervous bravado which so perplexed them—that he was helping the people down at the stock company; they were old friends of his.

The upshot of the matter was, that the Principal went to Paul's father, and Paul was taken out of school and put to work. The manager at Carnegie Hall was told to get another usher in his stead; the door-keeper at the theater was warned not to admit him to the house; and Charley Edwards remorsefully promised the boy's father not to see him again.

The members of the stock company were vastly amused when some of Paul's stories reached them—especially the women. They were hard-working women, most of them supporting indolent husbands or broth-ers, and they laughed rather bitterly at having stirred the boy to such fervid and florid inventions. They agreed with the faculty and with his father, that Paul's was a bad case.

The east-bound train was plowing through a January snowstorm; the dull lawn was beginning to show gray when the engine whistled a mile out of Newark. Paul started up from the seat where he had lain curled in uneasy slumber, rubbed the breath-misted window glass with his hand, and peered out. The snow was whirling in curling eddies above the white bottom lands, and the drifts lay already deep in the fields and along the fences, while here and there the long dead grass and dried weed stalks protruded black above it. Lights shone from the scattered houses, and a gang of laborers who stood beside the track waved their lanterns.

Paul had slept very little, and he felt grimy and uncomfortable. He had made the all-night journey in a day coach because he was afraid if he took a Pullman he might be seen by some Pittsburgh business man who had noticed him in Denny & Carson's office. When the whistle woke him, he clutched quickly at his breast pocket, glancing about him with an un-certain smile. But the little, clay-bespattered Italians were still sleeping, the slatternly women across the aisle were in open-mouthed oblivion, and even the crumby, crying babies were for the nonce stilled. Paul settled back to struggle with his impatience as best he could.

When he arrived at the Jersey City station, he hurried through his breakfast, manifestly ill at ease and keeping a sharp eye about him. After he reached the Twenty-third Street station, he consulted a cabman, and had himself driven to a men's furnishing establishment which was just opening for the day. He spent upward to two hours there, buying with endless reconsidering and great care. His new street suit he put on in the fitting-room; the frock coat and dress clothes he had bundled into the cab with his new shirts. Then he drove to a hatter's and a shoe house. His next errand was at Tiffany's, where he selected silver-mounted brushes and a scarf-pin. He would not wait to have his silver marked, he said. Lastly, he stopped at a trunk shop on Broadway, and had his purchases packed into various traveling bags.

It was a little after one o'clock when he drove up to the Waldorf, and, after settling with the cabman, went into the office. He registered from Washington; said his mother and father had been abroad, and that he had come down to await the arrival of their steamer. He told his story plausibly and had no trouble, since he offered to pay for them in advance, in engaging his rooms; a sleeping-room, sitting room and bath.

Not once, but a hundred times Paul had planned this entry into New York. He had gone over every detail of it with Charley Edwards, and in his scrap book at home there were pages of description about New York hotels, cut from the Sunday papers.

When he was shown to his sitting room on the eighth floor, he saw at a glance that everything was as it should be; there was but one detail in his mental picture that the place did not realize, so he rang for the bell boy and sent him down for flowers. He moved about nervously until the boy returned, putting away his new linen and fingering it delightedly as he did so. When the flowers came, he put them hastily into water, and then tumbled into a hot bath. Presently he came out of his white bathroom, resplendent in his new silk underwear, and playing with the tassels of his red robe. The snow was whirling so fiercely outside his windows that he could scarcely see across the street; but within, the air was deliciously soft and fragrant. He put the violets and jonquils on the tabouret beside the couch, and threw himself down with a long sigh, covering himself with a Roman blanket. He was thoroughly tired; he had been in such haste, he had stood up to such a strain, covered so much ground in the last twenty-four hours, that he wanted to think how it had all come about. Lulled by the sound of the wind, the warm air, and the cool fragrance of the flowers, he sank into deep, drowsy retrospection.

It had been wonderfully simple; when they had shut him out of the theater and concert hall, when they had taken away his bone, the whole thing was virtually determined. The rest was a mere matter of opportunity. The only thing that at all surprised him was his own courage— for he realized well enough that he had always been tormented by fear, a sort of apprehensive dread that, of late years, as the meshes of the lies he had told closed about him, had been pulling the muscles of his body tighter and tighter. Until now, he could not remember a time when he had not been dreading something. Even when he was a little boy, it was always there—behind him, or before, or on either side. There had always been the shadowed corner, the dark place into which he dared not look, but from which something seemed always to be watching him—and Paul had done things that were not pretty to watch, he knew.

But now he had a curious sense of relief, as though he had at last thrown down the gauntlet to the thing in the corner.

Yet it was but a day since he had been sulking in the traces; but yesterday afternoon that he had been sent to the bank with Denny & Carson's deposit, as usual—but this time he was instructed to leave the book to be balanced. There was above two thousand dollars in checks, and nearly a thousand in the bank notes which he had taken from the book and quietly transferred to his pocket. At the bank he had made out a new deposit slip. His nerves had been steady enough to permit of his returning to the office, where he had finished his work and asked for a full day's holiday tomorrow, Saturday, giving a perfectly reasonable pretext. The bank book, he knew, would not be returned before Monday or Tuesday, and his father would be out of town for the next week. From the time he slipped the bank notes into his pocket until he boarded the night train for New York, he had not known a moment's hesitation.

How astonishingly easy it had all been; here he was, the thing done; and this time there would be no awakening, no figure at the top of the stairs. He watched the snowflakes whirling by his window until he fell asleep.

When he awoke, it was four o'clock in the afternoon. He bounded up with a start; one of his precious days gone already! He spent nearly an hour in dressing, watching every stage of his toilet carefully in the mirror. Everything was quite perfect; he was exactly the kind of boy he had always wanted to be.

When he went downstairs, Paul took a carriage and drove up Fifth Avenue toward the Park. The snow had somewhat abated; carriages and tradesmen's wagons were hurrying soundlessly to and fro in the winter twilight; boys in woolen mufflers were shoveling off the doorsteps; the avenue stages made fine spots of color against the white street. Here and there on the corners whole flower gardens blooming behind glass windows, against which the snow flakes stuck and melted; violets, roses, carnations, lilies of the valley—somehow vastly more lovely and alluring that they blossomed thus unnaturally in the snow. The Park itself was a wonderful stage winter-piece.

When he returned, the pause of the twilight had ceased, and the tune of the streets had changed. The snow was falling faster, lights streamed from the hotels that reared their many stories fearlessly up into the storm, defying the raging Atlantic winds. A long, black stream of carriages poured down the avenue, intersected here and there by other streams, tending horizontally. There were a score of cabs about the entrance of his hotel, and his driver had to wait. Boys in livery were running in and out of the awning stretched across the sidewalk, up and down the red velvet carpet laid from the door to the street. Above, about, within it all, was the rumble and roar, the hurry and toss of thousands of human beings as hot for pleasure as himself, and on every side of him towered the glaring affirmation of the omnipotence of wealth.

The boy set his teeth and drew his shoulders together in a spasm of realization; the plot of all dramas, the text of all romances, the nerve-stuff of all sensations was whirling about him like the snowflakes. He burnt like a faggot in a tempest.

When Paul came down to dinner, the music of the orchestra floated up the elevator shaft to greet him. As he stepped into the thronged corridor, he sank back into one of the chairs against the wall to get his breath. The lights, the chatter, the perfumes, the bewildering medley of color—he had, for a moment, the feeling of not being able to stand it. But only for a moment; these were his own people, he told himself. He went slowly about the corridors, through the writing-rooms, smoking-rooms, reception-rooms, as though he were exploring the chambers of an enchanted palace, built and peopled for him alone.

When he reached the dining room he sat down at a table near a window. The flowers, the white linen, the many-colored wine glasses, the gay toilettes of the women, the low popping of corks, the undu-lating repetitions of the *Blue Danube* from the orchestra, all flooded Paul's dream with bewildering radiance. When the roseate tinge of his champagne was added—that cold, precious, bubbling stuff that creamed and foamed in his glass—Paul wondered that there were honest men in the world at all. This was what all the world was fighting for, he re-flected; this was what all the struggle was about. He doubted the reality of his past. Had he ever known a place called Cordelia Street, a place where fagged-looking business men boarded the early car? Mere rivets in a machine they seemed to Paul,—sickening men, with combings of children's hair always hanging to their coats, and the smell of cooking in their clothes. Cordelia Street—Ah, that belonged to another time and country! Had he not always been thus, had he not sat here night after night, from as far back as he could remember, looking pensively over just such shimmering textures, and slowly twirling the stem of a glass like this one between his thumb and middle finger? He rather thought he had.

He was not in the least abashed or lonely. He had no especial desire to meet or to know any of these people; all he demanded was the right to look on and conjecture, to watch the pageant. The mere stage properties were all he contended for. Nor was he lonely later in the evening, in his loge at the Opera. He was entirely rid of his nervous misgivings, of his forced aggressiveness, of the imperative desire to show himself different from his surroundings. He felt now that his surroundings explained him. Nobody questioned the purple; he had only to wear it passively. He had only to glance down at his dress coat to reassure himself that here it would be impossible for anyone to humiliate him.

He found it hard to leave his beautiful sitting room to go to bed that night, and sat long watching the raging storm from his turret window. When he went to sleep, it was with the lights turned on in his bedroom; partly because of his old timidity, and partly so that, if he should wake in the night, there would be no wretched moment of doubt, no horrible suspicion of yellow wall paper, or of Washington and Calvin above his bed.

On Sunday morning the city was practically snow-bound. Paul breakfasted late, and in the afternoon he fell in with a wild San Francisco boy, a freshman at Yale, who said he had run down for a "little flyer" over Sunday. The young man offered to show Paul the night side of the town, and the two boys went off together after dinner, not returning to the hotel until seven o'clock the next morning. They had started out in the confiding warmth of a champagne friendship, but their parting in the elevator was singularly cool. The freshman pulled himself together to make his train, and Paul went to bed. He awoke at two o'clock in the afternoon, very thirsty and dizzy, and rang for ice water, coffee, and the Pittsburgh papers.

On the part of the hotel management, Paul excited no suspicion. There was this to be said for him, that he wore his spoils with dignity and in no way made himself conspicuous. His chief greediness lay in his ears and eyes, and his excesses were not offensive ones. His dearest pleasures were the gray winter twilights in his sitting room; his quiet enjoyment of his flowers, his clothes, his wide divan, his cigarette and his sense of power. He could not remember a time when he had felt so at peace with himself. The mere release from the necessity of petty lying, lying every day and every day, restored his self-respect. He had never lied for pleasure, even at school; but to make himself noticed and admired, to assert his difference from other Cordelia Street boys; and he felt a good deal more manly, more honest, even, now that he had no need for boastful pretensions, now that he could, as his actor friends used to say, "dress the part." It was characteristic that remorse did not occur to him. His golden days went by without a shadow, and he made each as perfect as he could.

On the eighth day after his arrival in New York, he found the whole affair exploited in the Pittsburgh papers, exploited with a wealth of detail which indicated that local news of a sensational nature was at a low ebb. The firm of Denny & Carson announced that the boy's father had refunded the full amount of his theft, and that they had no intention of prosecuting. The Cumberland minister had been interviewed, and expressed his hope of yet reclaiming the motherless lad, and Paul's Sabbath-school teacher declared that she would spare no effort to that end. The rumor had reached Pittsburgh that the boy had been seen in a New York hotel, and his father had gone East to find him and bring him home.

Paul had just come in to dress for dinner; he sank into a chair, weak in the knees, and clasped his head in his hands. It was to be worse than jail, even; the tepid waters of Cordelia Street were to close over him finally and forever. The gray monotony stretched before him in hopeless, unrelieved years; Sabbath-school, Young People's Meeting, the yellow-papered room, the damp dish-towels; it all rushed back upon him with sickening vividness. He had the old feeling that the orchestra had suddenly stopped, the sinking sensation that the play was over. The sweat broke out on his face, and he sprang to his feet, looked about him with his white, conscious smile, and winked at himself in the mirror. With something of the childish belief in miracles with which he had so often gone to class, all his lessons unlearned, Paul dressed and dashed whistling down the corridor to the elevator.

He had no sooner entered the dining room and caught the measure of the music, than his remembrance was lightened by his old elastic power of claiming the moment, mounting with it, and finding it all sufficient. The glare and glitter about him, the mere scenic accessories had again, and for the last time, their old potency. He would show himself that he was game, he would finish the thing splendidly. He doubted, more than ever, the existence of Cordelia Street, and for the first time he drank his wine recklessly. Was he not, after all, one of these fortunate beings? Was he not still himself, and in his own place? He drummed a nervous accompaniment to the music and looked about him, telling himself over and over that it had paid.

He reflected drowsily, to the swell of the violin and the chill sweetness of his wine, that he might have done it more wisely. He might have caught an outbound steamer and been well out of their clutches before now. But the other side of the world had seemed too far away and too uncertain then; he could not have waited for it; his need had been too sharp. If he had to choose over again, he would do the same thing tomorrow. He looked affectionately about the dining room, now gilded with a soft mist. Ah, it had paid indeed!

Paul was awakened next morning by a painful throbbing in his head and feet. He had thrown himself across the bed without undressing, and had slept with his shoes on. His limbs and hands were lead heavy, and his tongue and throat were parched. There came upon him one of those fateful attacks of clear-headedness that never occurred except when he was physically exhausted and his nerves hung loose. He lay still and closed his eyes and let the tide of realities wash over him.

His father was in New York; "stopping at some joint or other," he told himself. The memory of successive summers on the front stoop fell upon him like a weight of black water. He had not a hundred dollars left; and he knew now, more than ever, that money was everything, the wall that stood between all he loathed and all he wanted. The thing was winding itself up; he had thought of that on his first glorious day in New York, and had even provided a way to snap the thread. It lay on his dressing-table now; he had got it out last night when he came blindly up from dinner,—but the shiny metal hurt his eyes, and he disliked the look of it, anyway.

He rose and moved about with a painful effort, succumbing now and again to attacks of nausea. It was the old depression exaggerated; all the world had become Cordelia Street. Yet somehow he was not afraid of anything, was absolutely calm; perhaps because he had looked into the dark corner at last, and knew. It was bad enough, what he saw there; but somehow not so bad as his long fear of it had been. He saw everything clearly now. He had a feeling that he had made the best of it, that he had lived the sort of life he was meant to live, and for half an hour he sat staring at the revolver. But he told himself that was not the way, so he went downstairs and took a cab to the ferry.

When Paul arrived at Newark, he got off the train and took another cab, directing the driver to follow the Pennsylvania tracks out of the town. The snow lay heavy on the roadways and had drifted deep in the open fields. Only here and there the dead grass or dried weed stalks projected, singularly black, above it. Once well into the country, Paul dismissed the carriage and walked, floundering along the tracks, his mind a medley of irrelevant things. He seemed to hold in his brain an actual picture of everything he had seen that morning. He remembered every feature of both his drivers, the toothless old woman from whom he had bought the red flowers in his coat, the agent from whom he had got his ticket, and all of his fellow-passengers on the ferry. His mind, unable to cope with vital matters near at hand, worked feverishly and deftly at sorting and grouping these images. They made for him a part of the ugliness of the world, of the ache in his head, and the bitter burning on his tongue. He stopped and put a handful of snow into his mouth as he walked, but that, too, seemed hot. When he reached a little hillside, where the tracks ran through a cut some twenty feet below him, he stopped and sat down.

The carnations in his coat were drooping with the cold, he noticed; all their red glory over. It occurred to him that all the flowers he had seen in the show windows that first night must have gone the same way, long before this. It was only one splendid breath they had, in spite of their brave mockery at the winter outside the glass. It was a losing game in the end, it seemed, this revolt against the homilies by which the world is run. Paul took one of the blossoms carefully from his coat and scooped a little hole in the snow, where he covered it up. Then he dozed a while, from his weak condition, seeming insensible to the cold.

The sound of an approaching train woke him, and he started to his feet, remembering only his resolution, and afraid lest he should be too late. He stood watching the approaching locomotive, his teeth chattering, his lips drawn away from them in a frightened smile; once or twice he glanced nervously sidewise, as though he were being watched. When the right moment came, he jumped. As he fell, the folly of his haste occurred to him with merciless clearness, the vastness of what he had left undone. There flashed through his brain, clearer than ever before, the blue of Adriatic water, the yellow of Algerian sands.

He felt something strike his chest,—his body was being thrown swiftly through the air, on and on, immeasurably far and fast, while his limbs gently relaxed. Then, because the picture-making mechanism was crushed, the disturbing visions flashed into black, and Paul dropped back into the immense design of things.

Theme Questions

1. In the story, Miss Cather wrote, "Perhaps it was because, in Paul's world, the natural always nearly wore the guise of ugliness, that a certain element of artificiality seemed to him necessary in beauty." What evidence is there to show both the ugliness of the natural and the artificiality in beauty? How is this statement a key to understanding Paul's personality?

2. Contrast the attitude of Paul's teachers toward him with your attitude. Analyze their hostility and its possible reasons. In what ways are the teachers representative of society? What has Miss Cather done in the story to make the reader (you) more compassionate than the people in Paul's world?

3. Find the various instances of foreshadowing in the story that point to Paul's death, and describe each. Which are just part of his active imagination? Which relate directly to his suicide?

4. At the point of his greatest contentment, "Paul wondered," the author wrote, "that there were honest men in the world at all. This was what the whole world was fighting for, he reflected; this was

what all the struggle was about." Comment on Paul's materialism and on the general validity of his observation. What is the author's attitude toward the materialistic world?

5. Discuss Paul's suicide—his motivation, his despair, and the act itself. What is the significance of the last sentence of the story?

. . . also by Willa Cather   *My Antonia*
O Pioneers
Death Comes for the Archbishop

In the modern poetic idiom, the elegiac tone is often more bitter-sweet or ironic than eulogistic and romantic. Those who have seen the tragic fadeaways of has-beens will understand Housman's attitude in "To an Athlete Dying Young." His advice in "If it chance . . ." may not fall on too many receptive ears. Roethke's poem is a contrast to the others, in thought and in tone. Hardy dramatizes what most people would rather not be reminded of—the short memory of the living for the dead.

To an Athlete Dying Young

A. E. Housman

The time you won your town the race
We chaired you through the market-place;
Man and boy stood cheering by,
And home we brought you shoulder-high.

To-day, the road all runners come,
Shoulder-high we bring you home,
And set you at your threshold down,
Townsman of a stiller town.

Smart lad, to slip betimes away
From fields where glory does not stay
And early though the laurel grows
It withers quicker than the rose.

Eyes the shady night has shut
Cannot see the record cut,
And silence sounds no worse than cheers
After earth has stopped the ears:

Now you will not swell the rout
Of lads that wore their honours out,
Runners whom renown outran
And the name died before the man.

So set, before its echoes fade,
The fleet foot on the sill of shade,
And hold to the low lintel up
The still-defended challenge-cup.

And round that early-laurelled head
Will flock to gaze the strengthless dead,
And find unwithered on its curls
The garland briefer than a girl's.

If It Chance Your Eye Offend You

A. E. Housman

If it chance your eye offend you,
    Pluck it out, lad, and be sound;
'Twill hurt, but here are salves to friend you,
    And many a balsam grows on ground.

And if your hand or foot offend you,
    Cut it off, lad, and be whole;
But play the man, stand up and end you,
    When your sickness is your soul.

Elegy for Jane

(My Student, Thrown by a Horse)

Theodore Roethke

> I remember the neckcurls, limp and damp as tendrils;
> And her quick look, a sidelong pickerel smile;
> And how, once startled into talk, the light syllables leaped for her,
> And she balanced in the delight of her thought,
> A wren, happy, tail into the wind,
> Her song trembling the twigs and small branches.
> The shade sang with her;
> The leaves, their whispers turned to kissing;
> And the mould sang in the bleached valleys under the rose.
>
> Oh, when she was sad, she cast herself down into such a pure
>   depth,
> Even a father could not find her:
> Scraping her cheek against straw;
> Stirring the clearest water.
>
> My sparrow, you are not here,
> Waiting like a fern, making a spiny shadow.
>
> The sides of wet stones cannot console me,
> Nor the moss, wound with the last light.
>
> If only I could nudge you from this sleep,
> My maimed darling, my skittery pigeon.
> Over this damp grave I speak the words of my love:
> I, with no rights in this matter,
> Neither father nor lover.

"Ah, Are You Digging on My Grave?"

Thomas Hardy

"Ah, are you digging on my grave
   My loved one?—planting rue?"
—"No; yesterday he went to wed
One of the brightest wealth has bred.
'It cannot hurt her now,' he said,
   'That I should not be true.'"

"Then who is digging on my grave?
   My nearest dearest kin?"
—"Ah, no; they sit and think, 'What use!
What good will planting flowers produce?
No rendance of her mound can loose
   Her spirit from Death's gin.'"

"But some one digs upon my grave?
   My enemy?—prodding sly?"
—"Nay; when she heard you had passed the Gate
That shuts on all flesh soon or late,
She thought you no more worth her hate,
   And cares not where you lie."

"Then, who is digging on my grave?
   Say—since I have not guessed!"
—"O it is I, my mistress dear,
Your little dog, who still lives near,
And much I hope my movements here
   Have not disturbed your rest?"

"Ah, yes! *You* dig upon my grave . . .
   Why flashed it not on me
That one true heart was left behind!
What feeling do we ever find

To equal among human kind
  A dog's fidelity!"

"Mistress, I dug upon your grave
  To bury a bone, in case
I should be hungry near this spot
When passing on my daily trot.
I am sorry, but I quite forgot
  It was your resting-place."

Theme Questions

1. Characterize as much as possible the individuals being described. Which poem gives the fullest portrait? In what ways?

2. Differentiate the messages of these poems on death. Which is the most life affirming? Why?

If for some, death is a release, for others it is a termination to be avoided no matter how difficult or unpleasant life is. A few recognize the paradox that the sourness of life is also its sweetness. The sixteen-year-old narrator of "On Saturday Afternoon" thus evaluates the meaning of an experience he had when he was ten.

On Saturday Afternoon

Alan Sillitoe

I once saw a bloke try to kill himself. I'll never forget the day because I was sitting in the house one Saturday afternoon, feeling black and fed-up because everybody in the family had gone to the pictures, except me who'd for some reason been left out of it. 'Course, I didn't know then that I would soon see something you can never see in the same way on the pictures, a real bloke stringing himself up. I was only a kid at the time, so you can imagine how much I enjoyed it.

I've never known a family to look as black as our family when they're fed-up. I've seen the old man with his face so dark and full of murder because he ain't got no fags or was having to use saccharine to sweeten his tea or even for nothing at all, that I've backed out of the house in case he got up from his fireside chair and came for me. He just sits, almost on top of the fire, his oil-stained Sunday-joint maulers opened out in front of him and facing inwards to each other, his thick shoulders scrunched forward, and his dark brown eyes staring into the fire. Now and again he'd say a dirty word, for no reason at all, the worst word you can think of, and when he starts saying this you know it's time to clear out. If mam's in it gets worse than ever, because she says sharp to him: "What are yo' looking so bleddy black for?" as if it might be because of something she's done and before you know what's happening he's tipped up a tableful of pots and mam's gone out of the house crying. Dad hunches back over the fire and goes on swearing. All because of a packet of fags.

I once saw him broodier than I'd ever seen him, so that I thought he'd gone crackers in a quiet sort of way—until a fly flew to within a yard of him. Then his hand shot out, got it, and slung it crippled into the roaring fire. After that he cheered up a bit and mashed some tea.

Well, that's where the rest of us get our black looks from. It stands to reason we'd have them with a dad who carries on like that, don't it? Black looks run in the family. Some families have them and some don't. Our family has them right enough, and that's certain, so when we're fed-up we're really fed-up. Nobody knows why we get as fed-up as we do or why it gives us these black looks when we are. Some people get fed-up and don't look bad at all: they seem happy in a funny sort of way, as if they've just been set free from clink after being in there for something they didn't do, or come out of the pictures after sitting plugged for eight hours at a bad film, or just missed a bus they ran half a mile for and seen it was the wrong one just after they'd stopped running—but in our family it's murder for the others if one of us is fed-up. I've asked myself lots of times what it is, but I can never get any sort of answer even if I sit and think for hours, which I must admit I don't do, though it looks good when I say I do. But I sit and think for long enough, until mam says to me, at seeing me scrunched up over the fire like dad: "What are yo' looking so black for?" So I've just got to stop thinking about it in case I get really black and fed-up and go the same way as dad, tippling up a tableful of pots and all.

Mostly I suppose there's nothing to look so black for: though it's nobody's fault and you can't blame anyone for looking black because I'm sure it's summat in the blood. But on this Saturday afternoon I was looking so black that when dad came in from the bookie's he said to me: "What's up wi' yo'?"

"I feel badly," I fibbed. He'd have had a fit if I'd said I was only black because I hadn't gone to the pictures.

"Well have a wash," he told me.

"I don't want a wash," I said, and that was a fact.

"Well, get outside and get some fresh air then," he shouted.

I did as I was told, double-quick, because if ever dad goes as far as to tell me to get some fresh air I know it's time to get away from him. But outside the air wasn't so fresh, what with that bloody great bike factory bashing away at the yard-end. I didn't know where to go, so I walked up the yard a bit and sat down near somebody's back gate.

Then I saw this bloke who hadn't lived long in our yard. He was tall and thin and had a face like a parson except that he wore a flat cap and had a moustache that drooped, and looked as though he hadn't had a square meal for a year. I didn't think much o' this at the time: but I remember that as he turned in by the yard-end one of the nosy gossiping women who stood there every minute of the day except when she trudged to the pawnshop with her husband's bike or best suit, shouted to him: "What's that rope for, mate?"

He called back: "It's to 'ang messen wi', missis," and she cackled at his bloody good joke so loud you'd think she never heard such a good 'un, though the next day she cackled on the other side of her fat face.

He walked by me puffing a fag and carrying his coil of brand-new rope, and he had to step over me to get past. His boot nearly took my shoulder off, and when I told him to watch where he was going I don't think he heard me because he didn't even look round. Hardly anybody was about. All the kids were still at the pictures, and most of their mams and dads were downtown doing the shopping.

The bloke walked down the yard to his back door, and having nothing better to do because I hadn't gone to the pictures I followed him. You see, he left his back door open a bit, so I gave it a push and went in. I stood there, just watching him, sucking my thumb, the other hand in my pocket. I suppose he knew I was there, because his eyes were moving more natural now, but he didn't seem to mind. "What are yer going to do wi' that rope, mate?" I asked him.

"I'm going ter 'ang messen, lad," he told me, as though he'd done it a time or two already, and people had usually asked him questions like this beforehand.

"What for, mate?" He must have thought I was a nosy young bogger.

"Cause I want to, that's what for," he said, clearing all the pots off the table and pulling it to the middle of the room. Then he stood on it to fasten the rope to the light-fitting. The table creaked and didn't look very safe, but it did him for what he wanted.

"It wain't hold up, mate," I said to him, thinking how much better it was being here than sitting in the pictures and seeing the Jungle Jim serial. But he got nettled now and turned on me. "Mind yer own business."

I thought he was going to tell me to scram, but he didn't. He made ever such a fancy knot with that rope, as though he'd been a sailor or summat, and as he tied it he was whistling a fancy tune to himself. Then he got down from the table and pushed it back to the wall, and put a chair in its place. He wasn't looking black at all, nowhere near as black as anybody in our family when they're feeling fed-up. If ever he'd looked only half as black as our dad looked twice a week he'd have hanged himself years ago, I couldn't help thinking. But he was making a good job of that rope all right, as though he'd thought about it a lot anyway, and as though it was going to be the last thing he'd ever do. But I knew something he didn't know, because he wasn't standing where I was. I knew the rope wouldn't hold up, and I told him so, again.

"Shut yer gob," he said, but quiet like, "or I'll kick yer out."

I didn't want to miss it, so I said nothing. He took his cap off and put it on the dresser, then he took his coat off, and his scarf, and spread them out on the sofa. I wasn't a bit frightened, like I might be now at sixteen because it was interesting. And being only ten I'd never had a chance to see a bloke hang himself before. We got pally, the two of us, before he slipped the rope around his neck.

"Shut the door," he asked me, and I did as I was told. "Ye're a good lad for your age," he said to me while I sucked my thumb, and he felt in his pockets and pull out all that was inside, throwing the handful of bits and bobs on the table: fag-packet and peppermints, a pawnticket, an old comb, and a few coppers. He picked out a penny and gave it to me saying: "Now listen ter me, young 'un. I'm going to 'ang messen, and when I'm swinging I want you to gi' this chair a bloody good kick and push it away. All right?"

I nodded.

He put the rope around his neck, and then took it off like it was a tie that didn't fit. "What are yer going to do it for, mate?" I asked again.

"Because I'm fed-up," he said, looking very unhappy. "And because I want to. My missus left me, and I'm out o'work."

I didn't want to argue, because the way he said it, I knew he couldn't do anything else except hang himself. Also there was a funny look in his face: even when he talked to me I swear he couldn't see me. It was different to the black looks my old man puts on, and I suppose that's why my old man would never hang himself, worse luck, because he never gets a look into his clock like this bloke had. My old man's look stares at you, so that you have to back down and fly out of the house: this bloke's look looked through you, so that you could face it and know it wouldn't do you any harm. So I saw now that dad would never hang himself because he could never get the right sort of look into his face, in spite of the fact that he'd been out of work often enough. Maybe mam would have to leave him first, and then he might do it; but no—I shook my head—there wasn't much chance of that even though he did lead her a dog's life.

"Yer wain't forget to kick that chair away?" he reminded me, and I swung my head to say I wouldn't. So my eyes were popping and I watched every move he made. He stood on the chair and put the rope around his neck so that it fitted this time, still whistling his fancy tune. I wanted to get a better goz at the knot, because my pal was in the scouts, and would ask to know how it was done, and if I told him later he'd let me know what happened at the pictures in the Jungle Jim serial, so's I could have my cake and eat it as well, as mam says, tit for tat. But I thought I'd better not ask the bloke to tell me, and I stayed back in my corner. The last thing he did was take the wet dirty buttend from his lips and sling it into the empty firegrate, following it with his eyes to the black fireback where it landed—as if he was then going to mend a fault in the lighting like any electrician.

Suddenly his long legs wriggled and his feet tried to kick the chair, so I helped him as I'd promised I would and took a runner at it as if I was playing centre-forward for Notts Forest, and the chair went scooting back against the sofa, dragging his muffler to the floor as it tipped over. He swung for a bit, his arms chafing like he was a scarecrow flapping birds away, and he made a noise in his throat as if he'd just took a dose of salts and was trying to make them stay down.

Then there was another sound, and I looked up and saw a big crack come in the ceiling, like you see on the pictures when an earthquake's happening, and the bulb began circling round and round as though it was a space ship. I was just beginning to get dizzy when, thank Christ, he fell down with such a horrible thump on the floor that I thought he'd broken every bone he'd got. He kicked around for a bit, like a dog that's got colic bad. Then he lay still.

I didn't stay to look at him. "I told him that rope wouldn't hold up," I kept saying to myself as I went out of the house, tut-tutting because he hadn't done the job right, hands stuffed deep into my pockets and nearly crying at the balls-up he'd made of everything. I slammed his gate so hard with disappointment that it nearly dropped off its hinges.

Just as I was going back up the yard to get my tea at home, hoping the others had come back from the pictures so's I wouldn't have anything to keep on being black about, a copper passed me and headed for the bloke's door. He was striding quickly with his head bent forward, and I knew that somebody had narked. They must have seen him buy the rope and then tipped-off the cop. Or happen the old hen at the yard-end had finally caught on. Or perhaps he'd even told somebody himself, because I supposed that the bloke who'd strung himself up hadn't much known what he was doing, especially with the look I'd seen in his eyes. But that's how it is, I said to myself, as I followed the copper back to the bloke's house, a poor bloke can't even hang himself these days.

When I got back the copper was slitting the rope from his neck with a pen-knife, then he gave him a drink of water, and the bloke opened his peepers. I didn't like the copper, because he'd got a couple of my mates sent to approved school for pinching lead piping from lavatories.

"What did you want to hang yourself for?" he asked the bloke, trying to make him sit up. He could hardly talk, and one of his hands was bleeding from where the light-bulb had smashed. I knew that rope wouldn't hold up, but he hadn't listened to me. I'll never hang myself anyway, but if I want to I'll make sure I do it from a tree or something like that, not a light-fitting. "Well, what did you do it for?"

"Because I wanted to," the bloke croaked.

"You'll get five years for this," the copper told him. I'd crept back into the house and was sucking my thumb in the same corner.

"That's what yo' think," the bloke said, a normal frightened look in his eyes now. "I only wanted to hang myself."

"Well," the copper said, taking out his book, "it's against the law, you know."

"Nay," the bloke said, "it can't be. It's my life, ain't it?"

"You might think so," the copper said, "but it ain't."

He began to suck the blood from his hand. It was such a little scratch though that you couldn't see it. "That's the first thing I knew," he said.

"Well I'm telling you," the copper told him.

'Course, I didn't let on to the copper that I'd helped the bloke to hang himself. I wasn't born yesterday, nor the day before yesterday either.

"It's a fine thing if a bloke can't tek his own life," the bloke said, seeing he was in for it.

"Well he can't," the copper said, as if reading out of his book and enjoying it. "It ain't your life. And it's a crime to take your own life. It's killing yourself. It's suicide."

The bloke looked hard, as if everyone of the copper's words meant six-months cold. I felt sorry for him, and that's a fact, but if only he'd listened to what I'd said and not depended on that light-fitting. He should have done it from a tree, or something like that.

He went up the yard with the copper like a peaceful lamb, and we all thought that that was the end of that.

But a couple of days later the news was flashed through to us— even before it got to the Post because a woman in our yard worked at the hospital of an evening dishing grub out and tidying up. I heard her spilling it to somebody at the yard-end. "I'd never 'ave thought it. I thought he'd got that daft idea out of his head when they took him away. But no. Wonders'll never cease. Chucked 'issen from the hospital window when the copper who sat near his bed went off for a pee. Would you believe it? Dead? Not much 'e ain't."

He'd heaved himself at the glass, and fallen like a stone on to the road. In one way I was sorry he'd done it but another I was glad, because he's proved to the coppers and everybody whether it was his life or not all right. It was marvellous though, the way the brainless bastards had put him in a ward six floors up, which finished him off, proper, even better than a tree.

All of which will make me think twice about how black I sometimes feel. The black coal-bag locked inside you, and the black look it puts on your face, doesn't mean you're going to string yourself up or sling yourself under a double-decker or chuck yourself out of a window or cut your throat with a sardine-tin or put your head in the gas-oven or drop your rotten sack-bag of a body on to a railway line, because when you're feeling that black you can't even move from your chair. Anyhow, I know I'll never get so black as to hang myself, because hanging don't look very nice to me, and never will, the more I remember old what's-his-name swinging from the light-fitting.

More than anything else, I'm glad now I didn't go to the pictures that Saturday afternoon when I was feeling black and ready to do myself in. Because you know, I shan't ever kill myself. Trust me. I'll stay alive half-barmy till I'm a hundred and five, and go out screaming blue murder because I want to stay where I am.

Theme Questions

1. "He wasn't looking black at all, nowhere near as black as anybody in our family when they're feeling fed up. If ever he'd looked only half as black as our dad looked twice a week he'd have hanged himself years ago, I couldn't help thinking." This passage reflects the ten-year-old boy's thinking. What was his attitude then toward his father? toward the suicide? What were his views at the age of sixteen? What changes had come about?

2. Part of the humor of the story is its irony. Discuss the basic thematic irony and any other smaller ironies that contribute to the theme.

3. The working class setting is important. What details does Sillitoe include to show that the story takes place in a slum? Consider the expressed attitudes of some of the characters in addition to the physical surroundings.

4. In what ways does the story measure the value of living? What are the essential differences between people like the bloke and the narrator? After all, who does own a man's life?

5. Does the vernacular aid the story? in what ways? Is it a disadvantage? in what ways? What does the use of the vernacular reveal about language?

. . . **also by Alan Sillitoe**   *The Loneliness of the Long Distance Runner*
Saturday Night and Sunday Morning
The Ragman's Daughter and Other Stories

PART FOUR

PASSAGE

Boy with His Hair Cut Short

Muriel Rukeyser

Sunday shuts down on a twentieth-century evening.
The El passes. Twilight and bulb define
the brown room, the overstuffed plum sofa,
the boy, and the girl's thin hands above his head.
A neighbor radio sings stocks, news, serenade.

He sits at the table, head down, the young clear neck exposed,
watching the drugstore sign from the tail of his eyes;
tattoo, neon, until the eye blears, while his
solicitous tall sister, simple in blue, bending
behind him, cuts his hair with her cheap shears.

The arrow's electric red always reaches its mark,
successful neon! He coughs, impressed by that precision.
His child's forehead, forever protected by his cap,
is bleached against the lamplight as he turns head
and steadies to let the snippets drop.

Erasing the failure of weeks with level fingers,
she sleeks the fine hair, combing : "You'll look fine tomorrow!
You'll surely find something, they can't keep turning you down;
the finest gentleman's not so trim as you!" Smiling, he raises
the adolescent forehead wrinkling ironic now.

He sees his decent suit laid out, new-pressed,
his carfare on the shelf. He lets his head fall, meeting
her earnest hopeless look, seeing the sharp blades splitting,
the darkened room, the impersonal sign, her motion,
the blue vein, bright on her temple, pitifully beating.

For some youth, and ideally for all, there is a gradual passage from play to study to work. Too often, however, the adult world intrudes too soon with economic necessity and/or social necessity, such as war, and forces a premature passage. In the process, a youth sometimes becomes older than his elders.

In Arthur Miller's short play focusing on two memorable Mondays, something of the relationships between work and education is demonstrated.

A Memory of Two Mondays

Arthur Miller

The shipping room of a large auto-parts warehouse. This is but the back of a large loft in an industrial section of New York. The front of the loft, where we cannot see, is filled with office machinery, records, the telephone switchboard, and the counter where customers may come who do not order by letter or phone.

The two basic structures are the long packing table which curves upstage at the left, and the factory-type windows which reach from floor to ceiling and are encrusted with the hard dirt of years. These windows are the background and seem to surround the entire stage.

At the back, near the center, is a door to the toilet; on it are hooks for clothing. The back wall is bare but for a large spindle on which orders are impaled every morning and taken off and filled by the workers all day long. At center there is an ancient desk and chair. Downstage right is a small bench. Boxes, a roll of packing paper on the table, and general untidiness. This place is rarely swept.

The right and left walls are composed of corridor openings, a louverlike effect, leading out into the alleys which are lined with bins reaching to the ceiling. Downstage center there is a large cast-iron floor scale with weights and balance exposed.

The nature of the work is simple. The men take orders off the hook, go out into the bin-lined alleys, fill the orders, bring the merchandise back to the table, where Kenneth packs and addresses everything. The desk is used by Gus and/or Tom Kelly to figure postage or express rates on, to eat on, to lean on, or to hide things in. It is just home base, generally.

A warning: The place must seem dirty and unmanageably cha- otic, but since it is seen in this play with two separate visions it is also ro- mantic. It is a little world, a home to which, unbelievably perhaps, these people like to come every Monday morning, despite what they say.

It is a hot Monday morning in summer, just before nine.

The stage is empty for a moment; then Bert enters. He is eighteen. His trousers are worn at the knees but not unrespectable; he has rolled- up sleeves and is tieless. He carries a thick book, a large lunch in a brown paper bag, and a New York Times. *He stores the lunch behind the packing table, clears a place on the table, sits and opens the paper, reads.*

Enter Raymond Ryan, the manager. He wears a tie, white shirt, pressed pants, carries a clean towel, a tabloid, and in the other hand a sheaf of orders.

Raymond is forty, weighed down by responsibilities, afraid to be kind, quite able to be tough. He walks with the suggestion of a stoop.

He goes directly to a large hook set in the back wall and impales the orders. Bert sees him but, getting no greeting, returns to his paper. Pre- occupied, Raymond walks past Bert toward the toilet, then halts in thought, turns back to Bert.

RAYMOND   Tommy Kelly get in yet?

BERT   I haven't seen him, but I just got here myself. (*Raymond nods slightly, worried.*) He'll probably make it all right.

RAYMOND   What are you doing in so early?

BERT   I wanted to get a seat on the subway for once. Boy, it's nice to walk around in the streets before the crowds get out . . .

RAYMOND   (—*he has never paid much attention to Bert, is now curious, has time for it*)   How do you get time to read that paper?

BERT   Well, I've got an hour and ten minutes on the subway. I don't read it all, though. Just reading about Hitler.

RAYMOND   Who's that?

BERT   He took over the German government last week.

RAYMOND   (*nodding, uninterested*)   Listen, I want you to sweep up that excelsior laying around the freight elevator.

BERT   Okay. I had a lot of orders on Saturday, so I didn't get to it.

RAYMOND   (*self-consciously; thus almost in mockery*)   I hear you're go- ing to go to college. Is that true?

BERT   (*embarrassed*)   Oh, I don't know, Mr. Ryan. They may not even let me in, I got such bad marks in high school.

RAYMOND   *You* did?

BERT   Oh, yeah. I just played ball and fooled around, that's all. I think I wasn't listening, y'know?

RAYMOND   How much it going to cost you?

BERT   I guess about four, five hundred for the first year. So I'll be here a long time—if I ever do go. You ever go to college?

RAYMOND   (*shaking his head negatively*)   My kid brother went to pharmacy though. What are you going to take up?

BERT   I really don't know. You look through that catalogue—boy, you feel like taking it all, you know?

RAYMOND   This the same book you been reading?

BERT   Well, it's pretty long, and I fall asleep right after supper.

RAYMOND (*turning the book up*)   "War and Peace"?

BERT   Yeah, he's supposed to be a great writer.

RAYMOND   How long it take you to read a book like this?

BERT   Oh, probably about three, four months, I guess. It's hard on the subway, with all those Russian names.

RAYMOND (*putting the book down*)   What do you get out of a book like that?

BERT   Well, it's—it's literature.

RAYMOND (*nodding, mystified*)   Be sure to open those three crates of axles that came in Saturday, will you? (*He starts to go toward the toilet.*)

BERT   I'll get to it this morning.

RAYMOND   And let me know when you decide to leave. I'll have to get somebody—

BERT   Oh, that'll be another year. Don't worry about it. I've got to save it all up first. I'm probably just dreaming anyway.

RAYMOND   How much do you save?

BERT   About eleven or twelve a week.

RAYMOND   Out of fifteen?

BERT   Well, I don't buy much. And my mother gives me my lunch.

RAYMOND   Well, sweep up around the elevator, will you?

(*Raymond starts for the toilet as Agnes enters. She is a spinster in her late forties, always on the verge of laughter.*)

AGNES   Morning, Ray!

RAYMOND   Morning, Agnes. (*He exits into the toilet.*)

AGNES (*to Bert*)   Bet you wish you could go swimming, heh?

BERT   Boy, I wouldn't mind. It's starting to boil already.

AGNES   You ought to meet my nephew sometime, Bert. He's a wonderful swimmer. Really, you'd like him. He's very serious.

BERT   How old is he now?

AGNES   He's only thirteen, but he reads the *New York Times* too.

BERT   Yeah?

AGNES (*noticing the book*)   You still reading that book?

BERT (*embarrassed*)   Well, I only get time on the subway, Agnes—

AGNES   Don't let any of them kid you, Bert. You go ahead. You read the *New York Times* and all that. What happened today?

BERT   Hitler took over the German government.

AGNES   Oh, yes; my nephew knows about him. He loves civics. Last week one night he made a regular speech to all of us in the living room, and I realized that everything Roosevelt has done is absolutely illegal. Did you know that? Even my brother-in-law had to admit it, and he's a Democrat.

(*Enter Patricia on her way to the toilet. She is twenty-three, blankly pretty, dressed just a little too tightly. She is not quite sure who she is yet.*)

PATRICIA   Morning!

AGNES   Morning, Patricia! Where did you get that pin?

PATRICIA   It was given. (*She glances at Bert, who blushes.*)

AGNES   Oh, Patricia! Which one is he?

PATRICIA   Oh, somebody. (*She starts past for the toilet; Bert utters a warning "Ugh," and she remains.*)

AGNES (*—she tends to laugh constantly, softly*)   Did you go to the dance Saturday night?

PATRICIA (*fixing her clothing*)   Well, they're always ending up with six guys in the hospital at that dance, and like that, so we went bowling.

AGNES   Did he give you that pin?

PATRICIA   No, I had a date after him.

AGNES (*laughing, titillated*)   Pat!

PATRICIA   Well, I forgot all about him. So when I got home he was still sitting in front of the house in his car. I thought he was going to murder me. But isn't it an unusual pin? (*To Bert, who has moved off*) What are you always running away for?

BERT (*embarrassed*)   I was just getting ready to work, that's all.

(*Enter Gus. He is sixty-eight, a barrel-bellied man, totally bald, with a long, fierce, gray mustache that droops on the right side. He wears a bowler, and his pants are a little too short. He has a ready-made clip-on tie. He wears winter underwear all summer long, changes once a week. There is something neat and dusty about him—a rolling gait, bandy legs, a belly hard as a rock and full of beer. He speaks with a gruff Slavic accent.*)

PATRICIA   Oh, God, here's King Kong. (*She goes out up one of the corridors.*)

GUS (*calling after her halfheartedly—he is not completely sober, not bright yet*)   You let me get my hands on you I give you King Kong!

AGNES (*laughing*)   Oh, Gus, don't say those things!

GUS (*going for her*)   Aggie, you make me crazy for you!

AGNES (*laughing and running from him toward the toilet door*)   Gus!

GUS   Agnes, let's go Atlantic City!

(*Agnes starts to open the toilet door. Raymond emerges from it.*)

AGNES (*surprised by Raymond*)   Oh!

RAYMOND (*with plaintive anger*)   Gus! Why don't you cut it out, heh?

GUS   Oh, I'm sick and tired, Raymond.

(*Agnes goes into the toilet.*)

RAYMOND   How about getting all the orders shipped out by tonight, heh, Gus—for once?

GUS   What I did? I did something?

RAYMOND   Where's Jim?

GUS   How do I know where's Jim? Jim is my brother?

(*Jim enters, stiff. He is in his mid-seventies, wears bent eyeglasses; has a full head of hair; pads about with careful tread.*)

JIM (*dimly*)   Morning, Raymond. (*He walks as though he will fall forward. All watch as Jim aims his jacket for a hook, then, with a sudden motion, makes it. But he never really sways.*)

GUS   Attaboy, Jim! (*To Raymond*)   What you criticize Jim? Look at that!

JIM (*turning to Raymond with an apologetic smile*)   Morning, Raymond. Hot day today. (*He goes to the spike and takes orders off it.*)

RAYMOND   Now look, Gus, Mr. Eagle is probably going to come today, so let's have everything going good, huh?

GUS   You can take Mr. Eagle and you shove him!

(*Agnes enters from the toilet.*)

RAYMOND   What's the matter with you? I don't want that language around here any more. I'm not kidding, either. It's getting worse and worse, and we've got orders left over every night. Let's get straightened out here, will you? It's the same circus every Monday morning. (*He goes out.*)

AGNES   How's Lilly? Feeling better?

GUS   She's all the time sick, Agnes. I think she gonna die.

AGNES   Oh, don't say that. Pray to God, Gus.

GUS (*routinely*)   Aggie, come with me Atlantic City. (*He starts taking off his shirt.*)

AGNES (*going from him*)   Oh, how you smell!

GUS (*loudly*)   I stink, Aggie!

AGNES (*closing her ears, laughing*)   Oh, Gus, you're so terrible! (*She rushes out.*)

GUS (*laughs loudly, tauntingly, and turns to Bert*)   What are you doin'? It's nine o'clock.

BERT   Oh. (*He gets off the bench.*) I've got five to. Is your wife really sick? (*He gets an order from the hook.*)

GUS   You don't see Jim wait till nine o'clock! (*He goes to Jim, who is looking through the orders, and puts an arm around him.*) Goddam Raymond. You hear what he says to me?

JIM   Ssh, Gus, it's all right. Maybe better call Lilly.

GUS (*grasping Jim's arm*)   Wanna beer?

JIM (*trying to disengage himself*)   No, Gus, let's behave ourselves. Come on.

GUS (*looking around*)   Oh, boy. Oh, goddam boy. Monday morning. Ach.

JIM (*to Bert, as he starts out*)   Did you unpack those axles yet?

GUS (*taking the order out of Jim's hand*)   What are you doing with axles? Man your age! (*He gives Bert Jim's order.*) Bert! Here! You let him pick up heavy stuff I show you something! Go!

BERT   I always take Jim's heavy orders, Gus. (*He goes out with the orders.*)

GUS   Nice girls, heh, Jim?

JIM   Oh, darn nice. Darn nice girls, Gus.

GUS   I keep my promise, hah, Jim?

JIM   You did, Gus. I enjoyed myself. But maybe you ought to call up your wife. She might be wonderin' about you. You been missin' since Saturday, Gus.

GUS (*asking for a reminder*)   Where we was yesterday?

JIM   That's when we went to Staten Island, I think. On the ferry? Remember? With the girls? I think we was on a ferry. So it must've been to Staten Island. You better call her.

GUS   Ach—She don't hear nothing, Jim.

JIM   But if the phone rings, Gus, she'll know you're all right.

GUS   All right, I ring the phone. (*He goes and dials. Jim leaves with his orders.*)

(*Patricia enters.*)

PATRICIA   Morning, Kong!

GUS   Shatap.

(*She goes into the toilet as Gus listens on the phone. Then he roars*) Hallo! *Hallo!* Lilly! Gus! *Gus!* How you feel? *Gus!* Working! Ya! Ya! *Gus!* Oh, shatap! (*He hangs up the phone angrily, confused. Jim enters with a few small boxes, which he sets in a pile on the table.*)

JIM   You call her?

GUS   Oh, Jim, she don't hear nothing. (*He goes idly to the toilet, opens the door. Patricia screams within, and Gus stands there in the open doorway, screaming with her in parody, then lets the door shut.*)

(*Jim starts out, examining his order, a pencil in his hand, as Kenneth enters, lunch in hand. Kenneth is twenty-six, a strapping, fair-skinned man, with thinning hair, delicately shy, very strong. He has only recently come to the country.*)

JIM   Morning, Kenneth.

KENNETH   And how are you this fine exemplary morning, James?

JIM   Oh, comin' along. Goin' to be hot today. (*He goes out.*)

(*Kenneth hangs up his jacket and stores his lunch. Gus is standing in thought, picking his ear with a pencil.*)

KENNETH   Havin' yourself a thought this morning, Gus? (*Gus just looks at him, then goes back to his thought and his excavation.*) Gus, don't you think something could be done about the dust constantly fallin' through the air of this place? Don't you imagine a thing or two could be done about that?

GUS   Because it's dusty, that's why. (*He goes to the desk, sits.*)

KENNETH   That's what I was sayin'—it's dusty. Tommy Kelly get in?

GUS   No.

KENNETH   Oh, poor Tommy Kelly. (*Bert enters.*) Good morning to you, Bert. Have you finished your book yet?

BERT (*setting two heavy axles on the bench*)   Not yet, Kenneth.

KENNETH   (*his jacket in his hand*)   Well, don't lose heart. (*He orates*):

"Courage, brother! do not stumble
 Though thy path be dark as night;
 There's a star to guide the humble;
 Trust in God, and do the Right."

By Norman Macleod.

BERT (*with wonder, respect*)   How'd you learn all that poetry?

KENNETH (*hanging up his jacket*)   Why, in Ireland, Bert; there's all kinds of useless occupations in Ireland. "When lilacs last in the dooryard bloomed . . ."

GUS (*from the desk*)   What the hell you doin'? (*Bert goes to order hook.*)

KENNETH   Why, it's the poetry hour, Gus, don't you know that? This is the hour all men rise to thank God for the blue of the sky, the roundness of the everlasting globe, and the cheerful cleanliness of the subway system. And here we have some axles. Oh, Bert, I never thought I would end me life wrappin' brown paper around strange axles. (*He wraps*) And what's the latest in the *New York Times* this morning?

BERT (*looking through orders on the hook*)   Hitler took over the German government.

KENNETH   Oh, did he! Strange, isn't it, about the Germans? A great people they are for mustaches. You take Bismarck, now, or you take Frederick the Great, or even take Gus over here—

GUS   I'm no Heinie.

KENNETH   Why, I always thought you were, Gus. What are you, then?

GUS   American.

KENNETH   I know that, but what *are* you?

GUS   I fought in submarine.

KENNETH   Did you, now? An American submarine?

GUS   What the hell kind of submarine I fight in, Hungarian? (*He turns back to his desk.*)

KENNETH   Well, don't take offense, Gus. There's all kinds of submarines, y'know. (*Bert starts out, examining his order.*) How's this to be wrapped, Bert? Express?

BERT   I think that goes parcel post. It's for Skaneateles.

GUS (*erupting at his desk*)   Axles parcel post? You crazy? You know how much gonna cost axles parcel post?

BERT   That's right. I guess it goes express.

GUS   And you gonna go college? Barber college you gonna go!

BERT   Well, I forgot it was axles, Gus.

GUS (*muttering over his desk*)   Stupid.

KENNETH   I've never been to Skaneateles. Where would that be?

BERT   It's a little town upstate. It's supposed to be pretty there.

KENNETH   That a sweet thought? Sendin' these two grimy axles out into the green countryside? I spent yesterday in the park. What did you do, Bert? Go swimmin' again, I suppose?

GUS (*turning*)   You gonna talk all day?

BERT   We're working. (*He goes out. Kenneth wraps.*)

KENNETH   You're rubbin' that poor kid pretty hard, Gus; he's got other things on his mind than parcel post and—

GUS   What the hell I care what he got on his mind? Axles he gonna send parcel post! (*He returns to his work on the desk.*)

KENNETH (*wraps, then*)   Can you feel the heat rising in this building! If only some of it could be saved for the winter. (*Pause. He is wrapping.*) The fiery furnace. Nebuchadnezzar was the architect. (*Pause.*) What do you suppose would happen, Gus, if a man took it into his head to wash these windows? They'd snatch him off to the nuthouse, heh? (*Pause.*) I wonder if he's only kiddin'—Bert. About goin' to college someday.

GUS (*not turning from his desk*)   Barber College he gonna go.

KENNETH (*—he works, thinking*)   He must have a wealthy family. Still and all, he don't spend much. I suppose he's just got some strong idea in his mind. That's the thing, y'know. I often conceive them myself, but I'm all the time losin' them, though. It's the holdin' on— that's what does it. You can almost see it in him, y'know? He's holdin' on to somethin'. (*He shakes his head in wonder, then sings*):

> Oh, the heat of the summer,
> The cool of the fall,
> The lady went swimming
> With nothing at all.

Ah, that's a filthy song, isn't it! (*Pause. He wraps.*) Gus, you suppose Mr. Roosevelt'll be makin' it any better than it is? (*He sings*):

> The minstrel boy to the war has gone,
> In the ranks of death . . .

(*Patricia enters from the toilet.*)

PATRICIA   Was that an Irish song?

KENNETH (*shyly*)   All Irish here and none of yiz knows an Irish song.

PATRICIA   You have a terrific voice, Kenneth.

GUS (*to Patricia*)   Why don't you make date with him?

KENNETH (*stamping his foot*)   Oh, that's a nasty thing to say in front of a girl, Gus!

(*Gus rises.*)

PATRICIA (*backing away from Gus*)   Now don't start with me, kid, because—

(*Gus lunges for her. She turns to run, and he squeezes her buttocks mercilessly as she runs out and almost collides with Larry, who is entering. Larry is thirty-nine, a troubled but phlegmatic man, good-looking. He is carrying a container of coffee and a lighted cigarette. On the collision he spills a little coffee.*)

LARRY (*with a slight humor*)   Hey! Take it easy.

PATRICA (*quite suddenly all concerned for Larry, to Gus*)   Look what you did, you big horse!

(*Larry sets the coffee on the table.*)

LARRY   Jesus, Gus.

GUS   Tell her stop makin' all the men crazy! (*He returns to his desk.*)

PATRICIA   I'm sorry, Larry. (*She is alone, in effect, with Larry. Both of them wipe the spot on his shirt.*) Did you buy it?

LARRY (*embarrassed but courageous, as though inwardly flaunting his own fears*)   Yeah, I got it yesterday.

PATRICIA   Gee, I'd love to see it. You ever going to bring it to work?

LARRY (*—now he meets her eyes*)   I might. On a Saturday, maybe.

PATRICIA   'Cause I love those Auburns, y'know?

LARRY   Yeah, they got nice valves. Maybe I'll drive you home some night. For the ride.

PATRICIA (*—the news stuns her*)   Oh, boy! Well—I'll see ya. (*She goes.*)

GUS   You crazy? Buy Auburn?

LARRY (*with depth—a profound conclusion*)   I like the valves, Gus.

GUS   Yeah, but when you gonna go sell it who gonna buy an Auburn?

LARRY   Didn't you ever get to where you don't care about that? I *always* liked those valves, and I decided, that's all.

GUS   Yeah, but when you gonna go sell it—

LARRY   I don't care.

GUS   You don't care!

LARRY   I'm sick of dreaming about things. They've got the most beautifully laid-out valves in the country on that car, and I want it, that's all.

(*Kenneth is weighing a package on the scales.*)

GUS   Yeah, but when you gonna go sell it—

LARRY   I just don't care, Gus. Can't you understand that? (*He stares away, inhaling his cigarette.*)

KENNETH   (*stooped over, sliding the scale weights*)   There's a remarkable circumstance, Larry. Raymond's got twins, and now you with the triplets. And both in the same corporation. We ought to send that to the *Daily News* or something. I think they give you a dollar for an item like that.

(*Bert enters, puts goods on the table.*)

BERT   Gee, I'm getting hungry. Want a sandwich, Kenneth? (*He reaches behind the packing table for his lunch bag.*)

KENNETH   Thank you, Bert. I might take one later.

GUS   (*turning from the desk to Bert*)   Lunch you gonna eat nine o'clock?

BERT   I got up too early this morning. You want some?

KENNETH   He's only a growing boy, Gus—and by the way, if you care to bend down, Gus (*—indicating under the scale platform—*) there's more mice than ever under here.

GUS   (*without turning*)   Leave them mice alone.

KENNETH   Well, you're always complainin' the number of crayons I'm using, and I'm only tellin' you they're the ones is eatin' them up. (*He turns to Larry.*) It's a feast of crayons goin' on here every night, Larry.

(*Enter Jim with goods, padding along.*)

JIM   Goin' to be hot today, Gus.

GUS   Take easy, what you running for? (*Jim stops to light his cigar butt.*)

KENNETH   (*reading off the scale weights*)   Eighty-one pounds, Gus. For Skaneateles, in the green countryside of upper New York State.

GUS   What? What you want?

KENNETH   I want the express order—eighty-one pounds to Skaneateles, New York.

GUS   Then why don't you say that, goddam Irishman? You talk so much. When you gonna stop talkin'? (*He proceeds to make out the slip.*)

KENNETH   Oh, when I'm rich, Gus, I'll have very little more to say. (*Gus is busy making out the slip; Kenneth turns to Larry.*) No sign yet of Tommy Kelly in the place, Larry.

LARRY   What'd you, cut a hole in your shoe?

KENNETH   A breath of air for me little toe. I only paid a quarter for them, y'know; feller was sellin' them in Bryant Park. Slightly used, but they're a fine pair of shoes, you can see that.

LARRY   They look small for you.

KENNETH   They are at that. But you can't complain for a quarter, I guess.

GUS   Here.

(*Gus hands Kenneth an express slip, which Kenneth now proceeds to attach to the package on the table. Meanwhile Jim has been leafing through the orders on the hook and is now leaving with two in his hand.*)

KENNETH   How do you keep up your strength, Jim? I'm always exhausted. You never stop movin', do ya? (*Jim just shakes his head with a "Heh, heh."*) I bet it's because you never got married, eh?

JIM   No, I guess I done everything there is but that.

LARRY   How come you never did get married, Jim?

JIM   Well, I was out West so long, you know, Larry. Out West. (*He starts to go again.*)

KENNETH   Oh, don't they get married much out there?

JIM   Well, the cavalry was amongst the Indians most of the time.

BERT   How old are you now, Jim? No kidding.

KENNETH   I'll bet he's a hundred.

JIM   Me? No. I ain't no hunderd. I ain't near a hunderd. You don't have to be a hunderd to've fought the Indians. They was more Indians was fought than they tells in the schoolbooks, y'know. They was a hell of a lot of fightin' up to McKinley and all in there. I ain't no hunderd. (*He starts out.*)

KENNETH   Well, how old would you say you are, Jim?

JIM   Oh, I'm seventy-four, seventy-five, seventy-six—around in there. But I ain't no hunderd. (*He exits, and Kenneth sneezes.*)

BERT (*—he has put his lunch bag away and is about to leave*)   Boy, I was hungry!

KENNETH (*irritated*)   Larry, don't you suppose a word might be passed to Mr. Eagle about the dust? It's rainin' dust from the ceiling!

(*Bert goes out.*)

GUS   What the hell Mr. Eagle gonna do about the dust?

KENNETH   Why, he's supposed to be a brilliant man, isn't he? Dartmouth College graduate and all? I've been five and a half months in this country, and I never sneezed so much in my entire life before. My nose is all—

(*Enter Frank, the truckdriver, an impassive, burly man in his thirties.*)

FRANK   Anything for the West Bronx?

KENNETH   Nothin' yet, Frank. I've only started, though.

(*Jim enters with little boxes, which he adds to the pile on the bench.*)

FRANK   You got anything for West Bronx, Jim? I've got the truck on the elevator.

GUS   What's the hurry?

FRANK   I got the truck on the elevator.

GUS Well, take it off the elevator! You got one little box of bearings for the West Bronx. You can't go West Bronx with one little box.

FRANK Well, I gotta go.

GUS You got a little pussy in the West Bronx.

FRANK Yeah, I gotta make it before lunch.

JIM (*riffling through his orders*) I think I got something for the East Bronx.

FRANK No, West Bronx.

JIM (*removing one order from his batch*) How about Brooklyn?

FRANK What part? (*He takes Jim's order, reads the address, looks up, thinking.*)

JIM Didn't you have a girl around Williamsburg?

FRANK I'll have to make a call. I'll be right back.

GUS You gonna deliver only where you got a woman?

FRANK No, Gus, I go any place you tell me. But as long as I'm goin' someplace I might as well—you know. (*He starts out.*)

GUS You some truckdriver.

FRANK You said it, Gus. (*He goes out.*)

GUS Why don't you go with him sometime, Kenneth? Get yourself nice piece ding-a-ling—

KENNETH Oh, don't be nasty now, Gus. You're only tryin' to be nasty to taunt me.

(*Raymond enters.*)

RAYMOND Didn't Tommy Kelly get here?

GUS Don't worry for Tommy. Tommy going to be all right.

LARRY Can I see you a minute, Ray? (*He moves with Raymond over to the left.*)

RAYMOND Eagle's coming today, and if he sees him drunk again I don't know what I'm going to do.

LARRY Ray, I'd like you to ask Eagle something for me.

RAYMOND What?

LARRY I've got to have more money.

RAYMOND You and me both, boy.

LARRY No, I can't make it any more, Ray. I mean it. The car put me a hundred and thirty bucks in the hole. If one of the kids gets sick I'll be strapped.

RAYMOND Well, what'd you buy the car for?

LARRY I'm almost forty, Ray. What am I going to be careful for?

RAYMOND See, the problem is, Larry, if you go up, I'm only making thirty-eight myself, and I'm the manager, so it's two raises—

LARRY Ray, I hate to make it tough for you, but my wife is driving me nuts. Now—

(*Enter Jerry Maxwell and Willy Hogan, both twenty-three. Jerry has a black eye; both are slick dressers.*)

JERRY AND WILLY Morning. Morning, Gus.

RAYMOND   Aren't you late, fellas?

JERRY (*glancing at his gold wristwatch*)   I've got one minute to nine, Mr. Ryan.

WILLY   That's Hudson Tubes time, Mr. Ryan.

GUS   The stopwatch twins.

RAYMOND (*to Jerry*)   You got a black eye?

JERRY   Yeah, we went to a dance in Jersey City last night.

WILLY   Ran into a wise guy in Jersey City, Mr. Ryan.

JERRY (*with his taunting grin; he is very happy with himself*)   Tried to take his girl away from us.

RAYMOND   Well, get on the ball. Mr. Eagle's—

(*Enter Tom Kelly. Gus rises from the desk. Bert enters, stands still. Raymond and Larry stand watching. Kenneth stops wrapping. Tom is stiff; he moves in a dream to the chair Gus has left and sits rigidly. He is a slight, graying clerk in his late forties.*)

GUS (*to Raymond*)   Go 'way, go 'head.

(*Raymond comes up and around the desk to face Tom, who sits there, staring ahead, immobile, his hands in his lap.*)

RAYMOND   Tommy.

(*Jerry and Willy titter.*)

GUS (*to them*)   Shatap, goddam bums!

JERRY   Hey, don't call me—

GUS   Shatap goddamit I break you goddam head! (*He has an anxle in his hand, and Raymond and Larry are pulling his arm down. Jim enters and goes directly to him. All are crying, "Gus! Cut it out! Put it down!"*)

JERRY   What'd we do? What'd I say?

GUS   Watch out! Just watch out you make fun of this man! I break you head, both of you! (*Silence. He goes to Tom, who has not moved since arriving.*) Tommy. Tommy, you hear Gus? Tommy? (*Tom is transfixed.*)

RAYMOND   Mr. Eagle is coming today, Tommy.

GUS (*to all*)   Go 'head, go to work, go to work! (*They all move; Jerry and Willy go out.*)

RAYMOND   Can you hear me, Tom? Mr. Eagle is coming to look things over today, Tom.

JIM   Little shot of whisky might bring him to.

GUS   Bert! (*He reaches into his pocket.*)   Here, go downstairs bring a shot. Tell him for Tommy. (*He sees what is in his hand.*) I only got ten cents.

RAYMOND   Here. (*He reaches into his pocket as Jim, Kenneth, and Larry all reach into their own pockets.*)

BERT (*taking a coin from Raymond*)   Okay, I'll be right up. (*He hurries out.*)

RAYMOND   Well, this is it, Gus. I gave him his final warning.

GUS (*—he is worried*)   All right, go 'way, go 'way.
(*Agnes enters.*)
AGNES   Is he—?
RAYMOND   You heard me, Agnes. I told him on Saturday, didn't I?
(*He starts past her.*)
AGNES   But Ray, look how nice and clean he came in today. His hair is
all combed, and he's much neater.
RAYMOND   I did my best, Agnes. (*He goes out.*)
GUS (*staring into Tommy's dead eyes*)   Ach. He don't see nothin',
Agnes.
AGNES (*looking into Tommy's face*)   And he's supposed to be saving
for his daughter's confirmation dress! Oh, Tommy. I'd better cool his
face. (*She goes into the toilet.*)
KENNETH (*to Larry*)   Ah, you can't blame the poor feller; sixteen years
of his life in this place.
LARRY   You said it.
KENNETH   There's a good deal of monotony connected with the life,
isn't it?
LARRY   You ain't kiddin'.
KENNETH   Oh, there must be a terrible lot of Monday mornings in six-
teen years. And no philosophical idea at all, y'know, to pass the
time?
GUS (*to Kenneth*)   When you gonna shut up?
(*Agnes comes from the toilet with a wet cloth. They watch as she
washes Tom's face.*)
KENNETH   Larry, you suppose we could get these windows washed
sometime? I've often thought if we could see a bit of the sky now
and again it would help matters now and again.
LARRY   They've never been washed since I've been here.
KENNETH   I'd do it myself if I thought they wouldn't all be laughin' at
me for a greenhorn. (*He looks out through the open window, which
only opens out a few inches.*) With all this glass we might observe the
clouds and the various signs of approaching storms. And there might
even be a bird now and again.
AGNES   Look at that—he doesn't even move. And he's been trying so
hard! Nobody gives him credit, but he does try hard. (*To Larry*)
See how nice and clean he comes in now?
(*Jim enters, carrying parts.*)
JIM   Did you try blowing in his ear?
GUS   Blow in his ear?
JIM   Yeah, the Indians used to do that. Here, wait a minute. (*He
comes over, takes a deep breath, and blows into Tom's ear. A faint
smile begins to appear on Tom's face, but, as Jim runs out of breath,
it fades.*)

KENNETH   Well, I guess he's not an Indian.

JIM   That's the truth, y'know. Out West, whenever there'd be a drunken Indian, they used to blow in his ear.

(*Enter Bert, carefully carrying a shotglass of whisky.*)

GUS   Here, gimme that. (*He takes it.*)

BERT (*licking his fingers*)   Boy, that stuff is strong.

GUS   Tommy? (*He holds the glass in front of Tom's nose.*) Whisky. (*Tom doesn't move.*) Mr. Eagle is coming today, Tommy.

JIM   Leave it on the desk. He might wake up to it.

BERT   How's he manage to make it here, I wonder.

AGNES   Oh, he's awake. Somewhere inside, y'know. He just can't show it, somehow. It's not really like being drunk, even.

KENNETH   Well, it's pretty close, though, Agnes.

(*Agnes resumes wetting Tom's brow.*)

LARRY   Is that a fact, Jim, about blowing in a guy's ear?

JIM   Oh, sure. Indians always done that. (*He goes to the order hook, leafs through.*)

KENNETH   What did yiz all have against the Indians?

JIM   The Indians? Oh, we didn't have nothin' against the Indians. Just law and order, that's all. Talk about heat, though. It was so hot out there we—

(*Jim exits with an order as Frank enters.*)

FRANK   All right, I'll go to Brooklyn.

GUS   Where you running? I got nothing packed yet.

(*Enter Jerry, who puts goods on the table.*)

FRANK   Well, you beefed that I want to go Bronx, so I'm tellin' you now I'll go to Brooklyn.

GUS   You all fixed up in Brooklyn?

FRANK   Yeah, I just made a call.

AGNES (*laughing*)   Oh, you're all so terrible! (*She goes out.*)

JERRY   How you doin', Kenny? You gittin' any?

KENNETH   Is that all two fine young fellas like you is got on your minds?

JERRY   Yeah, that's all. What's on your mind?

(*Frank is loading himself with packages.*)

GUS (*of Tommy*)   What am I gonna do with him, Larry? The old man's comin'.

LARRY   Tell you the truth, Gus, I'm sick and tired of worrying about him, y'know? Let him take care of himself.

(*Gus goes to Larry, concerned, and they speak quietly.*)

GUS   What's the matter with you these days?

LARRY   Two years I'm asking for a lousy five-dollar raise. Meantime my brother's into me for fifty bucks for his wife's special shoes; my sister's got me for sixty-five to have her kid's teeth fixed. So I buy a

car, and they're all on my back—how'd I dare buy a car! Whose
money is it? Y'know, Gus? I mean—

GUS   Yeah, but an Auburn, Larry—

LARRY (*getting hot*)   I happen to like the valves! What's so unusual
about that?

(*Enter Willy and Jerry with goods.*)

WILLY (*to Jerry*)   Here! Ask Frank. (*To Frank*) Who played shortstop
for Pittsburgh in nineteen-twenty-four?

FRANK   Pittsburgh? Honus Wagner, wasn't it?

WILLY (*to Jerry*)   What I tell ya?

JERRY   How could it be Honus Wagner? Honus Wagner—

(*Raymond enters with a mechanic, and Willy and Jerry exit, arguing.
Frank goes out with his packages. Gus returns to his desk.*)

RAYMOND   Larry, you want to help this man? He's got a part here.

(*Larry simply turns, silent, with a hurt and angry look. The mechanic
goes to him, holds out the part; but Larry does not take it, merely in-
spects it, for it is greasy, as is the man.*)

RAYMOND (*going to the desk, where Gus is now seated at work beside
Tom Kelly*)   Did he move at all, Gus?

GUS   He's feeling much better, I can see. Go, go 'way, Raymond.

(*Raymond worriedly stands there.*)

LARRY (*to mechanic*)   Where you from?

MECHANIC   I'm mechanic over General Truck.

LARRY   What's that off?

MECHANIC (*as Bert stops to watch, and Kenneth stops packing to observe*)   That's the thing—I don't know. It's a very old coal truck, see,
and I thought it was a Mack, because it says Mack on the radiator,
see? But I went over to Mack, and they says there's no part like that
on any Mack in their whole history, see?

LARRY   Is there any name on the engine?

MECHANIC   I'm tellin' you; on the engine it says American-LaFrance—
must be a replacement engine.

LARRY   That's not off a LaFrance.

MECHANIC   I know! I went over to American-LaFrance, but they says
they never seen nothin' like that in their whole life since the year one.

(*Raymond joins them.*)

LARRY   What is it, off the manifold?

MECHANIC   Well, it ain't exactly off the manifold. It like sticks out,
see, except it don't stick out, it's like stuck in there—I mean it's like
in a little hole there on top of the head, except it ain't exactly a hole,
it's a thing that comes up in like a bump, see, and then it goes down.
Two days I'm walkin' the streets with this, my boss is goin' crazy.

LARRY   Well, go and find out what it is, and if we got it we'll sell it
to you.

RAYMOND   Don't you have any idea, Larry?

LARRY   I might, Ray, but I'am not getting paid for being an encyclopedia. There's ten thousand obsolete parts upstairs—it was never my
job to keep all that in my head. If the old man wants that service, let
him pay somebody to do it.

RAYMOND   Ah, Larry, the guy's here with the part.

LARRY   The guy is always here with the part, Ray. Let him hire somebody to take an inventory up there and see what it costs him.

RAYMOND   (*taking the part off the table*)   Well, I'll see what I can find
up there.

LARRY   You won't find it, Ray. Put it down. (*Raymond does, and
Larry, blinking with hurt, turns to the mechanic.*) What is that truck,
about nineteen-twenty-two?

MECHANIC   That truck? (*He shifts onto his right foot in thought.*)

LARRY   Nineteen-twenty?

MECHANIC   (*in a higher voice, shifting to the left foot*)   That truck?

LARRY   Well, it's at least nineteen-twenty, isn't it?

MECHANIC   Oh, it's at least. I brung over a couple a friend of mines,
and one of them is an old man and he says when he was a boy already that truck was an old truck, and he's an old, old man, that guy.
(*Larry takes the part now and sets it on the packing bench. Now
even Gus gets up to watch as he stares at the part. There is a hush.
Raymond goes out. Larry turns the part a little and stares at it again.
Now he sips his coffee.*) I understand this company's got a lot of old
parts from the olden days, heh?

LARRY   We may have one left, if it's what I think it is, but you'll have
to pay for it.

MECHANIC   Oh, I know; that's why my boss says try all the other places
first, because he says youse guys charge. But looks to me like we're
stuck.

LARRY   Bert. (*He stares in thought.*) Get the key to the third floor from
Miss Molloy. Go up there, and when you open the door you'll see
those Model-T mufflers stacked up.

BERT   Okay.

LARRY   You ever been up there?

BERT   No, but I always wanted to go.

LARRY   Well, go past the mufflers and you'll see a lot of bins going up
to the ceiling. They're full of Marmon valves and ignition stuff.

BERT   Yeah?

LARRY   Go past them, and you'll come to a little corridor, see?

BERT   Yeah?

LARRY   At the end of the corridor is a pile of crates—I think there's
some Maxwell differentials in there.

BERT   Yeah?

LARRY   Climb over the crates, but don't keep goin', see. Stand on top of the crates and turn right. Then bend down, and there's a bin— No, I tell you, get off the crates, and you can reach behind them, but to the right, and reach into that bin. There's a lot of Locomobile headnuts in there, but way back—you gotta stick your hand way in, see, and you'll find one of these.

BERT   Geez, Larry, how do you remember all that?

(*Agnes rushes in.*)

AGNES   Eagle's here! Eagle's here!

LARRY   (*to the mechanic*)   Go out front and wait at the counter, will ya? (*The mechanic nods and leaves. Larry indicates the glass on the desk.*) Better put that whisky away, Gus.

GUS (*alarmed now*)   What should we do with him?

(*Larry goes to Tom, peeved, and speaks in his ear.*)

LARRY   Tommy. Tommy!

AGNES   Larry, why don't you put him up on the third floor? He got a dozen warnings already. Eagle's disgusted—

GUS   Maybe he's sick. I never seen him like this.

(*Jim enters with goods.*)

JIM   Eagle's here.

LARRY   Let's try to walk him around. Come on.

(*Gus looks for a place to hide the whisky, then drinks it.*)

GUS   All right, Tommy, come on, get up. (*They hoist him up to his feet, then let him go. He starts to sag; they catch him.*) I don't think he feel so good.

LARRY   Come on, walk him. (*To Agnes*) Watch out for Eagle. (*She stands looking off and praying silently.*) Let's go, Tom. (*They try to walk Tom, but he doesn't lift his feet.*)

AGNES   (*trembling, watching Tommy*)   He's so kindhearted, y'see? That's his whole trouble—he's too kindhearted.

LARRY   (*angering, but restrained, shaking Tom*)   For God's sake, Tom, come on! Eagle's here! (*He shakes Tom more violently.*) Come on! What the hell is the matter with you, you want to lose your job? God-damit, you a baby or something?

AGNES   Sssh!

(*They all turn to the left. In the distance is heard the clacking of heel taps on a concrete floor.*)

GUS   Put him down. Larry! (*They seat Tom before the desk. Agnes swipes back his mussed hair. Gus sets his right hand on top of an invoice on the desk.*) Here, put him like he's writing. Where's my pencil? Who's got pencil? (*Larry, Kenneth, Agnes search themselves for a pencil.*)

KENNETH   Here's a crayon.

GUS   Goddam, who take my pencil! Bert! Where's that Bert! He always take my pencil!

(*Bert enters, carrying a heavy axle.*)

BERT   Hey, Eagle's here!

GUS   Goddam you, why you take my pencil?

BERT   I haven't got your pencil. This is mine.

(*Gus grabs the pencil out of Bert's shirt pocket and sticks it upright into Tom's hand. They have set him up to look as if he is writing. They step away. Tom starts sagging toward one side.*)

AGNES (*in a loud whisper*)   Here he comes!

(*She goes to the order spike and pretends she is examining it. Larry meanwhile rushes to Tom, sets him upright, then walks away, pretending to busy himself. But Tom starts falling off the chair again, and Bert rushes and props him up.*)

(*The sound of the heel taps is on us now, and Bert starts talking to Tom, meantime supporting him with one hand on his shoulder.*)

BERT (*overloudly*)   Tommy, the reason I ask, see, is because on Friday I filled an order for the same amount of coils for Scranton, see, and it just seems they wouldn't be ordering the same exact amount again.

(*During his speech Eagle has entered—a good-looking man in his late forties, wearing palm beach trousers, a shirt and tie, sleeves neatly folded up, a new towel over one arm. He walks across the shipping room, not exactly looking at anyone, but clearly observing everything. He goes into the toilet, past Agnes, who turns.*)

AGNES   Good morning, Mr. Eagle.

EAGLE (*nodding*)   Morning. (*He goes into the toilet.*)

KENNETH (*indicating the toilet*)   Keep it up, keep it up now!

BERT (*loudly*)   Ah—another thing that's bothering me, Tommy, is those rear-end gears for Riverhead. I can't find any invoice for Riverhead. I can't find any invoice for gears to Riverhead. (*He is getting desperate, looks to the others, but they only urge him on.*) So what happened to the invoice? That's the thing we're all wondering about, Tommy. What happened to that invoice? You see, Tom? That invoice—it was blue, I remember, blue with a little red around the edges—

KENNETH (*loudly*)   That's right there, Bert, it was a blue invoice—and it had numbers on it—

(*Suddenly Tom stands, swaying a little, blinking. There is a moment's silence.*)

TOM   No, no, Glen Wright was shortstop for Pittsburgh, not Honus Wagner.

(*Eagle emerges from the toilet. Bert goes to the order spike.*)

LARRY   Morning, sir. (*He goes out.*)

TOM (*half bewildered, shifting from foot to foot*) Who was talking about Pittsburgh? (*He turns about and almost collides with Eagle.*) Morning, Mr. Eagle.

EAGLE (—*as he passes Tom he lets his look linger on his face*) Morning, Kelly.

(*Eagle crosses the shipping room and goes out. Agnes, Kenneth, and Gus wait an instant. Jim enters, sees Tom is up.*)

JIM Attaboy, Tommy, knew you'd make it.

TOM Glen Wright was shortstop. Who asked about that?

GUS (*nodding sternly his approbation to Bert*) Very good, Bert, you done good.

BERT (*wiping his forehead*) Boy!

TOM Who was talking about Pittsburgh? (*Agnes is heard weeping. They turn.*) Agnes? (*He goes to her.*) What's the matter, Ag?

AGNES Oh, Tommy, why do you do that?

PATRICIA (*calling from offstage left*) Aggie? Your switchboard's ringing.

AGNES Oh, Tommy! (*Weeping, she hurries out.*)

TOM (*to the others*) What happened? What is she cryin' for?

GUS (*indicating the desk*) Why don't you go to work, Tommy? You got lotta parcel post this morning.

(*Tom always has a defensive smile. He shifts from foot to foot as he talks, as though he were always standing on a hot stove. He turns to the desk, sees Kenneth. He wants to normalize everything.*)

TOM Kenny! I didn't even see ya!

KENNETH Morning, Tommy. Good to see you up and about.

TOM (*with a put-on brogue*) Jasus, me bye, y'r hair is fallin' like the dew of the evenin'.

KENNETH (*self-consciously wiping his hair*) Oh, Tommy, now—

TOM Kenny, bye, y'r gittin' an awful long face to wash!

KENNETH (*gently cuffing him*) Oh, now, stop that talk!

TOM (*backing toward his desk*) Why, ya donkey, ya. I bet they had to back you off the boat!

KENNETH (*with mock anger*) Oh, don't you be callin' me a donkey now!

(*Enter Raymond.*)

RAYMOND Tom? (*He is very earnest, even deadly.*)

TOM (*instantly perceiving his own guilt*) Oh, mornin', Ray, how's the twins? (*He gasps little chuckles as he sits at his desk, feeling about for a pencil.*)

(*Raymond goes up close to the desk and leans over, as the others watch —pretending not to.*)

RAYMOND (*quietly*) Eagle wants to see you.

TOM (*with foreboding, looking up into Raymond's face*)   Eagle? I got a lot of parcel post this morning, Ray. (*He automatically presses down his hair.*)

RAYMOND   He's in his office waiting for you now, Tom.

TOM   Oh, sure. It's just that there's a lot of parcel post on Monday. . . . (*He feels for his tie as he rises, and walks out. Raymond starts out after him, but Gus intercedes.*)

GUS (*going up to Raymond*)   What Eagle wants?

RAYMOND   I warned him, Gus, I warned him a dozen times.

GUS   He's no gonna fire him.

RAYMOND   Look, it's all over, Gus, so there's nothing—

GUS   He gonna fire Tommy?

RAYMOND   Now don't raise your voice.

GUS   Sixteen year Tommy work here! He got daughter gonna be in church confirmation!

RAYMOND   Now listen, I been nursing him along for—

GUS   Then you fire me! You fire Tommy, you fire me!

RAYMOND   Gus!

(*With a stride Gus goes to the hook, takes his shirt down, thrusts himself into it.*)

GUS   Goddam son-of-a-bitch.

RAYMOND   Now don't be crazy, Gus.

GUS   I show who crazy! Tommy Kelly he gonna fire! (*He grabs his bowler off the hook. Enter Agnes, agitated.*)

AGNES   Gus! Go to the phone!

GUS (*not noticing her, and with bowler on, to Raymond*)   Come on, he gonna fire me now, son-of-a-bitch! (*He starts out, shirttails flying, and Agnes stops him.*)

AGNES (*indicating the phone*)   Gus, your neighbor's—

GUS (*trying to disengage himself*)   No, he gonna fire me now. He fire Tommy Kelly, he fire me!

AGNES   Lilly, Gus! Your neighbor wants to talk to you. Go, go to the phone.

(*Gus halts, looks at Agnes.*)

GUS   What, Lilly?

AGNES   Something's happened. Go, go to the phone.

GUS   Lilly? (*Perplexed, he goes to the phone.*) Hallo. Yeah, Gus. Ha? (*He listens, stunned. His hand, of itself, goes to his hatbrim as though to doff the hat, but it stays there. Jim enters, comes to a halt, sensing the attention, and watches Gus.*) When? When it happen? (*He listens, and then mumbles*) Ya. Thank you. I come home right away. (*He hangs up. Jim comes forward to him questioningly. To Jim, perplexed*) My Lilly. Die.

JIM   Oh? Hm!

(*Larry enters. Gus dumbly turns to him.*)

GUS (*to Larry*)   Die. My Lilly.

LARRY   Oh, that's tough, Gus.

RAYMOND   You better go home. (*Pause.*) Go ahead, Gus. Go home.

(*Gus stands blinking. Raymond takes his jacket from the hook and helps him on with it. Agnes starts to push his shirtails into his pants.*)

GUS   We shouldn't've go to Staten Island, Jim. Maybe she don't feel good yesterday. Ts, I was in Staten Island, maybe she was sick. (*Tommy Kelly enters, goes directly to his desk, sits, his back to the others. Pause. To Tom*) He fire you, Tommy?

TOM (*holding tears back*)   No, Gus, I'm all right.

GUS (*going up next to him*)   Give you another chance?

TOM (*—he is speaking with his head lowered*)   Yeah. It's all right, Gus, I'm goin' to be all right from now on.

GUS   Sure. Be a man, Tommy. Don't be no drunken bum. Be a man. You hear? Don't let nobody walk on top you. Be man.

TOM   I'm gonna be all right, Gus.

GUS (*nodding*)   One more time you come in drunk I gonna show you something. (*Agnes sobs. He turns to her.*) What for you cry all the time? (*He goes past her and out. Agnes then goes. A silence.*)

RAYMOND (*breaking the silence*)   What do you say, fellas, let's get going, heh? (*He claps his hands and walks out as all move about their work. Soon all are gone but Tommy Kelly, slumped at his desk; Kenneth, wrapping; and Bert, picking an order from the hook. Now Kenneth faces Bert suddenly.*)

KENNETH (*—he has taken his feeling from the departing Gus, and turns now to Bert*)   Bert? How would you feel about washing these windows—you and I—once and for all? Let a little of God's light in the place?

BERT (*excitedly, happily*)   Would you?

KENNETH   Well, I would if you would.

BERT   Okay, come on! Let's do a little every day; couple of months it'll all be clean! Gee! Look at the sun!

KENNETH   Hey, look down there!
   See the old man sitting in a chair?
   And roses all over the fence!
   Oh, that's a lovely back yard!

(*A rag in hand, Bert mounts the table; they make one slow swipe of the window before them and instantly all the windows around the stage burst into the yellow light of summer that floods into the room.*)

BERT   Boy, they've got a tree!
   And all those cats!

KENNETH   It'll be nice to watch the seasons pass.
'That pretty up there now, a real summer sky
And a little white cloud goin' over?
I can just see autumn comin' in
And the leaves falling on the gray days.
You've got to have a sky to look at!
(*Gradually, as they speak, all light hardens to that of winter, finally.*)
BERT (*turning to Kenneth*)   Kenny, were you ever fired from a job?
KENNETH   Oh, sure; two-three times.
BERT   Did you feel bad?
KENNETH   The first time, maybe. But you have to get used to that,
Bert. I'll bet you never went hungry in your life, did you?
BERT   No, I never did. Did you?
KENNETH   Oh, many and many a time. You get used to that too,
though.
BERT (*turning and looking out*)   That tree is turning red.
KENNETH   It must be spectacular out in the country now.
BERT   How does the cold get through these walls?
Feel it, it's almost a wind!
KENNETH   Don't cats walk dainty in the snow!
BERT   Gee, you'd never know it was the same place—
How clean it is when it's white!
Gus doesn't say much any more, y'know?
KENNETH   Well, he's showin' his age. Gus is old.
When do you buy your ticket for the train?
BERT   I did. I've got it.
KENNETH   Oh, then you're off soon!
You'll confound all the professors, I'll bet!
(*He sings softly.*)
"The minstrel boy to the war has gone . . ."
(*Bert moves a few feet away; thus he is alone. Kenneth remains at the
window, looking out, polishing, and singing softly.*)
BERT   There's something so terrible here!
There always was, and I don't know what.
Gus, and Agnes, and Tommy and Larry, Jim and Patricia—
Why does it make me so sad to see them every morning?
It's like the subway;
Every day I see the same people getting on
And the same people getting off,
And all that happens is that they get older. God!
Sometimes it scares me; like all of us in the world
Were riding back and forth across a great big room,
From wall to wall and back again,

And no end ever! Just no end!

(*He turns to Kenneth, but not quite looking at him, and with a deeper anxiety.*)

Didn't you ever want to be anything, Kenneth?

KENNETH   I've never been able to keep my mind on it, Bert. . . .
I shouldn't've cut a hole in me shoe.
Now the snow's slushin' in, and me feet's all wet.

BERT   If you studied, Kenneth, if you put your mind to something great,
I know you'd be able to learn anything, because you're clever, you're
much smarter than I am!

KENNETH   You've got something steady in your mind, Bert;
Something far away and steady.
I never could hold my mind on a far-away thing . . .

(*His tone changes as though he were addressing a group of men; his manner is rougher, angrier, less careful of proprieties.*)

She's not giving me the heat I'm entitled to.
Eleven dollars a week room and board,
And all she puts in the bag is a lousy pork sandwich,
The same every day and no surprises.
Is that right? Is that right now?
How's a man to live,
Freezing all day in this palace of dust
And night comes with one window and a bed
And the streets full of strangers
And not one of them's read a book through,
Or seen a poem from beginning to end
Or knows a song worth singing.
Oh, this is an ice-cold city, Mother,
And Roosevelt's not makin' it warmer, somehow.

(*He sits on the table, holding his head.*)

And here's another grand Monday!

(*They are gradually appearing in natural light now, but it is a cold wintry light which has gradually supplanted the hot light of summer. Bert goes to the hook for a sweater.*)

Jesus, me head'll murder me. I never had the headache till this year.

BERT (*delicately*)   You're not taking up drinking, are you?

KENNETH (*—he doesn't reply. Suddenly, as though to retrieve something slipping by, he gets to his feet, and roars out*):

> "The Ship of State," by Walt Whitman!
> "O Captain! my Captain! our fearful trip is done!
> The ship has weathered every wrack,
> The prize we sought is won . . . "

Now what in the world comes after that?

BERT   I don't know that poem.

KENNETH   Dammit all! I don't remember the bloody poems any more the way I did! It's the drinkin' does it, I think. I've got to stop the drinkin'!

BERT   Well, why do you drink, Kenny, if it makes you feel—

KENNETH   Good God, Bert, you can't always be doin' what you're better off to do! There's all kinds of unexpected turns, y'know, and things not workin' out the way they ought! What in hell *is* the next stanza of that poem? "The prize we sought is won . . ." God, I'd never believe I could forget that poem! I'm thinkin', Bert, y'know—maybe I ought to go onto the Civil Service. The only trouble is there's no jobs open except for the guard in the insane asylum. And that'd be a nervous place to work, I think.

BERT   It might be interesting, though.

KENNETH   I suppose it might. They tell me it's only the more intelligent people goes mad, y'know. But it's sixteen hundred a year, Bert, and I've a feelin' I'd never dare leave it, y'know? And I'm not ready for me last job yet, I think. I don't want nothin' to be the last, yet. Still and all . . .

(*Raymond enters, going to toilet. He wears a blue button-up sweater.*)

RAYMOND   Morning, boys. (*He impales a batch of orders on the desk.*)

KENNETH (*in a routine way*)   Morning, Mr. Ryan. Have a nice New Year's, did you?

RAYMOND   Good enough. (*To Bert, seeing the book on the table.*) Still reading that book?

BERT   Oh, I'm almost finished now. (*Raymond nods, continues on. Bert jumps off the table.*) Mr. Ryan? Can I see you a minute? (*He goes to Raymond.*) I wondered if you hired anybody yet, to take my place.

RAYMOND (*pleasantly surprised*)   Why? Don't you have enough money to go?

BERT   No, I'm going. I just thought maybe I could help you break in the new boy. I won't be leaving till after lunch tomorrow.

RAYMOND (*with resentment, even an edge of sarcasm*)   We'll break him in all right. Why don't you just get on to your own work? There's a lot of excelsior laying around the freight elevator.

(*Raymond turns and goes into the toilet. For an instant Bert is left staring after him. Then he turns to Kenneth, perplexed.*)

BERT   Is he sore at me?

KENNETH (*deprecatingly*)   Ah, why would he be sore at you? (*He starts busying himself at the table, avoiding Bert's eyes. Bert moves toward him, halts.*)

BERT   I hope you're not, are you?

KENNETH (*with an evasive air*)   Me? Ha! Why, Bert, you've got the heartfelt good wishes of everybody in the place for your goin'-away! (*But he turns away to busy himself at the table—and on his line Larry has entered with a container of coffee and a cigarette.*)

BERT   Morning, Larry. (*He goes to the hook, takes an order.*)

LARRY (*leaning against the table*)   Jesus, it'd be just about perfect in here for penguins. (*Bert passes him.*) You actually leaving tomorrow?

BERT (*eagerly*)   I guess so, yeah.

LARRY (*with a certain embarrassed envy*)   Got all the dough, heh?

BERT   Well, for the first year anyway. (*He grins in embarrassment.*)   .
You mind if I thank you?

LARRY   What for?

BERT   I don't know—just for teaching me everything. I'd have been fired the first month without you, Larry.

LARRY (*with some wonder, respect*)   Got all your dough, heh?

BERT   Well, that's all I've been doing is saving.

(*Enter Tom Kelly. He is bright, clean, sober.*)

TOM   Morning!

KENNETH (*with an empty kind of heartiness*)   Why, here comes Tommy Kelly!

TOM (*passing to hang up his coat and hat*)   Ah, y're gettin' an awful long face to wash, Kenny, me bye.

KENNETH   Oh, cut it out with me face, Tommy. I'm as sick of it as you are.

TOM   Go on, ya donkey ya, they backed you off the boat.

KENNETH   Why, I'll tear you limb from limb, Tom Kelly! (*He mocks a fury, and Tom laughs as he is swung about. And then, with a quick hug and a laugh*) Oh, Tommy, you're the first man I ever heard of done it. How'd you do it, Tom?

TOM   Will power, Kenny. (*He walks to his desk, sits.*) Just made up my mind, that's all.

KENNETH   Y'know the whole world is talking about you, Tom—the way you mixed all the drinks at the Christmas party and never weakened? Y'know, when I heard it was you going to mix the drinks I was prepared to light a candle for you.

TOM   I just wanted to see if I could do it, that's all. When I done that—mixin' the drinks for three hours, and givin' them away—I realized I made it. You don't look so hot to me, you know that?

KENNETH (*with a sigh*)   Oh, I'm all right. It's the sight of Monday, that's all, is got me down.

TOM   You better get yourself a little will power, Kenny. I think you're gettin' a fine taste for the hard stuff.

KENNETH   Ah, no, I'll never be a drunk, Tommy.

TOM   You're a drunk now.

KENNETH   Oh, don't say that, please!

TOM   I'm tellin' you, I can see it comin' on you.

KENNETH (*deeply disturbed*)   You can't either. Don't say that, Tommy! (*Agnes enters.*)

AGNES   Morning! (*She wears sheets of brown paper for leggins.*)

KENNETH   Winter's surely here when Agnes is wearin' her leggins.

AGNES (*with her laughter*)   Don't they look awful? But that draft under the switchboard is enough to kill ya.

LARRY   This place is just right for penguins.

AGNES   Haven't you got a heavier sweater, Bert? I'm surprised at your mother.

BERT   Oh, it's warm; she knitted it.

KENNETH   Bert's got the idea. Get yourself an education.

TOM   College guys are sellin' ties all over Macy's. Accountancy, Bert, that's my advice to you. You don't even have to go to college for it either.

BERT   Yeah, but I don't want to be an accountant.

TOM (*with a superior grin*)   You don't want to be an accountant?

LARRY   What's so hot about an accountant?

TOM   Well, try runnin' a business without one. That's what you should've done, Larry. If you'd a took accountancy, you'd a—

LARRY   You know, Tommy, I'm beginning to like you better drunk? (*Tommy laughs, beyond criticism.*) I mean it. Before, we only had to pick you up all the time; now you got opinions about everything.

TOM   Well, if I happen to know something, why shouldn't I say—

(*Enter Raymond from the toilet.*)

RAYMOND   What do you say we get on the ball early today, fellas? Eagle's coming today. Bert, how about gettin' those carburetor crates open, will ya?

BERT   I was just going to do that.

(*Bert and Raymond are starting out, and Agnes is moving to go, when Gus and Jim enter. Both of them are on the verge of staggering. Gus has a bright new suit and checked overcoat, a new bowler, and new shoes. He is carrying upright a pair of Ford fenders, still in their brown paper wrappings—they stand about seven feet in height. Jim aids him in carefully resting the fenders against the wall.*)

(*Kenneth, Agnes, and Larry watch in silence.*)

(*Patricia enters and watches. She is wearing leggins.*)

(*Willy and Jerry enter in overcoats, all jazzed up.*)

WILLY   Morning!

JERRY   Morn—(*Both break off and slowly remove their coats as they note the scene and the mood. Gus, now that the fenders are safely stacked, turns.*)

GUS (*dimly*)   Who's got a hanger?

KENNETH   Hanger? You mean a coat-hanger, Gus?

GUS   Coat hanger.

JERRY   Here! Here's mine! (*He gives a wire hanger to Gus. Gus is aided by Jim in removing his overcoat, and they both hang it on the hanger, then on a hook. Both give it a brush or two, and Gus goes to his chair, sits. He raises his eyes to them all.*)

GUS   So what everybody is looking at?

(*Bert, Willy, Jerry go to work, gradually going out with orders. Jim also takes orders off the hook, and the pattern of going-and-coming emerges. Patricia goes to the toilet. Tom Kelly works at the desk.*)

LARRY (*half-kidding, but in a careful tone*)   What are you all dressed up about?

(*Gus simply glowers in his fumes and thoughts. Raymond goes over to Jim.*)

RAYMOND   What's he all dressed up for?

JIM   Oh, don't talk to me about him, Ray, I'm sick and tired of him. Spent all Saturday buyin' new clothes to go to the cemetery; then all the way the hell over to Long Island City to get these damned fenders for that old wreck of a Ford he's got. Never got to the cemetery, never got the fenders on—and we been walkin' around all weekend carryin' them damn things.

RAYMOND   Eagle'll be here this morning. See if you can get him upstairs. I don't want him to see him crocked again.

JIM   I'd just let him sit there, Ray, if I was you. I ain't goin' to touch him. You know what he went and done? Took all his insurance money outa the bank Saturday. Walkin' around with all that cash in his pocket —I tell ya, I ain't been to sleep since Friday night. 'Cause you can't let him loose with all that money and so low in his mind, y'know . . .

GUS   Irishman! (*All turn to him. He takes a wad out of his pocket, peels one bill off.*) Here. Buy new pair shoes.

KENNETH   Ah, thank you, no, Gus, I couldn't take that.

RAYMOND   Gus, Eagle's coming this morning; why don't you—

GUS (*stuffing a bill into Kenneth's pocket*)   Go buy pair shoes.

RAYMOND   Gus, he's going to be here right away; why don't you—

GUS   I don't give one goddam for Eagle! Why he don't make one more toilet?

RAYMOND   What?

(*Bert enters with goods.*)

GUS   Toilet! That's right? Have one toilet for so many people? That's very bad, Raymond. That's no nice. (*Offering Bert a bill*) Here, boy, go—buy book, buy candy.

(*Larry goes to Gus before he gives the bill, puts an arm around him, and walks away from the group.*)

LARRY Come on, Gussy, let me take you upstairs.

GUS I don't care Eagle sees me, I got my money now, goddam. Oh, Larry, Larry, twenty-two year I workin' here.

LARRY Why don't you give me the money, Gus? I'll put in the bank for you.

GUS What for I put in bank? I'm sixty-eight years old, Larry. I got no children, nothing. What for I put in bank? (*Suddenly, reminded, he turns back to Raymond, pointing at the floor scale.*) Why them goddam mice nobody does nothing?

RAYMOND (*alarmed by Gus's incipient anger*) Gus, I want you to go upstairs!

(*Patricia enters from toilet.*)

GUS (*at the scale*) Twenty-two years them goddam mice! That's very bad, Raymond, so much mice! (*He starts rocking the scale.*) Look at them goddam mice! (*Patricia screams as mice come running out from under the scale. A mêlée of shouts begins, everyone dodging mice or swinging brooms and boxes at them. Raymond is pulling Gus away from the scale, yelling at him to stop it. Agnes rushes in and, seeing the mice, screams and rushes out. Jerry and Willy rush in and join in chasing the mice, laughing. Patricia, wearing leggins, is helped onto the packing table by Larry, and Gus shouts up at her.*) Come with me Atlantic City, Patricia! (*He pulls out the wad.*) Five thousand dollars I got for my wife!

PATRICIA You rotten thing, you! You dirty rotten thing, Gus!

GUS I make you happy, Patricia! I make you—(*Suddenly his hand goes to his head; he is dizzy. Larry goes to him, takes one look.*)

LARRY Come, come on. (*He walks Gus into the toilet.*)

PATRICIA (*out of the momentary silence*) Oh, that louse! Did you see what he did, that louse? (*She gets down off the table, and, glancing angrily toward the toilet, she goes out.*)

RAYMOND All right, fellas, what do you say, heh? Let's get going.

(*Work proceeds—the going and coming.*)

TOM (*as Raymond passes him*) I tried talking to him a couple of times, Ray, but he's got no will power! There's nothing you can do if there's no will power, y'know?

RAYMOND Brother! It's a circus around here. Every Monday morning! I never saw anything like . . .

(*He is gone. Kenneth is packing. Tom works at his desk. Jim comes and, leaving goods on the packing table, goes to the toilet, peeks in, then goes out, studying an order. Bert enters with goods.*)

KENNETH There's one thing you have to say for the Civil Service; it seals the fate and locks the door. A man needn't wonder what he'll do with his life any more.

(*Jerry enters with goods.*)

BERT (*glancing at the toilet door*)   Gee, I never would've thought Gus liked his wife, would you?

(*Tom, studying a letter, goes out.*)

JERRY (*looking up and out the window*)   Jesus!

BERT (*not attending to Jerry*)   I thought he always hated his wife—

JERRY   Jesus, boy!

KENNETH (*to Jerry*)   What're you doin'? What's—?

JERRY   Look at the girls up in there. One, two, three, four windows— full a girls, look at them! Them two is naked!

(*Willy enters with goods.*)

KENNETH   Oh, my God!

WILLY (*rushing to the windows*)   Where? Where?

KENNETH   Well, what're you gawkin' at them for!

(*Gus and Larry enter from the toilet.*)

JERRY   There's another one down there! Look at her on the bed! What a beast!

WILLY (*overjoyed*)   It's a cathouse! Gus! A whole cathouse moved in!

(*Willy and Jerry embrace and dance around wildly; Gus stands with Larry, staring out, as does Bert.*)

KENNETH   Aren't you ashamed of yourself!!

(*Tom enters with his letter.*)

TOM   Hey, fellas, Eagle's here.

JERRY (*pointing out*)   There's a new cathouse, Tommy! (*Tom goes and looks out the windows.*)

KENNETH   Oh, that's a terrible thing to be lookin' at, Tommy! (*Agnes enters; Kenneth instantly goes to her to get her out.*) Oh, Agnes, you'd best not be comin' back here any more now—

AGNES   What? What's the matter?

(*Jerry has opened a window, and he and Willy whistle sharply through their fingers. Agnes looks out.*)

KENNETH   Don't, Agnes, don't look at that!

AGNES   Well, for heaven's sake! What are all those women doing there?

GUS   That's whorehouse, Aggie.

KENNETH   Gus, for God's sake! (*He walks away in pain.*)

AGNES   What are they sitting on the beds like that for?

TOM   The sun is pretty warm this morning—probably trying to get a little tan.

AGNES   Oh, my heavens. Oh, Bert, it's good you're leaving! (*She turns to them.*) You're not all going, are you? (*Gus starts to laugh, then Tom, then Jerry and Willy, then Larry, and she is unstrung and laughing herself, but shocked.*) Oh, my heavens! (*She is gone, as Jim enters with goods.*)

KENNETH   All right, now, clear off, all of you. I can't be workin' with a lot of sex maniacs blockin' off me table!

GUS   Look, Jim! (*Jim looks out.*)

JIM   Oh, nice.

JERRY   How about it, fellas? Let's all go lunchtime! What do you say, Kenny? I'll pay for you!

(*Gus goes to the desk, drags the chair over to the window.*)

KENNETH   I'd sooner roll meself around in the horse manure of the gutter!

JERRY   I betcha you wouldn't even know what to do!

KENNETH (*bristling, fists shut*)   I'll show you what I do! I'll show you right now!

(*Enter Raymond, furious.*)

RAYMOND   What the hell is this? What's going on here?

GUS (*sitting in his chair, facing the windows*)   Whorehouse. (*Raymond looks out the windows.*)

KENNETH   You'd better pass a word to Mr. Eagle about this, Raymond, or the corporation's done for. Poor Agnes, she's all mortified, y'know.

RAYMOND   Oh, my God! (*To all*) All right, break it up, come on, break it up, Eagle's here. (*Willy, Jerry, Bert, and Jim disperse, leaving with orders. Tommy returns to the desk.*) What're you going to do, Gus? You going to sit there? (*Gus doesn't answer; sits staring out thoughtfully.*) What's going on with you? Gus! Eagle's here! All right, cook in your own juice. Sit there. (*He glances out the windows.*) Brother, I needed this now! (*He goes out angrily.*)

LARRY   Give me the money, Gus, come on. I'll hold it for you.

GUS (*—an enormous sadness is on him*)   Go way.

(*Enter Patricia. She glances at Larry and Gus, then looks out the windows.*)

KENNETH (*wrapping*)   Ah, Patricia, don't look out there. It's disgraceful.

TOM   It's only a lot of naked women.

KENNETH   Oh, Tommy, now! In front of a girl!

PATRICIA (*to Kenneth*)   What's the matter? Didn't you ever see that before? (*She sees Gus sitting there.*) Look at Kong, will ya? (*She laughs.*) Rememberin' the old days, heh, Kong?

(*Larry is walking toward an exit at left.*)

GUS   Oh, shatap!

PATRICIA (*catching up with Larry at the edge of the stage, quietly*)   What's Ray sayin' about you sellin' the Auburn?

LARRY   Yeah, I'm kinda fed up with it. It's out of my class anyway.

PATRICIA   That's too bad. I was just gettin' to enjoy it.

LARRY (*very doubtfully*)   Yeah?

PATRICIA   What're you mad at me for?

LARRY   Why should I be mad?

PATRICIA   You're married, what're you—?

LARRY   Let me worry about that, will you?

PATRICIA   Well, I gotta worry about it too, don't I?

LARRY   Since when do you worry about anything, Pat?

PATRICIA   Well, what did you expect me to do? How did I know you were serious?

(*Gus goes to his coat, searches in a pocket.*)

LARRY   What did you think I was telling you all the time?

PATRICIA   Yeah, but Larry, anybody could say those kinda things.

LARRY   I know, Pat. But I never did. (*With a cool, hurt smile*) You know, kid, you better start believing people when they tell you something. Or else you're liable to end up in there. (*He points out the windows.*)

PATRICIA (*with quiet fury*)   You take that back! (*He walks away; she goes after him.*) You're going to take that back, Larry!

(*Eagle enters, nods to Larry and Patricia.*)

EAGLE   Morning.

PATRICIA (*with a mercurial change to sunny charm*)   Good morning, Mr. Eagle!

(*Larry is gone, and she exits. Eagle crosses, noticing Gus, who is standing beside his coat, drinking out of a pint whisky bottle.*)

EAGLE   Morning, Gus.

GUS (*lowering the bottle*)   Good morning. (*Eagle exits into the toilet.*)

TOM (*to Gus*)   You gone nuts?

(*Gus returns, holding the bottle, to his chair, where he sits, looking out the window. He is growing sodden and mean. Bert enters with goods.*)

KENNETH (*sotto voce*)   Eagle's in there, and look at him. He'll get the back of it now for sure.

TOM (*going to Gus*)   Gimme the bottle, Gus!

GUS   I goin' go someplace, Tommy. I goin' go cemetery. I wasn't one time in cemetery. I go see my Lilly. My Lilly die, I was in Staten Island. All alone she was in the house. Ts! (*Jerry enters with goods, sees him, and laughs.*)

BERT   Gus, why don't you give Tommy the bottle?

GUS   Twenty-two years I work here.

KENNETH (*to Jerry, who is staring out the window*)   Will you quit hangin' around me table, please?

JERRY   Can't I look out the window?

(*Willy enters with goods.*)

WILLY   How's all the little pussies?

KENNETH   Now cut that out! (*They laugh at him.*)

Tom (*sotto voce*) Eagle's in there!

KENNETH Is that all yiz know of the world—filthy women and dirty jokes and the ignorance drippin' off your faces? (*Eagle enters from the toilet.*) There's got to be somethin' done about this, Mr. Eagle. It's an awful humiliation for the women here. (*He points, and Eagle looks.*) I mean to say, it's a terrible disorganizing sight starin' a man in the face eight hours a day, sir.

EAGLE Shouldn't have washed the windows, I guess. (*He glances down at Gus and his bottle and walks out.*)

KENNETH Shouldn't have washed the windows, he says! (*They are laughing; Gus is tipping the bottle up. Jim enters with goods.*)

JERRY What a donkey that guy is!

(*Kenneth lunges for Jerry and grabs him by the tie, one fist ready.*)

KENNETH I'll donkey you! (*Jerry starts a swing at him, and Bert and Tom rush to separate them as Raymond enters.*)

RAYMOND Hey! Hey!

JERRY (*as they part*) All right, donkey, I'll see you later.

KENNETH You'll see me later, all right—with one eye closed!

RAYMOND Cut it out! (*Kenneth, muttering, returns to work at his table. Jerry rips an order off the hook and goes out. Willy takes an order. Bert goes out with an order. Raymond has been looking down at Gus, who is sitting with the bottle.*) You going to work, Gus? Or you going to do that? (*Gus gets up and goes to his coat, takes it off the hanger.*) What're you doing?

GUS Come on, Jim, we go someplace. Here—put on you coat.

RAYMOND Where you going? It's half-past nine in the morning.

(*Enter Agnes.*)

AGNES What's all the noise here? (*She breaks off, seeing Gus dressing.*)

GUS That's when I wanna go—half-past nine. (*He hands Jim his coat.*) Here. Put on. Cold outside.

JIM (*quietly*) Maybe I better go with him, Ray. He's got all his money in—

(*Bert enters with goods.*)

RAYMOND (*reasonably, deeply concerned.*) Gus, now look; where you gonna go now? Why don't you lie down upstairs?

GUS (*swaying, to Bert*) Twenty-two years I was here.

BERT I know, Gus.

(*Larry enters, watches.*)

GUS I was here before you was born I was here.

BERT I know.

GUS Them mice was here before you was born. (*Bert nods uncomfortably, full of sadness.*) When Mr. Eagle was in high school I was already here. When there was Winton Six I was here. When was Minerva car I was here. When was Stanley Steamer I was here, and

Stearns Knight, and Marmon was good car; I was here all them times. I was here first day Raymond come; he was young boy; work hard be manager. When Agnes still think she was gonna get married I was here. When was Locomobile, and Model K Ford and Model N Ford— all them different Fords, and Franklin was good car, Jordan car, Reo car, Pierce Arrow, Cleveland car—all them was good cars. All them times I was here.

BERT   I know.

GUS   You don't know nothing. Come on, Jim. (*He goes and gets a fen-der. Jim gets the other.*) Button up you coat, cold outside. Tommy? Take care everything good.

(*He walks out with Jim behind him, each carrying a fender upright. Raymond turns and goes out, then Larry. Agnes goes into the toilet. The lights lower as this movement takes place, until Bert is alone in light, still staring at the point where Gus left.*)

BERT   I don't understand;
I don't know anything:
How is it me that gets out?
I don't know half the poems Kenneth does,
Or a quarter of what Larry knows about an engine.

I don't understand how they come every morning,
Every morning and every morning,
And no end in sight.
That's the thing—there's no end!
Oh, there ought to be a statue in the park—
"To All the Ones That Stay."
One to Larry, to Agnes, Tom Kelly, Gus . . .

Gee, it's peculiar to leave a place—forever!
Still, I always hated coming here;
The same dried-up jokes, the dust;
Especially in spring, walking in from the sunshine,
Or any Monday morning in the hot days.

(*In the darkness men appear and gather around the packing table, eating lunch out of bags; we see them as ghostly figures, silent.*)
God, it's so peculiar to leave a place!
I know I'll remember them as long as I live,
As long as I live they'll never die,
And still I know that in a month or two
They'll forget my name, and mix me up
With another boy who worked here once,
And went. Gee, it's a mystery!

(*As full light rises Bert moves into the group, begins eating from a bag.*)

JERRY (*looking out the window*) You know what's a funny thing? It's a funny thing how you get used to that.

WILLY Tommy, what would you say Cobb's average was for lifetime?

TOM Cobb? Lifetime? (*He thinks. Pause. Kenneth sings.*)

KENNETH "The minstrel boy to the war has gone—

(*Patricia enters, crossing to toilet—*)

In the ranks of death you will find him."

PATRICIA Is that an Irish song?

KENNETH All Irish here, and none of yiz knows an Irish song!

(*She laughs, exits into the toilet.*)

TOM I'd say three-eighty lifetime for Ty Cobb. (*To Larry*) You're foolish sellin' that car with all the work you put in it.

LARRY Well, it was one of those crazy ideas. Funny how you get an idea, and then suddenly you wake up and you look at it and it's like— dead or something. I can't afford a car.

(*Agnes enters, going toward the toilet.*)

AGNES I think it's even colder today than yesterday.

(*Raymond enters.*)

RAYMOND It's five after one, fellas; what do you say?

(*They begin to get up as Jim enters in his overcoat and hat.*)

KENNETH Well! The old soldier returns!

RAYMOND Where's Gus, Jim?

(*Agnes has opened the toilet door as Patricia emerges.*)

AGNES Oh! You scared me. I didn't know you were in there!

JIM (*removing his coat*) He died, Ray.

RAYMOND What?

(*The news halts everyone—but one by one—in midair, as it were.*)

LARRY He what?

AGNES What'd you say?

JIM Gus died.

KENNETH Gus died!

BERT Gus?

AGNES (*going to Jim*) Oh, good heavens. When? What happened?

LARRY What'd you have an accident?

JIM No, we—we went home and got the fenders on all right, and he wanted to go over and start at the bottom, and go right up Third Avenue and hit the bars on both sides. And we got up to about Fourteenth Street, in around there, and we kinda lost track of the car someplace. I have to go back there tonight, see if I can find—

AGNES Well, what happened?

JIM Well, these girls got in the cab, y'know, and we seen a lot of places and all that—we was to some real high-class places, forty cents for a cup of coffee and all that; and then he put me in another cab, and we rode around a while; and then he got another cab to follow us. Case one of our cabs got a flat, see? He just didn't want to be held up for a minute, Gus didn't.

LARRY   Where were you going?

JIM   Oh, just all over. And we stopped for a light, y'know, and I thought I'd go up and see how he was gettin' along, y'know, and I open his cab door, and—the girl was fast asleep, see—and he—was dead. Right there in the seat. It was just gettin' to be morning.

AGNES   Oh, poor Gus!

JIM   I tell ya, Agnes, he didn't look too good to me since she died, the old lady. I never knowed it. He—liked that woman.

RAYMOND   Where's his money?

JIM   Oh—(*with a wasting wave of the hand*;—it's gone, Ray. We was stoppin' off every couple minutes so he call long distance. I didn't even know it, he had a brother someplace in California. Called him half a dozen times. And there was somebody he was talkin' to in Texas someplace, somebody that was in the Navy with him. He was tryin' to call all the guys that was in the submarine with him, and he was callin' all over hell and gone—and givin' big tips, and he bought a new suit, and give the cab driver a wristwatch and all like that. I think he got himself too sweated. Y'know it got pretty cold last night, and he was all sweated up. I kept tellin' him, I says, "Gus," I says, "you're gettin' yourself all sweated, y'know, and it's a cold night," I says; and all he kept sayin' to me all night he says, "Jim," he says, "I'm gonna do it right, Jim." That's all he says practically all night. "I'm gonna do it right," he says. "I'm gonna do it right." (*Pause. Jim shakes his head.*) Oh, when I open that cab door I knowed it right away. I takes one look at him and I knowed it. (*There is a moment of silence, and Agnes turns and goes into the toilet.*) Oh, poor Agnes, I bet she's gonna cry now.

(*Jim goes to the order hook, takes an order off, and, putting a cigar into his mouth, he goes out, studying the order. Raymond crosses and goes out; then Patricia goes. Willy and Jerry exit in different directions with orders in their hands; Kenneth begins wrapping. Tom goes to his desk and sits, clasps his hands, and for a moment he prays.*)

(*Bert goes and gets his jacket. He slowly puts it on.*)

(*Enter Frank, the truckdriver.*)

FRANK   Anything for West Bronx, Tommy?

TOM   There's some stuff for Sullivan's there.

FRANK   Okay. (*He pokes through the packages, picks some.*)

KENNETH   Gus died.

FRANK   No kiddin'!

KENNETH   Ya, last night.

FRANK   What do you know. Hm. (*He goes on picking packages out.*) Is this all for West Bronx, Tom?

TOM   I guess so for now.

FRANK (*to Kenneth*)   Died.

KENNETH   Yes, Jim was with him. Last night.

FRANK   Jesus. (*Pause. He stares, shakes his head.*) I'll take Brooklyn when I get back, Tommy. (*He goes out, loaded with packages. Bert is buttoning his overcoat. Agnes comes out of the toilet.*)

BERT   Agnes?

AGNES (*seeing the coat on, the book in his hand*)   Oh, you're leaving, Bert!

BERT   Yeah.

AGNES   Well. You're leaving.

BERT (*expectantly*)   Yeah.

(*Patricia enters.*)

PATRICIA   Agnes? Your switchboard's ringing.

(*Jerry enters with goods.*)

AGNES   Okay! (*Patricia goes out.*) Well, good luck. I hope you pass everything.

BERT   Thanks, Aggie. (*She walks across and out, wiping a hair across her forehead. Willy enters with goods as Jerry goes out. Jim enters with goods.*)

(*Bert seems about to say good-by to each of them, but they are engrossed and he doesn't quite want to start a scene with them; but now Jim is putting his goods on the table, so Bert goes over to him.*) I'm leaving, Jim, so—uh—

JIM   Oh, leavin'? Heh! Well, that's—

TOM (*from his place at the desk, offering an order to Jim*)   Jim? See if these transmissions came in yet, will ya? This guy's been ordering them all month.

JIM   Sure, Tom.

(*Jim goes out past Bert, studying his order. Bert glances at Kenneth, who is busy wrapping. He goes to Tom, who is working at the desk.*)

BERT   Well, so long, Tommy.

TOM (*turning*)   Oh, you goin', heh?

BERT   Yeah, I'm leavin' right now.

TOM   Well, keep up the will power, y'know. That's what does it.

BERT   Yeah. I—uh—I wanted to—

(*Raymond enters.*)

RAYMOND (*handing Tom an order*)   Tommy, make this a special, will you? The guy's truck broke down in Peekskill. Send it out special today.

TOM   Right.

(*Raymond turns to go out, sees Bert, who seems to expect some moment from him.*)

RAYMOND   Oh! 'By, Bert.

BERT   So long, Raymond, I— (*Raymond is already on his way, and he is gone. Jim enters with goods. Bert goes over to Kenneth and touches his back. Kenneth turns to him. Jim goes out as Willy enters with goods—Jerry too, and this work goes on without halt.*) Well, good-by, Kenny.

KENNETH (—*he is embarrassed as he turns to Bert*)   Well, it's our last look, I suppose, isn't it?

BERT   No, I'll come back sometime. I'll visit you.

KENNETH   Oh, not likely; it'll all be out of mind as soon as you turn the corner. I'll probably not be here anyway.

BERT   You made up your mind for Civil Service?

KENNETH   Well, you've got to keep movin', and—I'll move there, I guess. I done a shockin' thing last night, Bert; I knocked over a bar.

BERT   Knocked it over?

KENNETH   It's disgraceful, what I done. I'm standin' there, havin' a decent conversation, that's all, and before I know it I start rockin' the damned thing, and it toppled over and broke every glass in the place, and the beer spoutin' out of the pipes all over the floor. They took all me money; I'll be six weeks payin' them back. I'm for the Civil Service, I think; I'll get back to regular there, I think.

BERT   Well—good luck, Kenny. (*Blushing*) I hope you'll remember the poems again.

KENNETH (*as though they were unimportant*)   No, they're gone, Bert. There's too much to do in this country for that kinda stuff.

(*Willy enters with goods.*)

TOM   Hey, Willy, get this right away; it's a special for Peekskill.

WILLY   Okay.

(*Willy takes the order and goes, and when Bert turns back to Kenneth he is wrapping again. So Bert moves away from the table. Jerry enters, leaves; and Jim enters, drops goods on the table, and leaves. Larry enters with a container of coffee, goes to the order hook, and checks through the orders. Bert goes to him.*)

BERT   I'm goin', Larry.

LARRY (*over his shoulder*)   Take it easy, kid.

(*Patricia enters and crosses past Bert, looking out through the windows. Tom gets up and bumbles through a pile of goods on the table, checking against an order in his hand. It is as though Bert wished it could stop for a moment, and as each person enters he looks expectantly, but nothing much happens. And so he gradually moves—almost is moved —toward an exit, and with his book in his hand he leaves.*)

(*Now Kenneth turns and looks about, sees Bert is gone. He resumes his work and softly sings.*)

KENNETH   "The minstrel boy to the war has gone!" Tommy, I'll be needin' more crayon before the day is out.

TOM (*without turning from the desk*)   I'll get some for you.

KENNETH (*looking at a crayon, peeling it down to a nub*)   Oh, the damn mice. But they've got to live too, I suppose. (*He marks a package and softly sings*):

". . . in the ranks of death you will find him.
His father's sword he has girded on,
And his wild harp slung behind him."

CURTAIN

Theme Questions

1. Bert's entrance opens the play, his leaving for school marks its end; but consider whether he is a true protagonist. Why or why not? Is Kenneth the protagonist? Why or why not? How does one character serve as a foil for the other?

2. Bert says,

"There's something so terrible here!
There always was and I don't know what."

By analyzing the characters, discuss what it is that is terrible. What was Miller trying to indicate?

3. What is the significance of each of the two Mondays? What is Miller attempting to reveal about American life?

4. Miller's stage directions read: "A warning: The place must seem dirty and unmanageably chaotic, but since it is seen in this play with two separate visions it is also romantic. It is a little world, a home to which, unbelievably perhaps, these people like to come every Monday morning, despite what they say."

What are the two separate visions—the reality and the romance? Which predominates in the play? Why?

5. The importance of education is basic to the theme. Discuss the attitudes toward education of several of the characters. What ambivalence is expressed?

. . . **also by Arthur Miller**   *All my Sons*
Death of a Salesman
The Crucible
The Price

Shakespeare wrote of the reluctant schoolboy dragging his feet on the way to school and created a popular image. It is not, however, the only response to education. For some, learning is exciting, as it is for Keats in this sonnet. For some, like Ransom, learning about great writers elicits a wry sympathy. For some, school is a matter of being good and being quiet, but for John Ciardi that kind of student is no student at all.

Keen, Fitful Gusts

John Keats

Keen, fitful gusts are whispering here and there
Among the bushes half leafless, and dry;
The stars look very cold about the sky,
And I have many miles on foot to fare.
Yet feel I little of the cool bleak air,
Or of the dead leaves rustling drearily,
Or of those silver lamps that burn on high,
Or of the distance from home's pleasant lair:
For I am brimful of the friendliness
That in a little cottage I have found;
Of fair-haired Milton's eloquent distress,
And all his love for gentle Lycid drowned;
Of lovely Laura in her light green dress,
And faithful Petrarch gloriously crowned.

Survey of Literature

John Crowe Ransom

In all the good Greek of Plato
I lack my roastbeef and potato.

A better man was Aristotle,
Pulling steady on the bottle.

I dip my hat to Chaucer,
Swilling soup from his saucer,

And to Master Shakespeare
Who wrote big on small beer.

The abstemious Wordsworth
Subsisted on a curd's-worth,

But a slick one was Tennyson,
Putting gravy on his venison.

What these men had to eat and drink
Is what we say and what we think.

The influence of Milton
Came wry out of Stilton.

Sing a song for Percy Shelley,
Drowned in pale lemon jelly,

And for precious John Keats,
Dripping blood of pickled beets.

Then there was poor Willie Blake,
He foundered on sweet cake.

God have mercy on the sinner
Who must write with no dinner,

No gravy and no grub,
No pewter and no pub,

No belly and no bowels,
Only consonants and vowels.

On Flunking a Nice Boy Out of School

John Ciardi

> I wish I could teach you how ugly
> decency and humility can be when they are not
> the election of a contained mind but only
> the defenses of an incompetent. Were you taught
> meekness as a weapon? Or did you discover,
> by chance maybe, that it worked on mother
> and was generally a good thing—
> at least when all else failed—to get you over
> the worst of what was coming. Is that why you bring
> these sheepfaces to Tuesday?
>   They won't do.
> It's three months work I want, and I'd sooner have it
> from the brassiest lumpkin in pimpledom, but have it,
> than all these martyred repentances from you.

Theme Questions

1. Describe each poet's experiences, as you imagine them, that hypothetically led to the writing of each poem.

2. With which kind of student do you identify? Why? Why are the others different?

War—*the atrocity created by the old and suffered chiefly by the young—has aged boys overnight. Chiefly fools, hypocrites, and scoundrels glorify war; few writers, especially in the twentieth century, are so corrupted.*

World War I brought a great spate of antiwar poetry, some of which was written by poets who were killed in action, like Wilfred Owen and W. N. Hodgson. Their deaths punctuate their commentary.

Arms and the Boy

Wilfred Owen

Let the boy try along this bayonet-blade
How cold steel is, and keen with hunger of blood;
Blue with all malice, like a madman's flash;
And thinly drawn with famishing for flesh.

Lend him to stroke these blind, blunt bullet-heads
Which long to nuzzle in the heart of lads,
Or give him cartridges of fine zinc teeth,
Sharp with the sharpness of grief and death.

For his teeth seem for laughing round an apple.
There lurk no claws behind his fingers supple;
And god will grow no talons at his heels,
Nor antlers through the thickness of his curls.

Before Action

W. N. Hodgson

By all the glories of the day
   And the cool evening's benison,
By that last sunset touch that lay
   Upon the hills when day was done,
By beauty lavishly outpoured
   And blessings carelessly received,
By all the days that I have lived
   Make me a soldier, Lord.

By all of man's hopes and fears,
   And all the wonders poets sing,
The laughter of unclouded years,
   And every sad and lovely thing;
By the romantic ages stored
   With high endeavour that was his,
By all his mad catastrophes
   Make me a man, O Lord.

I, that on my familiar hill
   Saw with uncomprehending eyes
A hundred of Thy sunsets spill
   Their fresh and sanguine sacrifice,
Ere the sun swings his noonday sword
   Must say goodbye to all of this;—
By all delights that I shall miss,
   Help me to die, O Lord.

*written two days before his
death on July 1st, 1916*

"Gunners' Passage" takes place during World War II, the European theater of operations, although the setting is North Africa. War is so much associated in men's minds with noise—bomb blasts, siren screams, human screams—that the silence of anxiety, fear, and remembered disaster are overlooked. In this quiet story, Irwin Shaw shows us the boys who go to war, the men who return.

Gunners' Passage

Irwin Shaw

"In Brazil," Whitejack was saying, "the problem was girls. American girls."

They were lying on the comfortable cots with the mosquito netting looped gracefully over their heads and the barracks quiet and empty except for the two of them and shaded and cool when you remembered that outside the full sun of Africa stared down.

"Three months in the jungle, on rice and monkey meat." Whitejack lit a large, long, nickel cigar and puffed deeply, squinting up at the tin roof. "When we got to Rio, we felt we deserved an American girl. So the Lieutenant and Johnny and myself, we got the telephone directory of the American Embassy, and we went down the list, calling up likely names—secretaries, typists, interpreters, filing clerks. . . ." Whitejack grinned up at the ceiling. He had a large, sunburned, rough face, that was broken into good-looks by the white teeth of his smile, and his speech was Southern, but not the kind of Southern that puts a northerner's teeth on edge.

"It was the Lieutenant's idea, and by the time we got to the Q's he was ready to give up but we hit paydirt on the S's." Slowly he blew out a long draught of cigar smoke. "Uh-uh," he said, closing his eyes reflectively. "Two months and eleven days of honey and molasses. Three tender and affectionate American girls as loving as the day is long, with their own flat. Beer in the icebox from Sunday to Sunday, steaks big enough to saddle a mule with, and nothing to do, just lie on the beach in the afternoon and go swimmin' when the mood seized yuh. On per diem."

"How were the girls?" Stais asked. "Pretty?"

"Well, Sergeant," Whitejack paused and pursed his lips with thoughtful honesty. "To tell you the truth, Sergeant, the girls the Lieutenant and Johnny Moffat had were as smart and pretty as chipmunks. Mine . . ." Once more he paused. "Ordinarily, my girl would find herself hard put to collect a man in the middle of a full division of infantry soldiers. She was small and runty and she had less curves than a rifle barrel, and she wore glasses. But from the first time she looked at me, I could see she wasn't interested in Johnny or the Lieutenant. She looked at me and behind her glasses her eyes were soft and hopeful and humble and appealing." Whitejack flicked the cigar ash off into the little tin can on his bare chest he was using as an ash tray. "Sometimes," he said slowly, "a man feels mighty small if he just thinks of himself and turns down an appeal like that. Let me tell you something, Sergeant, I was in Rio two months and eleven days and I didn't look at another woman. All those dark-brown women walkin' along the beach three-quarters out of their bathing suits, just wavin' it in front of your face. . . . I didn't look at them. This runty, skinny little thing with glasses was the most lovin' and satisfactory and decent little person a man could possibly conceive of, and a man'd just have to be hog-greedy with sex to have winked an eye at another woman." Whitejack doused his cigar, took his ash tray off his chest, rolled over on his belly, adjusted the towel properly over his bare buttocks. "Now," he said, "I'm going to get myself a little sleep. . . ."

In a moment Whitejack was snoring gently, his tough mountaineer's face tucked childishly into the crook of his arm. Outside the barracks the native boy hummed low and wild to himself as he ironed a pair of suntan trousers on the shady side of the building. From the field, two hundred yards away, again and again came the sliding roar of engines climbing or descending the afternoon sky.

Stais closed his eyes wearily. Ever since he'd got into Accra he had done nothing but sleep and lie on his cot, day-dreaming, listening to Whitejack talk.

"Hi," Whitejack had said, as Stais had come slowly into the barracks two days before, "which way you going?"

"Home," Stais had said, smiling wearily as he did every time he said it. "Going home. Which way you going?"

"Not home." Whitejack had grinned a little. "Not home at all."

Stais liked to listen to Whitejack. Whitejack talked about America, about the woods of the Blue Ridge Mountains where he had been in the forestry service, about his mother's cooking and how he had owned great dogs who had been extraordinary at finding a trail and holding it, about how they had tried hunting deer in the hills from the medium bomber, no good because of the swirling winds rising from the gorges, about pleasant indiscriminate week-end parties in the woods with his friend Johnny Moffat and the girls from the mill in the next town. . . . Stais had been away from America for nineteen months now and Whitejack's talk made his native country seem present and pleasantly real to him.

"There was a man in my town by the name of Thomas Wolfe," Whitejack had said irrelevantly that morning. "He was a great big feller and he went away to New York to be an author. Maybe you heard of him?"

"Yes," said Stais. "I read two books of his."

"Well, I read that book of his," said Whitejack, "and the people in town were yellin' to lynch him for awhile, but I read that book and he got that town down fair and proper, and when they brought him back dead I came down from the hills and I went to his funeral. There were a lot of important people from New York and over to Chapel Hill down for the funeral and it was a hot day, too, and I'd never met the feller, but I felt it was only right to go to his funeral after readin' his book. And the whole town was there, very quiet, although just five years before they were yellin' to lynch him, and it was a sad and impressive sight and I'm glad I went."

And another time, the slow deep voice rolling between sleep and dreams in the shaded heat. . . . "My mother takes a quail and bones it, then she scoops out a great big sweet potato and lays some bacon on it, then she puts the quail in and cooks it slow for three hours, bastin' it with butter all the time. . . . You got to try that some time. . . ."

"Yes," said Stais, "I will."

Stais did not have a high priority number and there seemed to be a flood of colonels surging toward America, taking all the seats on the C-54's setting out westward, so he'd had to wait. It hadn't been bad. Just to lie down, stretched full-out, unbothered, these days, was holiday enough after Greece, and anyway he didn't want to arrive home, in front of his mother, until he'd stopped looking like a tired old man. And the barracks had been empty and quiet and the chow good at the transient mess and you could get Coca-Cola and chocolate milk at the PX. The rest of the enlisted men in Whitejack's crew were young and ambitious and were out swimming all day and going to the movies or playing poker in another barracks all night, and Whitejack's talk was smooth and amusing in the periods between sleep and dreams. Whitejack was an aerial photographer and gunner in a mapping-and-survey squadron and he'd been in Alaska and Brazil and back to the States and now was on his way to India, full of conversation. He was in a Mitchell squadron and the whole squadron was supposed to be on its way together, but two of the Mitchells had crashed and burned on the take-off at Natal, as Whitejack's plane had circled the field, waiting to form up. The rest of the squadron had been held at Natal and Whitejack's plane had been sent on to Accra across the ocean, by itself.

Vaguely and slowly, lying on the warm cot, with the wild song of the Negro boy outside the window, Stais thought of the two Mitchells burning between sea and jungle three thousand miles away, and other planes burning elsewhere, and what it was going to be like sitting down in the armchair in his own house and looking across the room at his mother, and the pretty Viennese girl in Jerusalem, and the DC3 coming down slowly, like an angel in the dusk to the rough secret pasture in the Peloponnesian hills. . . .

He fell asleep. His bones knit gently into dreams on the soft cot, with the sheets, in the quiet barracks, and he was over Athens again, with the ruins pale and shining on the hills, and the fighters boring in, and Lathrop saying, over the intercom, as they persisted in to a hundred, fifty yards, twisting, swiftly and shiftily in the bright Greek sky, "They grounded all the students today. They have the instructors up this afternoon . . ." And, suddenly, and wildly, fifty feet over Ploesti, with Liberators going down into the filth in dozens, flaming. . . . Then swimming off the white beach at Bengasi with the dead boys playing in the mild, tideless swell, then the parachute pulling at every muscle in his body, then the green and forest blue of Minnesota woods and his father, fat and small, sleeping on pine needles on his Sunday off, then Athens again, Athens . . .

"I don't know what's come over the Lieutenant," a new voice was saying as Stais came out of his dream. "He passes us on the field and he just don't seem to see us."

Stais opened his eyes. Novak, a farm boy from Oklahoma, was sitting on the edge of Whitejack's bed, talking. "It has all the guys real worried." He had a high, shy, rather girlish voice. "I used to think they never came better than the Lieutenant . . . Now . . ." Novak shrugged. "If he does see you, he snaps at you like he was General George Patton."

"Maybe," Whitejack said, "maybe seeing Lieutenant Brogan go down in Natal . . . He and Brogan were friends since they were ten years old. Like as if I saw Johnny Moffat go down . . ."

"It's not that." Novak went over to his own cot and got out his writing pad. "It began back in Miami four weeks ago. Didn't you notice it?"

"I noticed it," Whitejack said slowly.

"You ought to ask him about it." Novak started writing a letter. "You and him are good friends. After all, going into combat now, it's bad, the Lieutenant just lookin' through us when he passes us on the field. You don't think he's drunk all the time, do you?"

"He's not drunk."

"You ought to ask him."

"Maybe I will." Whitejack sat up, tying the towel around his lean middle. "Maybe I will." He looked forlornly down at his stomach. "Since I got into the Army, I've turned pig-fat. On the day I took the oath, I was twenty-eight and one-half inches around the waist. Today I'm thirty-two and three-quarters, if I'm an inch. The Army . . . Maybe I shouldn't've joined. I was in a reserved profession, and I was the sole support of an ailing mother."

"Why did you join?" Stais asked.

"Oh," Whitejack smiled at him, "you're awake. Feeling any better, Sergeant?"

"Feeling fine, thanks. Why did you join?"

"Well . . ." Whitejack rubbed the side of his jaw. "Well . . . I waited and I waited. I sat up in my cabin in the hills and I tried to avoid listenin' to the radio, and I waited and I waited, and finally I went downtown to my mother and I said, 'Ma'am, I just can't wait any longer,' and I joined up."

"When was that?" Stais asked.

"Eight days . . ." Whitejack lay down again, plumping the pillow under his head. "Eight days after Pearl Harbor."

"Sergeant," Novak said, "Sergeant Stais, you don't mind if I tell my girl you're a Greek, do you?"

"No," Stais said gravely. "I don't mind. You know, I was born in Minnesota."

"I know," said Novak, writing industriously. "But your parents came from Greece. My girl'll be very interested, your parents coming from Greece and you bombing Greece and being shot down there."

"What do you mean, your girl?" Whitejack asked. "I thought you said she was going around with a Technical Sergeant in Flushing, Long Island."

"That's true," Novak said apologetically. "But I still like to think of her as my girl."

"It's the ones that stay at home," said Whitejack darkly, "that get all the stripes and all the girls. My motto is: Don't write to a girl once you get out of pillow-case distance from her."

"I like to write to this girl in Flushing, Long Island," Novak said, his voice shy but stubborn. Then to Stais, "How many days were you in the hills before the Greek farmers found you?"

"Fourteen," said Stais.

"And how many of you were wounded?"

"Three. Out of seven. The others were dead."

"Maybe," Whitejack said, "he doesn't like to talk about it, Charley."

"Oh, I'm sorry." Novak looked up, his young, unlined face crossed with concern.

"That's all right," Stais said. "I don't mind."

"Did you tell them you were a Greek, too?" Novak asked.

"When one finally showed up who could speak English."

"That must be funny," Novak said reflectively. "Being a Greek, bombing Greece, not speaking the language . . . Can I tell my girl they had a radio and they radioed to Cairo . . . ?"

"It's the girl of a Technical Sergeant in Flushing, Long Island," Whitejack chanted. "Why don't you look facts in the face?"

"I prefer it this way," Novak said with dignity.

"I guess you can tell about the radio," Stais said. "It was pretty long ago. Three days later, the DC3 came down through a break in the clouds. It'd been raining all the time and it just stopped for about thirty minutes at dusk and that plane came down throwin' water fifteen feet in the air. . . . We cheered, but we couldn't get up from where we were sitting, any of us, because we were too weak to stand."

"I got to write that to my girl," Novak said. "Too weak to stand."

"Then it started to rain again and the field was hip-deep in mud and when we all got into the DC3, we couldn't get it started," Stais spoke calmly and thoughtfully, as though he were alone, reciting to himself. "We were just bogged down in that Greek mud. Then the pilot got out—he was a captain—and he looked around, with the rain coming down and all those farmers just standing there, sympathizing with him, and nothing anyone could do and he just cursed for ten minutes. He was from San Francisco and he really knew how to curse. Then everybody started breaking branches off the trees in the woods around that pasture, even two of us who couldn't stand one hour before, and we just covered that big DC3 complete with branches and waited for the rain to stop. We just sat in the woods and prayed no German patrols would come out in weather like that. In those three days I learned five words of Greek."

"What are they?" Novak asked.

"*Vouno,*" Stais said, "That means mountain. *Vrohi*: Rains. *Theos*: God. *Avrion*: Tomorrow. And *Yassov*: That means farewell."

"*Yassov,*" Novak said. "Farewell."

"Then the sun came out and the field started to steam and nobody said anything. We just sat there, watching the water dry off the grass, then the puddles started to go here and there, then the mud to cake a little. Then we got into the DC3 and the Greeks pushed and hauled for awhile and we broke loose and got out. And those farmers just standing below waving at us, as though they were seeing us off at Grand Central Station. Ten miles farther on we went right over a German camp. They fired at us a couple of times, but they didn't come anywhere close. The best moment of my whole life was getting into that hospital bed in Cairo, Egypt. I just stood there and looked at it for a whole minute, looking at the sheets. Then I got in very slow."

"Did you ever find out what happened to those Greeks?" Novak asked.

"No," said Stais. "I guess they're still there, waiting for us to come back some day."

There was silence, broken only by the slow scratching of Novak's pen. Stais thought of the thin, dark mountain faces of the men he had last seen, fading away, waving, standing in the scrub and short silver grass of the hill pasture near the Aegean Sea. They had been cheerful and anxious to please, and there was a look on the faces that made you feel they expected to die.

"How many missions were you on?" Novak asked.

"Twenty-one and a half," Stais said. He smiled. "I count the last one as half."

"How old are you?" Novak was obviously keeping the Technical Sergeant's girl carefully posted on all points of interest.

"Nineteen."

"You look older," said Whitejack.

"Yes," said Stais.

"A lot older."

"Yes."

"Did you shoot down any planes?" Novak peered at him shyly, his red face uncertain and embarrassed, like a little boy asking a doubtful question about girls. "Personally?"

"Two," Stais said. "Personally."

"What did you feel?"

"Why don't you leave him alone?" Whitejack said. "He's too tired to keep his eyes open, as it is."

"I felt—relieved," Stais said. He tried to think of what he'd really felt when the tracers went in and the Focke-Wolfe started to smoke like a crazy smudge pot and the German pilot fought wildly for half a second with the cowling and then didn't fight wildly any more. There was no way of telling these men, no way of remembering, in words, himself. "You'll find out," he said. "Soon enough. The sky's full of Germans."

"Japs," Whitejack said. "We're going to India."

"The sky's full of Japs."

There was silence once more, with the echo of the word "Japs" rustling thinly in the long, quiet room, over the empty rows of cots. Stais felt the old waving dizziness starting behind his eyes that the doctor in Cairo had said came from shock or starvation or exposure or all of these things, and lay back, still keeping his eyes open, as it became worse and waved more violently when he closed his eyes.

"One more question," Novak said. "Are—are guys afraid?"

"You'll be afraid," Stais said.

"Do you want to send that back to your girl in Flushing?" Whitejack asked sardonically.

"No," said Novak quietly. "I wanted that for myself."

"If you want to sleep," said Whitejack, "I'll shut this farmer up."

"Oh, no," said Stais, "I'm pleased to talk."

"If you're not careful," Whitejack said, "he'll talk about his girl in Flushing."

"I'd be pleased to hear it," said Stais.

"It's only natural I should want to talk about her," Novak said defensively. "She was the best girl I ever knew in my whole life. I'd've married her if I could."

"My motto," said Whitejack, "is never marry a girl who goes to bed with you the first time out. The chances are she isn't pure. The second time—that, of course, is different." He winked at Stais.

"I was in Flushing, Long Island, taking a five-weeks course in aerial cameras," Novak said, "and I was living at the YMCA. . . ."

"This is where I leave." Whitejack got off the bed and put on his pants.

"The YMCA was very nice. There were bathrooms for every two rooms, and the food was very good," said Novak, talking earnestly to Stais, "but I must confess, I was lonely in Flushing, Long Island. . . ."

"I will be back," Whitejack was buttoning up his shirt, "for the ninth installment."

"As long as you're going out," Novak said to him, "I wish you'd talk to the Lieutenant. It really makes me feel queer passing him, and him just looking through me like I was a window pane."

"Maybe I'll talk to the Lieutenant. And leave the Sergeant alone. Remember he's a tired man who's been to the war and he needs his rest." Whitejack went out.

Novak stared after him. "There's something wrong with him, too," he said. "Just lying on his back here for ten days, reading and sleeping. He never did that before. He was the liveliest man in the United States Air Force. Seeing those two planes go down . . . It's a funny thing, you fly with fellers all over the world, over America, Brazil, Alaska, you watch them shoot porpoises and sharks in gunnery practice over the Gulf Stream, you get drunk with them, go to their weddings, talk to them over the radio with their planes maybe a hundred feet away, in the air—and after all that flying, in one minute, for no reason, two planes go down. Fourteen fellers you've been livin' with for over a year. . . ." Novak shook his head. "There was a particular friend of Whitejack's in one of those planes. Frank Sloan. Just before we left Miami, they had a big fight. Frank went off and married a girl that Whitejack'd been going with off and on for a year, every time we hit Miami. Whitejack told him he was crazy, half the squadron had slept with the lady, and that was true, too, and just to teach him a lesson he'd sleep with her himself after they'd been married. And he did, too. . . ." Novak sighed. "A lot of funny things happen in the army, when fellers've been together a long time and get to know each other real well. And then, one minute, the Mitchell goes down. I guess Whitejack must've felt sort of queer, watching Frankie burn." Novak had put his writing pad down and now he screwed the top on his fountain pen. "The truth is," he said, "I don't feel so solid myself. That's why I like to talk. Especially to you . . . You've been through it. You're young, but you've been through it. But if it's any bother to you, I'll keep quiet. . . ."

"No," said Stais, still lying back, abstractedly wondering whether the waving would get worse or better, "not at all."

"This girl in Flushing, Long Island," Novak said slowly. "It's easy for Whitejack to make fun of me. The girls fall all over themselves chasing after him, he has no real conception of what it's like to be a man like me. Not very good-looking. Not much money. Not an officer. Not humorous. Shy."

Stais couldn't help grinning. "You're going to have a tough time in India."

"I know," Novak said. "I have resigned myself to not having a girl until the armistice. How did you do with the girls in the Middle East?" he asked politely.

"There was a nice Viennese girl in Jerusalem," Stais said dreamily. "But otherwise zero. You have to be very good unless you're an officer in the Middle East."

"That's what I heard," Novak said sorrowfully. "Well, it won't be so different to me from Oklahoma. That was the nice thing about this girl in Flushing, Long Island. She saw me come into the jewelry store where she worked and . . . I was in my fatigues and I was with a very smooth feller who made a date with her for that night. But she smiled at me, and I knew if I had the guts I could ask her for a date, too. But of course I didn't. But then later that night I was sitting in my room in the YMCA and my phone rang. It was this girl. The other feller had stood her up, she said, and would I take her out." Novak smiled dimly, thinking of that tremulous moment of glory in the small hotel room far away. "I got my fatigues off in one minute and shaved and showered and I picked her up. We went to Coney Island. It was the first time in my entire life I had ever seen Coney Island. It took three and a half weeks for me to finish my course and I went out with that girl every single night. Nothing like that ever happened to me before in my life—a girl who just wanted to see me every night of the week. Then the night before I was due to leave to join my squadron she told me she had got permission to take the afternoon off and she would like to see me off if I let her. I called at the jewelry shop at noon and her boss shook my hand and she had a package under her arm and we got into the subway and we rode to New York City. Then we went into a cafeteria and had a wonderful lunch and she saw me off and gave me the package. It was Schrafft's candy, and she was crying at the gate there, crying for me, and she said she would like me to write, no matter what . . ." Novak paused and Stais could tell that the scene at the gate, the hurrying crowds, the package of Schrafft's chocolates, the weeping young girl, were as clear as the afternoon sunlight to Novak there on the coast of Africa. "So I keep writing," Novak said. "She's written me she has a Technical Sergeant now, but I keep writing. I haven't seen her in a year and a half and what's a girl to do? Do you blame her?"

"No," said Stais, "I don't blame her."

"I hope I haven't bored you," Novak said.

"Not at all." Stais smiled at him. Suddenly the dizziness had gone and he could close his eyes. As he drifted down into that weird and ever-present pool of sleep in which he half-lived these days, he heard Novak say, "Now I have to write my mother."

Outside, the Negro boy sang and the planes grumbled down from the Atlantic and laboriously set out across the Sahara Desert.

Dreams again. Arabs, bundled in rags, driving camels along the perimeter of the field, outlined against the parked Liberators and waiting bombs, two Mitchells still burning on the shores of Brazil and Frank Sloan burning there and circling above him, Whitejack, who had told him he'd sleep with his wife and had, the hills around Jerusalem, gnarled, rocky, dusty, with the powdered green of olive groves set on slopes here and there, clinging against the desert wind, Mitchells slamming along the gorges of the Blue Ridge Mountains, bucking in the up-draughts, their guns going, hunting deer, the Mediterranean, bluer than anything in America, below them on the way home from Italy, coming down below oxygen level, with the boys singing dirty songs over the intercom and leave in Alexandria ahead of them. The girl from Flushing, Long Island, quietly going hand in hand with Novak to Coney Island on a summer's night. . . .

It was Whitejack who awakened him. He woke slowly. It was dark outside and the electric light was shining in his eyes and Whitejack was standing over him, shaking him gently.

"I thought you'd like to know," Whitejack was saying, "your name's on the bulletin board. You're leaving tonight."

"Thanks," Stais said, dimly grateful at being shaken out of the broken and somehow sorrowful dreams.

"I took the liberty of initialing it for you, opposite your name," Whitejack said. "Save you a trip up to the field."

"Thanks," said Stais. "Very kind of you."

"Also," said Whitejack, "There's fried chicken for chow."

Stais pondered over the fried chicken. He was a little hungry, but the effort of getting up and putting on his shoes and walking the hundred yards to the mess hall had to be weighed in the balance. "Thanks. I'll just lie right here," he said. "Any news of your boys?" he asked.

"Yes," said Whitejack. "The squadron came in."

"That's good."

"All except one plane." Whitejack sat down on the end of Stais' cot. His voice was soft and expressionless, under the bright electric light. "Johnny Moffat's plane."

In all the months that Stais had been in the air force, on fields to which planes had failed to return, he had learned that there was nothing to say. He was only nineteen years old, but he had learned that. So he lay quiet.

"They got separated in clouds on the way out of Ascension, and they never picked them up again. There's still a chance," Whitejack said, "that they'll drop in any minute." He looked at his watch. "Still a chance for another hour and forty minutes . . ."

There was still nothing to say, so Stais lay silent.

"Johnny Moffat," said Whitejack, "at one time looked as though he was going to marry my sister. In a way, it's a good thing he didn't. It'd be a little hard, being brothers-in-law, on some of the parties the air force goes on in one place and another." Whitejack fell silent, looked down at his belly. Deliberately, he let his belt out a notch. He pulled it to, with a severe little click. "That fried chicken was mighty good," he said. "You sure you want to pass it up?"

"I'm saving my appetite," Stais said, "for my mother's cooking."

"My sister," said Whitejack, "was passing fond of Johnny, and I have a feeling when he gets home from the war and settles down, she's going to snag him. She came to me right before I left and she asked me if I would let her have ten acres on the north side of my property and three acres of timber to build their house. I said it was OK with me." He was silent again, thinking of the rolling ten acres of upland meadow in North Carolina and the three tall acres of standing timber, oak and pine, from which it would be possible to build a strong country house. "There's nobody in the whole world I'd rather have living on my property than Johnny Moffat. I've known him for twenty years and I've had six fist fights with him and won them all, and been alone with him in the woods for two months at a time, and I still say that. . . ." He got up and went over to his own cot, then turned and came back. "By the way," he said softly, "this is between you and me, Sergeant."

"Sure," said Stais.

"My sister said she'd murder me for my hide and taller if I ever let Johnny know what was in store for him." He grinned a little. "Women're very confident in certain fields," he said. "And I never did tell Johnny, not even when I was so drunk I was singing 'Casey Jones' naked in the middle of the city of Tampa at three o'clock in the morning." He went over to his musette bag and got out a cigar and thoughtfully lit it. "You'd be surprised," he said, "how fond you become of nickel cigars in the Army."

"I tried smoking," said Stais. "I think I'll wait until I get a little older."

Whitejack sat heavily on his own cot. "Do you think they'll send you out to fight again?" he asked.

Stais stared up at the ceiling. "I wouldn't be surprised," he said. "There's nothing really wrong with me. I'm just tired."

Whitejack nodded, smoking slowly. "By the way," he said, "you heard us talking about the Lieutenant, didn't you?"

"Yes."

"I went out to the field and had a little conversation with him. He's just been sittin' there all day and most of the night since we got here, outside the Operations room, just lookin' and starin' across at the planes comin' in. Him and me, we've been good friends for a long time and I asked him pointblank. I said, 'Freddie,' I said, 'there's a question the boys're askin' themselves these days about you.' And he said, 'What's the matter?' And I said, 'The boys're asking if you've turned bad. You pass 'em and you don't even look at them as though you recognize 'em. What is it, you turn GI after a year?' I said. He looked at me and then he looked at the ground and he didn't say anything for maybe a minute. Then he said, 'I beg your pardon, Arnold. It never occurred to me.' Then he told me what was on his mind." Whitejack looked at his watch, almost automatically, then lifted his head again. "Ever since we got the order to go overseas he's been worrying. About the waist gunner and his navigator."

"What's he worrying about?" For a moment a crazy list of all the thousand things you can worry about in the crew of one airplane flashed through Stais' head.

"They're not fighting men," Whitejack said slowly. "They're both good fellers, you wouldn't want better, but the Lieutenant's been watchin' 'em for a long time on the ground, in the air, at their guns, and he's convinced they won't measure. And he feels he's responsible for taking the Mitchell in and getting it out with as many of us alive as possible and he feels the waist gunner and the navigator're danger- ous to have in the plane. And he's makin' up his mind to put in a request for two new men when we get to India, and he can't bear to think of what it'll do to the gunner and the navigator when they find out he's asked to have 'em grounded, and that's why he just sits there outside Operations, not even seein' us when we go by. . . ." Whitejack sighed. "He's twenty-two years old, the Lieutenant. It's a strain, something like that, for a man twenty-two years old. If you see Novak, you won't tell him anything, will you?"

"No," said Stais.

"I suppose things like this come up all the time in any army."

"All the time," said Stais.

Whitejack looked at his watch. Outside there was the growing and lapsing roar of engines that had been the constant sound of both their lives for so many months.

"Ah," said Whitejack, "they should've put me in the infantry. I can hit a rabbit at three hundred yards with a rifle, they put me in the Air Force and give me a camera. . . . Well, Sergeant, I think it's about time you were movin'."

Slowly, Stais got up. He put on his shoes and put his shaving kit into his musette bag and slung it over his shoulder.

"You ready?" asked Whitejack.

"Yes," said Stais.

"That all the baggage you got—that little musette bag?"

"Yes," said Stais. "I was listed as missing, presumed dead, and they sent all my stuff into the supply room and all my personal belongings home to my mother."

Stais looked around the barracks. It shone in the harsh army light of barracks at night all over the world, by now familiar, homelike, to all the men who passed through them. He had left nothing.

They walked out into the soft, engine-filled night. A beacon flashed nervously across the sky, dimming the enormous pale twinkle of Southern stars for a moment. They walked slowly, stepping cautiously over the ditches dug for the flood rains of the African West Coast.

As they passed the Operations room, Stais saw a young lieutenant slumped down in a wobbly old wicker chair, staring out across the field.

"They come yet?" Whitejack asked.

"No," said the lieutenant, without looking up.

Stais went into the building and into the room where they had the rubber raft and the patented radio and the cloth painted blue on one side and yellow on the other. A fat middle-aged ATC captain wearily told them about ditching procedure. There were more than thirty people in the room, all passengers on Stais' plane. There were two small, yellow Chinese who were going to be airsick and five bouncing fat Red Cross women, and three sergeants with a lot of Air Force medals, trying not to seem excited about going home, and two colonels in the Engineers, looking too old for this war. Stais only half listened as the fat captain explained how to inflate the raft, what strings to pull, what levers to move, where to find the waterproofed Bible. . . .

Whitejack was standing outside when Stais started for his plane. He gave Stais a slip of paper. "It's my home address," he said. "After the war, just come down sometime in October and I'll take you hunting."

"Thank you very much," said Stais gravely. Over Whitejack's

shoulder he saw the lieutenant, still slumped in the wicker chair, still staring fixedly and unrelievedly out across the dark field.

Whitejack walked out to the great plane with Stais, along the oil-spattered concrete of the runway, among the Chinese and loud Red Cross women and the sergeants. They stopped, without a word, at the steps going up to the doorway of the plane and the other passengers filed past them.

They stood there, silently, with the two days of random conversation behind them and Brazil and Athens behind them, and five hundred flights behind them, and Jerusalem and Miami behind them, and the girls from Vienna and the American Embassy and Flushing, Long Island, behind them, and the Greek mountaineers behind them and Thomas Wolfe's funeral, and friends burning like torches, and dogs under treed raccoons in the Blue Ridge Mountains behind them, and a desperate twenty-two year old lieutenant painfully staring across a dusty airfield for ten days behind them, and the Mediterranean and the hospital bed in Cairo and Johnny Moffat wandering that night over the Southern Atlantic, with ten acres of meadow and three acres of timber for his house, and Whitejack's sister waiting for him, all behind them. And, ahead of Stais, home and a mother who had presumed him dead and wept over his personal belongings, and ahead of Whitejack the cold bitter mountains of India and China and the tearing dead sound of the fifties and the sky full of Japs. . . .

"All right, Sergeant," the voice of the lieutenant checking the passengers. "Get on."

Stais waved, a little broken wave, at Whitejack standing there. "See you," he said, "in North Carolina."

"Some October." Whitejack smiled a little, in the light of the floodlamps.

The door closed and Stais sat down in the seat in front of the two Chinese.

"I think these planes are absolutely charming," one of the Red Cross women was saying loudly. "Don't you?"

The engines started and the big plane began to roll. Stais looked out of the window. A plane was landing. It came slowly into the light of the runway lamps and set down heavily, bumping wearily. Stais stared. It was a Mitchell. Stais sighed to himself. As the big C54 wheeled at the head of the runway, then started clumsily down, Stais put the slip of paper with Arnold Whitejack written on it, and the address, in scrawling, childlike handwriting, into his pocket. And as he saw the Mitchell pull to a stop near the Operations room, he felt for the moment a little less guilty for going home.

Theme Questions

1. What is the significance of the title? In how many ways does the story represent passage for Stais? Does this apply to the others?

2. The plotting of the story is rather intricate. What is the main plot? How does the subplot of Whitejack and Johnny Moffat contribute to the main plot? How does the subplot of the young lieutenant contribute to the main plot? In what ways do they all contribute to the main theme?

3. Both are in their teens, yet Novak is young and Stais is old. Why? Contrast the two characters in relation to their experiences and attitudes.

4. Study the time flow in the story. What techniques does Shaw use to move time? In what ways does time become a significant factor?

5. The style of the story is marked by its use of understatement. Discuss its use, particularly in reference to the descriptions of war. How does Shaw use contrast in the story as part of the technique of understatement?

. . . **also by Irwin Shaw**   *The Young Lions*
Act of Faith and Other Stories
Voices of a Summer Day

It doesn't matter which war or what cause, the following poems seem to apply to any or all. Yet historically they reflect three wars since the beginning of the twentieth century. Sassoon's poem deals with the conditions of battle itself. MacLeish and Crane offer broader comments in different ways. MacLeish wants death made meaningful; Crane's refrain line, "War is kind" shows his bitter irony.

The Dug-Out*

Siegfried Sassoon

Why do you lie with your legs ungainly huddled,
And one arm bent across your sullen, cold,
Exhausted face? It hurts my heart to watch you,
Deep-shadowed from the candle's guttering gold;
And you wonder why I shake you by the shoulder;
Drowsy, you mumble and sigh and turn your head. . . .
You are too young to fall asleep for ever;
And when you sleep you remind me of the dead.

The Young Dead Soldiers**

for Lieutenant Richard Myers

Archibald MacLeish

The young dead soldiers do not speak.
Nevertheless, they are heard in the still houses: who has not heard
    them?
They have a silence that speaks for them at night and when the
    clock counts.

They say: We were young. We have died. Remember us.
They say: We have done what we could but until it is finished it
    is not done.

* Reprinted by permission of George Sassoon.
** From *Actfive and Other Poems*, by Archibald MacLeish. Copyright 1948 by Archibald MacLeish. Reprinted by permission of Random House, Inc.

They say: We have given our lives but until it is finished no one
  can know what our lives gave.
They say: Our deaths are not ours; they are yours; they will mean
  what you make them.
They say: Whether our lives and our deaths were for peace and
  a new hope or for nothing we cannot say; it is you who must
  say this.
They say: We leave you our deaths. Give them their meaning.
We were young, they say. We have died. Remember us.

Do Not Weep, Maiden

Stephen Crane

Do not weep, maiden, for war is kind.
Because your lover threw wild hands toward the sky
And the affrighted steed ran on alone,
Do not weep.
War is kind.

   Hoarse, booming drums of the regiment,
   Little souls who thirst for fight,
   These men were born to drill and die.
   The unexplained glory flies above them,
   Great is the battle-god, great, and his kingdom—
   A field where a thousand corpses lie.

Do not weep, babe, for war is kind.
Because your father tumbled in the yellow trenches,
Raged at his breast, gulped and died,
Do not weep.
War is kind.

   Swift blazing flag of the regiment,
   Eagle with crest of red and gold,
   These men were born to drill and die.
   Point for them the virtue of slaughter,
   Make plain to them the excellence of killing
   And a field where a thousand corpses lie.

Mother whose heart hung humble as a button
On the bright splendid shroud of your son,
Do not weep.
War is kind.

Theme Questions

1. Consider the five war poems as a group, but state the theme for each separately. Draw the separate themes together for a general commentary.

2. Select the war poem that has the strongest impact for you. State your personal response, and then analyze what the poet did structurally and thematically to create the reaction.

There is no clear line of demarcation between immaturity and maturity, and no single point in life when the crossover occurs. Some of this fluctuation is reflected in "Sophistication" in George and Helen's last quiet fling, in which they communicate like adults but play like children.

Sophistication

Sherwood Anderson

It was early evening of a day in the late fall and the Winesburg County Fair had brought crowds of country people into town. The day had been clear and the night came on warm and pleasant. On the Trunion Pike, where the road after it left town stretched away between berry fields now covered with dry brown leaves, the dust from passing wagons arose in clouds. Children, curled into little balls, slept on the straw scattered on wagon beds. Their hair was full of dust and their fingers black and sticky. The dust rolled away over the fields and the departing sun set it ablaze with colors.

In the main street of Winesburg crowds filled the stores and the sidewalks. Night came on, horses whinnied, the clerks in the stores ran madly about, children became lost and cried lustily, an American town worked terribly at the task of amusing itself.

Pushing his way through the crowds in Main Street, young George Willard concealed himself in the stairway leading to Doctor Reefy's office and looked at the people. With feverish eyes he watched the faces drifting past under the store lights. Thoughts kept coming into his head and he did not want to think. He stamped impatiently on the wooden steps and looked sharply about. "Well, is she going to stay with him all day? Have I done all this waiting for nothing?" he muttered.

George Willard, the Ohio village boy, was fast growing into manhood and new thoughts had been coming into his mind. All that day, amid the jam of people at the Fair, he had gone about feeling lonely.

He was about to leave Winesburg to go away to some city where he hoped to get work on a city newspaper and he felt grown up. The mood that had taken possession of him was a thing known to men and unknown to boys. He felt old and a little tired. Memories awoke in him. To his mind his new sense of maturity set him apart, made of him a half-tragic figure. He wanted someone to understand the feeling that had taken possession of him after his mother's death.

There is a time in the life of every boy when he for the first time takes the backward view of life. Perhaps that is the moment when he crosses the line into manhood. The boy is walking through the street of his town. He is thinking of the future and of the figure he will cut in the world. Ambitions and regrets awake within him. Suddenly something happens; he stops under a tree and waits as for a voice calling his name. Ghosts of old things creep into his consciousness; the voices outside of himself whisper a message concerning the limitations of life. From being quite sure of himself and his future he becomes not at all sure. If he be an imaginative boy a door is torn open and for the first time he looks out upon the world, seeing, as though they marched in procession before him, the countless figures of men who before his time have come out of nothingness into the world, lived their lives and again disappeared into nothingness. The sadness of sophistication has come to the boy. With a little gasp he sees himself as merely a leaf flown by the wind through the streets of his village. He knows that in spite of all the stout talk of his fellows he must live and die in uncertainty, a thing blown by the winds, a thing destined like corn to wilt in the sun. He shivers and looks eagerly about. The eighteen years he has lived seem but a moment, a breathing space in the long march of humanity. Already he hears death calling. With all his heart he wants to come close to some other human, touch someone with his hands, be touched by the hand of another. If he prefers that the other be a woman, that is because he believes that a woman will be gentle, that she will understand. He wants, most of all, understanding.

When the moment of sophistication came to George Willard his mind turned to Helen White, the Winesburg banker's daughter. Always he had been conscious of the girl growing into womanhood as he grew into manhood. Once on a summer night when he was eighteen, he had walked with her on a country road and in her presence had given way to an impulse to boast, to make himself appear big and significant in her eyes. Now he wanted to see her for another purpose. He wanted to tell her of the new impulses that had come to him. He had tried to make her think of him as a man when he knew nothing of manhood and now he wanted to be with her and to try to make her feel the change he believed had taken place in his nature.

As for Helen White, she also had come to a period of change. What George felt, she in her young woman's way felt also. She was no longer a girl and hungered to reach into the grace and beauty of womanhood. She had come home from Cleveland, where she was attending college, to spend a day at the Fair. She also had begun to have memories. During the day she sat in the grandstand with a young man, one of the instructors from the college, who was a guest of her mother's. The young man was of a pedantic turn of mind and she felt at once he would not do for her purpose. At the Fair she was glad to be seen in his company as he was well dressed and a stranger. She knew that the fact of his presence would create an impression. During the day she was happy, but when night came on she began to grow restless. She wanted to drive the instructor away, to get out of his presence. While they sat together in the grandstand and while the eyes of former schoolmates were upon them, she paid so much attention to her escort that he grew interested. "A scholar needs money. I should marry a woman with money," he mused.

Helen White was thinking of George Willard even as he wandered gloomily through the crowds thinking of her. She remembered the summer evening when they had walked together and wanted to walk with him again. She thought that the months she had spent in the city, the going to theatres and the seeing of great crowds wandering in lighted thoroughfares, had changed her profoundly. She wanted him to feel and be conscious of the change in her nature.

The summer evening together that had left its mark on the memory of both the young man and woman had, when looked at quite sensibly, been rather stupidly spent. They had walked out of town along a country road. Then they had stopped by a fence near a field of young corn and George had taken off his coat and let it hang on his arm. "Well, I've stayed here in Winesburg—yes—I've not yet gone away but I'm growing up," he had said. "I've been reading books and I've been thinking. I'm going to try to amount to something in life.

"Well," he explained, "that isn't the point. Perhaps I'd better quit talking."

The confused boy put his hand on the girl's arm. His voice trembled. The two started to walk back along the road toward town. In his desperation George boasted, "I'm going to be a big man, the biggest that ever lived here in Winesburg," he declared. "I want you to do something, I don't know what. Perhaps it is none of my business. I want you to try to be different from other women. You see the point. It's none of my business I tell you. I want you to be a beautiful woman. You see what I want."

The boy's voice failed and in silence the two came back into town and went along the street to Helen White's house. At the gate he tried to say something impressive. Speeches he had thought out came into his head, but they seemed utterly pointless. "I thought—I used to think—I had it in my mind you would marry Seth Richmond. Now I know you won't," was all he could find to say as she went through the gate and toward the door of her house.

On the warm fall evening as he stood in the stairway and looked at the crowd drifting through Main Street, George thought of the talk beside the field of young corn and was ashamed of the figure he had made of himself. In the street the people surged up and down like cattle confined in a pen. Buggies and wagons almost filled the narrow thoroughfare. A band played and small boys raced along the sidewalk, diving between the legs of men. Young men with shining red faces walked awkwardly about with girls on their arms. In a room above one of the stores, where a dance was to be held, the fiddlers tuned their instruments. The broken sounds floated down through an open window and out across the murmur of voices and the loud blare of the horns of the band. The medley of sounds got on young Willard's nerves. Everywhere, on all sides, the sense of crowding, moving life closed in about him. He wanted to run away by himself and think. "If she wants to stay with that fellow she may. Why should I care? What difference does it make to me?" he growled and went along Main Street and through Hern's grocery into a side street.

George felt so utterly lonely and dejected that he wanted to weep but pride made him walk rapidly along, swinging his arms. He came to Wesley Moyer's livery barn and stopped in the shadows to listen to a group of men who talked of a race Wesley's stallion, Tony Tip, had won at the Fair during the afternoon. A crowd had gathered in front of the barn and before the crowd walked Wesley, prancing up and down and boasting. He held a whip in his hand and kept tapping the ground. Little puffs of dust arose in the lamplight. "Hell, quit your talking," Wesley exclaimed. "I wasn't afraid, I knew I had 'em beat all the time. I wasn't afraid."

Ordinarily George Willard would have been intensely interested in the boasting of Moyer, the horseman. Now it made him angry. He turned and hurried away along the street. "Old wind-bag," he sputtered. "Why does he want to be bragging? Why don't he shut up?"

George went into a vacant lot and as he hurried along, fell over a pile of rubbish. A nail protruding from an empty barrel tore his trousers. He sat down on the ground and swore. With a pin he mended the torn place and then arose and went on. "I'll go to Helen White's house, that's what I'll do. I'll walk right in. I'll say that I want to see her. I'll walk right in and sit down, that's what I'll do," he declared, climbing over a fence and beginning to run.

On the veranda of Banker White's house Helen was restless and distraught. The instructor sat between the mother and daughter. His talk wearied the girl. Although he had also been raised in an Ohio town, the instructor began to put on the airs of the city. He wanted to appear cosmopolitan. "I like the chance you have given me to study the background out of which most of our girls come," he declared. "It was good of you, Mrs. White, to have me down for the day." He turned to Helen and laughed. "Your life is still bound up with the life of this town?" he asked. "There are people here in whom you are interested?" To the girl his voice sounded pompous and heavy.

Helen arose and went into the house. At the door leading to a garden at the back she stopped and stood listening. Her mother began to talk. "There is no one here fit to associate with a girl of Helen's breeding," she said.

Helen ran down a flight of stairs at the back of the house and into the garden. In the darkness she stopped and stood trembling. It seemed to her that the world was full of meaningless people saying words. Afire with eagerness she ran through a garden gate and turning a corner by the banker's barn, went into a little side street. "George! Where are you, George?" she cried, filled with nervous excitement. She stopped running, and leaned against a tree to laugh hysterically. Along the dark little street came George Willard, still saying words. "I'm going to walk right into her house. I'll go right in and sit down," he declared as he came up to her. He stopped and stared stupidly. "Come on," he said and took hold of her hand. With hanging heads they walked away along the street under the trees. Dry leaves rustled under foot. Now that he had found her George wondered what he had better do and say.

At the upper end of the fair ground, in Winesburg, there is a half decayed old grandstand. It has never been painted and the boards are all warped out of shape. The fair ground stands on top of a low hill rising out of the valley of Wine Creek and from the grandstand one can see at night, over a cornfield, the lights of the town reflected against the sky.

George and Helen climbed the hill to the fair ground, coming by the path past Waterworks Pond. The feeling of loneliness and isolation that had come to the young man in the crowded streets of his town was both broken and intensified by the presence of Helen. What he felt was reflected in her.

In youth there are always two forces fighting in people. The warm unthinking little animal struggles against the thing that reflects and remembers, and the older, the more sophisticated thing had possession of George Willard. Sensing his mood, Helen walked beside him filled with respect. When they got to the grandstand they climbed up under the roof and sat down on one of the long bench-like seats.

There is something memorable in the experience to be had by going into a fair ground that stands at the edge of a Middle Western town on a night after the annual fair has been held. The sensation is one never to be forgotten. On all sides are ghosts, not of the dead, but of living people. Here, during the day just passed, have come the people pouring in from the town and the country around. Farmers with their wives and children and all the people from the hundreds of little frame houses have gathered within these board walls. Young girls have laughed and men with beards have talked of the affairs of their lives. The place has been filled to overflowing with life. It has itched and squirmed with life and now it is night and the life has all gone away. The silence is almost terrifying. One conceals oneself standing silently beside the trunk of a tree and what there is of a reflective tendency in his nature is intensified. One shudders at the thought of the meaninglessness of life while at the same instant, and if the people of the town are his people, one loves life so intensely that tears come into the eyes.

In the darkness under the roof of the grandstand, George Willard sat beside Helen White and felt very keenly his own insignificance in the scheme of existence. Now that he had come out of town where the presence of the people stirring about, busy with a multitude of affairs, had been so irritating the irritation was all gone. The presence of Helen renewed and refreshed him. It was as though her woman's hand was assisting him to make some minute readjustment of the machinery of his life. He began to think of the people in the town where he had always lived with something like reverence. He had reverence for Helen. He wanted to love and to be loved by her, but he did not want at the moment to be confused by her womanhood. In the darkness he took hold of her hand and when she crept close put a hand on her shoulder. A wind began to blow and he shivered. With all his strength he tried to hold and to understand the mood that had come upon him. In that high place in the darkness the two oddly sensitive human atoms held each other tightly and waited. In the mind of each was the same thought. "I have come to this lonely place and here is this other," was the substance of the thing felt.

In Winesburg the crowded day had run itself out into the long night of the late fall. Farm horses jogged away along lonely country roads pulling their portion of weary people. Clerks began to bring samples of goods in off the sidewalks and lock the doors of stores. In the Opera House a crowd had gathered to see a show and further down Main Street the fiddlers, their instruments tuned, sweated and worked to keep the feet of youth flying over a dance floor.

In the darkness in the grandstand Helen White and George Willard remained silent. Now and then the spell that held them was broken and they turned and tried in the dim light to see into each other's eyes. They kissed but that impulse did not last. At the upper end of the fair ground a half dozen men worked over horses that had raced during the afternoon. The men had built a fire and were heating kettles of water. Only their legs could be seen as they passed back and forth in the light. When the wind blew the little flames of the fire danced crazily about.

George and Helen arose and walked away into the darkness. They went along a path past a field of corn that had not yet been cut. The wind whispered among the dry corn blades. For a moment during the walk back into town the spell that held them was broken. When they had come to the crest of Waterworks Hill they stopped by a tree and George again put his hands on the girl's shoulders. She embraced him eagerly and then again they drew quickly back from that impulse. They stopped kissing and stood a little apart. Mutual respect grew big in them. They were both embarrassed and to relieve their embarrassment dropped into the animalism of youth. They laughed and began to pull and haul at each other. In some way chastened and purified by the mood they had been in they became, not man and woman, not boy and girl, but excited little animals.

It was so they went down the hill. In the darkness they played like two splendid young things in a young world. Once, running swiftly forward, Helen tripped George and he fell. He squirmed and shouted. Shaking with laughter, he rolled down the hill. Helen ran after him. For just a moment she stopped in the darkness. There is no way of knowing what woman's thoughts went through her mind but, when the bottom of the hill was reached and she came up to the boy, she took his arm and walked beside him in dignified silence. For some reason they could not have explained they had both got from their silent evening together the thing needed. Man or boy, woman or girl, they had for a moment taken hold of the thing that makes the mature life of men and women in the modern world possible.

Theme Questions

1. Define sophistication according to the dictionary, common usage, and Anderson's special use. In what ways does Anderson enrich or enlarge the definition?

2. "All that day, amid the jam of people at the Fair, he George had gone about feeling lonely." Why? In what ways does his loneliness relate to the theme of the story? What does Anderson offer as a solution to loneliness?

3. The plot structure shows parallels in the lives of George and Helen and then their unparallel convergence. What are the parallel elements? At what point is the convergence, or meshing? What does it signify?

4. The setting contributes to the plot, the tone, and the mood. Discuss its intrinsic value. How does it enrich the other elements?

5. Paragraph 4, which indicates certain naturalistic elements, states the philosophy of the story. Restate your understanding of it, and indicate how the experience of George and Helen illustrates Anderson's viewpoint.

. . . also by Sherwood Anderson   *Winesburg, Ohio*
The Triumph of the Egg
Death in the Woods

Passage occurs for some because of outside circumstances, for others because of inner readiness. Allowed to be irresponsible, many will remain irresponsible, but given the opportunity to be responsible, most will fulfill expectations. Shakespeare's Prince Hal, in the soliloquy that follows, shows his awareness of other people's opinions of him and how these opinions differ from his self-view. In Pound's poem, the selfless commitment to love provides something even deeper than love, richer perhaps because it comes from someone so young.

from "Henry IV," Part 1, Act I, Scene 2

William Shakespeare

PRINCE.   I know you all, and will awhile uphold
The unyok'd humour of your idleness:
Yet herein will I imitate the sun,
Who doth permit the base contagious clouds
To smother up his beauty from the world,
That when he please again to be himself,
Being wanted, he may be more wonder'd at,
By breaking through the foul and ugly mists
Of vapours that did seem to strangle him.
If all the year were playing holidays,
To sport would be as tedious as to work;
But when they seldom come, they wish'd for come,
And nothing pleaseth but rare accidents.
So, when this loose behaviour I throw off,
And pay the debt I never promised,
By how much better than my word I am
By so much shall I falsify men's hopes;
And like bright metal on a sullen ground,
My reformation, glittering o'er my fault,
Shall show more goodly and attract more eyes
Than that which hath no foil to set it off.
I'll so offend to make offence a skill;
Redeeming time when men think least I will.

The River-Merchant's Wife: A Letter

Rihaku

translated by Ezra Pound

While my hair was still cut straight across my forehead
I played about the front gate, pulling flowers.
You came by on bamboo stilts, playing horse,
You walked about my seat, playing with blue plums.
And we went on living in the village of Chokan:
Two small people, without dislike or suspicion.

At fourteen I married My Lord you.
I never laughèd, being bashful.
Lowering my head, I looked at the wall.
Called to, a thousand times, I never looked back.

At fifteen I stopped scowling,
I desired my dust to be mingled with yours
For ever and for ever and for ever.
Why should I climb the look out?

At sixteen you departed,
You went into far Ku-to-yen, by the river of swirling eddies,
And you have been gone five months.
The monkeys make sorrowful noise overhead.

You dragged your feet when you went out.
By the gate now, the moss is grown, the different mosses,
Too deep to clear them away!
The leaves fall early this autumn, in wind.
The paired butterflies are already yellow with August
Over the grass in the West garden;
They hurt me. I grow older.
If you are coming down through the narrows of the river Kiang,
Please let me know beforehand,
And I will come out to meet you
As far as Cho-fu-Sa.

Theme Questions

1. Each poem is a private communication. As such, what does each reveal about the speaker, the people in the speaker's life, and past and future actions?

2. Each poem reflects a distant time and place—Elizabethan England and pre-twentieth-century China. What is alien and strange in each? What is universal?

One of the hallmarks of the loss of youth is the loss of illusion. Basic to the initiation story, this theme has appeared frequently in this book. Now it is present again in this last story, Joseph Conrad's "Youth."

The theme is so persistent that perhaps we must come to the realization that the loss of illusion seems to be inexorably as much a part of the aging process as the biological death and replacement of the protoplasmic cell.

Youth

Joseph Conrad

This could have occurred nowhere but in England, where men and sea interpenetrate, so to speak—the sea entering into the life of most men, and the men knowing something or everything about the sea, in the way of amusement, of travel, or of breadwinning.

We were sitting round a mahogany table that reflected the bottle, the claret glasses, and our faces as we leaned on our elbows. There was a director of companies, an accountant, a lawyer, Marlow, and myself. The director had been a *Conway* boy, the accountant had served four years at sea, the lawyer—a fine crusted Tory, High Churchman, the best of old fellows, the soul of honor—had been chief officer in the P. & O. service in the good old days when mailboats were square-rigged at least on two masts, and used to come down the China Sea before a fair monsoon with stun'sails set alow and aloft. We all began life in the merchant service. Between the five of us there was the strong bond of the sea, and also the fellowship of the craft, which no amount of enthusiasm for yachting, cruising, and so on can give, since one is only the amusement of life and the other is life itself.

Marlow (at least I think that is how he spelt his name) told the story, or rather the chronicle, of a voyage:

"Yes, I have seen a little of the Eastern seas; but what I remember best is my first voyage there. You fellows know there are those voyages that seem ordered for the illustration of life, that might stand for a symbol of existence. You fight, work, sweat, nearly kill yourself, sometimes do kill yourself, trying to accomplish something—and you can't. Not from any fault of yours. You simply can do nothing, neither great nor little—not a thing in the world—not even marry an old maid, or get a wretched 600-ton cargo of coal to its port of destination.

"It was altogether a memorable affair. It was my first voyage to the East, and my first voyage as second mate; it was also my skipper's first command. You'll admit it was time. He was sixty if a day; a little man, with a broad, not very straight back, with bowed shoulders and one leg more bandy than the other, he had that queer twisted-about appearance you see so often in men who work in the fields. He had a nutcracker face—chin and nose trying to come together over a sunken mouth—and it was framed in iron-gray fluffy hair, that looked like a chinstrap of cotton-wool sprinkled with coaldust. And he had blue eyes in that old face of his, which were amazingly like a boy's, with that candid expression some quite common men preserve to the end of their days by a rare internal gift of simplicity of heart and rectitude of soul. What induced him to accept me was a wonder. I had come out of a crack Australian clipper, where I had been third officer, and he seemed to have a prejudice against crack clippers as aristocratic and high-toned. He said to me, 'You know, in this ship you will have to work.' I said I had to work in every ship I had ever been in. 'Ah, but this is different, and you gentlemen out of them big ships; . . . but there! I dare say you will do. Join tomorrow.'

"I joined tomorrow. It was twenty-two years ago; and I was just twenty. How time passes! It was one of the happiest days of my life. Fancy! Second mate for the first time—a really responsible officer! I wouldn't have thrown up my new billet for a fortune. The mate looked me over carefully. He was also an old chap, but of another stamp. He had a Roman nose, a snow-white, long beard, and his name was Mahon, but he insisted that it should be pronounced Mann. He was well connected; yet there was something wrong with his luck, and he had never got on.

"As to the captain, he had been for years in coasters, then in the Mediterranean, and last in the West Indian trade. He had never been round the Capes. He could just write a kind of sketchy hand, and didn't care for writing at all. Both were thorough good seamen of course, and between those two old chaps I felt like a small boy between two grandfathers.

"The ship also was old. Her name was the *Judea*. Queer name, isn't it? She belonged to a man Wilmer, Wilcox—some name like that; but he has been bankrupt and dead these twenty years or more, and his name don't matter. She had been laid up in Shadwell basin for ever so long. You may imagine her state. She was all rust, dust, grime—soot aloft, dirt on deck. To me it was like coming out of a palace into a ruined cottage. She was about 400 tons, had a primitive windlass, wooden latches to the doors, not a bit of brass about her, and a big square stern. There was on it, below her name in big letters, a lot of scrollwork, with the gilt off, and some sort of a coat of arms, with the motto 'Do or Die' underneath. I remember it took my fancy immensely. There was a touch of romance in it, something that made me love the old thing—something that appealed to my youth!

"We left London in ballast—sand ballast—to load a cargo of coal in a northern port for Bankok. Bankok! I thrilled. I had been six years at sea, but had only seen Melbourne and Sydney, very good places, charming places in their way—but Bankok!

"We worked out of the Thames under canvas, with a North Sea pilot on board. His name was Jermyn, and he dodged all day long about the galley drying his handkerchief before the stove. Apparently he never slept. He was a dismal man, with a perpetual tear sparkling at the end of his nose, who either had been in trouble, or was in trouble, or expected to be in trouble—couldn't be happy unless something went wrong. He mistrusted my youth, my common sense, and my seamanship, and made a point of showing it in a hundred little ways. I dare say he was right. It seems to me I knew very little then, and I know not much more now; but I cherish a hate for that Jermyn to this day.

"We were a week working up as far as Yarmouth Roads, and then we got into a gale—the famous October gale of twenty-two years ago. It was wind, lightning, sleet, snow, and a terrific sea. We were flying light, and you may imagine how bad it was when I tell you we had smashed bulwarks and a flooded deck. On the second night she shifted her ballast into the lee bow, and by that time we had been blown off somewhere on the Dogger Bank. There was nothing for it but go below with shovels and try to right her, and there we were in that vast hold, gloomy like a cavern, the tallow dips stuck and flickering on the beams, the gale howling above, the ship tossing about like mad on her side; there we all were, Jermyn, the captain, everyone, hardly able to keep our feet, engaged on that gravedigger's work, and trying to toss shovelfuls of wet sand up to windward. At every tumble of the ship you could see vaguely in the dim light men falling down with a great flourish of shovels. One of the ship's boys (we had two), impressed by the weirdness of the scene, wept as if his heart would break. We could hear him blubbering somewhere in the shadows.

"On the third day the gale died out, and by and by a north-country tug picked us up. We took sixteen days in all to get from London to the Tyne! When we got into dock we had lost our turn for loading, and they hauled us off to a pier where we remained for a month. Mrs. Beard (the captain's name was Beard) came from Colchester to see the old man. She lived on board. The crew of runners had left, and there remained only the officers, one boy and the steward, a mulatto who answered to the name of Abraham. Mrs. Beard was an old woman, with a face all wrinkled and ruddy like a winter apple, and the figure of a young girl. She caught sight of me once, sewing on a button, and insisted on having my shirts to repair. This was something different from the captains' wives I had known on board crack clippers. When I brought her the shirts, she said: 'And the socks? They want mending, I am sure, and John's—Captain Beard's—things are all in order now. I would be glad of something to do.' Bless the old woman. She overhauled my outfit for me, and meantime I read for the first time *Sartor Resartus* and Burnaby's *Ride to Khiva*. I didn't understand much of the first then: but I remember I preferred the soldier to the philosopher at the time; a preference which life has only confirmed. One was a man, and the other was either more—or less. However, they are both dead and Mrs. Beard is dead, and youth, strength, genius, thoughts, achievements, simple hearts—all dies. . . . No matter.

"They loaded us at last. We shipped a crew. Eight able seamen and two boys. We hauled off one evening to the buoys at the dock gates, ready to go out, and with a fair prospect of beginning the voyage next day. Mrs. Beard was to start for home by a late train. When the ship was fast we went to tea. We sat rather silent through the meal—Mahon, the old couple, and I. I finished first, and slipped away for a smoke, my cabin being in a deckhouse just against the poop. It was high water, blowing fresh with a drizzle; the double dock gates were opened, and the stream colliers were going in and out in the darkness with their lights burning bright, a great plashing of propellers, rattling of winches, and a lot of hailing on the pierheads. I watched the procession of headlights gliding high and of green lights gliding low in the night, when suddenly a red gleam flashed at me, vanished, came into view again, and remained. The fore end of a steamer loomed up close. I shouted down the cabin, 'Come up, quick!' and then heard a startled voice saying afar in the dark, 'Stop her, sir.' A bell jingled. Another voice cried warningly, 'We are going right into that bark, sir.' The answer to this was a gruff 'All right,' and the next thing was a heavy crash as the steamer struck a glancing blow with the bluff of her bow about our forerigging. There was a moment of confusion, yelling, and running about. Steam roared. Then somebody was heard saying, 'All clear, sir.' . . . 'Are you all right?' asked the gruff voice. I had jumped forward to see the damage, and hailed back. 'I think so.' 'Easy astern,' said the gruff voice. A bell jingled. 'What steamer is that?' screamed Mahon. By that time she was no more to us than a bulky shadow maneuvering a little way off. They shouted at us some name—a woman's name, Miranda or Melissa—or some such thing. 'This means another month in this beastly hole,' said Mahon to me, as we peered with lamps about the splintered bulwarks and broken braces. 'But where's the captain?'

"We had not heard or seen anything of him all that time. We went aft to look. A doleful voice arose hailing somewhere in the middle of the dock, '*Judea* ahoy!' . . . How the devil did he get there? . . . 'Hallo!' we shouted. 'I am adrift in our boat without oars,' he cried. A belated water-man offered his services, and Mahon struck a bargain with him for half-a-crown to tow our skipper alongside; but it was Mrs. Beard that came up the ladder first. They had been floating about the dock in that mizzly cold rain for nearly an hour. I was never so surprised in my life.

"It appears that when he heard my shout 'Come up' he understood at once what was the matter, caught up his wife, ran on deck, and across, and down into our boat, which was fast to the ladder. Not bad for a sixty-year-old. Just imagine that old fellow saving heroically in his arms that old woman—the woman of his life. He set her down on a thwart, and was ready to climb back on board when the painter came adrift somehow, and away they went together. Of course in the confusion we did not hear him shouting. He looked abashed. She said cheerfully, 'I suppose it does not matter my losing the train now?' 'No, Jenny— you go below and get warm,' he growled. Then to us: 'A sailor has no business with a wife—I say. There I was, out of the ship. Well, no harm done this time. Let's go and look at what that fool of a steamer smashed.'

"It wasn't much, but it delayed us three weeks. At the end of that time, the captain being engaged with his agents, I carried Mrs. Beard's bag to the railway station and put her all comfy into a third-class carriage. She lowered the window to say, 'You are a good young man. If you see John—Captain Beard—without his muffler at night, just remind him from me to keep his throat well wrapped up.' 'Certainly, Mrs. Beard,' I said. 'You are a good young man; I noticed how attentive you are to John—to Captain——' The train pulled out suddenly; I took my cap off to the old woman: I never saw her again. . . . Pass the bottle.

"We went to sea next day. When we made that start for Bankok we had been already three months out of London. We had expected to be a fortnight or so—at the outside.

"It was January, and the weather was beautiful—the beautiful sunny winter weather that has more charm than in the summertime, because it is unexpected, and crisp, and you know it won't, it can't, last long. It's like a windfall, like a godsend, like an unexpected piece of luck.

"It lasted all down the North Sea, all down Channel; and it lasted till we were three hundred miles or so to the westward of the Lizards; then the wind went round to the sou'west and began to pipe up. In two days it blew a gale. The *Judea*, hove to, wallowed on the Atlantic like an old candle-box. It blew day after day: it blew with spite, without interval, without mercy, without rest. The world was nothing but an immensity of great foaming waves rushing at us, under a sky low enough to touch with the hand and dirty like a smoked ceiling. In the stormy space surrounding us there was as much flying spray as air. Day after day and night after night there was nothing round the ship but the howl of the wind, the tumult of the sea, the noise of water pouring over her deck. There was no rest for her and no rest for us. She tossed, she pitched, she stood on her head, she sat on her tail, she rolled, she groaned, and we had to hold on while on deck and cling to our bunks when below, in a constant effort of body and worry of mind.

"One night Mahon spoke through the small window of my berth. It opened right into my very bed, and I was lying there sleepless, in my boots, feeling as though I had not slept for years, and could not if I tried. He said excitedly:

" 'You got the sounding rod in here, Marlow? I can't get the pumps to suck. By God! It's no child's play!'

"I gave him the sounding rod and lay down again, trying to think of various things—but I thought only of the pumps. When I came on deck they were still at it, and my watch relieved at the pumps. By the light of the lantern brought on deck to examine the sounding rod I caught a glimpse of their weary, serious faces. We pumped all the four hours. We pumped all night, all day, all the week—watch and watch. She was working herself loose, and leaked badly—not enough to drown us at once, but enough to kill us with the work at the pumps. And while we pumped the ship was going from us piecemeal: the bulwarks went, the stanchions were torn out, the ventilators smashed, the cabin door burst in. There was not a dry spot in the ship. She was being gutted bit by bit. The longboat changed, as if by magic, into matchwood where she stood in her gripes. I had lashed her myself, and was rather proud of my handiwork, which had withstood so long the malice of the sea. And we pumped. And there was no break in the weather. The sea was white like a sheet of foam, like a caldron of boiling milk; there was not a break in the clouds, no—not the size of a man's hand—no, not for so much as ten seconds. There was for us no sky, there were for us no stars, no sun, no universe—nothing but angry clouds and an infuriated sea. We pumped watch and watch, for dear life; and it seemed to last for months, for years, for all eternity, as though we had been dead and gone to a hell for sailors. We forgot the day of the week, the name of the month, what year it was, and whether we had ever been ashore. The sails blew away, she lay broadside on under a weather cloth, the ocean poured over her, and we did not care. We turned those handles and had the eyes of idiots. As soon as we had crawled on deck I used to take a round turn with a rope about the men, the pumps, and the mainmast, and we turned, we turned incessantly, with the water to our waists, to our necks, over our heads. It was all one. We had forgotten how it felt to be dry.

"And there was somewhere in me the thought: By Jove! This is the deuce of an adventure—something you read about; and it is my first voyage as second mate—and I am only twenty—and here I am lasting it out as well as any of these men, and keeping my chaps up to the mark. I was pleased. I would not have given up the experience for worlds. I had moments of exultation. Whenever the old dismantled craft pitched heavily with her counter high in the air, she seemed to me to throw up, like an appeal, like a defiance, like a cry to the clouds without mercy, the words written on her stern: '*Judea*, London. Do or Die.'

"O youth! The strength of it, the faith of it, the imagination of it! To me she was not an old rattletrap carting about the world a lot of coal for a freight—to me she was the endeavor, the test, the trial of life. I think of her with pleasure, with affection, with regret—as you would think of someone dead you have loved. I shall never forget her. . . . Pass the bottle.

"One night when tied to the mast, as I explained, we were pumping on, deafened with the wind, and without spirit enough in us to wish ourselves dead, a heavy sea crashed aboard and swept clean over us. As soon as I got my breath I shouted, as in duty bound, 'Keep on, boys!' when suddenly I felt something hard floating on deck strike the calf of my leg. I made a grab at it and missed. It was so dark we could not see each other's faces within a foot—you understand.

"After that thump the ship kept quiet for a while, and the thing, whatever it was, struck my leg again. This time I caught it—and it was a saucepan. At first, being stupid with fatigue and thinking of nothing but the pumps, I did not understand what I had in my hand. Suddenly it dawned upon me, and I shouted, 'Boys, the house on deck is gone. Leave this, and let's look for the cook.'

"There was a deckhouse forward, which contained the galley, the cook's berth, and the quarters of the crew. As we had expected for days to see it swept away, the hands had been ordered to sleep in the cabin—the only safe place in the ship. The steward, Abraham, however, persisted in clinging to his berth, stupidly, like a mule—from sheer fright I believe, like an animal that won't leave a stable falling in an earthquake. So we went to look for him. It was chancing death, since once out of our lashings we were as exposed as if on a raft. But we went. The house was shattered as if a shell had exploded inside. Most of it had gone overboard—stove, men's quarters, and their property, all was gone; but two posts, holding a portion of the bulkhead to which Abraham's bunk was attached, remained as if by a miracle. We groped in the ruins and came upon this, and there he was, sitting in his bunk, surrounded by foam and wreckage, jabbering cheerfully to himself. He was out of his mind; completely and forever mad, with this sudden shock coming upon the fag-end of his endurance. We snatched him up, lugged him aft, and pitched him headfirst down the cabin companion. You understand there was no time to carry him down with infinite precautions and wait to see how he got on. Those below would pick him up at the bottom of the stairs all right. We were in a hurry to go back to the pumps. That business could not wait. A bad leak is an inhuman thing.

"One would think that the sole purpose of that fiendish gale had been to make a lunatic of that poor devil of a mulatto. It eased before morning, and next day the sky cleared, and as the sea went down the leak took up. When it came to bending a fresh set of sails the crew demanded to put back—and really there was nothing else to do. Boats gone, decks swept clean, cabin gutted, men without a stitch but what they stood in, stores spoiled, ship strained. We put her head for home, and—would you believe it? The wind came east right in our teeth. It blew fresh, it blew continuously. We had to beat up every inch of the way, but she did not leak so badly, the water keeping comparatively smooth. Two hours' pumping in every four is no joke—but it kept her afloat as far as Falmouth.

"The good people there live on casualties of the sea, and no doubt were glad to see us. A hungry crowd of shipwrights sharpened their chisels at the sight of that carcass of a ship. And, by Jove! they had pretty pickings off us before they were done. I fancy the owner was already in a tight place. There were delays. Then it was decided to take part of the cargo out and calk her topsides. This was done, the repairs finished, cargo reshipped; a new crew came on board, and we went out —for Bankok. At the end of a week we were back again. The crew said they weren't going to Bankok—a hundred and fifty days' passage—in a something hooker that wanted pumping eight hours out of the twenty-four; and the nautical papers inserted again the little paragraph: '*Judea*. Bark. Tyne to Bankok; coals; put back to Falmouth leaky and with crew refusing duty.'

"There were more delays—more tinkering. The owner came down for a day, and said she was as right as a little fiddle. Poor old Captain Beard looked like the ghost of a Geordie skipper—through the worry and humiliation of it. Remember he was sixty, and it was his first command. Mahon said it was a foolish business, and would end badly. I loved the ship more than ever, and wanted awfully to get to Bankok. To Bankok! Magic name, blessed name. Mesopotamia wasn't a patch on it. Remember I was twenty, and it was my first second-mate's billet, and the East was waiting for me.

"We went out and anchored in the outer roads with a fresh crew— the third. She leaked worse than ever. It was as if those confounded shipwrights had actually made a hole in her. This time we did not even go outside. The crew simply refused to man the windlass.

"They towed us back to the inner harbor, and we became a fixture, a feature, an institution of the place. People pointed us out to visitors as

'That 'ere bark that's going to Bankok—has been here six months—put back three times.' On holidays the small boys pulling about in boats would hail, '*Judea*, ahoy!' and if a head showed above the rail shouted, 'Where you bound to?—Bankok?' and jeered. We were only three on board. The poor old skipper mooned in the cabin. Mahon undertook the cooking, and unexpectedly developed all a Frenchman's genius for preparing nice little messes. I looked languidly after the rigging. We became citizens of Falmouth. Every shopkeeper knew us. At the barber's or tobacconist's they asked familiarly, 'Do you think you will ever get to Bankok?' Meantime the owner, the underwriters, and the charterers squabbled amongst themselves in London, and our pay went on. . . . Pass the bottle.

"It was horrid. Morally it was worse than pumping for life. It seemed as though we had been forgotten by the world, belonged to nobody, would get nowhere; it seemed that, as if bewitched, we would have to live for ever and ever in that inner harbor, a derision and a byword to generations of longshore loafers and dishonest boatmen. I obtained three months' pay and a five days' leave, and made a rush for London. It took me a day to get there and pretty well another to come back—but three months' pay went all the same. I don't know what I did with it. I went to a music hall, I believe, lunched, dined, and supped in a swell place in Regent Street, and was back on time, with nothing but a complete set of Byron's works and a new railway rug to show for three months' work. The boatman who pulled me off to the ship said: 'Hallo! I thought you had left the old thing. *She* will never get to Bankok.' 'That's all *you* know about it,' I said, scornfully—but I didn't like that prophecy at all.

"Suddenly a man, some kind of agent to somebody, appeared with full powers. He had grog-blossoms all over his face, an indomitable energy, and was a jolly soul. We leaped into life again. A hulk came alongside, took our cargo, and then we went into dry dock to get our copper stripped. No wonder she leaked. The poor thing, strained beyond endurance by the gale, had, as if in disgust, spat out all the oakum of her lower seams. She was recalked, new-coppered, and made as tight as a bottle. We went back to the hulk and reshipped our cargo.

"Then, on a fine moonlight night, all the rats left the ship.

"We had been infested with them. They had destroyed our sails, consumed more stores than the crew, affably shared our beds and our dangers, and now, when the ship was made seaworthy, concluded to clear out. I called Mahon to enjoy the spectacle. Rat after rat appeared on our rail, took a last look over his shoulder, and leaped with a hollow thud into the empty hulk. We tried to count them, but soon lost the tale. Mahon said: 'Well, well! don't talk to me about the intelligence of rats. They ought to have left before, when we had that narrow squeak from foundering. There you have the proof how silly is the superstition about them. They leave a good ship for an old rotten hulk, where there is nothing to eat, too, the fools! . . . I don't believe they know what is safe or what is good for them, any more than you or I.'

"And after some more talk we agreed that the wisdom of rats had been grossly overrated, being in fact no greater than that of men.

"The story of the ship was known, by this, all up the Channel from Land's End to the Forelands, and we could get no crew on the south coast. They sent us one all complete from Liverpool and we left once more—for Bankok.

"We had fair breezes, smooth water right into the tropics, and the old *Judea* lumbered along in the sunshine. When she went eight knots everything cracked aloft, and we tied our caps to our heads; but mostly she strolled on at the rate of three miles an hour. What could you expect? She was tired—that old ship. Her youth was where mine is— where yours is—you fellows who listen to this yarn; and what friend would throw your years and your weariness in your face? We didn't grumble at her. To us aft, at least, it seemed as though we had been born in her, reared in her, had lived in her for ages, had never known any other ship. I would just as soon have abused the old village church at home for not being a cathedral.

"And for me there was also my youth to make me patient. There was all the East before me, and all life, and the thought that I had been tried in that ship and had come out pretty well. And I thought of men of old who, centuries ago, went that road in ships that sailed no better, to the land of palms, and spices, and yellow sands, and of brown nations ruled by kings more cruel than Nero the Roman, and more splendid than Solomon the Jew. The old bark lumbered on, heavy with her age and the burden of her cargo, while I lived the life of youth in ignorance and hope. She lumbered on through an interminable procession of days; and the fresh gilding flashed back at the setting sun, seemed to cry out over the darkening sea the words painted on her stern, '*Judea*, London. Do or Die.'

"Then we entered the Indian Ocean and steered northerly for Java Head. The winds were light. Weeks slipped by. She crawled on, do or die, and people at home began to think of posting us as overdue.

"One Saturday evening, I being off duty, the men asked me to give them an extra bucket of water or so—for washing clothes. As I did not wish to screw on the fresh-water pump so late, I went forward whistling, and with a key in my hand to unlock the forepeak scuttle, intending to serve the water out of a spare tank we kept there.

"The smell down below was as unexpected as it was frightful. One would have thought hundreds of paraffin lamps had been flaring and smoking in that hole for days. I was glad to get out. The man with me coughed and said, 'Funny smell, sir.' I answered negligently, 'It's good for the health, they say,' and walked aft.

"The first thing I did was to put my head down the square of the midship ventilator. As I lifted the lid a visible breath, something like a thin fog, a puff of faint haze, rose from the opening. The ascending air was hot, and had a heavy, sooty, paraffiny smell. I gave one sniff, and put down the lid gently. It was no use choking myself. The cargo was on fire.

"Next day she began to smoke in earnest. You see it was to be expected, for though the coal was of a safe kind, that cargo had been so handled, so broken up with handling, that it looked more like smithy coal than anything else. Then it had been wetted—more than once. It rained all the time we were taking it back from the hulk, and now with this long passage it got heated, and there was another case of spontaneous combustion.

"The captain called us into the cabin. He had a chart spread on the table, and looked unhappy. He said, 'The coast of West Australia is near, but I mean to proceed to our destination. It is the hurricane month, too; but we will just keep her head for Bankok, and fight the fire. No more putting back anywhere, if we all get roasted. We will try first to stifle this 'ere damned combustion by want of air.'

"We tried. We battened down everything, and still she smoked. The smoke kept coming out through imperceptible crevices; it forced itself through bulkheads and covers; it oozed here and there and everywhere in slender threads, in an invisible film, in an incomprehensible manner. It made its way into the cabin, into the forecastle; it poisoned the sheltered places on the deck; it could be sniffed as high as the mainyard. It was clear that if the smoke came out the air came in. This was disheartening. This combustion refused to be stifled.

"We resolved to try water, and took the hatches off. Enormous volumes of smoke, whitish, yellowish, thick, greasy, misty, choking, ascended as high as the trucks. All hands cleared out aft. Then the poisonous cloud blew away, and we went back to work in a smoke that was no thicker now than that of an ordinary factory chimney.

"We rigged the force pump, got the hose along, and by and by it burst. Well, it was as old as the ship—a prehistoric hose, and past repair. Then we pumped with the feeble head pump, drew water with buckets, and in this way managed in time to pour lots of Indian Ocean into the main hatch. The bright stream flashed in sunshine, fell into a layer of white crawling smoke, and vanished on the black surface of coal. Steam ascended mingling with the smoke. We poured salt water as into a barrel without a bottom. It was our fate to pump in that ship, to pump out of her, to pump into her; and after keeping water out of her to save ourselves from being drowned, we frantically poured water into her to save ourselves from being burnt.

"And she crawled on, do or die, in the serene weather. The sky was a miracle of purity, a miracle of azure. The sea was polished, was blue, was pellucid, was sparkling like a precious stone, extending on all sides, all round to the horizon—as if the whole terrestrial globe had been one jewel, one colossal sapphire, a single gem fashioned into a planet. And on the luster of the great calm waters the *Judea* glided imperceptibly, enveloped in languid and unclean vapors, in a lazy cloud that drifted to leeward, light and slow; a pestiferous cloud defiling the splendor of sea and sky.

"All this time of course we saw no fire. The cargo smoldered at the bottom somewhere. Once Mahon, as we were working side by side, said to me with a queer smile: 'Now, if she only would spring a tidy leak—like that time when we first left the Channel—it would put a stopper on this fire. Wouldn't it?' I remarked irrelevantly, 'Do you remember the rats?'

"We fought the fire and sailed the ship too as carefully as though nothing had been the matter. The steward cooked and attended on us. Of the other twelve men, eight worked while four rested. Everyone took his turn, captain included. There was equality, and if not exactly fraternity, then a deal of good feeling. Sometimes a man, as he dashed a bucketful of water down the hatchway, would yell out, 'Hurrah for Bankok!' and the rest laughed. But generally we were taciturn and serious—and thirsty. Oh! how thirsty! And we had to be careful with the water. Strict allowance. The ship smoked, the sun blazed. . . . Pass the bottle.

"We tried everything. We even made an attempt to dig down to the fire. No good, of course. No man could remain more than a minute below. Mahon, who went first, fainted there, and the man who went to fetch him out did likewise. We lugged them out on deck. Then I leaped down to show how easily it could be done. They had learned wisdom by that time, and contented themselves by fishing for me with a chainhook tied to a broom handle, I believe. I did not offer to go and fetch up my shovel, which was left down below.

"Things began to look bad. We put the longboat into the water. The second boat was ready to swing out. We had also another, a fourteen-foot thing, on davits aft, where it was quite safe.

"Then, behold, the smoke suddenly decreased. We redoubled our efforts to flood the bottom of the ship. In two days there was no smoke at all. Everybody was on the broad grin. This was on a Friday. On Saturday no work, but sailing the ship of course, was done. The men washed their clothes and their faces for the first time in a fortnight, and had a special dinner given them. They spoke of spontaneous combustion with contempt, and implied *they* were the boys to put out combustions. Somehow we all felt as though we each had inherited a large fortune. But a beastly smell of burning hung about the ship. Captain Beard had hollow eyes and sunken cheeks. I had never noticed so much before how twisted and bowed he was. He and Mahon prowled soberly about hatches and ventilators, sniffing. It struck me suddenly poor Mahon was a very, very old chap. As to me, I was pleased and proud as though I had helped to win a great naval battle. O youth!

"The night was fine. In the morning a homeward-bound ship passed us hull down—the first we had seen for months; but we were nearing the land at last, Java Head being about 190 miles off, and nearly due north.

"Next day it was my watch on deck from eight to twelve. At breakfast the captain observed, 'It's wonderful how that smell hangs about the cabin.' About ten, the mate being on the poop, I stepped down on the main deck for a moment. The carpenter's bench stood abaft the mainmast: I leaned against it sucking at my pipe, and the carpenter, a young chap, came to talk to me. He remarked, 'I think we have done very well, haven't we?' and then I perceived with annoyance the fool was trying to tilt the bench. I said curtly, 'Don't, Chips,' and immediately became aware of a queer sensation, of an absurd delusion—I seemed somehow to be in the air. I heard all round me like a pent-up breath released—as if a thousand giants simultaneously had said Phoo!—and felt a dull concussion which made my ribs ache suddenly. No doubt about it—I was in the air, and my body was describing a short parabola. But short as it was, I had the time to think several thoughts in, as far as I can remember, the following order: 'This can't be the carpenter—What is it?—Some accident—Submarine volcano?—Coals, gas!—By Jove! We are being blown up—everybody's dead—I am falling into the after-hatch—I see fire in it.'

"The coaldust suspended in the air of the hold had glowed dull-red at the moment of the explosion. In the twinkling of an eye, in an infinitesimal fraction of a second since the first tilt of the bench, I was sprawling full length on the cargo. I picked myself up and scrambled out. It was quick like a rebound. The deck was a wilderness of smashed timber, lying crosswise like trees in a wood after a hurricane; an immense curtain of soiled rags waved gently before me—it was the mainsail blown to strips. I thought: the masts will be toppling over directly; and to get out of the way bolted on all fours towards the poop ladder. The first person I saw was Mahon, with eyes like saucers, his mouth open, and the long white hair standing straight on end round his head like a silver halo. He was just about to go down when the sight of the main deck stirring, heaving up, and changing into splinters before his eyes, petrified him on the top step. I stared at him in unbelief, and he stared at me with a queer kind of shocked curiosity. I did not know that I had no hair, no eyebrows, no eyelashes, that my young mustache was burnt off, that my face was black, one cheek laid open, my nose cut, and my chin bleeding. I had lost my cap, one of my slippers, and my shirt was torn to rags. Of all this I was not aware. I was amazed to see the ship still afloat, the poop deck whole—and, most of all, to see anybody alive. Also the peace of the sky and the serenity of the sea were distinctly surprising. I suppose I expected to see them convulsed with horror. . . . Pass the bottle.

"There was a voice hailing the ship from somewhere—in the air, in the sky—I couldn't tell. Presently I saw the captain—and he was mad. He asked me eagerly, 'Where's the cabin table?' and to hear such a question was a frightful shock. I had just been blown up, you understand, and vibrated with that experience—I wasn't quite sure whether I was alive. Mahon began to stamp with both feet and yelled at him, 'Good God! don't you see the deck's blown out of her?' I found my voice, and stammered out as if conscious of some gross neglect of duty, 'I don't know where the cabin table is.' It was like an absurd dream.

"Do you know what he wanted next? Well, he wanted to trim the yards. Very placidly, and as if lost in thought, he insisted on having the foreyard squared. 'I don't know if there's anybody alive,' said Mahon, almost tearfully. 'Surely,' he said, gently, 'there will be enough left to square the foreyard.'

"The old chap, it seems was in his own berth winding up the chronometers, when the shock sent him spinning. Immediately it occurred to him—as he said afterwards—that the ship had struck something, and he ran out into the cabin. There, he saw, the cabin table had vanished somewhere. The deck being blown up, it had fallen down into the lazarette of course. Where we had our breakfast that morning he saw only a great hole in the floor. This appeared to him so awfully mysterious, and impressed him so immensely, that what he saw and heard after he got on deck were mere trifles in comparison. And mark, he noticed directly the wheel deserted and his bark off her course— and his only thought was to get that miserable, stripped, undecked, smoldering shell of a ship back again with her head pointing at her port of destination. Bankok! That's what he was after. I tell you this quiet, bowed, bandy-legged, almost deformed little man was immense in the singleness of his idea and in his placid ignorance of our agitation. He motioned us forward with a commanding gesture, and went to take the wheel himself.

"Yes; that was the first thing we did—trim the yards of that wreck! No one was killed, or even disabled, but everyone was more or less hurt. You should have seen them! Some were in rags, with black faces, like coal heavers, like sweeps, and had bullet heads that seemed closely cropped, but were in fact singed to the skin. Others, of the watch below, awakened by being shot out from their collapsing bunks, shivered incessantly, and kept on groaning even as we went about our work. But they all worked. That crew of Liverpool hard cases had in them the right

stuff. It's my experience they always have. It is the sea that gives it—
the vastness, the loneliness surrounding their dark stolid souls. Ah!
Well! We stumbled, we crept, we fell, we barked our shins on the wreckage, we hauled. The masts stood, but we did not know how much they
might be charred down below. It was nearly calm, but a long swell ran
from the west and made her roll. They might go at any moment. We
looked at them with apprehension. One could not foresee which way
they would fall.

"Then we retreated aft and looked about us. The deck was a tangle
of planks on edge, of planks on end, of splinters, of ruined woodwork.
The masts rose from that chaos like big trees above a matted undergrowth. The interstices of that mass of wreckage were full of something
whitish, sluggish, stirring—of something that was like a greasy fog. The
smoke of the invisible fire was coming up again, was trailing, like a
poisonous thick mist in some valley choked with dead wood. Already
lazy wisps were beginning to curl upwards amongst the mass of
splinters. Here and there a piece of timber, stuck upright, resembled
a post. Half of a fife rail had been shot through the foresail, and the
sky made a patch of glorious blue in the ignobly soiled canvas. A portion
of several boards holding together had fallen across the rail, and one
end protruded overboard, like a gangway leading upon nothing, like
a gangway leading over the deep sea, leading to death—as if inviting
us to walk the plank at once and be done with our ridiculous troubles. And still the air, the sky—a ghost, something invisible was hailing
the ship.

"Someone had the sense to look over, and there was the helms-
man, who had impulsively jumped overboard, anxious to come back. He
yelled and swam lustily like a merman, keeping up with the ship. We
threw him a rope, and presently he stood amongst us streaming with
water and very crestfallen. The captain had surrendered the wheel,
and apart, elbow on rail and chin in hand, gazed at the sea wistfully.
We asked ourselves, What next? I thought, Now, this is something like.
This is great. I wonder what will happen. O youth!

"Suddenly Mahon sighted a steamer far astern. Captain Beard said,
'We may do something with her yet.' We hoisted two flags, which said in
the international language of the sea, 'On fire. Want immediate assistance.' The steamer grew bigger rapidly, and by and by spoke with two
flags on her foremast, 'I am coming to your assistance.'

"In half an hour she was abreast, to windward, within hail, and
rolling slightly, with her engines stopped. We lost our composure,
and yelled all together with excitement, 'We've been blown up.' A man
in a white helmet, on the bridge, cried, 'Yes! All right! all right!' and
he nodded his head, and smiled, and made soothing motions with his
hand as though at a lot of frightened children. One of the boats dropped

in the water, and walked towards us upon the sea with her long oars. Four Calashes pulled a swinging stroke. This was my first sight of Malay seamen. I've known them since, but what struck me then was their unconcern: they came alongside, and even the bowman standing up and holding to our main chains with the boathook did not deign to lift his head for a glance. I thought people who had been blown up deserved more attention.

"A little man, dry like a chip and agile like a monkey, clambered up. It was the mate of the steamer. He gave one look, and cried, 'O boys —you had better quit!'

"We were silent. He talked apart with the captain for a time— seemed to argue with him. Then they went away together to the steamer.

"When our skipper came back we learned that the steamer was the *Sommerville*, Captain Nash, from West Australia to Singapore via Batavia with mails, and that the agreement was she should tow us to Anjer or Batavia, if possible, where we could extinguish the fire by scuttling, and then proceed on our voyage—to Bankok! The old man seemed excited. 'We will do it yet,' he said to Mahon, fiercely. He shook his fist at the sky. Nobody else said a word.

"At noon the steamer began to tow. She went ahead slim and high, and what was left of the *Judea* followed at the end of seventy fathom of towrope—followed her swiftly like a cloud of smoke with mastheads protruding above. We went aloft to furl the sails. We coughed on the yards, and were careful about the bunts. Do you see the lot of us there, putting a neat furl on the sails of that ship doomed to arrive nowhere? There was not a man who didn't think that at any moment the masts would topple over. From aloft we could not see the ship for smoke, and they worked carefully, passing the gaskets with even turns. 'Harbor furl'—aloft there!' cried Mahon from below.

"You understand this? I don't think one of those chaps expected to get down in the usual way. When we did I heard them saying to each other, 'Well, I thought we would come down overboard, in a lump— sticks and all—blame me if I didn't.' 'That's what I was thinking to myself,' would answer wearily another battered and bandaged scarecrow. And, mind, these were men without the drilled-in habit of obedience. To an onlooker they would be a lot of profane scallywags without a redeeming point. What made them do it—what made them obey me when I, thinking consciously how fine it was, made them drop the bunt of the foresail twice to try and do it better? What? They had no professional reputation—no examples, no praise. It wasn't a sense of duty; they all knew well enough how to shirk, and laze, and dodge—when they had a mind to it—and mostly they had. Was it the two pounds ten a month that sent them there? They didn't think their pay half good enough. No; it was something in them, something inborn and subtle and everlasting.

I don't say positively that the crew of a French or German merchantman wouldn't have done it, but I doubt whether it would have been done in the same way. There was a completeness in it, something solid like a principle, and masterful like an instinct—a disclosure of something secret—of that hidden something, that gift of good or evil that makes racial difference, that shapes the fate of nations.

"It was that night, at ten that, for the first time since we had been fighting it, we saw the fire. The speed of the towing had fanned the smoldering destruction. A blue gleam appeared forward, shining below the wreck of the deck. It wavered in patches, it seemed to stir and creep like the light of a glowworm. I saw it first, and told Mahon. 'Then the game's up,' he said. 'We had better stop this towing, or she will burst out suddenly fore and aft before we can clear out.' We set up a yell; rang bells to attract their attention; they towed on. At last Mahon and I had to crawl forward and cut the rope with an axe. There was no time to cast off the lashings. Red tongues could be seen licking the wilderness of splinters under our feet as we made our way back to the poop.

"Of course they very soon found out in the steamer that the rope was gone. She gave a loud blast of her whistle, her lights were seen sweeping in a wide circle, she came up ranging close alongside, and stopped. We were all in a tight group on the poop looking at her. Every man had saved a little bundle or a bag. Suddenly a conical flame with a twisted top shot up forward and threw upon the black sea a circle of light, with the two vessels side by side and heaving gently in its center. Captain Beard had been sitting on the gratings still and mute for hours, but now he rose slowly and advanced in front of us, to the mizzen-shrouds. Captain Nash hailed: 'Come along! Look sharp. I have mail-bags on board. I will take you and your boats to Singapore.'

" 'Thank you! No!' said our skipper. 'We must see the last of the ship.'

" 'I can't stand by any longer,' shouted the other. 'Mails—you know.'

" 'Ay! ay! We are all right.'

" 'Very well! I'll report you in Singapore. . . . Good-by!'

"He waved his hand. Our men dropped their bundles quietly. The steamer moved ahead, and passing out of the circle of light, vanished at once from our sight, dazzled by the fire which burned fiercely. And then I knew that I would see the East first as commander of a small boat. I thought it fine; and the fidelity to the old ship was fine. We should see the last of her. Oh, the glamor of youth! Oh, the fire of it, more dazzling than the flames of the burning ship, throwing a magic light on the wide earth, leaping audaciously to the sky, presently to be quenched by time, more cruel, more pitiless, more bitter than the sea—and like the flames of the burning ship surrounded by an impenetrable night.

"The old man warned us in his gentle and inflexible way that it was part of our duty to save for the underwriters as much as we could of the ship's gear. Accordingly we went to work aft, while she blazed forward to give us plenty of light. We lugged out a lot of rubbish. What didn't we save? An old barometer fixed with an absurd quantity of screws nearly cost me my life: a sudden rush of smoke came upon me, and I just got away in time. There were various stores, bolts of canvas, coils of rope; the poop looked like a marine bazaar, and the boats were lumbered to the gunwales. One would have thought the old man wanted to take as much as he could of his first command with him. He was very, very quiet, but off his balance evidently. Would you believe it? He wanted to take a length of old stream-cable and a kedge anchor with him in the longboat. We said, 'Ay, ay, sir,' deferentially, and on the quiet let the things slip overboard. The heavy medicine chest went that way, two bags of green coffee, tins of paint—fancy, paint!—a whole lot of things. Then I was ordered with two hands into the boats to make a stowage and get them ready against the time it would be proper for us to leave the ship.

"We put everything straight, stepped the longboat's mast for our skipper, who was to take charge of her, and I was not sorry to sit down for a moment. My face felt raw, every limb ached as if broken, I was aware of all my ribs, and would have sworn to a twist in the backbone. The boats, fast astern, lay in a deep shadow, and all around I could see the circle of the sea lighted by the fire. A gigantic flame arose forward straight and clear. It flared fierce, with noises like the whirr of wings, with rumbles as of thunder. There were cracks, detonations, and from the cone of flame the sparks flew upwards, as man is born to trouble, to leaky ships, and to ships that burn.

"What bothered me was that the ship, lying broadside to the swell and to such wind as there was—a mere breath—that boats would not keep astern where they were safe, but persisted, in a pigheaded way boats have, in getting under the counter and then swinging alongside. They were knocking about dangerously and coming near the flame, while the ship rolled on them, and, of course, there was always the danger of the masts going over the side at any moment. I and my two boatkeepers kept them off as best we could, with oars and boathooks; but to be constantly at it became exasperating, since there was no reason why we should not leave at once. We could not see those on board, nor could we imagine what caused the delay. The boatkeepers were swearing feebly, and I had not only my share of the work but also had to keep at it two men who showed a constant inclination to lay themselves down and let things slide.

"At last I hailed, 'On deck there,' and someone looked over. 'We're ready here,' I said. The head disappeared, and very soon popped up again. 'The captain says, All right, sir, and to keep the boats well clear of the ship.'

"Half an hour passed. Suddenly there was a frightful racket, rattle, clanking of chain, hiss of water, and millions of sparks flew up into the shivering column of smoke that stood leaning slightly above the ship. The catheads had burned away, and the two red-hot anchors had gone to the bottom, tearing out after them two hundred fathom of red-hot chain. The ship trembled, the mass of flame swayed as if ready to collapse, and the fore-topgallant mast fell. It darted down like an arrow of fire, shot under, and instantly leaping up within an oar's length of the boats, floated quietly, very black on the luminous sea. I hailed the deck again. After some time a man in an unexpectedly cheerful but also muffled tone, as though he had been trying to speak with his mouth shut, informed me, 'Coming directly, sir,' and vanished. For a long time I heard nothing but the whirr and roar of the fire. There were also whistling sounds. The boats jumped, tugged at the painters, ran at each other playfully, knocked their sides together, or, do what we would, swung in a bunch against the ship's side. I couldn't stand it any longer, and swarming up a rope, clambered aboard over the stern.

"It was as bright as day. Coming up like this, the sheet of fire facing me was a terrifying sight, and the heat seemed hardly bearable at first. On a settee cushion dragged out of the cabin Captain Beard, his legs drawn up and one arm under his head, slept with the light playing on him. Do you know what the rest were busy about? They were sitting on deck right aft, round an open case, eating bread and cheese and drinking bottled stout.

"On the background of flames twisting in fierce tongues above their heads they seemed at home like salamanders, and looked like a band of desperate pirates. The fire sparkled in the whites of their eyes, gleamed on patches of white skin seen through the torn shirts. Each had the marks as of a battle about him—bandaged heads, tied-up arms, a strip of dirty rag round a knee—and each man had a bottle between his legs and a chunk of cheese in his hand. Mahon got up. With his handsome and disreputable head, his hooked profile, his long white beard, and with an uncorked bottle in his hand, he resembled one of those reckless sea robbers of old making merry amidst violence and disaster. 'The last meal on board,' he explained solemnly. 'We had nothing to eat all day, and it was no use leaving all this.' He flourished the bottle and indicated the sleeping skipper. 'He said he couldn't swallow anything, so I got him to lie down,' he went on; and as I stared, 'I don't know whether you are aware, young fellow, the man had no sleep to speak of for days—and there will be dam' little sleep in the boats.' 'There will be no boats by and by if you fool about much longer,' I said, indignantly. I walked up to the skipper and shook him by the shoulder. At last he opened his eyes, but did not move. 'Time to leave her, sir,' I said quietly.

"He got up painfully, looked at the flames, at the sea sparkling round the ship, and black, black as ink farther away; he looked at the stars shining dim through a thin veil of smoke in a sky black, black as Erebus.

" 'Youngest first,' he said.

"And the ordinary seaman, wiping his mouth with the back of his hand, got up, clambered over the taffrail and vanished. Others followed. One, on the point of going over, stopped short to drain his bottle, and with a great swing of his arm flung it at the fire. 'Take this!' he cried.

"The skipper lingered disconsolately, and we left him to commune alone for a while with his first command. Then I went up again and brought him away at last. It was time. The ironwork on the poop was hot to the touch.

"Then the painter of the longboat was cut, and the three boats, tied together, drifted clear of the ship. It was just sixteen hours after the explosion when we abandoned her. Mahon had charge of the second boat, and I had the smallest—the fourteen-foot thing. The longboat would have taken the lot of us; but the skipper said we must save as much property as we could—for the underwriters—and so I got my first command. I had two men with me, a bag of biscuits, a few tins of meat, and a breaker of water. I was ordered to keep close to the longboat, and that in case of bad weather we might be taken into her.

"And do you know what I thought? I thought I would part company as soon as I could. I wanted to have my first command all to myself. I wasn't going to sail in a squadron if there were a chance for independent cruising. I would make land by myself. I would beat the other boats. Youth! All youth! The silly, charming, beautiful youth.

"But we did not make a start at once. We must see the last of the ship. And so the boats drifted about that night, heaving and setting on the swell. The men dozed, waked, sighed, groaned. I looked at the burning ship.

"Between the darkness of earth and heaven she was burning fiercely upon a disc of purple sea shot by the blood-red play of gleams; upon a disc of water glittering and sinister. A high, clear flame, an immense and lonely flame, ascended from the ocean, and from its summit the black smoke poured continuously at the sky. She burned furiously; mournful and imposing like a funeral pile kindled in the night, surrounded by the sea, watched over by the stars. A magnificent death had come like a grace, like a gift, like a reward to that old ship at the end of her laborious days. The surrender of her weary ghost to the keeping of stars and sea was stirring like the sight of a glorious triumph. The masts fell just before daybreak, and for a moment there was a burst and turmoil of sparks that seemed to fill with flying fire the night patient and watchful, the vast night lying silent upon the sea. At daylight she was only a charred shell, floating still under a cloud of smoke and bearing a glowing mass of coal within.

"Then the oars were got out, and the boats forming in a line moved round her remains as if in procession—the longboat leading. As we pulled across her stern a slim dart of fire shot out viciously at us, and suddenly she went down, head first, in a great hiss of steam. The unconsumed stern was the last to sink; but the paint had gone, had cracked, had peeled off, and there were no letters, there was no word, no stubborn device that was like her soul, to flash at the rising sun her creed and her name.

"We made our way north. A breeze sprang up, and about noon all the boats came together for the last time. I had no mast or sail in mine, but I made a mast out of a spare oar and hoisted a boat-awning for a sail, with a boathook for a yard. She was certainly over-masted, but I had the satisfaction of knowing that with the wind aft I could beat the other two. I had to wait for them. Then we all had a look at the captain's chart, and, after a sociable meal of hard bread and water, got our last instructions. These were simple: steer north, and keep together as much as possible. 'Be careful with that jury-rig, Marlow,' said the captain; and Mahon, as I sailed proudly past his boat, wrinkled his curved nose and hailed, 'You will sail that ship of yours under water, if you don't look out, young fellow.' He was a malicious old man—and may the deep sea where he sleeps now rock him gently, rock him tenderly to the end of time!

"Before sunset a thick rain-squall passed over the two boats, which were far astern, and that was the last I saw of them for a time. Next day I sat steering my cockleshell—my first command—with nothing but water and sky round me. I did sight in the afternoon the upper sails of a ship far away, but said nothing, and my men did not notice her. You see I was afraid she might be homeward bound, and I had no mind to turn back from the portals of the East. I was steering for Java—another blessed name—like Bankok, you know. I steered many days.

"I need not tell you what it is to be knocking about in an open boat. I remember nights and days of calm, when we pulled, we pulled, and the boat seemed to stand still, as if bewitched within the circle of the sea horizon. I remember the heat, the deluge of rain-squalls that kept us baling for dear life (but filled our water cask), and I remember sixteen hours on end with a mouth dry as a cinder and a steering oar over the stern to keep my first command head on to a breaking sea. I did not know how good a man I was till then. I remember the drawn faces, the dejected figures of my two men, and I remember my youth and the feeling that will never come back any more—the feeling that I could last forever, outlast the sea, the earth, and all men; the deceitful feeling that lures us on to joys, to perils, to love, to vain effort—to death; the triumphant conviction of strength, the heat of life in the handful of dust, the glow in the heart that with every year grows dim, grows cold, grows small, and expires—and expires, too soon, too soon—before life itself.

"And this is how I see the East. I have seen its secret places and have looked into its very soul; but now I see it always from a small boat, a high outline of mountains, blue and afar in the morning; like faint mist at noon; a jagged wall of purple at sunset. I have the feel of the oar in my hand, the vision of a scorching blue sea in my eyes. And I see a bay, a wide bay, smooth as glass and polished like ice, shimmering in the dark. A red light burns far off upon the gloom of the land, and the night is soft and warm. We drag at the oars with aching arms, and suddenly a puff of wind, a puff faint and tepid and laden with strange odors of blossoms, of aromatic wood, comes out of the still night—the first sigh of the East on my face. That I can never forget. It was impalpable and enslaving, like a charm, like a whispered promise of mysterious delight.

"We had been pulling this finishing spell for eleven hours. Two pulled, and he whose turn it was to rest sat at the tiller. We had made out the red light in that bay and steered for it, guessing it must mark some small coasting port. We passed two vessels, outlandish and high-sterned, sleeping at anchor, and, approaching the light, now very dim, ran the boat's nose against the end of a jutting wharf. We were blind with fatigue. My men dropped the oars and fell off the thwarts as if dead. I made fast to a pile. A current rippled softly. The scented obscurity of the shore was grouped into vast masses, a density of colossal clumps of vegetation, probably—mute and fantastic shapes. And at their foot the semicircle of a beach gleamed faintly, like an illusion. There was not a light, not a stir, not a sound. The mysterious East faced me, perfumed like a flower, silent like death, dark like a grave.

"And I sat weary beyond expression, exulting like a conqueror, sleepless and entranced as if before a profound, a fateful enigma.

"A splashing of oars, a measured dip reverberating on the level of water, intensified by the silence of the shore into loud claps, made me jump up. A boat, a European boat, was coming in. I invoked the name of the dead; I hailed: '*Judea* ahoy!' A thin shout answered.

"It was the captain. I had beaten the flagship by three hours, and I was glad to hear the old man's voice again, tremulous and tired. 'Is it you, Marlow?' 'Mind the end of that jetty, sir,' I cried.

"He approached cautiously, and brought up with the deep-sea lead line which we had saved—for the underwriters. I eased my painter and fell alongside. He sat, a broken figure at the stern, wet with dew, his hands clasped in his lap. His men were asleep already. 'I had a terrible time of it,' he murmured. 'Mahon is behind—not very far.' We conversed in whispers, in low whispers, as if afraid to wake up the land. Guns, thunder, earthquakes would not have awakened the men just then.

"Looking round as we talked, I saw away at sea a bright light traveling in the night. 'There's a steamer passing the bay,' I said. She was not passing, she was entering, and she even came close and anchored. 'I wish,' said the old man, 'you would find out whether she is English. Perhaps they could give us a passage somewhere.' He seemed nervously anxious. So by dint of punching and kicking I started one of my men into a state of somnambulism, and giving him an oar, took another and pulled towards the lights of the steamer.

"There was a murmur of voices in her, metallic hollow clangs of the engine room, footsteps on the deck. Her ports shone, round like dilated eyes. Shapes moved about, and there was a shadowy man high up on the bridge. He heard my oars.

"And then, before I could open my lips, the East spoke to me, but it was in a Western voice. A torrent of words was poured into the enigmatical, the fateful silence; outlandish, angry words, mixed with words and even whole sentences of good English, less strange but even more surprising. The voice swore and cursed violently; it riddled the solemn peace of the bay by a volley of abuse. It began by calling me Pig, and from that went crescendo into unmentionable adjectives—in English. The man up there raged aloud in two languages, and with a sincerity in his fury that almost convinced me I had, in some way, sinned against the harmony of the universe. I could hardly see him, but began to think he would work himself into a fit.

"Suddenly he ceased, and I could hear him snorting and blowing like a porpoise. I said:

" 'What steamer is this, pray?'

" 'Eh? What's this? And who are you?'

" 'Castaway crew of an English bark burnt at sea. We came here tonight. I am the second mate. The captain is in the longboat, and wishes to know if you would give us a passage somewhere.'

" 'Oh, my goodness! I say. . . . This is the *Celestial* from Singapore on her return trip. I'll arrange with your captain in the morning, . . . and, . . . I say, . . . did you hear me just now?'

" 'I should think the whole bay heard you.'

" 'I thought you were a shoreboat. Now, look here—this infernal lazy scoundrel of a caretaker has gone to sleep again—curse him. The light is out, and I nearly ran foul of the end of this damned jetty. This is the third time he plays me this trick. Now, I ask you, can anybody stand this kind of thing? It's enough to drive a man out of his mind. I'll report him. . . . I'll get the Assistant Resident to give him the sack, by—! See—there's no light. It's out, isn't it? I take you to witness the light's out. There should be a light, you know. A red light on the—'

" 'There was a light,' I said, mildly.

" 'But it's out, man! What's the use of talking like this? You can see for yourself it's out—don't you? If you had to take a valuable steamer along this God-forsaken coast you would want a light, too. I'll kick him from end to end of his miserable wharf. You'll see if I don't. I will—'

" 'So I may tell my captain you'll take us?' I broke in.

" 'Yes, I'll take you. Good night,' he said, brusquely.

"I pulled back, made fast again to the jetty, and then went to sleep at last. I had faced the silence of the East. I had heard some of its language. But when I opened my eyes again the silence was as complete as though it had never been broken. I was lying in a flood of light, and the sky had never looked so far, so high, before. I opened my eyes and lay without moving.

"And then I saw the men of the East—they were looking at me. The whole length of the jetty was full of people. I saw brown, bronze, yellow faces, the black eyes, the glitter, the color of an Eastern crowd. And all these beings stared without a murmur, without a sigh, without a movement. They stared down at the boats, at the sleeping men who at night had come to them from the sea. Nothing moved. The fronds of palms stood still against the sky. Not a branch stirred along the shore, and the brown roofs of hidden houses peeped through the green foliage, through the big leaves that hung shining and still like leaves forged of heavy metal. This was the East of the ancient navigators, so old, so mysterious, resplendent and somber, living and unchanged, full of danger and promise. And these were the men. I sat up suddenly. A wave of movement passed through the crowd from end to end, passed along the heads, swayed the bodies, ran along the jetty like a ripple on the water, like a breath of wind on a field—and all was still again. I see it now—the wide sweep of the bay, the glittering sands, the wealth of green infinite and varied, the sea blue like the sea of a dream, the crowd of attentive faces, the blaze of vivid color—the water reflecting it all, the curve of the shore, the jetty, the high-sterned outlandish craft floating still, and the three boats with the tired men from the West sleeping, unconscious of the land and the people and of the violence of sunshine. They slept thrown across the thwarts, curled on bottomboards, in the careless attitudes of death. The head of the old skipper, leaning back in the stern of the longboat, had fallen on his breast, and he looked as though he would never wake. Farther out old Mahon's face was upturned to the sky, with the long white beard spread out on his breast, as though he had been shot where he sat at the tiller; and a man, all in a heap in the bows of the boat, slept with both arms embracing the stemhead and with his cheek laid on the gunwale. The East looked at them without a sound.

"I have known its fascination since; I have seen the mysterious shores, the still water, the lands of brown nations, where a stealthy Nemesis lies in wait, pursues, overtakes so many of the conquering race, who are proud of their wisdom, of their knowledge, of their strength. But for me all the East is contained in that vision of my youth. It is all in that moment when I opened my young eyes on it. I came upon it from a tussle with the sea—and I was young—and I saw it looking at me. And this is all that is left of it! Only a moment; a moment of strength, of romance, of glamor—of youth! . . . A flick of sunshine upon a strange shore, the time to remember, the time for a sigh, and—good-by!—Night —Good-by . . . !"

He drank.

"Ah! The good old time—the good old time. Youth and the sea. Glamor and the sea! The good, strong sea, the salt, bitter sea, that could whisper to you and roar at you and knock your breath out of you."

He drank again.

"By all that's wonderful it is the sea, I believe, the sea itself—or is it youth alone? Who can tell? But you here—you all have something out of life: money, love—whatever one gets on shore—and, tell me, wasn't that the best time, that time when we were young at sea; young and had nothing, on the sea that gives nothing, except hard knocks—and sometimes a chance to feel your strength—that only—that you all re-gret?"

And we all nodded at him: the man of finance, the man of ac-counts, the man of law, we all nodded at him over the polished table that like a still sheet of brown water reflected our faces, lined, wrinkled; our faces marked by toil, by deceptions, by success, by love; our weary eyes looking still, looking always, looking anxiously for something out of life, that while it is expected is already gone—has passed unseen, in a sigh, in a flash—together with the youth, with the strength, with the romance of illusions.

Theme Questions

1. "You fellows know there are those voyages that seem ordered for the illustration of life, that might stand for a symbol of existence. You fight, work, sweat, nearly kill yourself, sometimes do kill yourself, trying to accomplish something—and you can't. Not from any fault of yours. You simply can do nothing, neither great nor little— . . ." In what ways does the story illustrate Marlow's statement? Does his experience "stand for a symbol of existence"?

Why or why not? What further implications may be derived by the reader?

2. Throughout the story there are repeated apostrophes to youth. What do they signify? What to Marlow—and to Conrad—is the essential meaning of youth? What does its loss represent?

3. The voyage from west to east is symbolic, as are such things and personages as the ship, Beard, and Mahon. Discuss what each signifies. What other symbols add to the interpretation or significance of the story?

4. The story is punctuated by Marlow's repeated, "Pass the bottle." Is there any pattern or reason for the various insertions? Considering that this is a story within a story, can you find any technical or structural reasons for Conrad's insertion of these words?

5. In his introduction to *The Nigger of the 'Narcissus'*, Conrad said that "all art . . . appeals primarily to the senses," and that the writer had to "aspire to the plasticity of sculpture, to the colour of painting, and to the magic suggestiveness of music—" particularly in order to make the reader *see*. Discuss the success of "Youth" in terms of Conrad's meeting his own standards.

. . . also by Joseph Conrad   *Heart of Darkness*
                                  Lord Jim
                                  Nostromo

Looking back, man faces his own experiences and the inexorable passage of time. Dylan Thomas apostrophes his youth in Wales in this moving lyric of apple-green times. Robert Frost simply states what youth and age both need to remember.

Fern Hill

Dylan Thomas

Now as I was young and easy under the apple boughs
About the lilting house and happy as the grass was green,
  The night above the dingle starry,
    Time let me hail and climb
  Golden in the heydays of his eyes,
And honoured among wagons I was prince of the apple towns
And once below a time I lordly had the trees and leaves
      Trail with daisies and barley
  Down the rivers of the windfall light.

And as I was green and carefree, famous among the barns
About the happy yard and singing as the farm was home,
  In the sun that is young once only,
    Time let me play and be
  Golden in the mercy of his means,
And green and golden I was huntsman and herdsman, the calves
Sang to my horn, the foxes on the hills barked clear and cold,
    And the sabbeth rang slowly
  In the pebbles of the holy streams.

All the sun long it was running, it was lovely, the hay-
Fields high as the house, the tunes from the chimneys, it was air
  And playing, lovely and watery
    And fire green as grass.
    And nightly under the simple stars

430

As I rode to sleep the owls were bearing the farm away,
All the moon long I heard blessèd among stables, the night-jars
   Flying with the ricks, and the horses
     Flashing into the dark.

And then to awake, and the farm, like a wanderer white
With the dew, come back, the cock on his shoulder: it was all
   Shining, it was Adam and maiden,
     The sky gathered again
   And the sun grew round that very day.
So it must have been after the birth of the simple light
In the first, spinning place, the spellbound horses walking warm
   Out of the whinnying green stable
   On to the fields of praise.

And honoured among foxes and pheasants by the gay house
Under the new made clouds and happy as the heart was long,
   In the sun born over and over,
     I ran my heedless ways,
   My wishes raced through the house-high hay
And nothing I cared, at my sky blue trades, that time allows
In all his tuneful turning so few and such morning songs
   Before the children green and golden
     Follow him out of grace,

Nothing I cared, in the lamb white days, that time would take me
Up to the swallow thronged loft by the shadow of my hand,
   In the moon that is always rising,
     Nor that riding to sleep
   I should hear him fly with the high fields
And wake to the farm forever fled from the childless land.
Oh as I was young and easy in the mercy of his means,
     Time held me green and dying
   Though I sang in my chains like the sea.

What Fifty Said

Robert Frost

When I was young my teachers were the old.
I gave up fire for form till I was cold.
I suffered like a metal being cast.
I went to school to age to learn the past.

Now I am old my teachers are the young.
What can't be moulded must be cracked and sprung.
I strain at lessons fit to start a suture.
I go to school to youth to learn the future.